READING MODERN DRAMA
Edited by Alan Ackerman

Exploring the relationship between dramatic language and its theatrical aspects, *Reading Modern Drama* provides an accessible entry point for general readers and academics into the world of contemporary theatre scholarship. This collection promotes the use of diverse perspectives and critical methods to explore the common theme of language as well as the continued relevance of modern drama in our lives.

Reading Modern Drama offers provocative close readings of both canonical and lesser-known plays, from *Hedda Gabler* to E.E. Cummings' *Him*. Taken together, these essays enter into an ongoing, fruitful debate about the terms "modern" and "drama" and build a much-needed bridge between literary studies and performance studies.

ALAN ACKERMAN is an associate professor in the Department of English at the University of Toronto.

Reading Modern Drama

Edited by Alan Ackerman

UNIVERSITY OF TORONTO PRESS
Toronto   Buffalo   London

© University of Toronto Press 2012
Toronto Buffalo London
www.utppublishing.com
Printed in the U.S.A.

ISBN 978-1-4426-1281-5 (paper)

Printed on acid-free paper.

Library and Archives Canada Cataloguing in Publication

Reading modern drama / edited by Alan Ackerman.

Includes bibliographical references and index.
ISBN 978-1-4426-1281-5

1. Drama – 19th century – History and criticism.   2. Drama – 20th century –
History and criticism.   I. Ackerman, Alan L. (Alan Louis)

PN1851.R43 2012   809.2   C2011-907700-0

University of Toronto Press acknowledges the financial assistance to its
publishing program of the Canada Council for the Arts and the Ontario Arts
Council.

University of Toronto Press acknowledges the financial support of the
Government of Canada through the Canada Book Fund for its publishing
activities.

Contents

Acknowledgments

Thanks to the hardworking editorial assistants at Modern Drama: Natalie Corbett, Michelle MacArthur, Katherine Foster, Natalie Papoutsis, and James McKinnon. Particular, extra thanks go to Caroline Reich, who has served not only as an outstanding editorial assistant for the journal but also as indexer for this book. I am also grateful to our excellent copyeditor Rosemary Clarke-Beattie. At the University of Toronto Press, Richard Ratzlaff, Barb Porter, and Anne-Marie Corrigan were instrumental in bringing this project to fruition. I am indebted to Jill Levenson, John Astington, and Stephen Johnson for their guidance and assistance. Finally, I gratefully acknowledge the warm support of Andrea Most.

READING MODERN DRAMA

Introduction

ALAN ACKERMAN

A sense of the struggle of language with itself forces a certain liberation in interpreting texts that seems to some to go beyond the apparent evidence of their words ... To understand serious writing will precisely require us to question what a text asserts in order to arrive at the conviction that we are covering the ground gained in what its words actually contrive to say.

– Stanley Cavell

ROSENCRANTZ What are you playing at?
GUILDENSTERN Words, words. They're all we have to go on.

– Tom Stoppard

Why publish a collection of essays entitled *Reading Modern Drama*? Individually, each of these words is apt to raise eyebrows. Yet "reading," "modern," and "drama" continue to play vital roles in organizing university curricula and defining activities of the broader culture. In the following pages, each of these words elicits new questions and definitions. This volume, moreover, is assembled from articles published in one journal, *Modern Drama*, and the title is also meant to suggest the value of reading this particular journal cohesively, in addition to the benefits of dipping into individual articles online (for pragmatic reasons, the articles were not revised for publication here). When I became editor of the journal five years ago, I aimed to respect its founding mandate "to stimulate interest in research and in the teaching of the drama since Ibsen" (Edwards 1), while prompting contributors to question its terms. In one chapter of this book, for instance, Joseph Roach argues that the modernity of modern drama begins in the eighteenth century rather than with Ibsen. The editorial vision of *Modern Drama* continues to evolve in a decades-long conversation about the meaning and value of "the drama" in modernity. This volume assembles some of the best work published in recent years, loosely organized around a common theme: the relationship of dramatic language to its theatrical aspects. Collected here, these close readings and critical interventions perform intellectual work that individual journal issues cannot.

Since the first issue of *Modern Drama* was published in 1958, criticism has seemed in a state of perpetual crisis. In "Criticism and Crisis," Paul de Man reflected on the apparent interdisciplinary expansion of literary studies in the early 1970s. In 1998 W.B. Worthen remarked, "There is a conceptual crisis in drama studies, a crisis reflected in the ways different disciplinary styles approach questions about dramatic texts, theatrical productions, and performance in general" ("Drama" 1093). Derived from the same Greek verb (κρίνειν, *krinein*: to separate, to discriminate, to choose), criticism and crisis present the critic with the continuing task of deciding between and defining not only objects but also methods of study. This year, in response to the proliferation of new media and modes of expression, the *Publication of the Modern Language Association* assembled a special issue on critical paradigms for the twenty-first century. It asked what possible new models of interpretation might arise if, with new technology, literature comes to be seen less as a fixed text and more as an event. For instance, how might performance studies shift attention from what texts mean to what texts do? In her contribution to that issue, " 'Just Want to Say': Performance and Literature, Jackson and Poirier," Peggy Phelan asserts that "literature has receded as a dominant cultural form in the past three decades while media culture has fostered our obsession with the performances" of celebrities (943). But, she also suggests, "If we lose the intimacy of the connection between literature and performance, we diminish something vital in and between them." The choice may be both/and rather than either/or. There is much to be said for "what [Phelan] feel[s] about the diminishment of literature as a cultural form," yet her celebration of "the thing not in the words" has methodological limits that *Reading Modern Drama* will explore. In the same issue, Joseph Roach also approaches what he perceives to be the "neglect of literature" by performance studies. He comments, "The widening gap between performance studies and literary studies is the source of a number of missed opportunities" ("Performance" 1080). In focusing on drama, which can be understood in the broadest possible terms, it has long been the aim of *Modern Drama* – and it is the aim of this book – to fill that gap.

This book strives to promote rigorous attention to the particular language(s) of dramatic texts. This goal does not assume that the text has an objective status apart from interpretation. On the contrary, it is supposed both to suggest and to reflect upon the creativity inherent in linguistic and literary self-reflexiveness, the productive tension between texts and performances, and the internal difference that is intrinsic to representation. Attending to texts is not the same as "sticking to the script" – at least not in these pages – if that expression is taken to mean a rigid, unimaginative approach to the temporal experience of a genre that is largely defined as intersubjective and intended for actualization in time and space. Yet the responsibility of close reading will here be advanced in sceptical, detailed, and philological terms.

Philology, the study (literally the *love*) of words may be, as Edward Said suggests, "just about the least with-it, least sexy, and most unmodern of any of the branches of learning associated with humanism" (57). But that is not as it should be. Nietzsche, the most radical of modern thinkers, as Said points out, thought of himself first and foremost as a philologist. And even the logophobic Antonin Artaud derives his rhetorical power not from overcoming what he identifies in *Le Théâtre et son double* as "*une rupture entre les choses, et les paroles* [a rupture between things and words]" (10 [7]),[1] but from dramatizing in his agonized, self-contradictory prose both the impossibility of that overcoming and the necessary "cruelty" of the effort. The medium (and hence the most common subject) of dramatists is language. Both ordinary language and more especially the language of drama and dramatic criticism are in continual, restless, constructive tension with themselves. As a result, what such texts assert – the experience that characters aim to express, that audiences and readers may imagine, in short, the *meaning* – can be understood only by attending first to the script and by working both to comprehend and to render intelligible, as Stanley Cavell remarks, "what its words actually contrive to say."

Writing in the *Tulane Drama Review* forty years ago, Richard Schechner reflected a central tension, even an antagonism, that has characterized studies of drama and theatre for the past half-century when he remarked, "The literary model is passing away and it is being replaced by a performance model whose shape, happily, is not yet fixed" (23). It is not clear that to have imagined such a vanquishing has been either correct or intellectually productive. *Modern Drama*, after more than fifty years, remains the most prominent journal in English to focus on dramatic literature of the past two centuries, although there are now numerous valuable journals that continue to distinguish themselves from *Modern Drama* along the lines Schechner and others have imagined. The articles collected here present provocative close readings of both canonical and lesser-known dramatic texts, from *Hedda Gabler* to E.E. Cummings's *Him*, through a range of methodological perspectives, and, in the case of Julie Stone Peters's chapter, "Jane Harrison and the Savage Dionysus," point to a new understanding of performance studies born from the productive tension between drama and theatre. *Reading Modern Drama* acknowledges that the terms "modern" and "drama" are the subjects of continuing and fruitful debate. It addresses familiar tensions between literary and theatre studies, resistance to privileging the "textual" or "linguistic" aspects of drama, and doubts about the project of reading plays. In the following pages, I will briefly discuss the crucial issues that arise from both the challenge of bringing moral intelligibility to historically determinable but linguistically (often) interpretable objects and the problem for critical judgment of navigating between meaning and interpretation, determinism and indeterminacy.

To say that drama is a form of literature and that the medium of drama is language is not to assume that it is isolated from the temporality of experience, from history, or that it does not pose, as a genre, unique and often disruptive challenges to reading itself. It also does not mean that drama can be understood apart from theatre. On the contrary, few would propose that we can make sense of drama without reference to specific forms and venues of theatrical performance. Thinking of drama as literature does not assume a theory of genre that is rigidly prescriptive, if it does imply shared formal structures among historically specific kinds of writing, production, and reception. Dramas are made of words, but the commonly noted "problem" of granting plays the cultural status of other literary forms, such as novels and poems – as well as the remarkable diversity of dramatic types – is directly related to the wide range of specific theatres for which plays are written as well as to the pluralism of modern, postcolonial, cosmopolitan societies. The consistency, therefore, with which diverse forms of drama, not just theatre, in the nineteenth and twentieth centuries have been *attacked*, even by theatre practitioners and drama critics, indicates a special instance of literary-historical dialecticalism, not to mention dialogism, that implies the inextricability of dramatic production and consumption (in books and theatres and often both at once). Plays can be read in an armchair by the fire, but they are not written principally to be read in that way.

How are we to understand and to experience both the pleasure and the responsibility of reading plays? What, dare we ask, is the value of modern dramas for life? Each of the following chapters considers these questions from a different perspective. Several investigate the constitutive opposition of language and silence. In " '*Vinløv i håret*': The Relationship between Women, Language, and Power in Ibsen's *Hedda Gabler*," Tanya Thresher shows that Hedda's consciousness of the manipulative power of words leads her to choose silence as a means of challenging her position in the patriarchal order. Similarly, in " '¡Silencio, he dicho!' Space, Language, and Characterization as Agents of Social Protest in Lorca's Rural Tragedies," Bilha Blum considers how dramatists subversively exploit silence. She interrogates the junctions where the explicit and the implicit, text and subtext, the said and the shown, meet and interact. Drawing on psychoanalysis in "The Money Shot: Economies of Sex, Guns, and Language in *Topdog/Underdog*," Myka Tucker-Abramson focuses on linguistic gaps, breakdowns, and disruptions in Suzan-Lori Parks's dramatizations of racial injustice to illustrate both the limitations of existing languages in America and ways of rebuilding relationships between literature and politics. Of course, it is vital to recognize that the spaces *between* words are constituted *by* words. Ethical critiques of silence thus raise a more basic question: what counts as evidence? This problem has been a particular bone of contention in the study of drama vis-à-vis the study of theatre, specifically when it comes to the oft-noted evanescence of performance.

To ask what counts as evidence, the data on which a judgment or conclusion may be based, is not the same as to ask what constitutes a valid archive. For arguments about literary texts, the repository of evidence may (in fact, often must) include visual images, recorded anecdotes, musical scores, legal documents, and so on. The point is that the arguments are strongly reasoned, basing their power to convince on shared knowledge, and not impressionistic or speculative, as we find too often in claims about the audience reception of certain plays or in arguments about the achievement in the theatre of *presence*, plenitude, or *authentic* thought that precedes articulate discourse. Each chapter in this book establishes its own standards of argumentation. However, while theatre and performance history are vital to the study of dramatic literature, the interpretation of the archives, the historical discourse itself, must be understood as constituted by and in language. Modern conceptions of language and literary theory have contributed valuably to historical research and historiography, to the understanding that, as Hayden White has put it, "every history is first and foremost a verbal artifact" (4).

A serious form of literary criticism applied to "modern drama" assumes, moreover, that, while drama must be understood in relation to theatre, reading drama is not the same as, in Anne Ubersfeld's words, "reading theater," where linguistic "signs" make up just one type of system among various sign systems that, as theatrical happening, are radically indeterminate, self-referential, and paradoxical, "both eternal (indefinitely reproducible and renewable) and of the instant (never reproduced identically)" (*Reading Theatre* 3). While remaining sensitive to tensions between text and performance, we must also both acknowledge that language is not just one sign system among others (indeed, it is the sign system from which, through structural linguistics, semiotics was born) and seek an empirical grounding for arguments, rather than a totalizing system, focusing not only on the gaps (*les trous*)[2] in the text but also on the words that are the means by which gaps are rendered. Kant and Hegel's ranking of literature above other, more sensuous arts continues to divide scholars of theatre and of drama, but *Reading Modern Drama* does not assume any such absolute priority of one medium or genre over another – of literature over music or dance or mime or sculpture – although it does assume, at the same time, that the literary aspect of theatre as expressed in drama requires separate, if not isolated, kinds of critical investigation that are alive to relations between the pragmatics and the semantics of expression (what language does and what language means). Literary criticism of drama can and should be enriched by studies of other arts, with their own vocabularies and methods. In "The Space Stage and the Circus: E.E. Cummings's *Him* and Frederick Kiesler's *Raumbühne*," for instance, Allison Carruth reveals the influences of circus and burlesque performers and of Bauhaus-trained set designer Frederick Kiesler on Cummings's dramatic work, as well as demonstrating the importance of theatre for understanding the poet's literary career. This book aims to further our understanding of specific instances of drama in relation to dance, to music, to the circus, to film, to archeology, to painting, and to poems and novels, as well as to genre theory.

"The term *dramatic*," wrote Cleanth Brooks and Robert Heilman, "which comes from the noun *drama*, can also be applied to poetry, not only to narrative poetry, such as that of Chaucer, which naturally has basic resemblances to drama and fiction, but also to lyric poetry, which is often thought of as being quite different from these forms. It may therefore be well to observe," they suggest, "just what characteristics the drama shares with other literary forms" (13). That Brooks and Heilman perceive "problems of the drama" ought not to lead us to assume that they are fastidious elitists or to project onto them an anxiety about the absence of clean categories. Instead, critical studies today might gain much by historicizing such "problems" and by adopting some measure of the careful formalism that characterized literary studies in the decades prior to and during *Modern Drama*'s founding in 1958. Brooks himself wrote that the critic "needs the help of the historian – all the help that he can get" ("Marvell's" 339). Yet the help that the historian has to offer may be of various kinds, and while the term "historicism" is on everyone's lips, it remains common to find narrative histories of theatre and drama that fail to interrogate the historicity of their own viewpoints and terminology – to acknowledge that each critique employs practices it exposes and participates in the economy it describes and to recognize that literary and non-literary texts inform each other.

The hermeneutic tension that arises from trying to discover meaning while acknowledging the difference between text and performance, as many have shown, is not confined to theatrical literature, but the appropriation of theatrical terms for literary criticism of non-theatrical genres also presents an opportunity for critical work specifically on drama because, as Benjamin Bennett has written, theatre is "the place where a . . . constitutive paradox of literature becomes an art in its own right, the art of drama" (4). This paradox, which commonly takes the form of attempting to define drama in terms of insufficiency or lack, what is *not* there, a sign of what is lost in performance (or, in Peter Szondi's neo-Hegelian terms, in history) has deeply informed the vocabulary of twentieth-century literary theory, criticism, and philosophy. But it is not necessary to think of what we do with words or of linguistic *action* in metaphysical terms, and in spite of the common misunderstanding and misapplication of their terminology, it was precisely against metaphysical theories of language that Kenneth Burke's "dramatistic" criticism, J.L. Austin's idea of "performative utterances," and Jacques Derrida's insistence on linguistic "play" in *différance* (different as they are) were directed. In his chapter, "How to Do Nothing with Words, or *Waiting for Godot* as Performativity," Richard Begam draws on the language philosophy of Austin and Ludwig Wittgenstein to analyse how *Waiting for Godot* exposes the structural logic of both rhetorical and dramatic performativity, reclaiming what he calls a "there-ness" for the dramatic event. This book also seeks to maintain a fruitful balance between practical and theoretical criticism, a relationship to texts that is concrete and abstract, particular and general, wedding close reading to theoretical generalization.

Reading Modern Drama aims to overcome what Frank Lentricchia and Andrew DuBois have identified as "the major clash in the practice of literary criticism in the past century: that between so-called formalist and so-called nonformalist (especially 'political') modes of reading" (ix). The term "close reading" is now often identified with the New Criticism, which has become a special target of theatre studies for supposedly privileging an "autotelic" text. This supposition is incorrect. First, it must be said that the so-called New Critics are by no means unified by a single critical method. In his 1941 book, *The New Criticism*, John Crowe Ransom effectively established the term in common usage, but he also disagreed strongly with the three (diverse) critics he examined: I.A. Richards, T.S. Eliot, and Yvor Winters. The cognitive approach of Richards, to take one example, hardly assumes that literature can be cut off from experience; in fact, he abolishes the distinction between the aesthetic and other emotions. Richards does not "[focus] on the autotelic object" or insist on the "essential separateness of the literary word," as Elin Diamond suggests (3, 4). T.S. Eliot, perhaps the most influential critic of his generation (and the one most likely to be scorned for his political and religious conservatism), goes so far as to remark, "No exponent of criticism . . . has, I presume, ever made the preposterous assumption that criticism is an autotelic activity. I do not deny that art may be affirmed to serve ends beyond itself" (69). Nor is it correct to assert, as Shannon Jackson does, that "New Criticism argued for literature less as the moral vehicle of liberal culture than as an object whose understanding required a formalized method of expert reading" ("Disciplinary Blind Spots" 37), although it is true that many of these critics (writing from the 1920s through the 1960s) advocate intellectual rigour and expertise in the practice of criticism, if we take that to mean a high degree of skill in and knowledge of their particular subject. "The common avoidance of all discussion of the wider social and moral aspects of the arts by people of steady judgment and strong heads," writes Richards, "is a misfortune, for it leaves the field free for folly, and cramps the scope of good critics unduly" (31). In this formulation, close reading is a moral obligation. Eliot, Richards, Brooks, and others of their generation largely reject the form/content distinction, focusing instead on defining the object of study as a whole and discerning meaning as it arises from the integrated work of art. These critics can teach us much about a rational rather than an impressionistic approach to literature. And they are by no means forgetful or disparaging of drama.

In an article recently published in *Modern Drama*, theatre theorist Marvin Carlson opposed two models of interpretation, the "literary" and the "theatrical," positing a boundary between studies of plays as dramatic texts and studies of plays as theatrical texts that he ostensibly aimed to critique and overcome ("A Difficult Birth" 487–89). I think that Carlson's oppositional schema is reductive and mistaken, but his view is widely held and, therefore, important. It has been my goal as editor to set the stage for such a debate – and to enter it – not to determine the results. Understood pragmatically, the tension Carlson imagines between the literary and the theatrical can be productive. The oversimplification of "literary interpretation," a phrase that does not suggest a particular critical method or hermeneutic model, is a disciplinary manoeuvre. No sophisticated literary critic today regards texts as unchanging objects, the same from moment to moment, whether in book or theatrical form. Interpretation itself is generally regarded as a fiction-making process. But there are many, such as representatives of the Samuel Beckett estate, who appear committed, in S.E. Gontarski's words, to "the decidedly untheatrical ideology of invariant texts." Gontarski's powerful critique of this position, which is included here, argues that Beckett's creative life was marked by continuous transformation. It is misguided to restrict productions of his plays to particular literary ideals. Beckett criticism cannot afford to deny the volatility of performance or the evolutionary vitality of adaptation in the interest of an arbitrary stability or an insistence on "accuracy." Along the same lines, in his excellent essay in this book, "Uncloseting Drama: Gertrude Stein and the Wooster Group," Nick Salvato convincingly describes the Wooster Group's engagement with Stein's text *Doctor Faustus Lights the Lights* as a sophisticated interpretation of it, "a mode of analysis more akin to the work of literary criticism than it is to the goals of traditional dramaturgy." He concludes that "the Wooster Group highlights the potential of performance to embody a way of reading." Their performance amplifies shades of meaning already at play in Stein's writing and offers another methodological model of close reading.

Of course, underlying Carlson's unhappiness with literary criticism is an assumption that plays *are* literature. He privileges the names Ibsen, Chekhov, Williams, and Miller because they are attached to texts and designate writers whose principal medium was language. Language evokes and creates scenic effects, whether in the mind's eye or on the stage, and in addition to being the playwright's medium, it is also the critic's – even as the critic's task is, like that of the playwright, to do cultural work. Ostensibly "non-textual" aspects of theatrical production (acting and design) are usually, themselves, products of language, especially for "modern drama" (as opposed to contemporary or seventeenth-century drama), which, as W.B. Worthen has said, epitomizes "the interdependence of the arts of writing and performance in the age of print" (*Print* 3). In his chapter, "Gossip Girls: Lady Teazle, Nora Helmer, and Invisible-Hand Drama," Joseph Roach argues that "modern drama" originates in the eighteenth century rather than in the age of Ibsen precisely because print and the development of the newspaper decisively shaped new dramatic writing, which participated in the changing structures of a society transformed by the increasing velocity of all kinds of information. The anti-textual bias of performance studies is wrong-headed not because the text must be revered as an autotelic object but because our *understanding* of a play begins and ends in language.[3]

The "specialized kind of script called drama" (Schechner, *Performance* 70) is, among other things, a kind of literature, which is to say a self-reflexive linguistic cultural form richly embedded in diverse literary histories and taught in literature departments everywhere (and not only in "drama courses").[4] Yet the diverse authors appearing in these pages attend closely to the fact that plays are produced onstage and to their social and cultural contexts. Of course, a work's theatrical value can be appreciated if it is also understood as literature. Drama's "literary" quality depends not on an essentialized literary discourse but on the fact that it has been regarded in this way (rightly or wrongly), at least in the important and diverse traditions of Europe and North America, since long before the advent of curricular or professional categorizations of literature around the turn of the twentieth century. In short, it remains relevant that people experience drama as literature and that they use the language of literature in referring to it, even in anti-literary disavowals, as the self-reflexive condition of its own origin.

Literary studies (and the model of disciplinarity it presents) has served as theatre studies' constitutive other. Theatre and performance studies persistently claim to have done away not only with foundational textual practices (which long ago came under radical critique in literature departments)[5] but also with disciplinarity altogether. Following Roach (who has called performance studies "postdisciplinary" [*Cities* xii]) and Dwight

Conquergood, Carlson calls performance an "antidiscipline" (*Performance* 189). I wish to suggest how we might begin to go about undoing that claim, not in order to show that it is wrong, but to propose that the anti-literary ideology or rhetoric undermines some of theatre studies' most valuable innovations. In her ambitious and sensitive study *Professing Performance: Theatre in the Academy from Philology to Performativity*, winner of ATHE's 2005 Outstanding Book Award in Theatre Practice and Pedagogy, Shannon Jackson both describes and instantiates some of these conflicts, beginning with the trendy application of theories of performance to literature today. The extremely various and contradictory connotations of the term "performance" (it makes community and breaks community; it is more fake and more real than "reality"; it repeats endlessly and never repeats; it is essentialist and anti-essentialist; and so on) paradoxically ground performance studies. As Jackson magnanimously writes, "Performance's many connotations and its varied intellectual kinships ensure that an interdisciplinary conversation around this interdisciplinary site rarely will be neat and straightforward. Perhaps it is time to stop assuming that it should" (15). Knowledge production requires boundaries or definitions, Jackson argues; performance is boundary busting, and this leads inevitably to tensions within institutional hierarchies. However, "performance discourse" has established a "liminal norm," a sameness-in-otherness, the centrality of marginality, that now characterizes the field, as theatre and performance studies scholars rush to assume increasingly marginal, oppositional, and occluded positions. They emphasize their own "difference" and employ a rhetoric of provocation but rarely disagree.

Jackson's work is sensitive to reductive characterizations by individuals practising within competing disciplines and sub-disciplines and the hazards of the synecdochic fallacy or the tendency to assume that one approach or piece of scholarship represents an entire discipline. But in spite of the book's rhetoric of generosity ("In the disciplining of performance, there are no clear good guys or bad guys" [38]) and its engaging prose style, its dominant affect is that of anxiety. Actually there are bad guys, and they tend to chair English Departments, like the putatively condescending and powerful George Lyman Kittredge at Harvard. Performance itself, we are told, is a site of "epistemological anxiety" (12), and it may make sense that a field that centres on such an idea inevitably reflects institutional anxieties, since knowledge formation and institutional construction are essentially conflated. The word "anxiety" appears with special frequency in the chapter entitled "Institutions and Performance," and there are so many examples that the reader comes away with the impression of a profoundly neurotic and defensive academic culture. Jackson argues that there is no escaping "the narcissistic and paranoid structures of an intellectual climate buffeted by a field of institutional power" (53) and that "paranoid and/or narcissistic delineations of sameness and difference are exacerbated by fields of institutional power" (42). Since institutional power is everywhere, academics in these fields suffer constantly "the interpersonal conflicts and inter-office paranoias that drive and derive from occupational change" (44) (the narcissists also tend to chair English Departments). Professor George Pierce Baker, who taught drama first at Harvard under Kittredge's chairmanship and later at Yale, where he founded the drama school, seems to endure constant anxiety. Yet, though he challenges the status quo and sometimes loses, the anxiety that Baker supposedly feels is inferred from "his institutional context" and not evidenced in specific expressions of anxiety per se. Jackson's basic model of knowledge formation and discipline is deeply indebted to Foucault, but, as such, it overstates the institutional force (or power) of the American academy in knowledge formation.

As a social form, drama is inherently comparative, requiring us to think about the structure and process of conflict in dialogue and to examine how characters share, learn, and teach new words. Of course, to share a moral vocabulary is not the same as to translate ideas from French to German; or, at least, a somewhat different and more difficult task of translation is required. Communities, and even individuals, can seem hermeneutically sealed off from each other. The notion that people living in a pluralistic society do not all "speak the same language" or that even people of different generations in the same family speak in different idioms has become a truism and a central subject of drama that is organized in thematic and formal terms by social conflict. But to say that people speak different languages does not mean that they have too little in common ever to understand each other at all. In his chapter entitled "Synge's *Playboy* and the Eugenics of Language," Nicholas Crawford examines the imaginatively hybrid diction of *The Playboy of the Western World*, an Irish drama written in English. Through a close reading of the play and its relationship to the Irish Literary Revival, Crawford shows how it critiques the eugenic and evolutionary discourses of heritage – biological, cultural, theatrical, and linguistic – that were contemporary with the play's debut. Synge was himself a student of languages, and his parodic oedipal drama both employs and resists an evolutionary fantasy of language. Specifically, the play subverts the notion that language can ever be pure or immune to mixture and mutation.

The process of learning to share language that dramas represent is literary, for in sharing fragments of languages rather than some kind of "universal" language (such as the "language of Shakespeare and Milton and The Bible," taught by Professor Higgins, author of "Higgins's Universal Alphabet," in Shaw's *Pygmalion* [206]), plays depend upon the associative quality of language, on tropes, on the mobility of metaphor. In his essay "Toward Black Liberation," Stokely Carmichael writes, "We shall have to struggle for the right to create our own terms through which to define ourselves and our relationship to the society, and to have these terms recognized" (119–20). The second half of the agenda is as important as the first. In a famous 1968 manifesto, "The Black Arts Movement," Larry Neal writes, "The Black Arts Movement . . . envisions an art that speaks directly to the needs and aspirations of Black America" (29). What such a speech would sound like, and the pedagogical aim of instructing a particular community in such speech, have been the project of playwrights around the world who have dramatized tensions between local and colonizing languages. Yet, to take a play that many associate with the Black Arts Movement, Amiri Baraka's *Dutchman* depends on more than a few bits and pieces of literary/linguistic material picked up from various traditional sources, tropes from Coleridge and Wagner as well as from Ralph Ellison, terms from Marx, none of which is to deny Baraka's importance in expanding a dramatic vocabulary around newly configured social practices. To say that a particular form of art speaks to a particular community is not the same as saying that the particular moral language associated with that art is relative or untranslatable. After all, central to *Reading Modern Drama* is the task of explicating and translating, or translating and explicating, a multilingual corpus from Ibsen to Parks. There is always a problem of translation, whatever the "original" language. It is the problem of moral intelligibility in the representation of (interpersonal) action.

I have spoken of the responsibility of reading plays; the ethics of all aspects of the experience of drama, from writing to reading to performing, are crucial to the diverse lines of inquiry in this book. In their essay, "*The Pillowman* and the Ethics of Allegory," Hana Worthen and W.B. Worthen show that Martin McDonagh's 2003 play allegorizes this question about the representation of stories and the structure of interpretation: what are the consequences of drama in the world beyond the stage? In its relation to the integrated arts of theatre, in its generally interpersonal form, its contingency to the social experience of an always implied audience, a concrete environment, the material bodies of actors, and the constraints of real time, drama has continuously challenged the segregation of epistemology and ethics, the true and the good, that has characterized modern (post-Kantian) philosophy. The fact that dramatic realism, still the mainstay of the commercial theatre, depends upon conversation, upon the credibility of everyday language – or, as Roach maintains, that "gossip is to modern drama what myth was to ancient tragedy" – is but one index of the problem of moral intelligibility that is central to modern drama, which requires of its readers and audience members the integration of thinking and feeling. Probing relations between the understanding and the will, modern drama represents the process by which individuals are changed by, and can change through, *sharing* language. The language of drama is, in this sense, different than the language of other literary genres, such as the lyric or the novel (though both lyrics and prose narratives are incorporated into plays), for, in its forms and in its contingency to a range of theatrical practices, it is closer to the world-constructing – the ordinary, non-metaphysical – work performed by non-literary language. Yet it also remains literary, self-reflexive, and disruptive. To understand drama in literary terms, therefore, is not to deny political readings, although it is to draw the readers' attention to the boundaries that define what is intrinsic and extrinsic to the work.

Close reading is entirely compatible with the drive to historicize. As Kenneth Burke shows, "linguistic analysis has opened up new possibilities in the correlating of producer and product – and these concerns have such important bearing upon matters of culture and conduct in general that no sheer conventions or ideals of criticism should be allowed to interfere with their development" (76). We should not insist that critical works manifest methodological purity, as long as the critical methods are plainly articulated. And what can be said today about the "producer" and the "product"? Literary and theatre studies of the past thirty years have been characterized by the intensive analysis of identity, as well as by the complaint that the New Critics, in their concern with the literary artefact, neglected to notice that race, class, gender, and nationality were vital factors in the production and consumption of culture. More recently, critics from Terry Eagleton to Homi Bhabha have acknowledged disaffection with identity politics, while pressing to further interrogate the metaphors and discursive forms through which power is deployed. In his contribution to a special issue of *Critical Inquiry* devoted to the future of criticism, Bhabha begins with an epigraph from Adrienne Rich's poem "Movement": "Race, class . . . all that . . . but isn't all that just history? / Aren't people bored with it all?" (qtd. on 342). One way to begin answering this question is to return to the concrete details of the texts that form the corpus of our study.

In spite of their emphasis upon the "performativity" of identity categories, as Walter Benn Michaels argues in *Our America*, critics who have focused on identity have not avoided essentialism (15). Michaels's polemic may seem to discredit political reading altogether; or it may more fruitfully be regarded as a caveat to balance subject positions (of readers and authors) carefully with a hermeneutic approach that discovers meaning in the text itself, the written word, or, as Michaels puts it in the title of his most recent book, the "shape of the signifier." For centuries, jeremiads against the degraded text have joined criticism of drama with a desire for spiritual renewal. But this literary critical discourse, like the plays themselves, is produced according to conventions it can transgress only because it finds them there. *Reading Modern Drama* calls for a kind of criticism that aims not to solve a text's problems but to read in a way that engages with their concrete, formal, and historical particularity, to recognize that the matter *of*, rather than *with*, drama is words, words, words.

At the same time, we must acknowledge and examine the idea that "drama" (from the Greek δράω, *dráō*: to do, act, perform) is a form of action, and insofar as ethics is intersubjective and active, even recent narratological studies have found this sense of the term drama inescapable. Adam Zachary Newton puts it this way: As "alterity" has come to "saturate the discourse of contemporary literary and cultural theory," "ethics" has come to signify "recursive, contingent, and interactive dramas of encounter and recognition . . . in acts of interpretive engagement" (11–12). The very grammar and structure of dramatic texts represent – we might go so far to say, *are* – forms of ethical encounter. By reading closely, in fact, we bridge the divide between "formal" and "nonformal" modes of criticism so that we can produce reasoned arguments about texts, even as we shed light on apparently extraliterary concerns such as race, gender, and class. In the process, we may discover that the challenge of understanding what the words contrive to say, like that of defining the insides and the outsides of texts, is richly complicated, ambiguous, and necessary.

It may be, as Lionel Trilling and others asserted in the 1950s, that all culture is oppositional, but one of the most infuriating (to some) features of drama – which is to say drama that succeeds with an audience – is that it forces us to dissolve such complacent descriptions of the adversarial, *pace* Robert Brustein and *The Theatre of Revolt*. Our eighteen- to twenty-five-year-old students are adversarial (if at all) in ways that are often unencumbered by the political orthodoxies of our academic fields – and the conflict between literature and performance, of course, largely stages or at least figures a projection of those politics. For most students, at least at large public universities like mine, a diploma is a passport to economic self-sufficiency, and the consumerist orientation that characterizes undergraduate experience can push instructors into positions that are themselves more adversarial, not to mention melancholic. *Reading Modern Drama* treats plays as sites within which to investigate ways not only of transmitting knowledge and examining method but also of preparing our students to take their place in a liberal, self-critical society. In analysing our own disciplinary assumptions and antagonisms, we can productively rethink what that means.

In his late work *The Conflict of the Faculties* (1798), Kant sought to distinguish the modern university from its medieval predecessors by elevating the role of reason above that of the simple mastery of authoritative texts. To rely upon textual authority is not to be truly rational; yet we must organize knowledge, and disciplines depend upon bodies of texts. In opposition to text-based faculties, Kant posits those, such as philosophy, dedicated to the public exercise of reason and scientific interests (*Wissenschaft*). Our universities and this book depend on the conflict between these faculties, which I do not reduce to literary and theatre studies, although literature and performance have been understood, simplistically, as allegorizing this binary opposition. Like Kant, we privilege reason over textual authority, but we don't do away with texts. Moreover, modern drama and the theoretical and critical writings related to it have modified our understanding of reason itself, as evidenced most compellingly in the following pages by R. Darren Gobert's analysis of the putative distinction between "feelings" and "reason" that are often taken to characterize Bertolt Brecht's theoretical approach to the theatre. In his chapter, entitled, "Cognitive Catharsis in *The Caucasian Chalk Circle*," Gobert locates Brecht's work up to *The Caucasian Chalk Circle* within a history of "emotion," a concept that underwent significant upheaval in the last century. A fuller appreciation of Brecht's evolving view of emotion within a cognitivist framework, as Gobert argues, allows a new reading of *The Caucasian Chalk Circle*, which highlights the integral role that emotions, more richly understood, might play in ethical decision-making.

Disciplines can (and must) evolve by interrogating their own foundations. The aim of self-interrogation, however – as it was developed by German philosophers after Kant – is not (or not only) to achieve Kant's abstraction of pure reason but also to serve the pedagogical project of *Bildung*, a process of knowledge acquisition and acculturation, a form of cultural work that includes our students. This project assumes neither the objectivity of the text nor the comforts of mastery. *Reading Modern Drama* concludes with Julie Stone Peters's brilliant essay, "Jane Harrison and the Savage Dionysus: Archeological Voyages, Ritual Origins, Anthropology, and the Modern Theatre." In one sense this chapter returns us to philology and its discontents, for Harrison has long been known primarily as a scholar of Greek drama and culture. Yet, as Peters shows, Harrison's real subject was ritual. A forerunner of later theatrical anthropologists, she believed that if Greek drama was "worth anything at all, it was an act of worship." In exploring this dimension of Harrison's work, Peters illuminates the primitivist rhetoric (and antitheatricality) of modern theatre and offers a model for modern theatre historiography which both challenges the provenance of the written text and renders modern conceptions of theatre as part of a broader continuum of performance practices. Peters treats Harrison, in short, as a template for "reading the nexus of preoccupations, desires, projections, and loathings that gave rise to some of the central strains of theatrical modernism and its offshoots." Strong readings, such as this one, surprise us with our own blind spots. But uncertainty must lead to analysis and argument, not anxiety. Performance is more than just an example of Kantian *Wissenschaft*. It is the central example for all of us, as critics, readers, and teachers.

NOTES

1 Translation from Artaud, *The Theater and Its Double*.

2 Ubersfeld writes that, "*comme tout texte littéraire, mais plus encore . . . le texte de théâtre est* troué, *T'* [the theatrical text] *s'inscrit dans les trous de T* [the literary text] (24; emphasis in original) [like any literary texts but even more so . . . the theatrical text has *gaps*, and that *T'* fits into the gaps of *T*" (translation from Ubersfeld, *Reading Theatre* [10]; emphasis in original). Julia Kristeva had already anticipated aspects of Ubersfeld's paradox when she wrote in 1977, "As a constructed model of a system of signs, semiology is a theory of the existent. Modern theater does not exist – it does not take (a) place – and consequently, its semiology is a mirage" (131). Kristeva's short essay was translated for the journal *SubStance* and the French text is not available.

3 I thank Darren Gobert for his conversation and correspondence on this subject.

4 For a nuanced materialist account of the absorption of drama into literature in the English-speaking world, see W.B. Worthen's *Print and the Poetics of Modern Drama*. Julie Stone Peters also gives a rich account of the relationship between printed drama and theatre in *Theatre of the Book*. For studies that productively complicate perceived antagonisms between literature and theatre, see Martin Puchner's *Stage Fright* and Jon Erikson's "The Ghost of the Literary." Puchner writes,

> Over the course of the eighteenth and nineteenth centuries contemporary drama (as opposed to Greek tragedy, Shakespeare, or "the classics") gradually constructed its "implied reader," to borrow from Wolfgang Iser, not only as a theater professional responsible for realizing it on stage but as a general reader: every dramatic text, then, is also, if not exclusively, a reading or closet drama. (20)

5 Here one thinks not only of de Man, Derrida, and deconstruction, or of Austin and later speech-act theory, but also of reader-response theory, the Konstanz school, Hans Robert Jauss, Wolfgang Iser, Michael Riffaterre, Stanley Fish, and many others.

WORKS CITED

Artaud, Antonin. *The Theater and Its Double*. Trans. Mary Caroline Richards. New York: Grove, 1958.

––––––. *Le Théâtre et son double*. Paris: Gallimard, 1938.

Benjamin, Walter. *The Origin of German Tragic Drama*. Trans. John Osborne. London: Verso, 1977.

Bennett, Benjamin. *Theater as Problem: Modern Drama and Its Place in Literature*. Ithaca: Cornell UP, 1990.

Bhabha, Homi K. "Statement for the Critical Inquiry Symposium." *Critical Inquiry* 30.2 (2004): 342–49.

Brooks, Cleanth. "Marvell's 'Horation Ode.'" 1946. *Seventeenth-Century English Poetry: Modern Essays in Criticism*. Ed. William R. Keast. London: Oxford UP, 1962. 321–40.

Brooks, Cleanth, and Robert B. Heilman. "Drama and Other Literary Forms." *Understanding Drama: Twelve Plays*. New York: Holt, 1948. 13–26.

Burke, Kenneth. "Symbolic Action in a Poem by Keats." Lentricchia and DuBois 72–87.

Carlson, Marvin. "A Difficult Birth: Bringing Staging Studies to the Pages of *Modern Drama*." *Modern Drama* 50.4 (2007): 487–99.

———. *Performance: A Critical Introduction*. London: Routledge, 1996.

Carmichael, Stokely. "Toward Black Liberation." *Black Fire: An Anthology of Afro-American Writing*. Ed. Leroi Jones and Larry Neal. New York: Morrow, 1968. 119–32.

Cavell, Stanley. *Cities of Words: Pedagogical Letters on the Register of the Moral Life*. Cambridge: Harvard UP, 2004.

de Man, Paul. *Blindness and Insight: Essays in the Rhetoric of Contemporary Criticism*. Minneapolis: U of Minnesota P, 1971.

———. "Criticism and Crisis." de Man 3–19.

———. Foreword. de Man vii–x.

Diamond, Elin. "Modern Drama / Modernity's Drama." *Modern Drama* 44.1 (2001): 3–15.

Edwards, A.C. Foreword. *Modern Drama* 1.1 (1958): 1.

———. Foreword. *Modern Drama* 1.2 (1958): 69.

Eliot, T.S. "The Function of Criticism." *Selected Prose of T.S. Eliot*. Ed. Frank Kermode. New York: Harcourt, 1975. 68–76.

Erikson, Jon. "The Ghost of the Literary in Recent Theories of Text and Performance." *Theatre Survey* 47.2 (2006): 245–51.

Fletcher, Angus. *Allegory: The Theory of a Symbolic Mode*. Ithaca: Cornell UP, 1964.

Jackson, Shannon. *Professing Performance: Theatre in the Academy from Philology to Performativity*. New York: Cambridge UP, 2004.

———. "Why Modern Plays Are Not Culture: Disciplinary Blind Spots." *Modern Drama* 44.1 (2001): 31–51.

Kant, Immanuel. *Der Streit der Fakultäten* [*The Conflict of the Faculties*]. Trans. Mary Gregor. New York: Abaris, 1979.

Kristeva, Julia. "Modern Theater Does Not Take (a) Place." Trans. Alice Jardine and Thomas Gora. *Sub-Stance* 18/19 (1977): 131–34.

Lentricchia, Frank. *After the New Criticism*. Chicago: U of Chicago P, 1980.

Lentricchia, Frank, and Andrew DuBois. Preface. *Close Reading: The Reader*. Ed. Frank Lentricchia and Andrew DuBois. Durham: Duke UP, 2003. ix.

Michaels, Walter Benn. *Our America: Nativism, Modernism, and Pluralism*. Durham: Duke UP, 1995.

———. *The Shape of the Signifier: 1967 to the End of History*. Princeton: Princeton UP, 2004.

Neal, Larry. "The Black Arts Movement." *The Drama Review* 12.4 (1968): 29–39.

Newton, Adam Zachary. *Narrative Ethics*. Cambridge: Harvard UP, 1995.

Peters, Julie Stone. *Theatre of the Book 1480–1880: Print, Text, and Performance in Europe*. Oxford: Oxford UP, 2000.

Phelan, Peggy. "'Just Want to Say': Performance and Literature, Jackson and Poirier." *PMLA* 125.4 (2010): 942–46.

Puchner, Martin. *Stage Fright: Modernism, Anti-theatricality, and Drama.* Baltimore: Johns Hopkins UP, 2002.

Ransom, John Crowe. *The New Criticism.* Norfolk, CT: New Directions, 1941.

Richards, I.A. *Principles of Literary Criticism.* London: Routledge, 2001.

Roach, Joseph. *Cities of the Dead: Circum-Atlantic Performance.* New York: Columbia UP, 1996.

———. "Performance: The Blunder of Orpheus." *PMLA* 125.4 (2010): 1978–86.

Said, Edward. *Humanism and Democratic Criticism.* New York: Columbia UP, 2003.

Schechner, Richard. *Performance Theory.* New York: Routledge, 1977.

———. "The New Look." *Tulane Drama Review* 11.1 (1966): 22–23.

Shaw, Bernard. *Pygmalion. Complete Plays with Prefaces.* Vol. 1. New York: Dodd, 1963. 189–296.

Stoppard, Tom. *Rosencrantz and Guildenstern Are Dead.* London: Faber, 1967.

Ubersfeld, Anne. *Lire le theater.* Tome 1. Paris: Belin, 1996.

———. *Reading Theatre.* Trans. Frank Collins. Toronto: U of Toronto P, 1999.

White, Hayden. *Figural Realism: Studies in the Mimesis Effect.* Baltimore: Johns Hopkins UP, 1999.

Worthen, W.B. "Drama, Performativity, and Performance." *PMLA* 113.5 (October, 1998): 1093–1107.

———. *Print and the Poetics of Modern Drama.* Cambridge: Cambridge UP, 2006.

1

Gossip Girls: Lady Teazle, Nora Helmer, and Invisible-Hand Drama

JOSEPH ROACH

Gossip is to modern drama what myth was to ancient tragedy. Gossip, like myth, offers playwrights a selection of favourite story types, well stocked with embarrassing details. Gossip, like myth, brings secrets into the public light, charming audiences with the socially cohesive pleasures of other people's pain. Gossip, like myth, unites communities against deviance in the cause of normality or, with equal efficiency, against normality on behalf of popular subversion. Ancient myth, however, handing down the world-historical heritage of atrocious deeds, concerned itself primarily with relations of kinship; modern gossip, by contrast, retailing damaging new information pertaining to just about anybody, strongly favours relations of negotiation and exchange. The only comparable currency today is money itself. Money, so often the subject of gossip, also behaves like gossip. As the word *credit* implies, money, like tit-bits of gossip, circulates arbitrarily in the form of fictional markers of value in which people must agree to believe in order to prosper.

Perhaps the most powerful effect of the gossip system – in which titillating information is banked, loaned, spent, purchased, and gambled – resides in the ambient pressure it continually exerts on attentive social beings. Such pressure stems, in part, from the possibility of becoming an "item" of gossip instead of its purveyor or consumer. Some people, for reasons of their own, seek such publicity. Many others dread it. But no one can escape entirely the often imperceptible and yet pervasive effects of its constant pressure, like the weight of air, resembling what Adam Smith, speaking of self-regulating economies in *An Inquiry into the Nature and Causes of the Wealth of Nations*, famously called, "an invisible hand" (1:456). The hand is invisible because the exchange of information at each transaction adds up to a total effect far larger than the sum of its parts, pooling into ever-deepening truth-effects – celebrity, notoriety, urban legends, ethnic stereotypes – blinding individuals to the full efficacy of their separate contributions, which are, nevertheless, still consequential to them collectively as part of "the great wheel of circulation" (Smith 1: 291). Smith takes care to explain the magical sleight of hand whereby some "pieces of money," like items of juicy gossip, amplify their effect simply by changing hands:

> A, for example, lends to W a thousand pounds, with which W immediately purchases of B a thousand pounds worth of goods. B having no occasion for the money himself, lends the identical pieces to X, with which X immediately purchases of C another thousand pounds worth of goods. C in the same manner, and for the same reason, lends them to Y, who again purchases goods with them of D. In this manner, the same pieces, either of coin or of paper, may, in the course of a few days, serve as the instrument of three different loans, and of three different purchases, each of which is, in value, equal to the whole amount of those pieces. (Smith 1: 351–52)

The special beauty of the great wheel of circulation is that it is reversible: "And as the same pieces of money can thus serve as the instrument of different loans to three, or for the same reason, to thirty times their value, so they may likewise successively serve as the instrument of repayment" (Smith 1: 352). When an individual attempts this kind of performance, it is likely to be stigmatized with ugly words like "check-kiting" or "Ponzi scheme," but when gangs of creditors like Smith's A, B, and C act together in ensemble with borrowers and buyers W, X, and Y, it is called "finance," and it is crucial to the growth of the larger economy. And so it is with gossipers A, B, and C, imparting their messages to listeners W, X, and Y, who are then obliged to reverse the exchange in self-interested reciprocity, like that of grooming behaviour in other primates.

The value of gossip, like that of money, also increases with its circulation, at least during the inflationary period before everyone who wants to hear it has heard it already. Awareness of gossip's effects is typically heightened when new media accelerate the speed of transmission and increase the potential audience, self-evidently so in the case of the recent rise of "social media." No modern subject, no matter how Luddite, escapes the reach of information's invisible hand. Anticipating its touch can trigger or suppress behaviours, while feeling its grasp can impose on diverse populations the conformist rigours of village life. Similar effects were noted, in the past, in connection with revolutionary developments in the world of print such as the advent of periodical literature. As early as the first decade of the eighteenth century, the pioneering journalist Sir Richard Steele signalled his understanding of how the coercive effects of gossip could increase circulation and "improve manners" when he titled his premiere journal *The Tatler*. Appositely, Steele made the theatre one of his principal beats. He knew that drama puts a vivid face, whether smiling or grimacing, on the faceless abstraction called "society," as is suggested by the time-honoured, uncanny hyperbole of masks, with their exaggerated eyes, and ears, and lips. Steele knew as well as we do that, while ancient drama mythologizes, modern drama tattles.

In imagining a gossip-based economy as represented by literature in general and drama in particular, I am indebted to Patricia Meyer Spacks's magisterial *Gossip* (1985). Spacks makes an historical argument in defence of "'serious' gossip," which she regards not only as a vital social practice but also as an art form, and she locates it squarely in the eighteenth century (20–23). This argument directly serves my larger purpose, which is to revise the commonly accepted period of what we call "modern drama." Beginning with a reassessment of the plays that Norman Holland long ago correctly called "the first modern comedies," I have argued elsewhere that the modernity of drama begins in the long eighteenth century, even as early as the English Restoration, multiplying its innovations continuously ever since (*It*, 12–21; "The Uncreating Word"). In one sense, this is merely to point out a matter of fact – that many of the revolutionary dramatic and theatrical techniques routinely ascribed to the nineteenth century have their genesis in the eighteenth. Such innovations include but are not limited to the candid naturalism with which Restoration comedy dealt with issues of sex and money, staging frontally – in realistic contemporary settings, indoors and out – the intimate activities of predatory social life among familiar protagonists dressed in the latest fashions (and undressed in them too). In another sense, it is to make a more speculative claim for the participation of drama in the changing structures of a society transformed by the increasing velocity of all kinds of information, including financial information. This includes the higher stakes attached to concealment and revelation, changing the ways in which people socially recognize one another and the ways in which they dramatize themselves doing so. Incidents of sex, love, marriage, and fortune are constant variables in dramatic history, as they are in social history, but I will argue here, for purposes of local illustration of a general trend, that the exemplary dramatist of the eighteenth century, Richard Brinsley Sheridan, fashioned a drama out of the pressures of the invisible hand, using some of the same techniques for which Henrik Ibsen has met adulation as *the* modern innovator. Gossip is the key to understanding the relationship of Sheridan's theatre to Ibsen's, because both dramatists seized upon the theatrical potential of the power of gossip in bourgeois life to inflate the currencies of money and information into the bubble known as scandal. Both playwrights knew how to use the entertainment value of scandal's runaway consequences to draw a crowd: it is fun to watch while other people gain and lose moral reputation just as it is fun to watch them gain and lose capital.

Though Sheridan's *The School for Scandal* (1777) and Ibsen's *A Doll House* (1879) might seem an odd couple on any syllabus, their common approach to gossip as modern myth joins them together in their own genre of serious social comedy – the blackmail play. Both dramas, not coincidentally, transpose austerely archetypical fables of moral and pecuniary improvidence into representative, tabloid master plots. *The School for Scandal*, which premiered a few months after the publication of *The Wealth of Nations*, originated as two separate preliminary sketches, "The Teazles" and "The Slanderers." Each of Sheridan's two plots consists of a biblically spare parable of truth: Lady Teazle, a vain young wife and feckless spendthrift is (almost) taken in adultery, but she is discovered, repents, and is redeemed; a bad brother (Joseph Surface) schemes against a good one (Charles Surface), but he is exposed, reprimanded, and disinherited. Joseph is the Pharisaical hypocrite, mouthing "sentiment," admired only by those he deceives and envied by those he does not – until his inflated reputation, like a financial bubble, bursts. Charles is the amiable ne'er-do-well, generous with his good wishes, profligate of his inheritance, but, in the end, worthy of romantic investment. The brothers' interests converge in the ingénue, the nubile heiress Maria, who circulates like money, and in a rich uncle from the wealth-producing plantations across the seas, who disguises himself as a loan shark and as a poor relation in order to plumb the depths of both Surfaces. In all these tests of social worth, gossip illuminates moral values by exposing private motives to the clarifying glare of public shame. The peccadilloes of the protagonists, including Lady Teazle's risqué visit to the lodgings of Joseph Surface, unfold before a kind of onstage public of representative scandal mongers. Lady Sneerwell, Sir Benjamin Backbite, Crabtree, and Mrs. Candour appear as the visible incarnations of the invisible hand, standing in for a larger, off-stage chorus of wagging tongues, as slanderous as Aristophanes's, chattering like *The Birds*, croaking like *The Frogs*. The playwright enlarges the audience's sense of the scale of the cabal by dropping the names of unseen collaborators. Their principal onstage spokesperson Sheridan names "Snake," lest the mythic resemblances of parable be lost.

In *The School for Scandal*, the blackmail is pervasive and diffuse, hovering as a potential threat (251); in *A Doll House*, it is more malevolently concentrated, but the allegory is no less biblical and the tabloid appeal no less prurient. Here, a vain young wife and feckless spendthrift risks the censure of an offstage society of scandal-mongers, apostrophized by Ibsen as "the whole wide world" (194); but the pressure exerted by their judgments, real and imagined, is even more claustrophobic than that imposed by Sheridan's carping chorus. On the surface, Torvald Helmer, a recently promoted bank vice-president, and his wife Nora inhabit a bourgeois Eden. He provides and pronounces, she consumes and complies, while the suburban deity smiles down in Miltonic complacency: he for the bank; she for the banker in him. But Nora has a secret. Or rather, in her startlingly complicated web of deceptions, lies, and child-like evasions, none as innocent as it seems, one big secret lurks, like a snake in the garden, threatening to poison the paradise at its source. She has criminally compromised herself by surreptitiously borrowing money from a shady bank clerk, Nils Krogstad, and worse, by forging her father's name on the note as security. Now Krogstad, on the verge of being sacked by the newly promoted and unsuspecting Helmer, threatens to expose Nora if he gets fired. Until he is diverted from his purpose of full public exposure at the last moment by the redemptive love of Christine Linde, Nora's confidante, Krogstad's blackmail terrorizes the Helmer household. Nora, whose first word in the play is "hide" (125), trembles behind a tissue of lies through most of three acts, like Lady Teazle hiding behind Joseph Surface's library screen, while her ridiculous husband prattles on downstage, clueless. The structural depth of this scenario of spousal fraud and threatened public exposure is proved by its persistence in subsequent dramatizations of bourgeois domestic life hovering on the threshold of myth and gossip. It is epitomized in American popular culture by the celebrated "Job Switching" episode of *I Love Lucy*, first aired on 15 September 1952:

> In need of money, Lucy writes on the back of a rubber check: "Dear Teller. Be a lamb and don't put this through until next month." Infuriated, Ricky declares: "Well, Lucy, what have you got to say?" Lucy: "Now I know why they call them tellers. They go around babbling everything they know." (Andrews 202)

In the carefully prepared, obligatory scene of each blackmail drama, televisual as well as theatrical, the screen of lies suddenly comes crashing down, with similarly unnerving discoveries for each of the husbands after the fall as well as contrasting but equally decisive outcomes for each of the wives. For blackmail to prosper – indeed, for blackmail to emerge as a distinctly modern phenomenon – potential threats of public exposure must be backed up by the availability of effective media of dissemination (Welsh ch. 4). These media have arrived punctually on the historical scene, ushering in a reign of terror for some, anxiety for many, and prurience for all. Along with the development of the newspaper, came justified fears – fears about the invasion of privacy, fears about the speedy dissemination of misinformation, fears about the irremediable destruction of innocent reputations, and fears about the degrading effects of unregulated consumption of idle talk. This list does not even take into account fears about the publication of damaging truths.

The prologue to *The School for Scandal*, written by the great actor David Garrick, wittily traces these alarms to the invidious effects, especially on women, of mass-circulation periodicals:

> So strong, so swift, the monster there's no gagging:
> Cut Scandal's head off – still the tongue is wagging. (Sheridan 228)

Garrick, himself a master of creating and maintaining a public image tantamount to a brand, deprecates "papers" by rhyming them with "vapors" (227). *The Town and Country Magazine*, a real eighteenth-century scandal sheet, makes a cameo appearance in act one, scene one of *The School for Scandal*, as Snake reports that Mrs. Candour has planted a morsel of insinuating gossip in its pages, linking a couple salaciously, even "when the parties perhaps had never seen each other's faces before in the course of their lives" (229). Providing Lady Sneerwell with a modern psychological motive for her vindictive participation in such malicious practices, such as collaborating with Joseph Surface in ruining his brother's reputation even though she is herself in love with Charles Surface, Sheridan has her explain, "Wounded myself in the early part of my life, by the envenomed tongue of slander, I confess I have since known no pleasure equal to the reducing of others to the level of my own injured reputation" (230). The scandal mongers take professional pride in their distinguished skills – there are no rivals, the audience learns, to Lady Sneerwell's singular "*delicacy of hint*, and *mellowness of sneer*," for instance, "even when they have a little truth on their side to support it" (230). But they also organize themselves so that their specialties complement and reinforce one another – an economy of scale as well as abundance.

The sophisticated interdependence of their specialized skills in the manufacture of a single product – gossip – recalls Smith's famous insistence on the efficacy of the modern division of labour, such as that carried out by the prototypical modern assembly line in Joshua Wedgewood's pottery factory, as a pre-condition for the success of the industrial revolution:

> The different operations into which the making of a pin, or of a metal button, is subdivided, are all of them much more simple, and the dexterity of the person, of whose life it has been the sole business to perform them, is usually much greater. The rapidity with which some of the operations of those manufactures are performed, exceeds what the human hand could, by those who had never seen them, be supposed capable of acquiring. (Smith 1: 18)

One extra insight implicit in this passage is that there existed human technologies, organized around social cooperation, which, to some extent, preceded material technologies, organized around machinery. Sheridan's scandal mongers, like the button makers, represent a proto-industrial organization, a set of manufacturing skills and practices that anticipates the divisions of labour in print journalism and ultimately electronic media – finding, reporting, and editing the news. Sheridan realized early in the communications revolution that there might be a falling-off of quality under conditions of mass production. When wildly distorted word of the contretemps in Joseph Surface's library spreads, for instance, twisting and turning on every tongue, Mrs. Candour, a traditionalist hold-over from the handicraft guild of oral culture, recognizes the superior speed and productivity, though not the fineness of detail, of the burgeoning print technology: "We shall have the whole affair in the newspapers, with the names of the parties at length, before I have dropped the story at a dozen houses" (293). While Smith extols the increased quantity and speed of production attainable through a division of labour into discrete specialties, Sheridan plays on fears that the same principles will come to govern the dissemination of gossip, with unforeseeable and perhaps ominous results.

Ibsen, a dedicated newspaper reader himself, dramatizes the long-term consequences of mass-produced information. In the revealing expository scene between Nora and Mrs. Linde in act one of *A Doll House*, the two women, old school friends, sit down together and gossip. They have not seen one another in ten years (130), nor have they corresponded; but they know a lot about one another, nonetheless. The intimacy of their exchanges is shadowed by the prior publication of the details for anyone to read. Nora knows that Christine is three years a widow: "I read it in the papers" (131). Christine, source unspecified, knows that Nora and Torvald spent a year in Italy (132). Nora, source unspecified, seems to know that Christine's marriage was loveless and that she had known Krogstad before marrying (133). Nora, source unspecified, knows that Krogstad's marriage was unhappy (139). Looking for a bank job through her connection to Nora, Christine knows that Helmer has been promoted, because, as Nora explains to her startled husband, "the story was wired out to the papers" (142). All the parties seem to be aware that Nora's father had ruined his public reputation in a banking scandal, for Nora later reminds her husband "how those nasty gossips wrote in the papers about Papa and slandered him so cruelly" (159). While imparting vital information about Nora's secret, which she naively can't help revealing to Christine, Ibsen also skillfully evokes the invisible hand – the ambient pressure of public scrutiny of private affairs. That pressure raises the stakes of being found out, first for Nora, who has lived with her dirty little secret for years, and then for Torvald, who panics when the blackmailer reveals the truth in a letter delivered to their door. His fear is intensified because he knows that Krogstad also maintains a sideline as a muckraking journalist

(159). The only possible remedy Helmer can imagine is an immediate pay-off and cover-up: "I've got to appease him somehow or other. The thing has to be hushed up at any cost. And as for you and me, it's got to seem like everything between us is just as it was – to the outside world, that is" (188). Nora had been counting on a more ennobling and self-sacrificial response, in which the inside world of her marriage would have outweighed the "outside world" of bad publicity, but no soap; and so she changes her plan of committing suicide, if necessary, by throwing herself into an icy fjord on his behalf.

If it isn't sex, money seems to be the root of all gossip, at the bottom of the innocence-shattering knowledge of good and evil. In a way that links the material preoccupations of invisible-hand drama from *The Man of Mode* (1676) to *Shopping and Fucking* (1996), Sheridan sees to it that every character in *The School for Scandal* is introduced with an expository digression on his or her financial situation. Snake remarks that Lady Sneerwell enjoys the status of a widow with a "good jointure" or spousal legacy (230). Two lines later Lady Sneerwell identifies Maria as heiress to a "fortune" (230). Charles Surface, however, beloved of both these well-to-do women, is "bankrupt of fortune and reputation," an early instance of the play's integration of the economies of money and information (231). Lady Sneerwell warns that Joseph Surface intends to make money the really old-fashioned way, by marrying it – in the person of Maria (230). Sir Peter Teazle remarks on the wealth of Sir Oliver Surface, whose "Eastern liberality" has given both his nephews, Charles and Joseph, "early independence," although the former has, of course, squandered his "bounty" (241). The level of financial detail in *The School for Scandal* extends all the way to the salary of Charles's servant Trip, whose gross take-home pay, we learn, is pegged at fifty pounds a year, less deductions for "bags and bouquets," items of personal grooming (262). Sheridan pro-vides such detailed personal financial information because it clearly inter-ests people – both the characters who people the play and the spectators who people the pit, box, and gallery. Sheridan well knew, as Ibsen did after him, that every X, Y, and Z in the audience – especially bankers A, B, or C – was in debt to someone else and probably deeply so.

Torvald Helmer's predicament as a banker–debtor is particularly poign-ant as the drama of the invisible hand plays out in his parlour. Women are assumed to drive bourgeois consumption. True to form, Helmer's wife is ostentatiously living beyond their means – that is apparent from the shop-ping spree that brings another load of consumer goods into an already well-appointed room. When Nora makes her first entrance, it takes a porter and a servant to help her carry her purchases. Like Ricky Ricardo, Torvald chimes in on spousal cue: "Has the little spendthrift been out throwing money around again?" (126). Like Lucy Ricardo, Nora wheedles and whines about money, reminding Helmer that his raise will soon bring them "piles and piles" of it:

> HELMER Yes – starting New Year's. But then it's a full three months until the raise comes through.
> NORA Pooh! We can borrow that long. (126)

As revenge propelled the actions of many ancient and Elizabethan tragedies, so credit provides invisible-hand drama with a sure-fire plot driver. Dozens of mortgage melodramas prepared the way for *The Cherry Orchard* (1904), and *A Doll House* was one of them, for Ibsen relentlessly exploits the anxieties about over-extended credit, putting, not the Helmers' house, but certainly their home on the block. Nora, in deep, way over her head, explains to Mrs. Linde, "In the business world, there's what they call quarterly interest and what they call amortization, and these are always so terribly hard to manage" (137). The dead-pan professional Mrs. Linde, however, has already patiently explained the law, "A wife can't borrow without her husband's consent" (135), while Nora, in full gossip-girl extravagance of attitude, chatters on blithely, demonstrating the good reasons why. "It *is* such a joy," she emphasizes to her frumpy interlocutor, "to wear fine things" (137). Nora explains that she secretly obtained the money mainly to fund a year-long vacation in Italy to save her husband's health. Nowhere else in the play is Helmer's physical health mentioned as a worry, past or present, but his financial health is on life support. He is threatened both comically by his wife's over-consumption and melodramatically by the dark hand of the blackmailer, which secretly holds the forged note, invisible even to the banker until near the end, but ultimately leveraging the menace of scandal for all it's worth. Thus, Krogstad threatens Nora, warning her that there is no escape from the invisible hand, even in death: "I'll be in control of your final reputation" (170).

When money and sex combine under the magical spell of misogyny, the opportunity to dramatize gossip breeds gossip, as does the likelihood that gossip-worthy incidents will occur. Sheridan had all the crucial details lined up a century before Ibsen. On her first entrance (2.1), sputtering in mid-row with her husband, Lady Teazle invites comic attack from Sir Peter on charges of her "extravagance," the female counterpoise to the "libertine" prodigality of Charles Surface. Sir Peter insists that she "shall throw away no more sums on unmeaning luxury," such as filling her dressing room with flowers out of season. It cannot be numbered among her faults, she retorts, that "flowers are dear in cold weather" (242–43). In act three, scene one, she hits him up for two-hundred pounds (259) and regretfully fixes the total size of his estate as equal to that of one of her other aging former suitors, who, unlike her husband, has since been considerate enough to have dropped dead (261).

Eighteenth-century essayists referred to "Lady Credit" by way of expressing their ambivalence about lending and borrowing. Sheridan understood this ambivalence and dramatized it. The introduction of the "honest Israelite" Moses, the stereotypical Jewish moneylender, into the auction scene of *The School for Scandal* appealed to more than the uncomplicated anti-Semitic prejudices of Sheridan's audience, though it appealed to that too (Ragussis). The wealth of nations depends on the availability of credit. Ethnic stereotyping depends on the availability of gossip. Both move to the guiding touch of the invisible hand, and Sheridan shows how one hand washes the other. The system of credit itself, once the only profession allowed to Jews and conventionally preserved for Jews alone, emerged from the medieval past tainted as usury. Despite the progressive trends evident in the Enlightenment (*Ernst und Falk* [*Ernst and Falk*], Lessing's plea for religious tolerance, dates from the same year as *The School for Scandal*), the position of Jews in eighteenth-century England was uncertain, especially after the repeal of the Jewish Naturalization Act of 1753, which had provided for them to become naturalized subjects without having to swear a Christian oath. Sheridan sheds light on the motives for retaining ghettoizing proscriptions against Jews, even as their financial services became more and more valuable: they were needed as scapegoats on whom to blame high rates of interest, the financial axle around which "the great wheel of circulation" turned but still a cultural embarrassment to gentiles. Perfecting his disguise in preparation for his assumed role as the Broker "Mr. Premium," Sir Oliver Surface takes lessons in "the cant of usury" from Moses, who instructs him on how to cast the blame for usurious rates on "a friend." This unnamed friend is an "unconscionable dog," who must "sell stock at great loss" in order to raise the money for the loan (257). Through the fictive model of the sequential exchange of credit (in the sense of a high-risk loan, but also in the sense of an unsecured belief about others), Sheridan thus dramatizes, with intermingled characters and caricatures, Adam Smith's "monied men A, B, and C" and "borrowers W, X, and Y" (1: 352), who keep the circulatory system flowing. The ultimate source of money, like the source of gossip, remains abstract, if not invisible, but its effects are everywhere apparent.

Sheridan's most significant stroke, however, is to make the most sympathetic character in *The School for Scandal*, Charles Surface, the most prolific borrower. His voracious consumption of credit is the vacuum that the nature of surplus capital abhors, into which it flows, and by means of which it circulates. Charles, in his amiable way, introduces himself to the supposed Mr. Premium:

> I am an extravagant young fellow who wants money to borrow; you I take to be a prudent old fellow who has got money to lend. I am blockhead enough to

give fifty per cent sooner than not have it; and you, I presume, are rogue enough
to take a hundred if you can get it. (267)

This prompts Sir Oliver/Mr. Premium to perform his "unconscionable dog"
routine, deflecting the opprobrium onto an offstage character, whose
affiliations, in case the point might somehow be missed, are represented
onstage by Moses. Such a scandal of indebtedness allows Sheridan to
make topical reference to the annuity bill of 1777, a law designed to
protect youthful spendthrifts, like both Charles and his servant Trip, from
signing over their as yet uninherited fortunes to usurers (257, 262). That
Charles Surface is vital to the national financial system as well as the
gossip system, Sheridan leaves no doubt. Urban legend has it that, when
the young gentleman falls ill, "[T]hey have prayers for the recovery of his
health in the Synagogue" (238). That Charles embraces the credit system
as he bids adieu to the kinship system, Sheridan comically emphasizes
by having him auction off the family portraits. "To be sure!" says Charles
to his disguised Uncle Oliver, "when a man wants money, where the
plague should he get assistance, if he can't make free with own relations?"
(270). That Charles retains the sympathy of the audience Sheridan also
affirms by rewarding him, at the final curtain, not only with Maria and
Maria's fortune but also with his Uncle Oliver's fortune – and thereby
hangs a tale of the global reach of the invisible hand.

Sheridan retails as financial gossip a fact of world history that Adam
Smith had trumpeted just a few months earlier in *The Wealth of Nations*:
"The discovery of America, and that of a passage to the East Indies by
the Cape of Good Hope, are the two greatest and most important events
recorded in the history of mankind" (Smith 2: 626). In *The School for
Scandal*, gossip affirms with facts and figures that Sir Oliver's sixteen-year
sojourn in Bengal has been very lucrative, indeed. His munificence funds
both Surface households, with 12,000 pounds to Joseph alone, and his
transmissions back to the motherland include "bullion," "rupees" (silver
coins of India), and "pagodas" (gold coins of India) (291). The hoarding
of bullion in the home country represents, for Adam Smith, the ultimately
ruinous policies of the old mercantilist system, but the political economist
is specific about the success of the British exploitation of India by finan-
ciers of the kind represented in the person of Oliver Surface:

The great fortunes so suddenly and so easily acquired in Bengal and other
British possessions in the East Indies may satisfy us that, as the wages of labour
were very low, so the profits of stock were very high. The interest on money was
proportionately so. In Bengal, money was frequently loaned to the farmers at
40, 50, or 60 per cent interest and the crop thus financed was mortgaged for the
payment. (Smith 1: 111)

Smith's information about Bengalese interest rates, contemporary with the play, shines a revealing light on Uncle Oliver's supposed naïveté about usury despite his many years in India. This comes out in the scene where Moses and Sir Peter coach Sir Oliver in the art of money-lending, as to the fine points of which the Nabob pleads ignorance:

> SIR PETER Oh, there's not much to learn – the great point, as I take it, is to be exorbitant enough in your demands – hey, Moses?
> MOSES Yes, that's a very great point.
> SIR OLIVER I'll answer for't I'll not be wanting in that. I'll ask him eight or ten per cent on the loan, at least.
> MOSES If you ask him no more than that, you'll be discovered immediately.
> OLIVER Hey! what the plague! how much then!
> MOSES That depends upon the circumstances. If he appears not very anxious for the supply, you should require only forty or fifty per cent; but if you find him in great distress, and want moneys very bad – you may ask him double. (257)

This is one of the moments in a popular work of culture when a contradiction in the socio-economic system is made to show itself only so that it can disappear quickly into invisibility. Sheridan presents plenty of gossip to suggest that Sir Oliver's role in the wealth of nations is to remove it from Bengal and put it into play in Britain, especially when he passes it through the slippery fingers of Charles. But his effort remains invisible even to himself. "Do you take me for Shylock in the play[?]" the mock-userer Premium wonders. Sir Oliver calls attention to his own misrecognition when he begins rehearsals for this role with the question: "How the plague shall I be able to pass for a Jew?" There's a bitingly ironic laugh-line in Moses's dead-pan answer: "There's no need – the principal is Christian" (256–57).

Both *The School for Scandal* and *A Doll House* build to a credit crash at the climax, which is what happens to Surface, Inc. and Helmer, Inc. when the screen falls. Sir Peter Teazle and Torvald Helmer know the dangers of credit fraud long before the former recognizes Joseph Surface and the latter recognizes his wife as skilled perpetrators of it. Hiding in plain sight, it is invisible to them. Indeed, Sir Peter is so preoccupied with one brother's over-extended finances that he cannot see the other's over-extended reputation. Sir Peter's remark to Mrs. Candour about the circulation of gossip, which he compares to notes of credit, is ironically on the mark at that point in the play (2.2), but its full appropriateness is not recognized until the screen scene (4.3):

> MRS. CANDOUR But sure you would not be quite so severe on those who only report what they hear.

SIR PETER Yes, madam, I would have law merchant [mercantile law, now called "regulation"] for them too: and in all cases of slander currency, whenever the drawer of the lie was not to be found, the injured parties should have a right to come on any of the endorsers. (250)

Adam Smith's doctrine of *laissez-faire*, the freedom of the invisible hand to grope anyone anywhere, has its great analogue in the eighteenth-century idea of freedom of speech. When Sir Peter rails at the scandal-mongers in the language of the prohibition of monetary fraud – "utterers of forged tales, coiners of scandal" – Lady Teazle replies in language anticipatory of the American Bill of Rights: "What! would you restrain the freedom of speech?" (244). Her courage in this regard, like Nora's, will be tested at the denouement. After the screen falls, both women "take the stage" with an opportunity to speak the truth in a way they never have before.

Nora's speech of realization and farewell – "But I can't go on believing what the majority says, or what's written in books" (193) – needs no recapitulation here, except to underscore her very last line before the famous door slam, when she offers Torvald the slender hope of a utopian "[m]iracle": "That our living together would be a true marriage" (196). Less famous by far, though similarly eloquent in its way, is Lady Teazle's response when she is caught *flagrante delicto*. Joseph Surface immediately starts concocting a plausible but wholly spurious story for Sir Peter to excuse her presence in his chambers. Chastened, she will have none it, and she cuts the hypocrite off cold, appealing honestly to her husband and yet sparing him nothing about her actions and motives:

Hear me Sir Peter! I came here on no matter relating to your ward [Maria], and even ignorant of this gentleman's pretensions to her – but I came, seduced by his insidious arguments, at least to listen to his pretended passion, if not to sacrifice *your* honor to his baseness. (288)

Joseph Surface interrupts to say, "The woman is mad!" Lady Teazle cuts him off again, "No, sir; she has recovered her senses," and so she has, with a similar commitment to the actual state of her relationships that Nora evinces, even though each woman makes a different decision about the future of her marriage. Lady Teazle goes on to explain that Sir Peter's expression of tenderness for her, which she overheard while she was hiding behind the screen and which he put in the tangible terms of a very generous financial settlement, has "penetrated to my heart" (288). As is not unusual in gossipy tales about an older husband making an accommodation for a younger wife, Lady Teazle is glad to get the cash – and she makes no pretence otherwise, rendering the invisible hand visible. Sir Peter, for his part, gets a wife whose awakening requires no "miracle" except a handsome jointure and the dignified freedom to spend it as she sees fit. At this unromantic plot point and moral turn, it is fair to ask which invisible-hand drama, *The School for Scandal* or *A Doll House*, is more realistic? Either way, the thrill of the denouement in each case derives from a sense that something like the truth has prevailed against long odds and that the gossip girls have transformed themselves into strong, clear-eyed women, each self-possessed in her own way and unafraid of the judgments of a world that seems ever more determined to drown itself in a bottomless sea of lies.

WORKS CITED

Andrews, Bart. *The Story of I Love Lucy*. New York: Dutton, 1976.

Holland, Norman. *The First Modern Comedies: The Significance of Etherege, Wycherley, and Congreve*. 1959. Bloomington: Indiana UP, 1967.

Ibsen, Henrik. *A Doll House*. *Ibsen: The Complete Major Prose Plays*. Trans. Rolf Fjelde. New York: New American Library, 1965. 119–96.

Ragussis, Michael. *Theatrical Nation: Jews and Other Outlandish Englishmen in Georgian Britain*. Philadelphia: U of Pennsylvania P, 2010.

Roach, Joseph. *It*. Ann Arbor: U of Michigan P, 2007.

———. "The Uncreating Word: Silence and Unspoken Thought in Fielding's Drama." *Henry Fielding: Novelist, Playwright, Journalist, Magistrate*. Ed. Claude Rawson. Newark: U of Delaware P, 2008. 40–57.

Sheridan, Richard Brinsley. *The School for Scandal in Six Plays*. Ed. Louis Kronenberger. New York: Hill, 1957.

Smith, Adam. *An Inquiry into the Nature and Causes of the Wealth of Nations*. 1776. Ed. R.H. Campbell, A.S. Skinner and W.B. Todd. 2 vols. Oxford: Clarendon, 1976.

Spacks, Patricia Meyer. *Gossip*. New York: Knopf, 1985.

Welsh, Alexander. *George Eliot and Blackmail*. Cambridge: Harvard University Press, 1985.

2

"Vinløv i håret": The Relationship between Women, Language, and Power in Ibsen's *Hedda Gabler*

TANYA THRESHER

The difficulty Ibsen's women experience accessing the dominant male discourse finds its most acute example in *Hedda Gabler* (1890), the play in which Ibsen's dramatic dialogue is at its most condensed and circumlocution is the dominant narrative technique.[1] The paucity of Hedda's words has been a matter of critical concern since the very inception of the play. In an 1891 review of *Hedda Gabler*, Edmund Gosse stated that

> I will dare to say that I think in this instance Ibsen has gone perilously far in his
> desire for rapid and concise expression. The *stichomythia* of the Greek and French
> tragedians was lengthy in comparison with this unceasing display of hissing
> conversational fireworks, fragments of sentences without verbs, clauses that come
> to nothing, adverbial exclamations and cryptic interrogatories. It would add,
> I cannot but think, to the lucidity of the play if some one character were
> permitted occasionally to express himself at moderate length ... (5)

While Gosse considers the entire play, other critics, like James McFarlane, focus on the central character herself, noting that the protagonist "must surely be one of the least eloquent heroines in the whole of the world's dramatic literature" (285). In line with McFarlane, Else Høst, in her 1958 monograph about the piece, considers that Hedda is

> *[a]ntagelig verdenslitteraturens mest ordknappe heltinne ... ikke det beskjedneste*
> *tilløp til en monolog er henne bevilget for å tolke sin indre verden; bare ved et par*
> *anledninger bryter hun med stykkets rolige konversasjonstone. Det aller mest av hva*
> *hun sier, går inn som nødvendige ledd i en høyst ordinær replikkveksling om*
> *daglidagse materier. Som en ren unntagelse faller en avstikkende formulering henne*
> *i munnen: symboluttrykket "vinløv i håret." (197)*

> [most likely the most reticent heroine in world literature ... [N]ot the most modest
> hint of a monologue is granted her in order to interpret her inner world: only in a

couple of instances does she break with the calm conversational tone of the piece. Most of what she says appears as necessary links in a highly ordinary exchange of words about everyday matters. A pure exception is the conspicuous formulation that falls from her mouth: the symbolic expression "vine leaves in the hair."][2]

Hedda's lack of garrulity is striking, but, nevertheless, the general's daughter shows an acute awareness of the power of words, knowing that they carry with them an emancipatory potential. Words hold the possibility of liberation from the ennui of bourgeois married existence and offer Hedda the opportunity to control the fate of other people, something for which she has a strong desire, as she admits to Fru Elvsted – *"jeg vil for en eneste gang i mit liv ha' magt over en menneskeskæbne* [for once in my life I want to have power over a human destiny] (*Hedda, Hundreårsutgave* 11: 355).[3] In spite of Hedda's consciousness of the manipulative potential of words, she never-theless fails to negotiate that potential adequately and ultimately chooses to appropriate silence as a means of challenging her position within the patriarchal order. This choice results from her comprehension of the emptiness of her words and of her resulting inability to attain the comradeship defined by Løvborg, an understanding facilitated by the death of Løvborg and the suspension of her belief in vine-leaves. Hedda's basic misunderstanding of language as a negotiation of power and her ultimate choice of silence are a stage in Ibsen's analysis of the mechanisms of meaning, an analysis originating most clearly in *Vildanden [The Wild Duck]* (1884) and culminating in *Når vi døde vågner [When We Dead Awaken]* (1899). This analysis, in turn, is closely connected to the self-reflexive nature of Ibsen's works and further highlights the aesthetic self-consciousness that situates the playwright more as a modernist than a realist.[4]

From the moment Hedda enters the stage, the play develops into a series of linguistic attempts on the part of the heroine at controlling reality and a growing realization that the relationship between language and reality is conditioned by the dominant ideology, in this case patriarchy. Hedda tries repeatedly, and with some success, to gain power through words and uses them to form an effective defensive barrier between herself and the Tesman family, a family that, for the general's daughter, as Ibsen wrote in a letter to Kristine Steen, *"danner tilsammen et helheds – og enhedsbillede. De har fælles tankegang, fælles erindringer, fælles livssyn. For Hedda står de som en mod hendes grundvæsen rettet fiendtlig og fremmed magt* [together forms a complete and unifying picture. They have a common way of thinking, common memories, a common view of life. For Hedda, they stand against her essential being as one hostile and alien power]" (*Hundreårsutgave* 18: 280). Hedda's rejection of familial affiliation comes about not only in the sustained use of "Gabler" as a surname but also in her refusing to use a personalized form of address for Tante Julle; in her verbally rejecting that epitome of Tesmanesque domesticity, Tesman's embroidered slippers (*Hedda, Hundreårsutgave* 11: 305–06); and, finally, in her purposely, as she later admits to Assessor Brack, insulting Tante Julle by pretending to believe her newly acquired hat belongs to the maid Berthe. In these instances, Hedda uses words to avoid becoming party to a social contract and to reinforce her social position as a member of the upper class, something that is increasingly threatened by her surroundings.

In order to take control of surroundings she increasingly finds "*tarvelige* [wretched]" (*Hedda, Hundreårsutgave* 11: 337), Hedda resorts to the coercive potential of words. Initially, this is apparent as Hedda, through simple questions, successfully elicits information from Thea concerning her current situation. In spite of an acknowledgment that she formerly feared General Gabler's daughter, an initial reluctance to talk with her, and a clear indication (in Hedda's misnaming her Thora) that the two have not been intimate, Thea willingly reveals to Hedda details of her relationship to Løvborg. Resisting Hedda's initial request, "*[f]ortæll mig nu lidt om hvorledes De har det i hjemmet* [now tell me a little about how it is at home]" (315), and her later insistence that "*nu skal du fortælle mig alting – således som det er* [now you must tell me everything – just as it really is]" (317), Thea finally agrees not merely to take part in the conversation but moreover to accept a kind of interrogation, saying, "*Ja, så får du spørge da* [Yes, then you can ask]" (317). In spite of some hesitation and speaking brokenly, Thea does, then, admit to Hedda the details of her life at home and the shocking (at least, for Hedda) fact that she has left her husband in order to follow Løvborg into town.

The linguistic control Hedda exerts over Thea in this instance has its precedent in her conversations with Løvborg, conversations that are verbal enactments, or theatricalizations, of his sexual exploits under the distant surveillance of General Gabler. Hedda and Løvborg self-consciously replicate these earlier conversations when they browse through a photograph album of Hedda and Tesman's wedding trip and talk of their earlier relationship, a relationship Hedda remembers as one of "*to gode kammerater. To rigtige fortrolige venner* [two good comrades. Two really intimate friends]" (*Hedda, Hundreårsutgave* 11: 347). Charles R. Lyons underscores the importance of Hedda's interaction with Løvborg in the Tesman living room, as it is here that

> we see both the mask, Hedda's pretense of showing Løvborg the photos performed for Tesman and Brack, and a rare honesty of language as Hedda relives the earlier experience. In Hedda's imagination, the experience she realized in these concealed conversations seems to remain the most vital segment of her life. At least, we see her engaged with the memory of a moment from the past with a greater display of energy than at any other point in the text. (106)

While Hedda recalls the earlier conversations with Løvborg as *"noget skønt, noget lokkende, – noget modigt synes jeg der var over – over denne løndomsfulde fortrolighed – dette kammeratskab* [something beautiful, something tempting/seductive – I believe there was something courageous about – about this secret intimacy – this comradeship]" (*Hedda, Hundreårsutgave* 11: 347), Løvborg is conscious of the power Hedda held over him:

LØVBORG   *Å Hedda – hvad var der dog for en magt i Dem, som tvang mig til at bekende sligt noget?*

HEDDA   *Tror De, det var en magt i mig?*

LØVBORG   *Ja, hvorledes skal jeg ellers forklare mig det? Og alle disse – disse omsvøbsfulde spørgsmål, som De gjorde mig –*

HEDDA   *Og som De så inderlig godt forstod–*

LØVBORG   *At De kunde sidde og spørge således! Ganske frejdigt!*

HEDDA   *Omsvøbsfuldt, må jeg be.*

LØVBORG   *Ja, men frejdigt alligevel. Spørge mig ud om – om alt sligt noget!*

(347–48)

[LØVBORG   Oh, Hedda – what kind of power was in you that forced me to confess such things?

HEDDA   Do you think there was a power in me?

LØVBORG   Well, how else can I explain it? And all those – those evasive questions you asked me –

HEDDA   And which you understood so well –

LØVBORG   That you could sit and ask like that! Quite boldly!

HEDDA   I had to ask evasively.

LØVBORG   Yes, but boldly all the same. Interrogate me about – about such things!]

As in the situation with Thea, Hedda was able, in this instance, to extort sensitive information through careful questioning, giving Løvborg the impression of participating in some kind of religious confession, an impression intensified by the use of the verbs *"at bekende"* and *"at skrifte,"* both of which mean to confess, in a religious sense. The implication that Hedda exerted a spiritual force is further strengthened in Løvborg's later inquiry as to whether it was not *"som om De vilde ligesom tvætte mig ren, – når jeg tyed til dem i bekendelse?* [as if you somehow wanted to absolve me – when I turned to you and confessed]" (348). For a woman whose acknowledged desire is to have power over another person's fate, this kind of expiation through storytelling must certainly have been attractive to Hedda.

Due to their content, Hedda's intimate conversations with Løvborg are clear transgressions of the moral boundaries of correct behaviour for a nineteenth-century middle-class woman. Similar in transgressive potential is Hedda's persuading Løvborg the alcoholic to take a glass of punch, persuasion masterfully effected through the revelation of Thea's concern for her friend, which necessarily calls into question Løvborg's understanding of the comradeship based on trust and open dialogue he believes the two share. Likewise, the incident with Julle's hat and that when the heroine says she longs to burn Thea's hair are evidence of a dislocation of words and moral responsibility characteristic of Hedda, something that the heroine transfers to Tesman with apparent ease when she convinces him to overlook the ethical implications of destroying a colleague's work by admitting she burned the manuscript due to her perception of his jealousy of Løvborg. Tesman's willing complicity is strengthened by the suggestion that Hedda is pregnant, and while his guilty conscience may ultimately inform his decision to piece together Løvborg's manuscript with Thea after the author's death, he nevertheless fails, during the course of the play, to disclose the true fate of the original piece of work. The power of words to hide reality is confirmed in Tesman's rash conclusion that Hedda acted out of burning passion for him, a passion associated with socially sanctioned love or the marriage contract.

An alternative to the marriage contract is offered in the comradeship between Løvborg and Thea, whose relationship best exemplifies the emancipatory potential of language and, in particular, speech. While publishing Løvborg's manuscript offers him the possibility of reinstating himself in society and will permit him a social victory, it is the act of conversing openly with others that, according to Løvborg, defines "*kammerater,*" the comrades of the future outlined in the new manuscript. Ibsen elucidates the relevance of comradeship in his notes for the play:

> Ejlert Løvborgs tanke er at der må skaffes tilveje et kammeratskabsforhold mellem man og kvinde, hvoraf det sande åndelige menneske kan fremgå. Det øvrige, som to bedriver, ligger udenfor som det uvæsentlige. Dette er det, som omgivelserne ikke forstår. Han er for dem en udsvævende person. I det indre ikke. (509)

> [Ejlert Løvborg's idea is that a relationship of comradeship between men and women has to be created, from which the truly intellectual person may result. Whatever else two people may engage in is insignificant. This is what the people around him do not understand. He is, for them, a debauched person. Not on the inside.]

Classifying comradeship between the sexes as "*Redningstanken!* [the rescue thought]," Ibsen further states in his notes that "*[d]et nye i E.L.s bog er læren om udvikling på grundlag af kammeratskab mellem mand og kvinde* [the new element in E.L.'s book is the tenet about development based on comradeship between man and woman]" (512). This development is closely associated with intellectual cooperation in the draft of the play, in which Hedda jealously imagines Løvborg and Thea working together in the Elvsted house (468). Hedda's hasty rejection of Tesman's offer to work similarly with him is evidence of her perception of her husband's unsuitability for such a relationship, something that the final version of the play readdresses when Thea and Tesman embark on recreating the lost manuscript in the memory of Løvborg.

In stark contrast to his relationship to Hedda, Løvborg characterizes his relationship to Thea as "*to rigtige kammerater. Vi tror ubetinget på hinanden. Og så kan vi sidde og tale så frejdigt sammen* – [two real comrades. We believe unconditionally in each other. And then we can sit and talk so boldly together –]" (*Hedda, Hundreårsutgave* 11: 350). Such an open dialogue has, for Thea, turned her into a "*virkeligt mennekse* [real human being]" (319),[5] as Løvborg has taught her to think not only by reading with her but also by talking about all sorts of things. Thea's desire to maintain her new-found status is revealed as she sets about piecing together Løvborg's manuscript after his death, for in recreating the object she has described as "*barnet* [the child]" (373), she is reproducing the consummation of the comradeship she earlier enjoyed with Løvborg, this time with Tesman.

This comradeship with Thea is, perhaps, an idealization on the part of Løvborg, and he later comes to regard their relationship in a different manner, claiming that "*[d]et er livsmodet og livstrodsen, som hun har knækket i mig* [she has broken the courage to live and to defy life in me]" (373). Such an ideal comradeship with Hedda, on the other hand, is unattainable, as talking with the general's daughter is an activity filled with "*omsvøb* [circumlocution]," a trait that affects her potential to become a true comrade and results in an inability to act. Løvborg suggests that with an openness of language comes action, by saying of Thea and her relationship to her comrade that "*[o]g så er det handlingens mod, som hun har, fru Tesman!* [and then she has the courage to act, Mrs. Tesman!]" (350). The inference that it is actions that, indeed, speak louder than words is supported by Thea's blatant disregard for what people might say regarding her abandonment of her husband in favour of Løvborg. To Hedda's question, "*Men hvad tror du så folk vil sige om dig, Thea?* [But then what do you think people will say about you, Thea?]," Thea replies, "*De får i guds navn sige, hvad de vil. For jeg har ikke gjort andet end jeg måtte gøre* [In God's name, they can say what they like. Because I haven't done anything other than what I had to do]" (319).

While Hedda's fear of what other people might say about her reveals her preoccupation with the spoken word and her awareness of language as a constraining, disciplinary mechanism, it is, nevertheless, Thea who comprehends the complex relationship between words and actions. After Hedda has manipulated Løvborg into drinking punch by causing him to doubt the comradeship the two share, Thea asks of the general's daughter, "*Hvad er det du siger! Hvad er det du gør!* [What are you saying! What are you doing!]"

(352). The clear association between word and deed – and hence the relationship of words to reality – is something Hedda has been indoctrinated by her peers to deny, as is most clearly evidenced when she threatens Løvborg with her pistols at his suggestion that they change their relationship into something physical. Hedda's motivation, as stated by the general's daughter herself, is the *"overhængende fare for at der vilde komme virkelighed ind i forholdet* [imminent danger that reality would enter into the relationship]" (348).

The relationship between reality and language is at its most dislocated in the motif of the *"vinløv i håret* [vine leaves in the hair]," an expression used to voice Hedda's vision of Løvborg once he has supposedly *"fåt magten over sig selv igen* [gained power over himself again]" (355) and become *"en fri mand for alle sine dage* [a free man for all his days]" (355). The expression, which is entirely absent from Ibsen's drafts for the piece and appears only six times in the entire play, contrasts sharply with Hedda's other language, particularly if we interpret the image as a Romantic one and consider Hedda's absolute disgust with words such as *"elsker* [love/loves (vb.)]," which she refers to as *"det klissete ord* [that sentimental word]" (331).[6] The vine-leaf expression occurs twice at the close of Act Two as Hedda explains to Thea her vision of Løvborg at Brack's soirée, reading his manuscript to her husband, and it is repeated, again to Thea, the following morning. When Tesman returns home, Hedda uses the phrase once more to ask her husband about the events of the previous night. Subsequently, as Hedda hears from Brack about the actual events of the party, she surmises that Løvborg did not have vine leaves in his hair. The final mention of the image occurs as Løvborg questions Hedda about her vision of his beautiful death.

Hedda has established herself from the outset of the play as uninterested, to say the least, in the natural world – conscious of the withering leaves outside, she is dismayed at the overabundance of cut flowers in the villa, for example, and requests that the curtains be drawn in order to block out the sunlight. Likewise, her physical aversion to her pregnancy adds to the incongruity of a natural image like vine leaves. Moreover, as John Northam points out, Ibsen does not fully develop the imagery of vine leaves in the play, something unusual in such a well-crafted piece, in which there is a subtle, gradual exposition of, for example, the curtain or hair motifs (70). Rather, the vine leaves occur abruptly at the end of Act Two, something that, in association with Ibsen's notes for the play, which say that there is a *"dyb poesi* [deep poetry]" in Hedda, Northam interprets as an indication of a "vision, a set of values in Hedda that is, for her, absolute, and therefore unchangeable" (501). These values, according to Northam, oppose the social imperatives that force Hedda into conformity with the conventions of society.

Clearly the vine-leaf imagery represents some kind of ideology in Hedda and may constitute part of her underlying deep poetry, but it remains difficult to assign it an essential nature, as the image remains under-developed and Hedda easily rejects it. After hearing from Brack the details of Løvborg's drunken exploits, Hedda admonishes Løvborg in Act Three to shoot himself beautifully. Løvborg responds, "*I skjønhed. (Smiler.) Med vinløv i håret, som De før i tiden tænkte Dem* – [In beauty. (*Smiles.*) With vine leaves in my hair, as you imagined in the past]," to which Hedda replies with the final mention of vine leaves in the piece, "*Å nei* – *Vinløvet,* – *det tror jeg ikke længer på. Men i skønhed alligevel!* [Oh no – Vine leaves – I don't believe in that any more. But in beauty nevertheless!]" (375). Hedda's renunciation of the vine imagery lessens the critical temptation to invest it with a sophisticated interpretation by way of Euripides's *The Bacchae* or readings of the Dionysus myth. Rather, as Lyons has said about such attempts, "the text itself gives us no evidence that she [Hedda] commands this kind of knowledge or that this paradigm infuses her language. Hedda identifies and celebrates Løvborg's rebellion, not its ideology" (87).

Hedda's ultimate rejection of the vine-leaf imagery is concomitant with the weakening power of her words, as, after all, Løvborg does not leave her with the intention of shooting himself beautifully at all but rather returns to Madame Diana's boudoir in hopes of retrieving his manuscript. Moreover, it clearly illustrates Hedda's evolving distrust of the liberating and poetical potential of words. Such a belief in the power of words to liberate, if we consider the fact that Hedda and Thea are the only characters who accept the vine-leaf image unquestioningly, appears to be female gendered and related to a willingness to transgress the limitations of patriarchy. Both Tesman and Brack respond with questions when Hedda uses the vine-leaf imagery in their presence (418, 421). They are representatives of a socially sanctioned use of language and uphold the dominant ideology through Tesman's written documentation of history and Brack's verbal interpretation of the law. Løvborg's use of the vine-leaf expression, while referring to Hedda's own and uttered perhaps ironically (as the stage directions may indicate), is evidence (along with the manuscript) of his comprehension, at least, of the desire to test the limits of the patriarchal ideology. Nevertheless, as his manuscript and earlier discussions of comrades suggest, he finds transgressive potential and an associated movement towards becoming a true human being in the practice of talking openly.

Unlike Løvborg, Hedda Gabler is unwilling to transgress the socially sanctioned linguistic indoctrination that has effectively taught her silence. While Hedda's vigilance with regard to open expression is shown in the way she rarely delivers simple straightforward statements but rather frames her utterances with questions in order to first ascertain the opinions of her conversational partner, her final appropriation of silence disrupts the disciplinary mechanism that society has taught her. Her relationship to silence is foreshadowed in the opening dialogue of the play, in which a brief interaction between Tante Julle and Berthe encapsulates the myth that is the general's daughter and underscores the distance between the myth and the reality that is the Tesman family. This dialogue frames Hedda in silence, for, while she is the topic of the conversation, she is absent – a situation paralleling that of the end of the drama. Moreover, her silence is tacitly connected to her newly acquired social status as Tesman's wife, as Julle and the maid mention that Hedda is still asleep in the marital bed with her spouse (295). Supporting her silencing within marriage is Hedda's own unwillingness to talk openly of her pregnancy or of any aspect of her sexuality; indeed, she actively tries to silence Tesman, when he begins to tell Tante Julle of the fullness of her figure, by interrupting him three times while moving towards the glass veranda, the space that symbolizes her desire for freedom (391). Likewise, the discussion with Brack regarding her wedding trip tacitly utilizes metaphor, here the train journey and the possibility of a third person's joining a married couple in their compartment, to suggest an extra-marital affair. As Lyons indicates, "This exchange demonstrates the skillful control with which both Hedda and Brack manage their sexual references within the safety of an almost-neutralized vocabulary" (123).

The careful neutralization of words has slowly relegated Hedda to a position of silence. The dangerous potential of such a position is most evident in Brack's silence regarding ownership of the pistol that fatally wounds Løvborg, for Brack's silence will place Hedda forever in his power, a power he intends to use for sexual exploitation. Hedda's diminishing power in this instance is underscored by Brack's increasingly intimate forms of address, as he switches from the formal "Hedda Gabler" and "*Fru Tesman* [Mrs. Tesman]" to "Hedda" and "*kæreste Hedda* [dear Hedda]." While Brack's silence with regard to the pistol is the most opaquely threatening, Hedda's social subordination through silence is evident throughout the play. Her situation as mistress of the Falk Villa, which is itself a spatial representation of silence due to its association with death and absence, has resulted from her desire to break silence with Tesman as he accompanies her home one evening (336). Her status as Tesman's wife is likewise the outcome of her silence regarding her sexual attraction to Løvborg, a silence the draft of the play intensifies, when Løvborg explains that he pursued a relationship with Thea as a result of hearing nothing from Hedda: "*Men da jeg så aldrig mere fik høre fra Dem, – aldrig fik et ord til svar på mine breve –* [But when I never heard from you again– never got a word in answer to my letters –]" (452). Hedda's response to this accusation – "*Det er uforsigtigt at gi' noget skriftlig fra sig. Og desuden – til slut – så svared jeg Dem da tilstrækkelig tydeligt – i handling* [It is not careful to give something written from oneself. And besides – in the end – I answered you sufficiently clearly – in action]" (452) – shows yet again Hedda's propensity to dissociate word and action.

It is Hedda's final choice to appropriate silence that allows her to re-establish the connection between word and deed and effectively neutralize the masterful threat Brack poses. Moreover, this new silence transforms her initial silence regarding her true feelings for Løvborg, something that she confesses to be her "*argeste feighet* [bitterest cowardice]" (349), into an act of courage. Her choice is made as she refuses to say, without any real coercion on Brack's part, that the pistol found on Løvborg was stolen from her. For a woman who, in the past, has shown a disregard for the truth-value of words and used them to manipulate and control others, this seems an all-too-easy confession, especially once we understand the dire consequences of it. While we cannot eliminate the possibility of a correspondence between Hedda's uncharacteristic insistence on the truth and an unwillingness on her part to surrender her past and/or her masculine power (of which the pistol is the most obvious symbol), Hedda's choice of silence, made all the more apparent by the playing of a wild dance melody on the piano, her disappearance into the back room, and her line "*[h]erefter skal jeg være stille* [after this I will be quiet]" (392) provide us with Ibsen's most provoking challenge. These words are not, in fact, the last time we hear from Hedda, for she actually delivers two more lines, the final one being her suggestion to Brack that he continue hoping to be entertained in her house as the cock of the walk, a suggestion abruptly broken by the sound of the gunshot. Likewise, her erasure from the stage does not denote the end of the conversation that is Hedda. Rather, it encourages Brack, as the representative of patriarchy, to search for a meaning behind words, something evident if we take the suicide as a defiant negation of his earlier assertion that "*Sligt noget siger man. Men man gør det ikke* [One says such things. But one does not do them]" (390), and his subsequent final line "*Men, gud sig forbarme, – sligt noget gør man da ikke!* [But, good lord, one doesn't do such things!]" (393).

With Hedda's final action Ibsen appeals to his audience to investigate the correspondence between words and actions, those elements that constitute the very foundation of theatrical art. At the same time, Hedda's theatrical erasure from the stage signals his fundamental distrust of the linguistic signifying system and reveals his "deep-seated skepticism with regard to our possibilities of knowing another human being" (Moi, 34). Hedda's final act is, thus, both a liberation from the absurdity of existence that tells us more than her words ever could and a deafening interrogation of the limits of the linguistic medium in relationship to otherness – an affirmation, thus, of the unspeakable beauty of vine leaves in one's hair.

NOTES

1   Charles R. Lyons gives a detailed account of the rhetorical strategy of circumlocution; see 110–35.

2 All translations from Norwegian, including those from Ibsen's plays, are my own in order to ensure the most literal translation of the original.

3 In Ibsen's draft for the piece, Hedda wants power over a person's *"sind* [mind]*"* (460) rather than fate. This strengthens her ambition for intellectual stimulation and offers a possible further explanation as to her choice and subsequent disappointment in marriage.

4 Recent Ibsen scholarship has sought to re-evaluate Ibsen's relationship to modernism. Atle Kittang's *Ibsens heroisme* and Toril Moi's *Henrik Ibsen and the Birth of Modernism* are two apt examples.

5 The importance of being a human being as opposed to a man or woman has been a recurring theme in Ibsen's work since *Et Dukkehjem*, in which Nora responds to Helmer's accusation that *"Du er først og fremst hustru og moder* [You are first and foremost a wife and mother]," with *"Det tror jeg ikke længere på. Jeg tror, at jeg er først og fremst et menneske, jeg likesåvel som du, – eller ialdfald, at jeg skal forsøge på at bli'e det* [I don't believe that any longer. I believe that I am first and foremost a human being just like you – or at any rate that I should try to become one]" (*Hundreårsutgave* 8: 359).

6 In the draft of the play, Hedda is much more assertive in her rejection of love, deriding Løvborg when he suggests she loves Tesman and explaining that she believes love does not really exist. Of love, she states that *"Jeg tror det er bare noget, som folk finder på. Og som de går omkring og snakker om* [I think it is just something people make up. And that they go around and talk about]" (*Hedda, Hundreårsutgave* 11: 448–49).

WORKS CITED

Gosse, Edmund. "Ibsen's New Drama." Rev. of *Hedda Gabler* Fortnightly Review ns 49 (1 Jan.–1 June 1891): 4–13.

Høst, Else. "Utdrag fra Hedda Gabler (1958). [Excerpt from Hedda Gabler (1958)]" In *Et skjær av uvilkårlig skjønnhet. Om Henrik Ibsens Hedda Gabler. [A Touch of Spontaneous Beauty. About Henrik Ibsen's Hedda Gabler].* Ed. Anne Marie Rekdal. Gjøvik: LNU, Cappelen Akademisk 2001. 85–91.

Ibsen, Henrik. Draft of *Hedda Gabler. Hundreårsutgave: Henrik Ibsens Samlede Verker.* Vol. 11. Ed. Francis Bull Halvdan Koht, Didrik Arup Siep. Oslo: Gyldendal Norsk Forlag, 1928–1957. 402–95.

Et dukkehjem. Ibsen, *Hundreårsutgave* Vol. 8. 271–364.

———. *Hedda Gabler.* Ibsen, *Hundreårsutgave* Vol. 11 261–556.

———. Notes to *Hedda Gabler.* Ibsen, *Hundreårsutgave* Vol. 11 496–556.

———. "Til Kristine Steen [To Kristine Steen]." Ibsen, *Hundreårsutgave* Vol. 18. 279–80.

Kittang, Atle. *Ibsens heroisme.* Oslo: Gyldendal, 2002.

Lyons, Charles R *"Hedda Gabler: Gender, Role, and World.* Boston: Twayne, 1990.

Northam, John. "Hedda Gabler." Ibsen Årbok 68/69 60–81.

McFarlane, James. *Ibsen and Meaning.* Norwich: Norvik, 1989.

Moi, Toril. Henrik *Ibsen and the Birth of Modernism: Art, Theatre, Philosophy.* Oxford: Oxford UP, 2006.

3

"¡Silencio, he dicho!" Space, Language, and Characterization as Agents of Social Protest in Lorca's Rural Tragedies[1]

BILHA BLUM

"The art of our time," said Susan Sontag, "is noisy with appeals for silence" (12). Although originally meant as an assessment of the cultural function of modern art, Sontag's juxtaposition of such antithetical terms as "noise" and "silence" places the work of art at a stylistic and thematic crossroads where the explicit and the implicit, the visible and the invisible, text and subtext or, indeed, what is said, shown, or done (and therefore "noisy") and what is not, can meet and interact. Each one of these levels constitutes an integral part of the work of art and, as such, it equally affects the construction of its meaning, in perfect accordance with the artist's intentionality. The additional task of the noisy elements, however, functioning as "appeals for silence," is to raise the addressee's awareness of those elements that were silenced, tacitly granting them primacy while foregrounding their position as the thematic core of the work. That is, from Sontag's angle, it would seem that in modern art, meaning is generated not only by a work of art's explicit components but also by those very elements the artist deliberately excluded precisely because he or she considers them highly important and meaningful. Choosing to silence whatever social or behavioural issues are silenced by cultural norms, taboos, and conventions, the artist can thus intentionally point to them and underscore their importance. With this strategy, commonly used by nineteenth-century artists such as Courbet, Ibsen, Zola, or Balzac in works informed by the "slice-of-life" principle of representation, a critical and even subversive attitude toward reality develops, while those features of society the artist wishes to criticize, remain explicit, visible, or, in Sontag's words, "noisy."

From a theatrical perspective, the tension that emerges between what is included and what is excluded from a dramatic artwork can also be viewed as an artistic technique for extending the significance of what seems to be a merely formal differentiation between stage (what the spectators are able to see) and offstage (what is withheld from their sight). In the dramatic work of Federico García Lorca this differentiation is particularly significant, as it matches the stark contrast between an authentically portrayed reality, typical of many of his plays (which he infused with a rich Catholic scent often verging on folklorism), functioning as a "signo icónico de extraordinaria coherencia" ("an iconic sign of extraordinary coherence"; Fernández Cifuentes 15),[2] and an alternative, rather imaginary existential sphere, implied by the text. The latter, paralleling the silenced aspects of society, Lorca either completely banishes from the stage (as in *The House of Bernarda Alba*) or relegates to only one part of the play (as in *Blood Wedding*), using an abrupt stylistic shift from prose to poetry to set it apart from all the rest. Given Lorca's unique use of dramatic language, in both the above plays, as well as in *Yerma*, which completes what is known as the "rural tragic trilogy" he wrote in the 1930s, this imaginative alternative world is further created through the evocative power of his poetry and rich metaphoric formulations. As he himself stated in 1927 in a lecture on the Spanish poet Góngora, only the language of poetry can express this two-pronged perception, which constitutes one of its most outstanding generic features:

Para que una metáfora tenga vida necesita dos condiciones esenciales, forma y radio de acción. Su núcleo central y una redonda perspectiva en torno de él. El núcleo se abre como una flor que nos sorprende por lo desconocido, pero en el radio de luz que lo rodea hallamos el nombre de la flor y conocemos su perfume. ("La Imagen Poética," 3: 230)

[For a metaphor to prevail, two essential conditions are required: form and radius of action; its central core and a circular perspective surrounding it. Its nucleus opens up like a flower that surprises us because we don't recognize it, but in the circle of light that surrounds it we will find the flower's name and also recognize its perfume.] (my translation)

Used by Lorca to describe the nature of metaphor, this mysterious flower suggests the link between the known and the unknown that is required to produce a chain of associations that travel from solid ground to the much more fragile, ideal, and mysterious level of existence, which Lorca believes should be reality, but isn't. This dialectical outlook prompted Lorca to create onstage a world with such components as characters, sets, costumes, and social hierarchies, chosen primarily according to their resemblance to reality, while the audience is also offered, subversively enough, an entirely different world, accessible only through an associative chain of thought.

As in other dramatic works focused on staging a realistic representation of the world, the social implications suggested by Lorca's rural tragedies manifest themselves in his manipulation of two of the most basic structural components of drama: space and language. The thematic factor added to both the formal division of space between stage and offstage and the shift between prose and poetry, meant to encourage the audience to move between the real and the ideal, sets Lorca's plays beyond the limits of realism. The need arises for a different critical approach underpinned by a theoretical confrontation between the constituents of these two binaries – stage/offstage and prose/poetry – as implied by the text itself, further reinforced by yet a third binary – life/death – also deeply implanted in the dramatic text. Moreover, as a result of death's intimate relation with silence (being, as it is, the result of its counterpart's exclusion just like offstage and poetry),[3] and its exclusively abstract nature determined mainly by cultural paradigms and contextual beliefs, the life/death binary, as we shall presently see, is made to fulfill a most important role in deciphering the meaning of Lorca's plays from a synchronic perspective. Given my concern with characterization as a substantial structural component of drama, I refer to this binary as the central parameter of my analysis of these plays.

I believe that such an analytical approach offers a new contextual reading of Lorca's rural tragedies, commonly regarded as his most mature plays, especially because, borrowing Baz Kershaw's phrase, they should indeed be considered "as a cultural construct and as a means of cultural production" (5). Functioning as such, Lorca's plays not only respond and react to their social entourage by artistically embodying society's features and content, but they also create a world of their own.[4] They become what Elin Diamond refers to as "cultural practices." In this sense, although my methodology is based essentially on play analysis, I will follow her assessment that performances, as reconstructions of their cultural milieu, are not only "reinscriptions" that "passionately reinvent the ideas, symbols, and gestures that shape social life" but are also the outcome of "negotiations with regimes of power, be they proscriptive conventions of gender and bodily display . . . or racist conventions sanctioned by state power" (2).

SPACE: STAGE VERSUS OFFSTAGE

The differentiation between the real and the ideal characteristic of Lorca's tragedies, in both its literal and figurative meanings (stage versus offstage and real world versus its idealistic alternative, respectively), is most tangible in *The House of Bernarda Alba*, a play imbued with silence and set in the house of a rural family inhabited only by females after the father's death. In this play, where a widowed mother wields inexorable power over her five daughters, Lorca draws a neat dividing line between the visible and the invisible, as perceived by the audience. Set onstage, the former corresponds to traditional norms and takes the concrete form of the public rooms of the house where the dramatic action takes place, including its furniture and mundane objects, which Lorca's Spanish audience of the 1930s, albeit urban and middle class, could easily identify as reflecting the peasant population's milieu, then considered the most genuinely loyal to tradition.[5] On the other hand, hidden from the spectators' eyes, the invisible is meant to seep into their consciousness through the carefully constructed implications of the events onstage. Placed in the offstage area, it primarily echoes the transgression of the social rules so meticulously obeyed onstage, and materializes mainly in the private rooms of the house to which the characters withdraw in their flight from social disapproval. Having banished privacy to the offstage area, the playwright additionally suggests that intimacy, feelings, and even poetry remain off-limits as well.

This unseen realm, which includes a place "a la orilla del mar" (2: 1004) ("by the shore of the sea"; 168) where María Josefa, the lunatic grandmother, wants to get married, is filled with the disturbing results of disobeying social norms: children born out of wedlock and forbidden relationships, as well as several amorous encounters, the most notorious of which are Adela's clandestine meetings with Pepe el Romano, her older sister's betrothed. Adela's erotic liaison with Pepe is screened off from both the spectators and the other characters in the play. It is precisely this secretiveness that, besides defining passion as sinful and repulsive, also echoes Lorca's well-designed differentiation between the two levels of reality he wishes to forge: one obedient to the dictates of tradition and the other, favoured by him despite its tragic results, centred on freedom of the self.

The lack of expression of human feelings in the society depicted onstage becomes especially poignant as one follows Bernarda's relationship with her daughters, marked by her unremitting efforts to silence them and suppress their ability to feel and express both happiness and grief. Even after their father's funeral she orders one of the girls to be quiet, advising her to crawl under her bed, obviously placed offstage in her private room, if she wishes to cry: "Si quieres llorar te metes debajo de la cama" (2: 980) ("If you want to cry, get under your bed"; 155). Obsessed with the fear of public opinion and swayed by prejudice, Bernarda, who functions here as the executor of the playwright's dramatic strategy, also swears her daughters to silence even when forced to confront her youngest daughter's suicide, committed because she had mistaken her mother for her lover's murderer:

Y no quiero llantos. La muerte hay que mirarla cara a cara. ¡Silencio! ¡A callar he dicho! ¡Las lágrimas cuando estés sola! ¡Nos hundiremos todas en un mar de luto! . . . ¡Me habéis oído? Silencio, silencio, he dicho! ¡Silencio! (2: 1066)

[And I want no weeping. Death must be looked at face to face. Silence! Be still, I said! Tears when you're alone! We'll drown ourselves in a sea of mourning . . . Did you hear me? Silence, silence, I said, Silence!] (201)

Society's grip on the characters' privacy is so tight, however, that not only the harsh characterization of Bernarda as a despot ruling over her daughters' lives enhances the differentiation between stage and offstage. The utter exclusion of feelings from the theatrical stage, which she so cruelly inflicts upon the other characters, is also self-inflicted, as suggested on various occasions by the daughters' reluctance to speak their hearts because they either fear punishment or feel uneasy about breaking traditional norms. Indeed, in most encounters that take place in the public rooms in front of the audience, they refrain from expressing their true feelings. The dialogue between Martirio and Amelia, which vaguely hints at Adela's illicit relationship with Pepe, is but one example of Lorca's tacit and explicit recourse to silence as a kind of offstage, in which he transfers the characters' intentions from text to subtext (or from stage to offstage) and at the same time interweaves speech with silence:

MARTIRIO. No. No. No digas nada, puede ser un barrunto mío.
AMELIA. Quizá. (*Pausa. Amelia inicia el mutis.*)
MARTIRIO. Amelia.
AMELIA. (*en la puerta*) ¿Qué? (*Pausa*)
MARTIRIO. Nada. (*Pausa*)
AMELIA. ¿Por qué me llamaste? (*Pausa*)
MARTIRIO. Se me escapó. Fue sin darme cuenta. (*Pausa*) (2: 1023–24)

[MARTIRIO. No. No. Don't say anything. It may be I've just imagined it.
AMELIA. Maybe. (*Pause. Amelia starts to go.*)
MARTIRIO. Amelia!
AMELIA. (*at the door*): What? (*Pause*)
MARTIRIO. Nothing. (*Pause*)
AMELIA. Why did you call me? (*Pause*)
MARTIRIO. It just came out. I didn't mean to. (*Pause*)]   (178)

A theatre artist, Lorca must have been well aware of the effect staged silence would have on the audience. The absence of sound is at once visual and auditory, and is certain to cause those sitting in the theatre, as well as the characters themselves, some embarrassment or, at the very least, slight discomfort. Some of Chekhov's plays and certainly those of Beckett, both by modern playwrights who question the effectiveness of language as a means of genuine human communication, corroborate this assumption. In this dialogue, text and subtext are clearly enmeshed, with the words themselves covering up the hidden message alluding to Adela's love affair, too slanderous for overt references.[6] Moreover, the numerous pauses between the lines reveal Martirio's inner struggle between her fear of revealing her sister's outrageous behaviour and her growing inclination to hurt her out of jealousy. It should be noted that Martirio, depicted as an ugly, slightly deformed young woman, is also secretly as well as hopelessly in love with Pepe. The passionate, albeit illicit, relationship between a woman and a man, as hinted at in the recurring pauses, the veiled subtext, and the awkwardness of the audience caused by the use of silence where noise is expected, place the spectators in the rather difficult position of having to test their loyalty to the prevailing value system. Putting passion and natural needs side by side with emotional restraint and honourable behaviour, both strongly damaging to the soul, is, I believe, one of Lorca's ways of questioning the moral validity of prevalent values while suggesting that living according to the rules may be destructive.

LANGUAGE: PROSE VERSUS POETRY

Blood Wedding, a story of love, betrayal, and revenge taking place in an Andalusian village, also examines social and personal priorities and their effect on both the characters and the audience. The transition from the painstaking representation of reality of the two first acts in the play, to the alternative world that Lorca exalted, is conveyed by a radical change of scenery and by an abrupt stylistic passage from prose to poetry.[7] At the end of the second of the three acts that compose the play, the dramatic action indeed shifts from a suffocating barren desert where the villagers live in houses whose walls "echan fuego" (2: 736) ("give off heat"; 53), to a poetic forest, described as a dark, damp, and cool place, whose denizens are the personification of the moon, three woodcutters, and death, which appears on stage as a beggar. All of these speak poetry, as do the "sinful" lovers, Leonardo and the Bride, who, by eloping on the day of her wedding to the Bridegroom, foiled the consummation of marital vows. Carried away by their mutual physical attraction and having broken the rules of normative conduct, the two lovers are the only realistic characters allowed to become an integral part of the forest. All the others, such as the Bridegroom, the Mother, or the Father, who are overpowered by social forces, speak prose, the only language used in the realm of reality. Moreover, it seems that Lorca chose the forest as it is the only place where the lovers can find shelter from persecution by those villagers in charge of enforcing the social contract. Home to fantastic figures impelled solely by instinct and passions, the wild forest is naturally the place furthest from civilization and closest to poetry and creation, and thus the most suitable to shield the illicit lovers from harm.

In *Blood Wedding*, the two different levels of existence suggested by the play thus emerge through the stylistic shift from prose to poetry. In *The House of Bernarda Alba*, written in 1936, four years after the completion of *Blood Wedding*, the same result was achieved through a different dramatic technique, one that often ranks the play with realistic works: the suspension of poetry altogether. This move and the chronological order of these two plays, with *Yerma* in between both stylistically and chronologically, point to a development in Lorca's artistic and social attitude. It seems that by 1936, Franco's Falangist forces of reaction were steadily eroding Lorca's dreams of social change, spurring him to offer his audience an accurate picture of society, free of illusions, "un documental fotográfico" (2: 973) ("a photographic document"; 150), as he himself defined it. In both plays, however, the visible realistic level, the most familiar to the spectators, is regulated by the normative codes set by society, while the invisible, silent, non-realistic, and poetic level is generated by the creative power of imagination, as well as by instinct, passion, and freedom of thought. In Lorca's hands, Sontag's "silence" has thus become an artistic tool used to express the inexpressible, that is, to create a meaningful encounter between the spectator and what is impossible, socially forbidden, or traditionally ignored because of cultural taboos and social norms calling for compliance. In this sense, it is the highly mimetic emphasis of Lorca's plays that clamours for social change: offered a replica of its own way of life and surroundings, both visually and in content, the audience immediately identifies with the familiar elements onstage, yet is forced, at the same time, to face the fatal consequences of its blind submission to the social order with which it has just identified.

The wake ceremony at the beginning of *The House of Bernarda Alba* underscores Lorca's sense of reality, as it was certainly inspired by similar ceremonies taking place in Spain at that time. The same is true of the scene depicting the ritual mourning for the two men, Leonardo and the Bridegroom, who kill each other in the forest in the closing act of *Blood Wedding*. Highly realistic too are the time-honoured black dresses worn by many of Lorca's female characters and the extreme loyalty to the dead displayed by the various widows, such as Bernarda, the Mother, and the Neighbour Woman. The wedding celebrations in *Blood Wedding*, the colourful and graceful "lavanderas" (laundresses) in *Yerma*, and even the rather orgiastic fertility rituals at the end of this latter play, are all deeply entrenched in Spanish tradition and were thus familiar to the plays' synchronic audience. As the effect of familiarity on an audience is usually confirmation of the world represented onstage, it could be argued that as a result, the spectators are tempted passively to accept the legitimacy of prevailing social conventions. Following the string of grim events in these plays, however, this faithful representation of reality eventually turns their acceptance into rejection until the normative values of society are at last completely overturned. That is, the reversal in the spectators' attitude that Lorca obviously wishes to achieve stems mainly from the severe damage the social rules have inflicted on the characters, with some doomed to live and some to die. I argue that this radical change ensues from the reversal of the concept of life and death embedded in the plays, which parallels Sontag's "noise/silence" antithesis and tacitly privileges death in its modern conception.

CHARACTERIZATION: LIFE VERSUS DEATH

Although it has garnered frequent changes in attitude spawned by cultural and religious developments, modernity regards death mainly as the irreversible and enigmatic end of earthly life and as a unique phenomenon in human perception, whose most eminent characteristic is that it cannot be experienced and then described. Alan Warren Friedman claims that death, now viewed as "distant, other, abstract, a mythical construct" (3), is actually unreal. "[U]nlike all other experiences," he rightly argues, "death is fictional even when closest because it is always vicarious, never truly our own" (3), and though it may occur in our immediate vicinity, to our most beloved, it is still difficult to comprehend, as it has no familiar, agreed on, or proven referent in the real world to which we can relate. In fact, death has no palpable existence beyond the images created in our minds and souls by its various representations common within the cultural and social group we belong to, such as religious rituals or ceremonies, secular traditions, legends and stories, verbal clichés, or even certain dress codes that members of the same community tend to easily recognize. Yet, as Freud noted, most obscure of all is the concept of death when it concerns us personally. "It is indeed impossible to imagine our own death," he wrote, "and whenever we attempt to do so we can perceive that we are in fact still present as spectators" (77).

In this sense, a certain analogy can be drawn between death as an abstract entity, described by Friedman as a "mythical construct," and the unreal or fictional world usually connected with theatre as an art, to which we indeed generally relate as "spectators." It seems quite natural then that Lorca, like Freud, saw death as detached from daily reality and associated it with that same ideal reality he created in his plays and presented to his audience as a substitute for the prosaic world in which they all lived. Furthermore, death in these plays is so intimately intertwined with the ideal that only those characters who reject or are rejected by society are "allowed" to die. On the other hand, those who do not die reflect normative conduct when judged by the behavioural parameters of synchronic Spanish society. The Mother and the Bride in *Blood Wedding*, Yerma in *Yerma*, and Bernarda and her daughters (except Adela) in *The House of Bernarda Alba*, all display an almost obsessive loyalty to the norms and are willing to forgo their personal freedom for the sake of complying with them, just as the theatre audience would. The Mother is probably the most extreme case of normative conduct, as she is the one to pay the highest price. She literally sacrifices her only son's life by sending him to pursue Leonardo in the forest after his escape with the Bride, simply because saving his honour (clearly a socially conditioned principle) is more important than saving his life. Likewise, the Bride, by agreeing to marry the Bridegroom, gives up her overwhelming passion for Leonardo, whose presence, she admits, makes her feel intoxicated with love: "Es como si me bebiera una botella de anís y me durmiera en una colcha de rosas" (2: 743) ("It's as though I'd drunk a bottle of anise and fallen asleep wrapped in a quilt of roses" [57–58]). Despite her undeniable desire, she acts as she does to preserve her seeming decency.

Faced with the imperative choice between appearances and motherhood, both Yerma and Bernarda opt for the former. In Yerma's case, even her obsessive yearning for a child, depicted in the play as the very core of her existence, seems to be modulated by her inordinate sense of honour rather than by love and affection.[8] For her, motherhood is more a woman's primary social obligation than the road to happiness and self-fulfillment rooted in love. This stance is implied by her description of her imaginary son, whose unusual verbal images elicit feelings of sheer coldness and pain rather than the tenderness that might be expected. Alone in her house, with a sewing basket dutifully placed at her feet, she sings to her non-existent son, pleading with him to come, while revealing to the spectators her true attitude:

> ¿De dónde vienes, amor, mi niño?,
> ¿De la cresta del duro frío,
> Qué necesitas, amor, mi niño?
> La tibia tela de tu vestido.
> . . . .
> Te diré, niño mio, que sí,
> Tronchada y rota soy para ti.
> ¡Cómo me duele esta cintura
> Donde tendrás primera cuna!
> ¿Cuándo, mi niño, vas a venir?
> Cuando tu carne huela a jazmín. (2: 807–808)

> [From where do you come, my love, my baby?
> "From the mountains of icy cold."
> What do you lack, sweet love, my baby?
> "The woven warmth in your dress."
> . . . .
> I shall say to you, child, yes,
> for you I'll torn and broken be.

How painful is this belly now,
where first you shall be cradled!
When, boy, when will you come to me?
"When sweet your flesh of jasmine smells."]   (101–102)

What does Lorca mean when he lets Yerma's potential child decree that her dream of motherhood will come true only when her flesh is redolent of the scent of jasmine? If we put aside the literal meaning of these lines, it would seem that such a direct link between Yerma's motherhood and the delicate perfume of the small white flower is meant to highlight the profound gap that separates her prosaic world from its poetic alternative. In terms of plot, Lorca is actually sentencing his protagonist, already at this early stage, to eternal sterility, as it transpires gradually from her successive actions, which show that no intimate encounter is possible between Yerma, a distinct member of the real world, and the jasmine, an obvious element of the poetic one. Indeed, under no circumstances will Yerma consent to give up her "honra" ("honour") and follow her instincts, even for the sake of the child she yearns for. Therefore, to avoid violating her duties as Juan's lawful wife, she obstinately refuses to overcome her sterility by either taking a lover, as the Old Woman suggested to her, or yielding to her repressed love for Víctor, the only man who has ever made her flesh shiver:

Una vez . . . Víctor . . . [. . .] Me cogió de la cintura y no pude decirle nada porque no podía hablar. Otra vez el mismo Víctor, teniendo yo catorce años (él era un zagalón), me cogió en sus brazos para saltar una acequia y me entró un temblor que me sonaron los dientes. Pero es que yo he sido vergonzosa. (2: 819)

[Perhaps . . . one time . . . with Victor. . . [. . .] He took me by the waist and I couldn't say a word to him, because I couldn't talk. Another time this same Victor, when I was fourteen years old – he was a husky boy – took me in his arms to leap a ditch and I started shaking so hard my teeth chattered. But I've always been shy.] (109)

As to the surviving characters, the denouement of the three plays points to a common denominator running through them, their differences notwithstanding. To retain their safe and honourable social position, the Bride, the Mother, Bernarda, and Yerma are prepared to waive their natural right to happiness engendered by filial love, passion, or motherhood. As a result, despite their obedience to social norms, they are all severely punished for their self-betrayal; yet life, not death, is their punishment at the end of each play. As they belong exclusively to the real world, by being kept alive they are condemned to lifelong spiritual and emotional sterility, as well as to mental stagnation. All doors to salvation are closed before them by the very rules they have tried so hard to abide by: as a sinner, the Bride will not love or be loved ever again; the Mother, who lost eternity along with her only son, will never have grandchildren; Bernarda is doomed to perennial mourning after losing not only her daughter but also her family's honour; and Yerma, who strangled to death both her husband and her ability to love, will never experience motherhood.

A rather different fate is in store for the characters who are allowed to die, namely, Leonardo and the Bridegroom in *Blood Wedding* and Adela in *The House of Bernarda Alba,* as they have balked at the restrictive, life-regulating rules. Leonardo, the passionate lover who defies social authority by running away with the Bride on her wedding day, and the Bridegroom, an innocent victim of society's sinister plotting, driven to death by his own mother's obsession with rules, kill each other in the forest and are thus eternally submerged, so to speak, in the imaginary realm of passion. Adela, the sensuous young woman who would not let society waste away her youth, puts an end to her life in the same invisible barn, from which, at the beginning of Act Three, the family's stallion, in desperate want of a mare, shakes the walls of the house with its pounding hooves. Spanish tradition considers Leonardo's and Adela's unnatural deaths a well-deserved punishment for their sins, while the death of the Bridegroom is deemed a noble sacrifice: he is killed as it were while rightfully trying to mend matters and restore social order by avenging Leonardo's offence. Lorca views all three as fugitives, however, trying to escape through death the pitiless world of the living, which has thwarted their ability to love. For them, dying is, paradoxically, tantamount to salvation.

At first glance, Lorca's intimate and almost obsessive artistic involvement with death, with plays where it not only occurs but is also feared, talked about, and even impersonated (as in *Blood Wedding*), could be considered as a way of reflecting accepted Spanish social attitudes.[9] Particularly in the author's time, Spain's relationship with death exceeded by far strict compliance with the rituals of religious canons, which was (and still is) prevalent in most cultures. For the pious Catholic Spanish society of Lorca's time, death was a terrifying component of life, a potent element that determined human conduct, and an important incentive for people's actions, manifested not only in each individual's daily behaviour but also in the spiritual and philosophical premises underlying the very fabric of society. From the most basic up to the highest level of everyday life, where values and moral norms were shaped, death constituted an integral part of Spanish life, whose expression covered all walks of human existence. An obvious example, illustrated in Lorca's plays, is the code of behaviour imposed on widows, who were condemned to be loyal to their dead husbands and wear widow's weeds to the end of their lives. Other examples include the persistent demand for capital punishment for any transgression of family honour, the prohibition of any overt expression of sentiment, and the blind obedience to the dictates of the Church and its representatives, even if they were clearly meant to strangle individual freedom.

This attitude toward death, which thrived in Spain in the 1930s but had its roots much further back (it is already depicted in the plays by Lope de Vega and Calderón de la Barca) seems unique when pitted against the background of Europe as a whole. By then, most European societies were making steady efforts to remove death from the domain of the living. As Philippe Ariès remarks, the complete physical and spiritual banishment of death from the proximity of the living (cemeteries began to be built on the outskirts of cities already toward the end of the eighteenth century), stimulated by the simultaneous decline of religion, is typical of the rise of modernism (580). On the eve of the twentieth century this led to an entirely new approach to death, which, according to Friedman, ceased to be tragic or heroic and became rather incoherent and even unexpected (23–24). Spain, however, remained ideologically faithful to its medieval cultural heritage, despite the effects of modernism as indicated by its devotion to the past. Julian Marias indeed remarks,

> In Spain balladry, the classical theatre, and the novel of the Golden Age have been the great instruments that have made Spaniards understand and project themselves as Spaniards, and have contributed decisively toward the establishment of Spain as a society, as a nation. (30–31)

Most Spaniards consequently retained a keen awareness of death intermingled with the loss of the joy of life and a strong sense of death as punishment, despite the changes afflicted by modern thought. Lorca himself, as stated by Pedro Salinas, his fellow poet, could certainly feel the presence of death and the depth of its impact on Spanish life everywhere around him,

> in the native air that gives him breath, in the singing of the servants in his house, in books written in his tongue, in the churches of his city; he finds [death] in all of his individual personality that has to do with people, with the inheritance of the past. Lorca was born in a country that for centuries has been living out a special kind of culture that I call the "culture of death." (277)

As in Christian belief, in Lorca's view too, Leonardo's, the Bridegroom's, and Adela's deaths signal their assimilation into an enchanted, poetic world free of any constraining rules, just like the world of the imaginary forest in *Blood Wedding*. However, while Christianity promises eternal bliss after death only to those who have followed its strict dictates, in Lorca's alternative world bliss is granted solely to those brave enough to defy them. In his plays, death always occurs in the fantastic, imaginary, poetic world placed offstage, far from the prosaic reality depicted on it. As a result, those who die conceive of death as enchanting rather than threatening, as a safe haven rather than a means of punishment, and as a genuine promised land accessible to those faithful to their own feelings. This is how Lorca's plays ensure the primacy of "silence" over "noise" or, in fact, of death over life.

CONCLUSION

The structure and content of *The House of Bernarda Alba*, *Yerma*, and *Blood Wedding* suggest that in the eyes of the synchronic spectators, exposed through Lorca's creative imagination to the beauty of death and, conversely, to the ugliness of life, the moral superiority of the alternative world staged for their sake was asserted. By using exclusion and relegation, or indeed silencing, as dramatic tools that generate meaning, along with the construction of a renewed concept of death, Lorca sought to raise the spectators' awareness of their lives, urging them to acknowledge the possibility of living according to a different social order. In the process, he wielded three pairs of antithetical elements that are among the basic components of the theatrical medium – space, language, and characterization – and systematically blocked the validity of one element in each pair in favour of the other.

As the plays are the direct outcome of their cultural background, Lorca's artistic choices are regulated mostly by his own world view: the spatial design directs the spectators to what is concealed in the offstage area; poetry, as the language of artistic creation whose "external and internal form acquire a weight and value of their own instead of referring indifferently to reality" (Jakobson 174), is connected both with the illusory invisible (in *The House of Bernarda Alba*) and the fantastic visible (in *Blood Wedding*); and the characters, defined by their actions and fate, live or die by their recognition of the supremacy of both his original arrangement of the theatrical space and his choice of language. As for the plays' style, it would seem that Lorca's dramatic technique in the rural tragic trilogy places them in a stylistic twilight zone swinging between realistic and poetic drama, which has fitted well into Spain's theatrical tradition since the Golden Age and also echoes its people's idiosyncratic character. The mixture of styles in Lorca's plays parallels the fusion of tragedy and comedy, singing and dancing, typical of the works of Lope de Vega or Calderón de la Barca, in whose plays, said Lorca, "está todo el ámbito de la escena y todas las posibilidades teatrales habidas y por haber" ("Alocución Previa" 1: 1192) ("the entire spectrum of the stage and all the theatrical possibilities of past and future can be found"; my translation). Similarity can be noticed also in the plays' content, as both Lorca and the Golden Age playwrights equally deal profusely with the doings and undoings of Spanish "honra" and its privileged position within the local set of values, not too drastically changed since then.

Despite their intrinsic local hue, however, Lorca's plays have acquired great universal value, and to date most of them, and his rural tragedies in particular, are produced and studied all over the Western world. Entrenched as they are in Spanish tradition, this may seem quite an intriguing accomplishment. Their relevance exceeds the boundaries of time and place, I suggest, precisely because in these plays the traditional elements of dramatic structure such as space, language, and characterization were geared toward the substitution of the tangible and concrete, embodying the "noisy" elements of the work of art, with the invisible and abstract, or, indeed, with silence itself. As a result, what seems to be the strictly local quality of the plays becomes the excluded, relegated, or enhanced antithesis of that same quality, granting the plays universal value, as illustrated by the relation of stage to offstage, prose to poetry, and life to death. Thus, Lorca's noisy "appeals for silence," used to proclaim his critical attitude toward his fellow countrymen, were able to become significant and relevant to societies and cultures other than that of 1930s Spain, and will probably remain so for years to come.

NOTES

1   "Silence, I said!" (201). These are Bernarda Alba's words in the closing scene of *The House of Bernarda Alba*. Subsequent quotations will be cited parenthetically. Translation into English is from *Three Tragedies*, translated by James Graham-Luján and Richard L. O'Connell. The Spanish version of all plays cited is from *Obras Completas*, Vol. 2.

2   Translation mine. On the subject of realism in the works of Lorca, view also C. Christopher Soufas' *Audience and Authority in the Modernist Theater of Federico Garcia Lorca*. Soufas refers here to the difficulty theatre critics have found in defining Lorca's plays as realistic, despite their traditional emphasis. "A frequent strategy," he argues, "is to ascribe those elements that are not easily assimilable into a realist format (e.g., symbolic figures and even the motivations of specific characters) to the intrusion of the dramatist's personality in the work" (9). Antonio Sánchez Trigueros solves the problem by referring to Lorca's dramatic style as "realismo poético, un realismo voluntariamente alejado de la mímesis pura, con claras intenciones de trascender la representación plana de la vida" (185) ["poetic realism, a kind of realism voluntarily distanced from pure mimesis, whose intention is to transcend a simple representation of life"].

3   On the role of silence and its relation with death in Lorca's *The House of Bernarda Alba*, view also Bilha Blum and Liora Malka's "The Poetics of Silence: Dancing Lorca." For a thorough discussion of the function of silence in Lorca's drama in general, view Drew Dougherty's "El Lenguaje del Silencio en el Teatro de García Lorca."

4   José Ortega, in "Conciencia Social en las Tres Dramas Rurales de Lorca," in which he offers an extensive analysis of these plays, refers to them as "una recreación de

conflictos humanos que expresan una situación social" (147) ["a re-creation of human conflicts that expresses a social situation"; translation mine].

5 On realism applied to *The House of Bernarda Alba*, view José Rubia Barcia's "El Realismo Mágico de *La Casa de Bernarda Alba*." By defining Lorca's realism as "magic," Rubia Barcia too is actually questioning the effectiveness of the term when trying to categorize Lorca's plays.

6 Although dealing with voices and sounds and not with silence, C. Brian Morris in his "Voices in a Void: Speech in *La Casa de Bernarda Alba*" chose to quote this same dialogue between Amelia and Martirio, about which he states, "The five pauses specified by Lorca, apart from decelerating the conversation, create an interplay of speech and silence in which silences generate more tensions than words." Besides, he argues, sounds (or actually words) "relieve the visual flatness of the play and punctuate its claustrophobic setting with a soundtrack in which a series of pauses constitute little pockets of suspense" (501).

7 The use of poetry in dramatic works has been widely discussed by T. S. Eliot, among others, who, in his *Poetry and Drama* insisted that in order to be effective, "[i]t must justify itself dramatically" (12). Two opposite opinions about the effectiveness of Lorca's use of poetry in his plays, especially in *Blood Wedding*, are the one sustained by Robert Barnes, in "The Fusion of Poetry and Drama in *Blood Wedding*," who claims it enriches and widens the scope of the play, and the one supported by William I. Oliver, in "The Trouble with Lorca," who accuses the playwright of "placing style before content" (6). Oliver believes that stylistic shifts in a play "must represent changes in the very subject and substance of the art work" and that in *Blood Wedding* "they are in no way justified by the characters, action, and theme" (6).

8 See Carlos Feal, "La Idea del Honor en las Tragedias de Lorca."

9 For a broader view of twentieth-century Spanish history and society, see Herr, Tuñon de Larra, Nash, Pierson, Gies, and Carr. On the influence of Andalucía on Lorca's work, see C. Brian Morris' *Son of Andalucía.*

WORKS CITED

Ariès, Phillipe. *The Hour of Our Death.* Trans. Helen Weaver. London: Allen Lane, 1981.

Barnes, Robert. "The Fusion of Poetry and Drama in *Blood Wedding*." *Modern Drama* 2 (1960): 395–402.

Blum, Bilha, and Liora Malka. "The Poetics of Silence: Dancing Lorca." *Assaph: Studies in the Theatre* 16 (2000): 109–34.

Carr, Raymond. *Spain: A History.* Oxford: Oxford UP, 2000.

Diamond, Elin, ed. *Performance and Cultural Politics.* London: Routledge, 1996.

Dougherty, Drew. "El Lenguaje del Silencio en el Teatro de García Lorca." *Anales de la Literatura Española Contemporánea* 11 (1986): 91–110.

Eliot, T. S. *Poetry and Drama.* London: Faber and Faber, 1950.

Feal, Carlos. "La Idea del Honor en las Tragedias de Lorca." "*Cuando yo me muera . . .*" *Essays in Memory of F. G. Lorca.* Ed. C. Brian Morris. Lanham: UP of America, 1988. 277–90.

Fernández Cifuentes, Luis. *García Lorca en el Teatro: La Norma y la Diferencia.* Zaragoza: Prensas Universitarias de Zaragoza, 1986.

Freud, Sigmund. "Thoughts for the Times on War and Death." *Civilization, Society and Religion.* Trans. James Strachey. Harmondsworth: Penguin, 1985. 61–89.

Friedman, Alan Warren. *Fictional Death and the Modernist Enterprise.* Cambridge: Cambridge UP, 1995.

García Lorca, Federico. "Alocución Previa a una Representación del Auto *La Vida es Sueño*, de Calderón." *Obras Completas.* Vol. 1. Madrid: Aguilar, 1986. 1192–94.

———. *Bodas de Sangre. Obras Completas.* Vol. 2. 701–99.

———. *La Casa de Bernarda Alba. Obras Completas.* Vol. 2. 973–1066.

———. "La Imagen Poética de Don Luis de Góngora." *Obras Completas.* Vol. 3. 223–47.

———. *Three Tragedies:* Blood Wedding, Yerma, The House of Bernarda Alba. Trans. James Graham-Luján and Richard L. O'Connell. Harmondsworth: Penguin, 1961.

———. *Yerma. Obras Completas.* Vol. 2. 803–80.

Gies, David T., ed. *Modern Spanish Culture.* Cambridge: Cambridge UP, 1999.

Herr, Richard. *Spain.* New York: Praeger, 1970.

Jakobson, Roman. "What Is Poetry?" *Semiotics of Art.* Eds. Ladislav Matejka and Irwin R. Titunik. Cambridge, MA: MIT P, 1976. 164–75.

Kershaw, Baz. *The Politics of Performance: Radical Theatre as Cultural Invention.* London: Routledge, 1992.

Marias, Julian. *Understanding Spain.* Trans. Frances M. López-Morillas. Ann Arbor: U of Michigan P, 2000.

Morris, C. Brian. *Son of Andalucía.* Nashville: Vanderbilt UP, 1997.

———. "Voices in a Void: Speech in *La Casa de Bernarda Alba.*" *Hispania* 72 (1989): 498–510.

Nash, Mary. *Defying Male Civilization: Women in the Spanish Civil War.* Denver: Arden, 1995.

Oliver, William I. "The Trouble with Lorca." *Modern Drama* 7 (1964): 2–15.

Ortega, José. "Conciencia Social en los Tres Dramas Rurales de Lorca." *Nuevas Perspectivas Sobre la Generación del 27 (Ensayos Literarios).* Ed. Hector R. Romero. Miami: Ediciones Universal, 1983. 147–60.

Pierson, Peter. *The History of Spain.* Westport, CT: Greenwood P, 1999.

Rubia Barcia, José. "El Realismo Mágico de *La Casa de Bernarda Alba.*" *Revista Hispánica Moderna* 31 (1965): 385–98.

Salinas, Pedro. "Lorca and the Poetry of Death." *Theatre in the Twentieth Century.* Ed. R. Corrigan. New York: Grove P, 1965. 273–81.

Sánchez Trigueros, Antonio. "Federico García Lorca en Escena (Una Invitación al Teatro)." *El Teatro de Lorca: Tragedia, Drama y Farsa.* Ed. Cristóbal Cuevas García. Malaga: Publicaciones del Congreso de Litaratura Española Contemporánea, 1995. 179–98.

Sontag, Susan. "The Aesthetic of Silence." *Styles of Radical Will.* New York: Farrar, Straus and Giroux, 1969. 3–34.

Soufas, C. Christopher. *Audience and Authority in the Modernist Theater of Federico García Lorca.* Tuscaloosa: U of Alabama P, 1996.

Tuñon de Larra, Manuel. *La España del Siglo XX.* Paris: Librería Española, 1973.

4

The Money Shot: Economies of Sex, Guns, and Language in *Topdog/Underdog*[1]

MYKA TUCKER-ABRAMSON

In "An Equation for Black People Onstage," playwright Suzan-Lori Parks lays out the difficulty of writing plays about black people without falling into an essentializing "Black Aesthetic." Theatre, she argues, is useful for black people because it "can 'tell it like it is'; 'tell it as it was'; 'tell it as it could be'" (21); and, indeed, Parks's plays are continually exploring the limits and intersections of all three. "[T]he writing is rich," she continues, "because we are not an impoverished people, but a wealthy people fallen on hard times" (21). When we consider this metaphor in light of Parks's well-known dramaturgical focus on black male characters, it becomes a highly charged one. In *Topdog/Underdog*, for example, Lincoln, a previously married and relatively prosperous hustler, has been left by his wife and is now working in a mall, dressing up as the historical Lincoln; his brother, Booth, has likewise been abandoned by his girlfriend, Grace, and is wholly dependent on Lincoln for money other than what he can make pawning stolen goods. Both characters are in crisis – economically and with respect to their masculinity – and Parks's notion of wealth is both a cause of and a metaphor for the crisis.

Held in tension throughout *Topdog/Underdog* is the relationship between the personal psychodramas of the two brothers and the larger issues of economics, race, and masculinity. In *Postmodernism, or the Cultural Logic of Late Capitalism*, Fredric Jameson famously articulated the split between modernism and postmodernism in Lacanian terms as the "breakdown in the signifying chain" (26); in other words, between the Symbol of money and its Real or material support. If we apply Jameson's economic diagnosis to *Topdog/Underdog*, we see how late capitalism also affects constructions of "masculinity"; if masculinity is based on economic worth and economics become unhinged from their Real value, then that notion of masculinity itself becomes increasingly difficult to maintain. By locating the drama in a one-bedroom apartment and focusing on only two characters – brothers Lincoln and Booth – Parks

Modern Drama, 50:1 (Spring 2007)

forces us to confront the vast issues of racial and economic inequalities in America through their impact on the psyches of two characters. In this way, Parks transforms the "larger" notions of postmodernity, late-capitalism, and racism into psychoanalytic and diagnostic tools for studying both her characters and society at large. *Topdog/Underdog* is both a social drama confronting the issues of racism and classism in modern America, and a psychodrama in its focus on the individual unravelling of Lincoln and Booth as well as of their relationship. And, in fact, it could be no other way. Parks suggests that, for the black man in a racist and classist society, the psychological and the social are inextricably linked. His assessment of his worth depends on his ability to identify both with the symptom of his oppression and with the symbol of recognition: money.

In classical psychoanalytic theory, the "symptom," or kernel of the neurosis, is formed by a gap in language, a space where the patient is unable to fit his or her experience into the greater social structure; as Žižek explains in *The Sublime Object of Ideology*, Freudian analysis claimed that the symptom could be "dissolved" by "re-establish[ing] the broken network of communication by allowing the patient to verbalize the meaning of his symptom" (73). However, identification is not resolution, and Lacan usefully reconceived the notion of symptom as "sinthome," that which the patient latches onto because "the only alternative to the symptom is nothing: pure autism, a psychic suicide, surrender to the death drive, even to the total destruction of the symbolic universe" (Žižek, *Sublime Object* 75). In other words, if Freud saw the end of psychoanalysis as the identification *of* the symptom, for Lacan, it is "*identification with the symptom*" (Žižek, *Sublime Object* 73; emphasis in original). The symptom represents the tension between the Symbolic and the Real, the tension between the fully formed appearance of self and the chaotic unconscious: the patient's confrontation with his own formation. This confrontation, however, is not an act that occurs only in one's head or on the couch. The symbolic order is a linguistic, and thus a deeply social and political, structure. The way in which a person identifies with the symptom is entirely framed by the linguistic and cultural structures surrounding the "gap."

Frantz Fanon's great insight in *Black Skin, White Masks* is that someone identifying with a society that is sick is him- or herself sick with the same ailments (i.e., someone identifying with a capitalist and racist society suffers from all the illnesses of capitalism and racism). Indeed, Fanon argues, if a black patient were ever to conclude the Lacanian process, he would end up identifying with whiteness itself, something he illustrates when he says that Antillean men identify with Tarzan rather than with the Natives on screen "because no black voice exists" (153).

While, of itself, this distortion is perhaps only moderately problematic, the identification is also highly unstable because as soon as the black man from the Antilles goes to France, he finds not "the final stage of his personality" but the tragic realization of his own blackness (Fanon 153n16). By carrying Lacan's process to its final conclusion, Fanon demonstrates the explicitly political content of identification; in this instance, the symptom is annihilated and the sufferer is left with *nothing – pure autism.*

In "Suzan-Lori Parks and the Empty (W)hole of Memory," Jeanette Malkin argues that "trauma does not remember its source, but rather replays the moment of cognitive disruption" (164). The symptom, then, is the articulation of that disruption. Furthermore, the word "trauma" could just as easily read "history." Located entirely in Lincoln and Booth's apartment, *Topdog/Underdog* enacts this psychoanalytic process of identification, and as Lincoln and Booth spiral towards their symptom, they get closer – not to the historical source, but to the moment of disruption and to their own psychic annihilation. The symptom is crucial to a reading of Parks, then, because it allows us to maintain that there is a Real (of history, of trauma), while emphasizing that we cannot access it – instead, we access a moment of disruption, and, moreover, we access this disruption through language. In other words, it is the social construction of language that both masks the trauma (history) but is also our only access to it and the only tool we have with which to diagnose (and potentially treat) the trauma. *Topdog/Underdog both* offers a damning diagnosis of American society *and* forces us to confront important questions about the limitations of language in such a diagnosis; it forces us to confront the difficulty of having only the master's tools for the necessary task of dismantling his house.

I

Southern trees bear strange fruit,
Blood on the leaves and blood at the root,
Black bodies swinging in the southern breeze,
Strange fruit hanging from the poplar trees.

—"Strange Fruit" (Abel Meeropol)

While the overwhelming majority of critics agree that Parks's dramaturgy is heavily invested and rooted in a postmodern aesthetic, the ways in which the term "postmodernity" gets defined differ wildly. This is problematic in that the notion of postmodernism itself is a politically fraught term, and in discussing works as politically invested as Parks's are, the distinction between Linda Hutcheon's airy "historiographic metafiction" postmodernism; Baudrillard's simulacra, where the gulf war, will not, is not, and did not happen(ing) (Baudrillard 2001 work was called *The Gulf War Did Not Take Place*); and Jameson's diagnostic economic postmodernism (*Postmodernism*) needs to be articulated. While Parks is undoubtedly invested in a deconstruction of history and the ability to write and rewrite it, she is also aware that there is actually a material history, and although we can't necessarily define it, it has very real consequences – especially when that history is the economic and social history of blacks in the United States – for the lives of her characters. That Lincoln is a poor black man who works in a mall and dresses up as a dead white president speaks to Parks's playing both with history and with the usual hallmarks of an aesthetic postmodernity – pastiche, parody, and so on. However, *Topdog/Underdog* is rooted first and foremost in the economic and political reality shaping their lives – in other words, the postmodernity of Lincoln's position is a result of the very real material, economic conditions in which he lives.

In "Culture and Finance Capital," Jameson lays out his definition of postmodernity as the entrance of society into late capitalism, which occurs once

> content ... has definitively been suppressed in favor of the form, in which the inherent nature of the product becomes insignificant, a mere marketing pretext, while the goal of production no longer lies in any specific market, any specific set of consumers or social and individual needs, but rather in its transformation into that element which by definition has no context or territory, and indeed no use value as such, namely, money. (260)

For Jameson, the key is the break of late capitalism from capitalism, the transformation of money from representing content to being pure form or, to bring it back to the language of psychoanalysis, a Symbol emptied of any Real or Imaginary support. While he acknowledges that there are aesthetic or artistic breaks between modernism and postmodernism, these breaks are results of, and expressions of, the economic transformations that have occurred with the ideological victory of the market, the de-industrialization of American labour, the rapid increase in what David Harvey so aptly termed "paper entrepreneurialism" (163) and the increasing crises of capitalism that must occur when, to riff on Marx, all that seems solid is revealed to be air. Through Lincoln's job as a three-card monte player, his employment in a mall, and his subsequent lay-off due to cheaper, mechanical labour, through Booth's attempt to move from petty thieving to card hustling, Parks gives us a powerful representation of the American de-industrialized worker. More importantly, Parks is able to move from the often overly abstract theories of Marxist postmodernism into the personal psychological, while still maintaining the complexity and specificity of her characters.

As theorists, both Jameson and Harvey demand a certain distancing, a systematization of their subjects. bell hooks points out the limits of such a systematizing in her discussion of her own movement towards class consciousness. hooks writes that "[a]s a student I read Marx, Gramsci, and a host of other male thinkers on the subject of class. These works provided theoretical paradigms, but rarely offered tools for confronting the complexity of class in daily life" (*where we stand* 43). Parks also emphasizes the need to root academic work in material and political circumstances when, speaking to Joshua Wolf Shenk, she says that "the great mistake of American culture and the mistake of history" is to "de-emphasize the relationship of the person right in the room with you ... We have to deal with what's happening right now" (qtd. in Shenk). While Parks borrows heavily from the language of Jameson, she continually underscores the need to refocus these ideas on community. In what follows, I would like to suggest that *Topdog/Underdog* acts as an intermediary text between Jameson's and Harvey's paradigmatic theories and the lived, material experiences those theories are seeking to explain, one that provides a roadmap not only of the psychological dysfunction besetting the brothers Lincoln and Booth but also of the broken and battered idea of a "united" America toward which their names inevitably gesture.

II

> The black cop is the only real obstacle
> Black slave turned black cop is not logical
> But very psychological
>
> – "Black Cop," KRS-One

Topdog/Underdog is not the first play in which Parks explores the metonymical link between family and nation. Nor is it the first place in her dramatic writings where we encounter a black man who dresses up as Lincoln. The main character of *The America Play*, named "The Foundling Father as Abraham Lincoln," is a grave-digger whose resemblance to the president inspires him to quit his job and move out West to open a theme park called "The Great Hole of History," where people pay him, "The Lesser Known," to act out the assassination of the historical Lincoln, "The Greater Known," over and over again – a job that can't help but recall Žižek's diagnosis of our society's love of "products deprived of their malignant property: coffee without caffeine, cream without fat" (Žižek, "Passion") or, in this case, violence without blood, a historical moment without its consequences or what Jameson would call form without content. The Foundling Father, or "Lesser Known," opens *The America Play* with two statements: "[t]o stop too fearful and too faint to go," is an example of chiasmus Parks finds in Webster's dictionary; she then remixes this with her own, "[h]e digged the hole and the whole held him" (159). By having a black man, "The Lesser Known," dressed as Lincoln, "The Greater Known," utter both a classic "chiasmus" and a rewritten one, Parks introduces us to her idea of "repetition and revision," a technique she borrows from jazz, where "the composer or performer will write or play a musical phrase once and again and again; etc. – with each revisit the phrase is slightly revised" ("Repetition and Revision"). Parks plays with "rep and rev" both linguistically and structurally, as her idea of the w/hole of history reappears and redefines itself throughout the play; specific phrases as well as the very conceptions of history and language are rewritten.

In *The Politics of Postmodernism*, Hutcheon locates postmodernity as the point "where documentary historical actuality meets formalist self-reflexivity and parody" (7), which Hutcheon defines as that which "works to foreground the *politics* of representation" (94). For Hutcheon, parody is the mechanism through which postmodernism reveals its political potential: "through a double process of installing and ironizing, parody signals how present representations come from past ones and what ideological consequences derive from both continuity and difference" (93). In other words, parody forces us to recognize our location within history, while also reminding us of the arbitrariness by which history is created. Within this context, Parks's project of "repetition and revision" can be considered another form of "parody." From the linguistic plays on "Fathuh" (175), which is remixed with Lincoln as forefather to become "foe-father" (178) and "fauxfather" (184), or from the "w/holes of history" to the very re-enactment of Lincoln's assassination, Parks asks us to re-examine our own relationship to history. As well, Parks continually re-contextualizes both the script of *Our American Cousin* (the play performed while Lincoln was assassinated) and the lines spoken by the historical characters involved in the assassination. When the Lesser Known tells the story of the Greater Known's death, he points out, "It would have been helpful to our story if, say, the Lesser Known were summoned to Big Town by the Great Mans wife: '*Emergency*, oh *Emergency*, please put the Great Man in the ground'" (160). The footnote for this quotation reads, "*Possibly* the words of Mary Todd Lincoln after the death of her husband" (160; emphasis added). Parks's recontextualization is two-fold. First, as Harry Elam and Alice Rayner point out, "Academic footnotes confirm meanings, elaborate ideas, and assign authorship but are peripheral to the textual body" (186). By adding the footnote "possibly" to a historical quotation, Parks undermines these acts of confirmation and thus "points out the impossibility of determining the Real [of history]" (186). Moreover, Parks has the Lesser Known acknowledge the failure of history to live up to what he wants it to be. After all, the event didn't actually happen: "none of this was meant to be" (161). While the Real cannot be determined, it also can't be ignored; Parks cannot say these *were* the words of Mary Todd Lincoln, only that they were *probably* the words. However, in writing this play, Parks undermines this acknowledgment by creating a successful link between Mary Todd and the Lesser Known. Mary Todd's call to bury her husband is answered years later when the Lesser Known, a man who digs graves, stands outside, "his ear cocked" (161) for her cry. This collapsing of past and present, of historical and performative truths, performs Hutcheon's "double process"; it both mocks history and also acknowledges its substantive existence and its formative importance in the lives of contemporary characters.

Consider, in this regard, the ending of the first act of the play. Once more, we have the Lesser Known calling out "*Emergency*, oh, *Emergency*, please put the Great Man in the ground" (173). Once more we have an ersatz (this time) Booth take aim at him. But this time he is shot "for real" and falls into the hole he has dug for himself. By being shot, the Lesser Known not only follows in the footsteps of the Great Man, but he also follows the demand to "put the Great Man in the ground;" the demand – after the fact – is addressed to him: by being put in the ground, he actually becomes the Great Man. It is this reversal Parks refers to when the Lesser Known explains his life story:

> all this while the Lesser Known digging his holes bearing the burden of his resemblance all the while trying somehow to equal the Great Man in stature, word and deed going forward with his lesser life trying somehow to follow in the Great Mans footsteps footsteps that were of course behind him. The Lesser Known trying somehow to catch up to the Great Man all this while and maybe running too fast in the wrong direction. Which is to say that maybe the Great Man had to catch him. Hhhh. Ridiculous. (171)

On the one hand, the Lesser Known has managed to reverse the direction of history, but, on the other hand, it is "ridiculous." So while parody can, as Hutcheon points out, investigate the "history and historical power of ... cultural representations" (99), it does so only on the level of narrative, of what is already known; it can't actually alter those processes of history.

This becomes even more apparent in the second act of the play when the Lesser Known's Wife, Lucy, and their son, Brazil, go west to exhume the Lesser Known's body and give him a proper burial. Staring into the

Great Hole of History, which is also her husband's final resting place, Lucy says, "You could look intuh that Hole and see your entire life pass before you. Not your own life but someones life from history, you know ... somebody who killed somebody important, uh face on uh postal stamp, you know, someone from History. *Like* you, but *not* you. You know: *Known*" (196). The absurd structure of this statement is underwritten with a more profound meaning: the Lesser Known becomes known when he repeats the Great Man's lines – "*Emergency*, oh, *Emergency*, please put the Great Man in the ground" (196) – and Lucy and Brazil obey his instructions. In reburying the Lesser Known, not only do Lucy and Brazil make him "known" generally to future generations of customers, but he also becomes knowable to his son, Brazil, who assumes his father's legacy by becoming a tour guide to "The Great Hall of Wonders." Here, in passing daily the case that displays his shot father, he's able to announce, "To my right: our newest Wonder: One of thuh greats Hisself" (199).

If, as Hutcheon argues, "Postmodernism paradoxically manages to legitimize culture (high and mass) even as it subverts it" (15), then it also subverts our notion of history, while legitimizing it. In this sense, postmodernism has a regenerative potential. In *The America Play*, Parks is able, through the family unity, both to mock the historical process and take ownership of it, showing its liberating and transformative potential. Jeanette Malkin makes the argument that *The America Play* is corrective (182) in that, through the archaeological metaphor that Lucy and Brazil act out, "[b]lack history [is] not 'lost' in some irretrievable kingdom ... [but] covered ... buried by a historical narrative" (181–82). For Malkin, then, history is something that can be retrieved. The problem with such an argument, however, is how do we "right and rewrite history in a postmodern culture that has dismantled the idea of history?" (179) as Harry Elam and Alice Rayner so nicely put it.

While Elam and Rayner also see *The America Play* presenting an alternative version of history, the alternative version is a performative and fractured one. They are careful to balance the success of the black author's appropriations and challenges to history with an insistence that the material effects of history be accounted for, no matter how history is subverted or rewritten. They argue that

> [t]here is a gap between the constructed myths and the lived experience, between the stories told and the day-to-day detail that is excluded. The 'Real' of history cannot be seen or repeated, yet it continues in the experience of those who live after, like the ghost of slavery. The excluded reality, however, caught between myth and matter, constitutes the gap or blank slate that is open to rewriting. It must be 'made up' or filled in with ideas, memories, imagination, and matter. (181)

Their reading is a compelling one in that it creates space for both "the potentials as well as the limitations in the written text and the performance" (186). If the work that *The America Play* does is "making up" or "filling in" this hole, then Parks soon finds herself with a new problem. If the material experience of those who live after is already visibly in effect, what purpose does the "making up" of history serve?

When Parks revisits the same themes of a black family's relationships to American history in *Topdog/Underdog*, the site of history is stripped of its potentially transformative or liberating character and history is transformed, reconceptualized as that which has laid the economic and social groundwork for the racism and wage-slavery in the lives of her very contemporary characters. No longer does the "postmodern absence of a Real in history" allow the "previously disenfranchised to construct a history through acts of writing, representing" (Elam and Rayner 189). Instead, the job of the written word in *Topdog/Underdog* is to confront history at the site of the present. If *The America Play* conforms to Hutcheon's model of using parody to interrogate our relationship to history, then *Topdog/Underdog* marks a Jamesonian transition from a parodic postmodern aesthetic to an economically critical one. In "Postmodernism and Consumer Society," Jameson argues that society has "begun to lose its capacity to retain its own past, has begun to live in a perpetual present and in a perpetual change that obliterates traditions of the kind which all earlier social formations have had in one way or another to preserve" (125). In other words, Jameson is giving up the possibility of reconstructing history and thus the potential productivity of postmodernity. The unhinging of Symbolic money from its Real value is also the unhinging of Symbolic History from its content. Hutcheon has taken Jameson to task for being too narrow in his ideas of history. She complains that Jameson's "lament" of the loss of history in postmodernism is actually a lament for the loss of "Marxist *History*" (113). But what Hutcheon calls "Marxist history" is really a materialist history, and Jameson's radical break from thinkers like Hutcheon demonstrates how this is so in three specific ways. First, by locating the modern/postmodern shift in economics, he re-inscribes the need for material factors in cultural paradigms. Second, instead of trying to *prescribe* a vision of postmodernism, his writings are diagnostic; he refuses to excuse postmodernism any more than a doctor would try to excuse bronchitis or influenza and, in this way, Jameson is able to articulate a need for change. Finally, Jameson radically abandons the hope that is found throughout Hutcheon's work. In *Iraq: The Borrowed Kettle*, Žižek makes the important point that the leftist rhetoric which trumpets that "another world is possible" is perhaps what is actually holding us back from radical social change, when he asks, "What if it is only full acceptance of the desperate closure of the present global situation that can push us towards actual change?" (114). In other words, the invocation of hope is a crutch that undermines our recognition of the need for change; it is only through Jameson's radical acceptance of the (fore)closure of capitalism that we can actually see the need for change. It is precisely this desperation that Parks captures so powerfully in *Topdog/Underdog*.

III

Now we the American working population
Hate the fact that eight hours a day
Is wasted on chasing the dream of someone that isn't us.
– "9–5ers Anthem," Aesop Rock

In *Topdog/Underdog*, the setting moves from a theme park to an urban slum and focuses on the lives of two poor black men – Booth and Lincoln – who are both economically and socially removed from the "productive" sector of society. Booth, a low level thief, decides he wants to move up in the world by following in Lincoln's footsteps as a card hustler. Lincoln, following the death of his friend, has retired from three-card monte and has taken a job dressing up as the historical Lincoln at a mall, where people once again pay to pretend to shoot him. This change in location (theme park to mall or urban slum) mirrors the radical break in form that occurs between *The America Play* and *Topdog/Underdog*. In "Elements of Style," Parks writes that "as I write along the container dictates what sort of substance will fill it and, at the same time, the substance is dictating the size and shape of the container" (7–8). *The America Play* roots itself, as David DeRose puts it, in "the highly stylized poetics of . . . post-modern American ideolects" (412) through its use of chiasmus and pastiche to examine "the relationship . . . of African Americans, to the formative cultural images of their history" (409). By comparison, then, *Topdog/Underdog* uses a more traditional, linear narrative in order to change the focus from the "cultural images" of history to the economic and psychological repercussions of the past.

Returning to "Repetition and Revision," Parks asks, "What does it mean for characters to say the same thing twice? 3 times? Over and over and over and oh-vah?" (Parks, "Elements" 10). Well, for one thing, she says, it causes us to "refigure the idea of forward progression" (10). In the act of repeating, not only do the words change while moving forward (over to oh-vah), but the later words actually alter the words uttered before through persistent re-contextualization. In repeating and revising *The America Play* into *Topdog/Underdog*, what are revealed are the material circumstances that created the historical crisis of *The America Play.*

In *Topdog/Underdog*, we can re-imagine the actual Lincoln pageant as this perpetual present, where the customers come in every week to shoot their president and the past returns not only as a farce but as a nostalgic looping of an event bearing almost no relationship to the historical instant. As Lincoln explains, "People like they historical shit in a certain way. They like it to unfold the way they folded it up. Neatly like a book. Not raggedy and bloody and screaming" (52). However, by bringing us behind the scenes of the pageant, Parks uses repetition and revision to tear history from the book. The historical pageant is now stripped to reveal what's behind it: namely, a black man – paid awful wages to dress up as the white man who "emancipated" him – who is being threatened with a mechanical replacement. The nostalgia for the present is replaced with a concrete symbol of our time. History is no longer relegated to books or theme parks but is re-visioned in the current socio-economic conditions of the man who plays Lincoln. This connection is both Symbolic (via their shared name) and also causal. (Parks shows the history of slavery to be directly linked to the economic slavery of black men in America, as is represented through the double signification of Lincoln.) By changing the linguistic relationship of the Lincoln of history to the Lincoln of the present, Parks radically alters our relationship to Lincoln and America at large and brutally re-inscribes history onto the perpetual present.

For Jameson, the link between economics, culture, and history is likewise a linguistic one. Our conceptions of the breakdown of form and content in economics, of past and present in history, occur at the level of language. In "Postmodernism and Consumer Society," he writes, "For Lacan, the experience of temporality, human time, past, present, memory, the persistence of personal identity over months and years – this existential or experiential feeling of time itself – is also an effect of language" (119). As with the doubling of Lincoln's name, Parks is always exploring the ways in which we use and are used by language. Motivated by a disgust with Lincoln's job and a desire to have him as a business partner, Booth attempts to convince Lincoln to return to cards. "I aint going back to that, bro. I aint going back" Lincoln responds (22); to which Booth replies, "You play Honest Abe. You aint going back but you going all the way back. Back to way back then when folks was slaves and shit" (22). This collapse in time plays off a linguistic inability to decipher between "back" (two months ago) and "back" (140 years ago). Language's collapse of history – its inability to extinguish past pasts and recent pasts – also collapses differences between historical slavery and modern wage slavery; and thus aligns Lincoln's job with that of the slave.

When Lincoln takes the job as "Lincoln," he is told that he will "have to wear a little makeup and accept less than what they would offer a – another guy" (29). What Lincoln doesn't say, but Booth does, is that "another" guy is always white. And, indeed, there is something more than a bit ironic about a poor black man dressing up as the supposed emancipator of black slaves for an income that barely allows two men to share a bachelor suite.

bell hooks, in "Reconstructing Black Masculinity," connects contemporary black masculine psychological enslavement to traditional "slavery," when she argues, "The image of black masculinity that emerges from slave narratives is one of hardworking men who longed to assume full patriarchal responsibility for families and kin" (*Black Looks* 90). In other words, emancipation from slavery and entrance into American society demanded the internalization of white ideals of masculinity, where the man provided for the family, which the woman raised. However, as problematic as this idea is when jobs are available, it becomes all but untenable when there are no economic opportunities. And, as late capitalism has continued to devalue product-based labour (and the 1950s American, and largely suburban, ideal of respectable working-class labour, in general), conceptions of masculine power have changed from primarily economic to phallocentric. Or, as bell hooks puts it, "[The black man's] ability to use that penis in the arena of sexual conquest could bring him as much status as being a wage earner and provider" (94). However, for Booth, economics still figures in constructions of sexuality. Booth draws a direct line between Lincoln's working for a white man and impotency, when, comparing his own desire to play three-card with Lincoln's preference to keep working at the mall, he erupts and calls Lincoln, "you shiteating motherfucking pathetic limpdick uncle tom" (21). While hooks locates the change of power from pocket to penis, so to speak, Booth reminds us that, under capitalism, economics is always involved in constructions of masculinity, through its associations with power and success.

IV

There's a new girl on my street
And I'mma introduce her to my meat
Told my homeboy I was scoping hoping
To crack them legs wide open
Ready to break that thang in half
Get it in with the shaft
Take a bath and I'm out, yeah

– "Dirty Mack," Ice Cube

How you studying these hoes
Need to talk what you know
And stop talking bout who I'm sticking and licking jus mad it ain't yours
I know ya'll poor ya'll broke
Ya'll job jus hanging up clothes
Step to me get burnt like toast
Muthafuckas adios amigos
Halves halves wholes wholes

– "Gossip Folks," Missy Elliott

It is in the works of Fanon that we find our clearest articulation of the difficulties disempowered men have trying to grapple with the complexities of their own relationships with women while struggling to secure economic and physical freedom in times of decolonization. In her essay, "Who Is That Masked Woman? Or, The Role of Gender in Fanon's *Black Skin, White Masks*," Gwen Bergner catalogues the ways in which Fanon locates women, and especially racialized women, as "objects of exchange in the homosocial, heterosexual colonial economy" (85). In other words, the ability to obtain and control women is symbolic of the ability to obtain and control money, and by extension, power. Fanon is unable to deal with the effects of colonialism on women's economic and sexual choices because he needs women's desires to come from subconscious spaces, which men's projects of decolonization attempt both to free and to define. Black women, then, must either align their desires with those of their black brothers or be considered neurotic victims of colonialism (as is the case with his diagnosis of Mayotte Capecia). The impetus behind these fears are eloquently laid out by bell hooks, who points out that "[m]uch black male anti-feminism is linked to a refusal to acknowledge that the phallocentric power black men wield over black women is 'real' power, the assumption being that only the power white men have that black men do not have is real" (*Black Looks* 108). Once women have to be accounted for, black men confront not only issues of racial oppression but the impact their success or failure has on black women. Furthermore, what effect does this structure have on black women and what structures are black women themselves being forced into? All Fanon can reply is that, of the woman of colour, "I know nothing about her" (180). If Fanon's silence demands the question, Parks's omission provides a partial answer. Women are completely absent from this play. While they are mentioned frequently, not once do they appear. They literally are signifiers, symbols of the brothers' failed attempts to achieve a stable masculinity.

Thus, when Booth talks about his "fuck books," he explains that it's out of a need "for unresolved sexual release. I'm a hot man. I aint apologizing for it" (45). He compares himself with Lincoln: "[w]hen you don't got a woman you just sit there. Letting yr shit fester" (45). His insistent comparisons of his own virility with Lincoln's impotence are nothing less than an often desperate assertion of his manhood. When he claims that the woman he is trying to get back together with, Grace, "[L]et me do her how I wanted. And no rubber" (41), when Lincoln and Booth both swear they use Magnum condoms for "the larger man"(42), and when Booth gets stood up and claims the next day that it was all a misunderstanding and "Grace got down on her knees"(86), what we are seeing, as hooks explains, is the compensatory substitution of one form of masculine power for another. In lieu of being a man in the economic sense, Booth tries to assert his manliness through sex. This is especially poignant if we consider the doubling of Grace, as "Grace," the person Booth desires, and "grace," the synonym for salvation; for Booth, the two are actually conflated. As Shawn-Marie Garrett points out, Parks insists that all her plays "share one vital quality: 'the yearning for salvation'" (134). Booth's desire for Grace is at once sexual and symbolic: he wants to have sex with Grace, but that sexual act represents the salvation of his masculinity. The absence of Grace from this play, then, signifies both Booth's failure sexually and also the failure of his sense of self. In fact, all of Booth's stories about Grace's coming back to him are a lie, a lie he uses to cover up, on the symbolic level, his failed masculinity and, on the literal level, his murdering her in response to her rejecting him. In "Nappy Happy," Angela Davis takes Ice Cube to task, when she tells him, "[Y]ou can't speak up for yourselves until you can also speak up for [your black] sisters" (Ice Cube and Davis 182). Booth, by killing Grace, by silencing his black sister, sinks deeper into the traps of racist society, further reducing the possibility that grace will enter his life.

This doubling (and even tripling) of names occurs throughout *Topdog/ Underdog*. If Grace is "named" by the desiring male gaze (in this case, the desire for sex and salvation), then Lincoln and Booth are "named" by their economic roles. However, in discussing the importance of names in *Topdog/Underdog*, it is crucial to recognize Parks's insistence that this is a story about two brothers who are incidentally named after the president of the United States and his assassin (*Topdog/Underdog Diaries*). While we have to take these words at least slightly tongue-in-cheek, it is important to heed her warning that Lincoln and Booth are not stereotypes or archetypes; they are brothers, workers, fighters, lovers – they are complete characters and need to be treated as such. But perhaps we can reconcile this with our own desires to construct meaning if we thread our study through Žižek's observation that "[n]aming is necessary but it is, so to speak, necessary afterwards, retroactively, once we are already 'in it'" (*Sublime Object* 95). In this sense, then, Parks's characters are not as they are as a result of their names; rather, as a result of their actions, their names are imbued with meaning, and in *Topdog/Underdog*, the importance of naming resurfaces time and again. While Booth is contemplating a name change, Lincoln warns him not to change his name to "something they cant say . . . I mean you dont want yr new handle to obstruct yr employment possibilities" (14), an extremely ironic comment, considering that Booth chooses the name three-card, a name that *is* his new-found employment; furthermore, it is positively uncanny that Lincoln is named (one might even say predestined) for the paid job he takes on. In a world where even our names – our symbolic identities – are formed through the economic, it is unsurprising that the rest of our lives and relationships are also formed and altered by class.

In *where we stand: class matters*, hooks takes up the psychological implications of a society where people are valued through money. She writes that

> our nation is full of young people, especially teenagers, who deny the reality
> of class, even as they identify solely with the values and mores of a predatory
> ruling class. Children from poor backgrounds are isolated and self-isolated
> because being poor is always and only a cause for shame. (84)

Lincoln and Booth both see poverty as a source of shame and are also without class allegiance. Lincoln muses that, while playing three-card, not only did they "take" tourists, but they also "took a father for the money he was gonna get his new kids a bike with and he cried in the street when we vanished. We took a mother's welfare check" (55). Even within the family, solidarity is contingent on economics. Every Thursday, Booth tells Lincoln, "Yr lucky I let you stay" (15); and every Friday, Lincoln is welcome because "[e]very Friday you come home with yr paycheck" (15). This lack of allegiance is even more disturbing because the entire system of economics that circulates throughout this text is a metaphor for, and an extension of, violence. As a hustler who "plays" welfare mothers, Lincoln is engaging in economic violence against his community, a violence that is finally returned physically when his partner, Sonny, is shot. This literal act of violence makes Lincoln change jobs to one where he is the object both of the symbolic violence of being "shot" at all day and of economic violence: he is penalized with a wage deduction for his skin colour and he lives under the threat that his job will be outsourced to a wax dummy. Eventually Lincoln is laid off, and he returns to three-card for one last game. This time, the customer isn't someone on the street; it's his brother, and when the game back-fires and Booth finds himself played, he kills Lincoln.

This collapse of symbolic into economic and literal violence is, Jameson argues, the foundation of late capitalism, and it is only through the materiality of violence that the immateriality of our economic system can be supported: "This whole global, yet American, postmodern culture is the internal and superstructural expression of a whole new wave of American military and economic domination throughout the world: in this sense, as throughout class history, the underside of culture is blood, torture, death, and terror" (*Postmodernism* 5). If the symbolic violence of Lincoln's jobs (Lincoln as both target and hustler who targets) represents this postmodern culture of money that is separated from the material, then it expresses not only the "blood, torture, death, and terror" of American foreign policy but also that of America's domestic policy.

Indeed, when Lincoln quits the economically profitable business of hustling and fails to make money working legitimately, his failure is filtered through metaphors of sex and violence. Lincoln's mall job is based on guns that don't shoot, and, throughout the play, Booth tells Lincoln that Cookie left him because he "couldn't get it up" (93). Considering that both Lincoln and Booth claim to use "Magnum" condoms "for the larger man" (42), Booth is effectively telling Lincoln his magnum won't shoot, or, to take it one step further, that it won't even cock. However, there is one place where Lincoln is not impotent. Lincoln tells Booth that "the customer is actually called the 'Mark'" (71), and when Lincoln wins money off Booth at the climax of the play, his magnum fires, and he hits his mark. Lincoln argues that his role as Lincoln is different from his role in street hustling because "[w]hen people know the real deal it aint a hustle" (22). But Booth doesn't know the real deal, and Lincoln hustles Booth out of his money. This act of hustling not only takes $500 from Booth but also transfers "manhood" back from Booth to Lincoln. This play on phalluses and guns is furthered through both Booth's claim that he slept with Lincoln's wife and his actual shooting of Lincoln. Both of Booth's magnums work, and through the metaphor of the penis as gun, sex too becomes a violent act.

In *Black Skin, White Masks*, Fanon claims that the "Oedipus complex is far from coming into being among Negroes" (151–52). This is a world where a brother will play a brother for money, and, in the very use of the word "brother," we see the further entanglement of economics and race and family trauma. On the one hand, instead of Booth's taking out his anger on the system that is oppressing him (at least symbolically, such as by robbing someone on Wall Street), he, instead, plays another ghettoized black "brother," who is as poor and trapped as Booth himself. David Marriott, in his study of psychoanalysis and race, points out that "not only did [Fanon] choose to question the universality of oedipal neuroses, but he also refused the rigid connection between the family and social consciousness. These two refusals consisted in an acknowledgment of the colonial influence on kinship and social ties" (110). From the "predestined" tragedy in their names to their sexual/economic power relations, Lincoln and Booth act out a sort of oedipal psychodrama and one that rigidly connects the family and social consciousness, but, as in Fanon, the connection between social and familial crisis is one not of analogy but of cause and effect. While we are not shown social consciousness, that consciousness *is* the unconscious of the brothers. It is social consciousness that creates the conditions within which the whole family reacts (and here, I think, we can assume that this also explains the absence of the parents); it is the rage of disempowerment and loss, that moves Booth to kill his brother, and, in this way, the burden of responsibility for Lincoln's death lies at least as much on the shoulders of systemic and economic racism as it does on Booth.

However, even the notion of brothers is called into question. As Lincoln points out, at precisely the point when Booth puts his money on the table, "I know we *brothers*, but is we really brothers, you know, blood brothers or not...?" (103). This is a world without known or stable fathers, and thus the Oedipus complex, instead of conforming to the traditional paternal paradigm of the white, Freudian psychodrama, is acted out between the maybe-brothers. It is also a world without mothers, and it is incredibly important that, when both parents vanished, they gave their kids money, literally putting monetary signifiers in place of their family roles; the entire Oedipus complex in *Topdog/Underdog* is acted out through economic signifiers. At first, Lincoln is connected to his father through his involvement in his father's affairs – he tells Booth that "one of his ladies liked me so I would do her after he'd done her" (90). But when the father leaves, he gives Lincoln $50, changing the link from sexual to economic and, in this sense, Lincoln's spending the money symbolizes his getting rid of, and perhaps even identifying with, the role of the father. If Lincoln is associated with the father, then Booth is associated with the mother through the $500 inheritance their mother gave him before she left – money Booth does not spend in order symbolically to maintain his maternal connection. When Lincoln wins Booth's inheritance, he both reasserts his claim to manhood and usurps Booth's connection to their mother. Booth does the only thing he can to regain his money, his link to his mother, and his manhood – he shoots Lincoln. And at the risk of further arguing for oedipal predestination, I would say that Lincoln appears to spend the entire play preparing to die. His refusal to go back to cards is based on the connection he makes, through Sonny, between cards and violence. In his song, Lincoln sings, "My luck was bad but now it turned to worse/Don't call me up a doctor, just call me up a hearse" (23). The first time we see Lincoln is when he enters the room and Booth pulls a gun on him; Booth asks Lincoln, "You ever wonder if someones gonna come in there with a real gun? A real gun with real slugs?" (48). And when Lincoln practises getting shot, Booth is terrified because "it was looking too real" (52). So, what do we make of this? Is this a Greek foreshadowing of the tragic oedipal drama? Perhaps – but I want to conclude this essay by arguing that his death is also part of something far more complex: the complete collapse of the Symbolic and the Real – the annihilation of the symptom.

V

Cause everybody is a nigga to a nigga!
America was sole from the Indians show and prove,
what was th[a]t? A straight up nigga move
A low down shame Yo it's straight insane
Yet they [complain] when a nigga snatch their gold chains
What is nigga suppose to do? Wait around for a handout
From a nigga like you?

– Ice T, "Straight Up Nigga"

Right before Booth shoots Lincoln, Lincoln complains that he is unable to open the stocking of money, which apparently never has been opened. He taunts Booth, "She coulda been jiving you, bro. Jiving you that there really *was* money in this thing" (106). Booth replies, "We *know* what's in it. Don't open it" (106). But Lincoln keeps trying, and this makes Booth crazy. Why? It has nothing to do with the actual money – after all, Booth has never opened the stocking. Rather, for Booth, the money in the stocking is, to return to Žižek, a symbol *with* Imaginary and Real support – it is Booth's symptom, and when Lincoln attempts to cut open the money, he threatens the symptom by threatening to collapse the tension among the Symbolic/Imaginary/Real. This causes Booth himself to collapse. He tells Lincoln, "I popped her. Grace" (107), collapsing the distinction between sex and violence, between the Symbolic Magnum condoms and the Real magnum gun. He also tells Lincoln, "That Booth shit is over. 3-Cards thuh man now" (108), collapsing the distinction between the Real of his own personal content and his Symbolic economic form. Furthermore, does not this collision between Booth and the stocking mirror the collision Fanon talks about when the black man encounters himself through the white man? Is not that tearing off of the white mask analogous to the tearing open of the stocking – an item that is also doubled in its meaning if we consider the proliferation of pop-culture images of black men wearing stockings as masks in hold-ups. In *Enjoy*

Your Symptom, Žižek writes that "wearing a mask actually *makes us* what we feign to be" (34). To pull off a mask, then, is to reveal not a truth but the abyss, and so Booth shoots Lincoln before he can open the stocking, in a desperate attempt to preserve the mask, the symptom. Yet, in this desperate attempt to ward off total psychic annihilation, Booth implicitly acknowledges that the stocking has already lost its meaning. Even if he prevents the opening of the stocking, in his panic, in his willingness to shoot Lincoln, Booth faces the disjunction between the Symbolic object (money) and its Real value (his connection with his mother), and in doing so, empties the money of its Real value, collapses it into pure Symbol. In this last shot, Booth loses his symptom, his brother, and, indeed, his ability to use language. Language fails. All he can do at the end is let out a helpless wail.

It is not predestination that has led to this tragedy but the confluence of economic degradation, systemic racism, and definitions of masculinity inscribed from without. In the speech "What America Would Be Like without Blacks," Ralph Ellison asserted that "whatever else the true American is, he is also somehow black. Materially, psychologically and culturally, part of the nation's heritage is Negro American and whatever it becomes will be shaped in part by the Negro's presence." The moment the shot leaves Booth's gun, Parks's social diagnosis is complete, and it is a diagnosis not of what is black but of what is American. The end of *Topdog/Underdog* is a failure – the game fails, language fails, performativity fails. This is not to say that the words, the text, do not matter, but rather that their transformative power can't exist beyond the pressures of material, social, and economic conditions. In *Topdog/Underdog*, Parks comes up against the limits of language and the limits of performance but, in doing so, begins the necessary project of rebuilding the relationship between literature and politics, between histories and the Real.

NOTE

1   The author would like to thank the editors and proofreaders at *Modern Drama* for all their work; Julie Crawford and Liza Yukins for their invaluable comments and advice; and most of all, Peter Dickinson, for his time, care, insights, and grammatical patience, without which this article would be a shell of its present self.

WORKS CITED

Aesop Rock. "9–5ers Anthem." *Labor Days*. Def Jux, 2001.

Bergner, Gwen. "Who Is That Masked Woman? Or, The Role of Gender in Fanon's Black Skin, White Masks." PMLA 110.1 (1995): 75–88.

DeRose, David. Rev. of *The America Play*. *Theatre Journal* 46.3 (October, 1994): 409–12.

Elam Harry and Rayner Alice. "Echoes from the Black (W)hole: An Examination of *The America Play* by Suzan-Lori Parks." *Performing America: Cultural Nationalism in American Theatre*. Ed. Jeffrey Mason and Ellen Gainor. Ann Arbor: U of Michigan P, 2002. 178–92.

Elliott, Missy. "Gossip Folks." *Under Construction*. Goldmind; Elektra, 2002.

Ellison, Ralph. "What America Would Be Like without Blacks." 6 April 1970. 13 October 2006 <http://teachingamericanhistory.org/library/index.asp?document=574>.

Fanon, Frantz. *Black Skin, White Masks*. Trans. Charles Lam Markmann. New York: Grove, 1967.

Garnett Shawn-Marie."The Possession of Suzan-Lori Parks." *American Theatre* 17.8 (2000): 22–26, 132–34.

Harvey, David. *The Condition of Postmodernity*. Cambridge: Blackwell, 1989.

hooks, bell. *where we stand: class matters*. New York: Routledge, 2000.

———*Black, Looks*. Boston: South End, 1992.

Hutcheon, Linda. *The Politics of Postmodernism*. New York: Routledge, 1989.

Ice Cube. "Dirty Mack." *The Predator*. Priority, 1992.

Ice Cube and Angela Davis. "Nappy Happy: A Conversation with Ice Cube and Angela Y. Davis." *Transition* 58 (1992): 174–92.

Ice T. "Straight Up Nigga." *OG: Original Gangster*. Sire/Warner, 1991.

Jameson, Fredric. "Culture and Finance Capital." *Critical Inquiry* 24.1 (1997): 246–65.

———. "Postmodernism and Consumer Society" *The Anti-Aesthetic: Essays on Post-modern Culture*. Ed. Foster, Hall. Seattle: Bay, 1983.

———. *Postmodernism or the Cultural Logic of Late Capitalism*. Durham: Duke UP, 1991.

KRS-One. Black Cop *Return of the Boom Bap*. Jive 1993.

Malkin, Jeanette. "Suzan-Lori Parks and the Empty (W)hole of Memory." *Memory-Theater and Postmodern Drama*. Ann Arbor: U of Michigan P, 1999. 155–82.

Marriott, David. "Border Anxieties: Race and Psychoanalysis." *Comparing Postcolonial Literatures: Dislocations*. Ed. Ashok Bery and Patricia Murray. London: MacMillan, 2000.

Meeropol, Abel. "Strange Fruit." Recorded by Billie Holiday. Commodore, 1939.

Parks, Suzan-Lori. *The America Play and Other Works*. New York: Theater Communications, 1995.

———. *The America Play*. Parks, *America* 157–99.

———. "An Equation for Black People Onstage." Parks, *America* 9–22.

———. From 'Elements of Style." Parks, *America* 9–18.

———. "Repetition and Revision." Parks, *America* 8–9.

———. *Topdog/Underdog*. New York: Theatre Communications, 2002.

———. *Topdog Diaries: An Intimate Portrait of Playwright Suzan-Lori Parks.* Prod. and Dir. Oren Jacoby. DVD. Image Entertainment, 2004.

Wolf Shenk, Joshua."Beyond a Black-and-White Lincoln." *New York Times* 7 Apr. 2002. 15 Jan. 2007 <http://www.shenk.net/parks.htm>.

Žižek, Slavoj. *Enjoy Your Symptom! Jacques Lacan in Hollywood and Out.* London: Routledge, 1992.

———. *Iraq: The Borrowed Kettle.* London: Verso, 2004.

———. "Passion in the Age of Decaffeinated Belief." 2004. 13 October 2006 <http://www.lacan.com/passion.htm>.

———. *The Sublime Object of Ideology.* Verso, 1989.

5

The Space Stage and the Circus: E.E. Cummings's *Him* and Frederick[1] Kiesler's *Raumbühne*

ALLISON CARRUTH

We have no contemporary theatre. No agitator's theatre, no tribunal, no force which does not merely comment on life, but shapes it. Our theatres are copies of obsolete architecture. Systems of superannuated copies. Copies of copies. Barococo theatres ... Space is space only for the person who moves about in it. For the actor, not for the spectator. The peep-show stage functions as relief, not as space.

– Frederick Kiesler[2]

In 1926, two experimental theatre companies in Greenwich Village sponsored an international exposition to showcase avant-garde work in dramaturgy, stagecraft, and acting. In the exposition's keynote address, Bauhaus-trained architect Frederick Kiesler, whose circus-inspired "space stage" had debuted two years previously in Vienna, called on New York theatre practitioners to develop an "agitator's theatre" that would be radical in form and ideology and that would be rooted not in the conventions of the proscenium-arch stage but in the practices of popular subcultures. This essay argues that Kiesler's polemic profoundly influenced modernist poet E.E. Cummings,[3] who attended the exposition as a theatre critic for the *Dial*. Already at work on his play *Him*, Cummings had been exploring the poetic and theatrical possibilities of popular performance since the early twenties.[4] In columns for both the *Dial* and *Vanity Fair*, Cummings also promoted modernist artists such as Eric Satie, Pablo Picasso, Gaston Lachaise, and Kiesler for their adaptations of burlesque, circus, and other popular forms. As biographer Richard Kennedy acknowledges, Cummings's poetry reflects these extra-literary interests by melding graphical verse forms with the "colloquial" language of variety acts and slapstick comedy (28).[5] Critics of Cummings's poetry often fault his work for precisely this hybridity, suggesting that his emulation of popular performers explains his status as a relatively minor poet in the high modernist canon.[6] Kennedy, for example, discounts the poet's light verse entirely, claiming that their style makes such poems "unworthy of print by a serious poet" (79).

However, the resonances between Cummings and Kiesler demonstrate that this investment in the popular is far from "light." Both Cummings and Kiesler attend to the formal sophistication, political potential, and grotesque subversions of popular culture in general and the circus in particular, conceptualizing performative spaces like the big top as at once serious and comic – dark and light. Cummings's essays for the *Dial* and *Vanity Fair* comprise a de facto manifesto for a theatre that would occupy a liminal space between such popular entertainments and avant-garde art. I argue that Kiesler's and others' theatrical designs and theories crucially inform this manifesto and illuminate, moreover, the formal oddities of *Him* as well as Cummings's larger interest in staging experimental plays that adapt the forms of both three-ring circus and burlesque variety shows.[7] Although not without his own elitist conceptions of "low" and "high" culture, Cummings turned to performance as the medium in which to reconstruct the culture divide, imagining avant-garde theatre as more suited to this project than modernist poetry.

THE PLAY OF DANGER

In a 1946 review for the *Harvard Wake*, William Carlos Williams defends Cummings against detractors, contending that his typographic experiments do not disfigure existing poetic conventions but rather offer an entirely new lexicon for poetry. Williams goes on to characterize Cummings's work as inherently performative, comparing the poet to a circus acrobat: "[H]e has fixed [this new poetic language so] that he can't be imitated"; instead, "you've got to learn the *basis* for his trapeze tricks" ("Lower Case" 405). Just as the acrobat's "trapeze tricks" defy gravity, in other words, Cummings's poetry transmutes poetic language. The comparison Williams draws between Cummings and a high-wire performer must have pleased the latter tremendously, who laboured from the publication of *Him* in 1927 until the production of *Santa Claus* in 1957 to reconstruct the little stage according to the principles of the big top.

Like other writers and artists of the period, Cummings was a huge fan of the circus, which he experienced as at once sublime, dangerous, and enormously entertaining. In a 1925 essay for *Vanity Fair* inspired by Ringling Brothers and Barnum and Bailey shows in the United States and by the world-renowned Fratellini clowns in Paris, Cummings characterizes the circus as "compris[ing] certain untranslatable idioms" that upend conventional modes of discourse and everyday praxis ("The Adult" 114). Cummings further asserts that the idioms of the clowns and trapeze artists are "immune to forgetfulness" and, as such, "resemble the spiritual essence of poetry" ("The Adult" 113–14). At the same time, Cummings's interest in the circus and other popular performance forms convinced him that drama, rather than poetry, was the most important form for avant-garde art. In the first of six "nonlectures" delivered at Harvard between 1952 and 1953, Cummings provocatively declares that his most important work inheres less in his nine volumes of poetry than in his relatively scant works of drama (4).[8] Throughout the Harvard talks, Cummings also argues for a "live art" that resists both abstraction and mimesis and that provides the artist and the audience with an opportunity to "actually feel" (79).

In his columns for *Vanity Fair* and the *Dial* from 1925 to 1927, Cummings writes prolifically about both performance culture and avant-garde art. These eccentric and irreverent pieces range widely from Jean Cocteau, Pablo Picasso, and Constantin Stanislavski to Coney Island, Josephine Baker, and the comic strip *Krazy Kat*. In this eclectic group, Cummings finds exempla for his emerging conception of circus-theatre. Moreover, Cummings critiques "serious" art forms, such as realist drama and sentimental fiction, as well as "respectable" entertainments, such as the *Ziegfeld Follies* and Broadway musicals. He argues that these organs of official culture appropriate popular and avant-garde subcultures by censoring, for example, both Mae West's performances and James Joyce's novels. To maintain social order, the "censor" – Cummings's icon for the American Comstock laws and conservative social reformers – must repress any form of the carnivalesque.

Cummings promotes the circus as a corrective to bourgeois censorship and the forms of art and leisure it produces. In a 1925 essay, provocatively titled "The Adult, the Artist, and the Circus," Cummings contrasts the kinetic power of the circus with the practices of conventional theatre:

> [I]n contrast to our modern theatres, where an audience and a spectacle merely confront each other ... [the circus], we immediately notice, has a definite kind of bigness. By "definite kind," I mean that the bigness of the circus-show is intrinsic – like the bigness of an elephant or of a skyscraper – not superficial, as in the case of an enlarged snapshot. The nature of this bigness becomes apparent when we perceive that it is never, for so much as the fraction of an instant, motionless. (112)

Cummings argues here that the circus intervenes in the staid experience of theatregoing by "surrounding" its audience with gigantic forms, dangerous stunts, and constant motion. As we will see, this emerging call for a theatre based on the circus anticipates Antonin Artaud's prescription for the theatre of cruelty. Cummings's ideal circus deploys its "bigness" – through sounds, sets, animals, and human bodies – to move the audience physically as well as cognitively. While many of his *Vanity Fair* readers might perceive the circus as "nothing but a big and colourful toy" and so opt for the "enlightened" shows of Broadway or the "passive" films of Hollywood, Cummings inverts this cultural hierarchy by depicting these middle-class recreations as passive diversions that displace the participatory and ritualistic structure of carnival. In a related essay entitled "Coney Island," Cummings extends this social critique when he asserts that both the circus and the amusement park are subcultures precisely because they are working-class entertainments and, thus, pose an implicit threat to what Mikhail Bakhtin terms "official culture."

To the extent that avant-garde theatre can crystallize the participatory idioms of the circus without assimilating its entertainment into sanctioned forms of leisure, Cummings suggests that drama might recuperate its ties to ritual, producing a space of "liminality" in other words (Turner). With this aim in view, Cummings attempts to articulate the sensational qualities of the big top in his prose writings. "The Adult, the Artist, and the Circus," for example, thickens with descriptions of the rides, smells, tastes, and sounds of a recent circus show, and the essay crescendos in a reference to a famous bicycle stuntman: "DANGER DERIDING DEATH DEFYING DESPERATE DAREDEVIL DIAVOLO LOOPS THE LOOP ON A BICYCLE" (114). Here, Cummings replicates his own breathless response to Diavolo's "death-defying" stunts by using an all-caps typescript – a striking departure from the insistent use of lower case in his poetry – to signal both the scale and the ritualistic quality of the bicycle act. At such a show, the audience does not simply watch but rather experiences bodily the risk and virtuosity of the stuntman. In contrast to conventional theatre, which is carefully staged and hierarchically structured, Cummings further maintains that "at this great spectacle, as nowhere else, the adult onlooker knows that unbelievably skillful and inexorably beautiful and unimaginably dangerous things are continually happening. But this is not all: he feels that there is a little too much going on at any [given] moment ... [And] *this is as it should be*" (113; emphasis in original). A space like "nowhere else," the circus violates the proscenium-arch stage and, in its place, offers an arena for decentralized and multiple forms of play. Janet Davis, in her recent cultural history of the American big top, affirms that the modern circus did offer a carnival of unprecedented scale and scope. Even before its merger with Ringling Brothers in 1920, Barnum and Bailey featured a crew of "1,200 people, 400 horses, and scores of other animals," a "wonderland" that promised "a startling stupendous revolution" in popular entertainment (Davis 23). For Cummings, at least, the modern circus seems to have delivered on this promise, a performative mish-mash that transforms the circus-goer's body and mind.

However, Cummings's experience of the circus as radically liminal vis-à-vis bourgeois culture is somewhat misleading, at least in terms of the politics and economics of the circus in the United States. Like operas and theatres, circus shows had hierarchical seating arrangements that ranged from reserved box seats to unreserved bleachers to open-pit seats between the track and the stands (Davis 32; Levine). Similarly, while Cummings figures the circus performer as culturally subversive, Davis observes that the "social structure of the railroad circus was built upon an occupational hierarchy akin to a caste system" (Davis 62). Aerialists and other headline performers often knew little about the sideshow acts, "because the big-top players and sideshow performers worked at opposite ends of the show grounds" (Davis 62), while sideshow performers were often chosen to affirm racist and gendered ideas of the "primitive," the "noble savage," and the "freak."[9]

In contrast to this historicized account of the early twentieth-century circus, Cummings experiences the big top as a subversive subculture and nascent avant-garde form. Cummings persistently promotes the participatory, performative, and grotesque character of the circus, qualities he observed in both the American and the European circus tours during the twenties. Although Cummings thus obfuscates the social hierarchies and exploitive realities of the circus, he envisions the big top as a subversive space vis-à-vis its bourgeois audience. Akin to the medieval carnival that Bakhtin theorizes in *Rabelais and His World*, Cummings's circus traffics in a generative zone of extremes: art and entertainment, fear and pleasure, the beautiful and the ugly. In attempting to recast the circus for the little theatre, Cummings constructs a maxim for such carnival art: "[T]he expression of ... supreme alive-ness" (114). Cummings returns often to this principle of "alive-ness," a principle that he opposes to the "pretend" world of bourgeois culture and the attendant economy based on consumer goods. As an attack on and an invitation to that culture, Cummings promotes the circus. In the big top, he claims, we find an ancient form of theatre, one that mobilizes the rituals of human play generally and the marginal space of popular carnival specifically:

> Within the "big top," as nowhere else on earth, is to be found Actuality. Living players play with living. There are no tears produced by onion-oil and Mr. Nevin's Rosary, no pasteboard hovels and *papier-mâché* palaces, no 'cuts,' 'retakes,' or 'N.G.'s' – and no curtain calls after suicide. At positively every performance Death Himself lurks, glides, struts, breathes, is. ("The Adult, the Artist, and the Circus" 113)

Repeating the phrase "as nowhere else," this didactic passage imagines a theatre whose stage and acting emanates from the circus. This "living" theatre would produce a liminal space of play, moreover, by incorporating the audience into its acts and estranging them from habitual modes of both conventional theatregoing and everyday performance. Unlike "going to the movies or putting out the cat," the "thrilling experiences of a life-or-death order" witnessed under the big top and adapted to the avant-garde stage offer a form of action more authentic and transformative than the formulaic actions of daily American life (113).

It was this theory of circus and of a circus-inspired theatre that Cummings put into practice with *Him*. For many contemporaneous critics, *Him* was, at best, an accomplished literary experiment and, at worst, an incoherent failure. Whether reviewing the published script in 1927 or the Provincetown Players' production in 1928, reviewers repeatedly cast *Him* as a "closet drama" that should have remained closeted. Ironically, but perhaps not surprisingly, these reviewers panned the play for the very elements that Cummings most admired in the circus: excess, multiplicity, participation, and stunts. In contrast to reviewers, the Provincetown Players viewed the play as one of their most daring and significant performances to date. Evocative of the many performers and sideshows of the circus, Cummings's script calls for 71 speaking parts, 9 jazz players, and a crowd topping out at over 100 people. The stage itself requires moving parts, such as a room where the lovers, Him and Me, interact; this living room set "rotates" 90 degrees with each set change to simulate an imaginary fourth wall as well as a circus arena. More complex still, the character Him stages a play for Me, which unfolds in Act Two and requires a dozen set changes. This play-within-a-play takes the form of a variety show, which culminates in a circus sideshow requiring that the entire cast and audience participate either as "freaks" or as members of the crowd. Ostensibly authored by Him's double "O. Him," Act Two thus works as a foil for Him's conceptual and unstageable play-in-progress.

Throughout Act Two, O. Him's "variety show" unsettles the boundaries between theatre and circus and between performers and audience. For example, a travesty of mass consumerism (a vignette in which a soapbox marketer pitches a magic pill to a passing crowd of cast members) leads into a fantastical satire of Fascism (a scene in which Mussolini battles rebel nymphs in classical Greece). Similarly, an actor who plays "the Doctor" in the two framing acts (Act One and Act Two), plays eight parts in the variety show of Act Two, including that of a censor who emerges from the theatre house to halt the progression of profanity in a performance of the blues song "Frankie and Johnnie." In this multi-part role, the doctor occupies a borderland between surrealism and slapstick, as does the play as a whole. While the play opens, for example, with the doctor anesthetizing Me on a table – an oblique reference to T.S. Eliot's 1917 poem "The Love Song of J. Alfred Prufrock"[10] – the scene occurs against a carnival cut-out of a doctor, a patient, and a table, with only the heads of each actor visible. In the next scene, this same doctor character introduces Him to the three "weirds," aging women who represent the three fates and yet speak in the language of advertising slogans and radio jingles. Similarly, the penultimate vignette of Act Three enacts a sideshow in which the doctor, costumed as a barker, unveils twelve prototypical circus "exotics," including an *"eighteen inch lady," "six hundred pounds of passionate pulchritude," "the King of Borneo,"* and the *"tattooed man"* (131). While other actors gather onstage as the audience, the doctor/barker addresses the theatre's real audience. This scene thus works to critique both the sideshow and the middle-class theatre in that the barker's final "unveiling" of an exotic reveals the character Me costumed as Princess Anankay – the mother of the three fates – costumed in turn as a pregnant exotic dancer. Me's performance in this scene has several complex effects. First, it confirms a latent allusion throughout the framing acts to her pregnancy. Second, it critiques the actual circus and its pandering to bourgeois conceptions of the grotesque and the exotic. And finally, it deploys surrealism to imbue the circus-inspired theatre with a tonal seriousness. As we will see, *Him* thus puts Kiesler's notion of an "agitator's theatre" into practice by jarring the audience out of stock emotional responses to both the theatre and the circus.

THE SPACE STAGE

The conception of theatre that *Him* attempts to realize connects Cummings's dramatic work to that of Austrian-born architect and set designer Frederick Kiesler. Kiesler came to New York in 1926 at the invitation of the Theatre Guild and the Provincetown Players to direct the International Theatre Exposition and to exhibit his *Raumbühne* – or "space stage" (see Figure 1). Cummings attended the Exposition while finalizing the typescript for *Him* and guest-writing the *Dial's* theatre column, evidently to review the space-stage design and Kiesler's keynote address on the future of modernist theatre.[11] As apparent in the *Dial* review, Kiesler's manifesto for avant-garde theatre resonated profoundly with Cummings's emerging dramatic corpus. The influence of Kiesler on Cummings proved to be a lasting one, moreover. Although Kennedy, Cummings's biographer, does not mention the relationship, Kiesler painted a portrait of Cummings entitled "e.e. cummings Galaxy" in 1947, two decades after the International Theatre Exposition (Spender 87).

Despite the initial attention that the space stage received both at its Vienna debut and at the International Theatre Exposition, today Kiesler is known primarily for Peggy Guggenheim's 57th Street art gallery in New York, Art of This Century. Completed in 1942, the gallery became a hub for mid-century art (Davidson and Rylands; "Peggy and Kiesler").[12] In both design and function, the space was radical, an extension of the principles Kiesler had begun developing for the theatre in the 1920s.

Figure 1: Frederick Kiesier, *Raumbühne;* Vienna International Theatre Exposition, 1924; © 2008 Austrian Frederick and Lillian Kiesler Private Foundation, Vienna.

Inspired partly by Bauhaus design principles and partly by Art Deco styles, Kiesler constructed the gallery to be a flexible and participatory environment, as a contemporaneous *New York Times* art critic aptly explains,

> Paintings are displayed there without frames, against curved walls or suspended in the opening. Sculpture is suspended in the air. Chairs double as sculpture pedestals. Series of pictures are arranged in viewing boxes and kaleidoscopes. There are movable canvas walls. Some of the lighting can be controlled by the spectator. ("Modern Art")

As described here, Kiesler's gallery was a public art space as no other, one that inverted the structures and protocols of the museum by encouraging visitors to touch, move, and physically interact with major works of art.[13] In the Surrealist Room, for example, visitors could rotate a kaleidoscopic wheel to view multiple objects by Marcel Duchamp, Kiesler's close friend and collaborator. In other so-called informal rooms, visitors could similarly pull up folding chairs and flip through racks of paintings by emerging postmodern artists.

For Kiesler, Art of This Century represented a theatre of the future akin to his earlier space stage in that the Guggenheim space enacted an avant-garde architectural critique of the New York art gallery that also evoked the nineteenth-century dime museum. Just as the space stage aimed to dismantle the proscenium arch theatre, Art of This Century aimed to revolutionize the New York art scene. Rather than offering a space of flat walls displaying glass-encased works, Art of This Century dispensed with both hierarchy and distance by inviting the viewer to reshape the viewing space.[14]

Kiesler had begun to develop this architectural vision twenty years earlier in his experiments with set design and stage-craft. While living in Berlin in the early twenties, Kiesler was an occasional member of both the Bauhaus school of design and the De Stijl group. During this period, Kiesler designed his first "space stage" for the Berlin production of Eugene O'Neill's *Emperor Jones*, and two years later, the Vienna Konzerthaus invited him to display the stage in the main hall. The *Raumbühne* (literally translated as "railway stage") consisted of a circular and elevated platform above which a smaller circular tower was suspended. The stage itself was constructed of open wooden beams that suggested the rafters and pits of conventional theatres. Actors would access the platforms via spiral-shaped ramps, ladders, and elevators, while spectators gathered in a round above the stage. Evocative of both an amusement park ride and the circus arena, the space stage literally exposed the infrastructure of the proscenium arch "peep-show-stage," and did so in Vienna's principal concert hall. Analogously to Art of This Century, Kiesler's experimental set design closed the distance between downstage and backstage as well as between audience and actor.

Kiesler's designs illustrate the complex relationship between constructivism and organic form in Bauhaus theatre designs such as those of leading figure Walter Gropius, who designed the "Total Theatre" in 1927 (Smith).[15] Kiesler's major design projects – the space stage and Art of This Century – were simultaneously industrial and organic, functional and aesthetic. As one critic persuasively argues, these spaces were "biomorphic and sculptural," integrating biological, mechanical, and theatrical forms (Gundrum). Just as the Bauhaus School as a whole became more interested in organic form in the late 1920s, the "biomorphic" quality of Kiesler's design practice is less evident in his early statements on the space stage, as articulated at the International Theatre Exposition:

The [space] stage is empty; it functions as space; it has ceased to appeal as decoration. The play itself is required to give it life. Everything now depends upon the play ... The energies of the components [sound, structure, objects, stage mechanisms, light] heighten one another; they grow and crystallize beneath the eyes of the public. No mystery. The stage structure develops step by step: the simultaneity of the picture-stage is abandoned. There is no curtain, nor is the

house darkened in lieu of a curtain. The performance is orchestral. The movement
is carried from one element to another. The movements begin abruptly;
accelerated and retarded, they continue without interruption until the play is
ended. (qtd. in Cummings "The Theatre" 147–48)

In this directive to New York's little theatres, Kiesler transmutes the theatre
from a stage for human drama and feeling to a system of moving parts.
Partly espousing the tenets of constructivism, Kiesler figures the actor as
one of the stage's mechanical components – an "agent of movement" analogous to sound and lighting effects.[16] Kiesler was certainly enamoured of
industrial technology and its possibilities for both architecture and
theatre. In his 1922 designs for Karl Capek's R.U.R, for example, Kiesler
undercut the play's apocalyptic representation of machines by articulating
the utopian aesthetic of machine-age art (Huhtamo). At the same time,
Kiesler imagined a theatre that would "abandon" the devices of traditional
theatre by expanding the physical space of performance and by orchestrat-
ing new kinds of bodily and psychic involvement on the part of actors and
audience members. To put his theory into practice, Kiesler turned from
avant-garde theatre to popular culture, drawing on carnival subculture. In
the case of R.U.R., Kiesler borrowed a device from European sideshows
called the Tanagra, a tiny stage on which actors appeared in miniature
through an arrangement of mirrors (Pringle).[17] The audience's response
to the Tanagra delighted Kiesler, who speculated after the fact that such
devices allow avant-garde theatre "to present the interplay of reality and
illusion" (qtd. in Pringle). Like Cummings then, Kiesler imagines that
both the structure and the technologies of carnival could produce sen-
sations on the little stage that would be at once playful and profound.
Also like Cummings, Kiesler integrated carnival technologies into his set
designs not so much to reconstruct the theatre as a mechanized space as
to alter the conditioned habits of actor and audience.

As evident in both Art of This Century and the space stage, Kiesler's
vision for the theatre was *kinetic* more than mechanistic, in the sense
that he melded together biological and industrial forms. Both his and
Cummings's theories thus anticipate those of Antonin Artaud, who completed the first manifesto of "Le Théâtre de la Cruauté" in the late thirties.
In Artaud's theatre of cruelty, the actor becomes "a neutral, pliant factor . . .
rigorously denied any individual initiative" (117). At the same time, Artaud
critiques conventional theatre for over-mechanizing the actor, explaining
that "there is a wide margin dividing a man from an instrument, between
an actor required to give nothing more than a certain number of sobs
and one who has to deliver a speech using his own powers of persuasion"
(117). This theatre of cruelty demands more from its actors than, to cite
Cummings, "tears produced by onion-oil": it demands a rigorous form of

presence and action. Artaud, like Kiesler and Cummings, wishes to redesign the theatre and retrain the actor by emphasizing kinetic movement and non-stylized affect while shunning the backdrops and props of conventional drama (its "décor," in other words). As Kiesler asserts, conventional theatre is hopelessly "barococo," alienating and dulling the audience for whom the intermission is the only "social event." In response to these conditions, Kiesler and Artaud envision a stage structured around organic forms, corporeal action, and performed rituals – a more technical expression of Cummings's "bigness" and "danger." "No décor," Artaud declares; rather, "[h]ieroglyphic characters, ritual costume, thirty foot high effigies of King Lear's beard in the storm, musical instruments as tall as men, objects of unknown form and purpose" will produce a theatre free from "stereotyped physical representation" (113). A conceptual analogue to Kiesler's built stage, the theatre of cruelty offers a performative field in which "direct contact ... between the audience and the show, between actors and audience, [comes] from the very fact that the audience is seated in the centre of the action, [and] is encircled and furrowed by it" (Artaud 115). Similarly, Kiesler's space stage aspires to be a "tribunal": a space that agitates and moves its audience by enacting rather than mimicking human drama.

In this sense, Kiesler's space stage anticipates Artaud's manifesto for theatre, a vision that captivated Cummings when he attended the Exposition in 1926. That Kiesler drew from the European carnival only solidified his influence on Cummings. To this point, Kiesler's central metaphor for the space stage is that of a roller coaster: "a kind of four-sided funnel opening towards the audience" ("The Theatre" 147).[18] Furthermore, while Artaud's theatre of cruelty remained, as Martin Puchner argues, a "utopian and phantasmatic" vision (527), Kiesler yoked theory to praxis – the avant-garde to the popular. Beyond his review of Kiesler's 1926 address, Cummings references the space stage indirectly in essays written for *Vanity Fair* later that year. In the Coney Island essay cited earlier, for example, Cummings aligns the amusement park and the big top with "the worldwide 'new movement' in the theatre" as represented at the Exposition ("Coney Island" 151). According to Cummings, this movement recognizes "first, that the circus is an authentic 'theatric' phenomenon[,] second, that the conventional 'theatre' is a box of negligible tricks. [And third, that] the existing relationships between actor, audience and theatre have been discovered to be rotten at their very cores" (151).[19] Responding to Kiesler's work implicitly, Cummings recommends Coney Island as the prototype for a theatre of the future:

The incredible temple of pity and terror, mirth and amazement, which is popularly known as Coney Island, really constitutes a perfectly unprecedented fusion of the circus and the theatre. It resembles the theatre, in that it fosters every known species of illusion. It suggests the circus, in that it puts us in touch with whatever is hair-raising, breath-taking and pore-opening. But Coney has a distinct drop on both the theatre and the circus. Whereas at the theatre we merely are deceived, at Coney we deceive ourselves. Whereas at the circus we are merely spectators of the impossible, at Coney we ourselves perform impossible feats. (150)

As when Kiesler promotes Tanagra as a technological "device" for avant-garde theatre, Cummings here promotes the roller coaster as an engineering feat that heightens even as it deceives the senses. Both Kiesler and Cummings cite such carnival forms as models for a non-mimetic theatre because they do not represent but rather present the body in action.[20]

BAUHAUS MEETS BURLESQUE: CUMMINGS'S THEATRE OF THE FUTURE

As Cummings's response to Kiesler's stagecraft suggests, the alliance between avant-garde theatre and popular performance in the 1920s was central to the American poet's work in the two or three years preceding the production of *Him*. Interested in merging the spectacles of carnival and circus with the forms of modernist literature and art, Cummings looked also to burlesque as a complementary model for avant-garde theatre. As with the three-ring circus, Cummings was a devoted fan of burlesque, frequenting first the Old Howard in Boston and then the National Winter Garden in New York during the 1910s and 1920s. While Cummings censured the Old Howard as a "respectable" theatre, he praised the Minsky Brothers' National Winter Garden and its headline performers – comedian Jack Shargel and striptease-dancer "Cleo" – for subverting both leisure-class mores and New York censorship laws. However, while Cummings was frequenting the National Winter Garden with John Dos Passos and others in the early twenties, burlesque was becoming an increasingly controversial and liminal entertainment form; and its profane comedy routines and racy striptease acts repeatedly led to censorship "busts," such as those of Mae West's Broadway plays, *Sex* and *Drag*.

Burlesque interested Cummings because its male comedians and female performers trafficked in grotesque displays that, like the carnival spaces of the circus and the amusement park, flouted middle-class social norms. In a 1925 *Vanity Fair* review of the National Winter Garden, for example, Cummings opposes burlesque to the formal and thematic "flatness" of middle-class art and theatre:

First let us take the art of three-dimensional painting. Here, as in "nature," not only do we never see around a solid person or object, but the very solidity of the

> object or person is conditioned by our inability to see around it, her, or him. More simply, in the case of sculpture: only one aspect of a statue is presented to us – in perceiving the rest, we are compelled to lose sight of what we have already seen; to revolve the figure, or else move around it ourselves. But the graphic arts and the theatre have an analogous limitation – that is, a thing or character cannot possibly be presented as beautiful, noble, or desirable and also as ugly, ignoble and despicable. ("You Aren't Mad" 126)

Billed by *Vanity Fair* as "certain observations on the extremely modern art of 'burlesk,'" this essay inverts the division between popular entertainment and high art, refiguring the culture divide as a dialectic. In Cummings's terms, "academic" forms of visual art and theatre rely on stereotyped bodies and stock characters and, as such, are "thoroughly dead." In contrast, burlesque performance is both "intensely alive" and "highly stylized," at once a popular entertainment and an avant-garde form. In 1920–21 line drawings for the *Dial*, entitled *National Winter Garden*, Cummings presents burlesque as modernist and carnivalesque.[21] As the drawings suggest, the Minsky Brothers' style of burlesque constitutes a bawdy and yet experimental performance form, one marked by a concern for *le mot juste* (in both its verbal satires and physical performances), a sort of Cubist montage (in its abrupt set changes and comedic non-sequiturs), and futuristic forms (in its mechanized stage effects and kinetic chorus line numbers).[22] In sum, Cummings implies that burlesque is a model for avant-garde theatre as it is based on three central techniques of modernism: precision, montage, and dynamism.

In the 1926 preface to his poetry volume *Is 5*, Cummings similarly references burlesque as a model for his poetic technique: "like the burlesk comedian, I am abnormally fond of that precision which creates movement" (*i: six nonlectures* 64). The curious connection Cummings makes here between precision and movement is echoed by Gilbert Seldes, who attended National Winter Garden performances with both Cummings and Dos Passos.[23] In *The Seven Lively Arts*, Seldes compares such popular performance venues to both architecture and engineering. About the Ziegfeld Follies revue, Seldes contends that "it shows a mania for perfection; it aspires to be precise and definite, it corresponds to those *de luxe* railway trains which are always exactly on time, to the millions of spare parts that always fit, to the ease of commerce when there is a fixed price; ... to the incorruptible purr of the dynamo" (132). In this analogy between the Follies' chorus lines and newly engineered railway trains, technical precision figures as a force that orders the frenetic assemblage of "spare parts." Seldes suggests here that such "engineering" produces aesthetic forms that are not "dead," as they are in much academic art, but dynamic and participatory. However, the differences between Cummings and Seldes on this point are significant. While the two friends frequented the National Winter Garden together, Seldes claims in *The Seven Lively Arts* to know little about burlesque, promoting instead the middle-class revue (251; qtd. in Shteir 90). More importantly, while Seldes admires the precision not only of Ziegfeld's up-market chorus line but also of capitalist industry, Cummings repeatedly satirizes both the culture and the economy of the bourgeoisie ("Burlesque" 292). That said, Cummings seems to agree with Seldes – as with Kiesler – that modernist art should adopt the techniques and technologies of popular performance to structure and to revitalize its fragmented forms.

To clarify his intentions for the production of *Him*, Cummings describes a routine by the Jewish burlesque comedian Jack Shargel, Minsky's most famous male performer. In the routine, as Cummings describes it, the "misfit-clothed" Shargel receives a perfect red rose from a "beauteous lady" (weighing several hundred pounds). Having accepted the rose "rapturously, deliriously even" and inhaled its fragrance, Shargel throws the rose "exquisitely, lightly from him" to the stage floor, producing a "terrific, soul-shaking, earthquake-like *crash*: as if all the glass and masonry on earth, all the most brittle and most ponderous things of this world, were broken to smithereens" ("You Aren't Mad" 128). The description underscores Cummings's admiration for the comedian's artistic invention, comedic virtuosity, and social impact. In Cummings's view, Shargel's burlesque routine leverages a dynamic play of actor, object, and sound effect to enact avant-garde practices of both montage and shock. Like Kiesler's "four-sided funnel," this burlesque stage thus figures in Cummings's work as a frenetic yet aesthetic space of live performance, one in which seemingly endless and often unscripted acts are performed "around" rather than in front of the audience. Rather than "peep" at the flat stages of conventional theatre, burlesque spectators can "know around" scenes and characters.

At the time of *Him*, the burlesque stage was perhaps the closest to Kiesler's "space stage" of any in New York. In 1917, for example, the Minsky Brothers installed a runway to bring female performers closer to their audience (Shteir 83).[24] In contrast, the Ziegfeld Follies, launched in 1909 as a respectable version of the Parisian Folies Bergère, featured svelte young girls uniformly dressed in lavish yet translucent costumes and cordoned off from the audience. As Rachel Shteir puts it, the Minsky Brothers "featured girls ... on a budget," producing fifty-two shows per year at a cost of $3,500 per show, as compared to the Follies, which produced several shows a year as ongoing runs at a cost of $30,000 per show (64). From the perspective of many middle-class onlookers at the time, the performers at the National Winter Garden and in the touring burlesque "circuits" were older and less attractive than revue dancers. At the same time, these qualities were the very source of the burlesque dancer's performative power. As Shteir explains, the "head-waggling, arm-whirling, big-mouthed moments of Minsky girl acts ... contrasting with burlesque comedy, provided raw sex and laughs," making the striptease a carnival-esque performance that subverted the "atomized" theatre of the middle-class (70).

***

As articulated in his essays of the early 1920s, Cummings produced *Him* as a testing ground for the performance forms he had been avidly enjoying as a fan: the three-ring circus and the burlesque variety show. With *Him*, Cummings staged an avant-garde play that was at once carnivalesque and lyric, burlesque and serious, fantastic and realistic. Thus the initial production of *Him* by Jim Light and Robert Edmond Jones at the Provincetown Playhouse and audiences' reception of the play were of utmost importance to the poet. Sadly for Cummings, most of the play's early reviewers doubted whether *Him* was a play at all. Although the 1927 book publication of *Him* received some praise for its "literary" innovations, the play itself was ultimately deemed a closet drama. These critics viewed the size of the cast and the perceived excesses of Cummings's borrowings from both burlesque and the circus as "problems," problems that prevented thematic unity and disrupted the central story of a modernist artist torn between the burdens of his art and his relationship with his lover. Given the limitations of a small proscenium stage and a low budget, director James Light had to devise elaborate flowcharts to convince Provincetown principals of its feasibility. The casting was particularly significant, as actors played multiple roles, in many cases switching racial and social identities (see appendices 1–2). In a scene enacting the "Frankie and Johnnie" blues song, for example, Light cast both white and black actors to play the parts of "black figures," some of whom played parts later in the variety show as diverse as Mussolini, an Englishman, and a Porter. In the view of Cummings, Light, and other theatre company members, the play was ultimately a success: an avant-garde performance that radically changed the lines between experimental theatre and popular entertainment.

While Cummings was discouraged enough with later productions of the play to foreclose on future collaborations or adaptations, he was tremendously pleased with Light's 1928 production. The primary reason for his satisfaction seems to have been Light's success in integrating the play's adaptations of burlesque and circus performance forms, on the one hand, and avant-garde principles of acting and set design, on the other, principles that emanated above all from Frederick Kiesler's theatrical manifestos and space-stage designs. In essence, the reviewers who lambasted Cummings and the Provincetown Players in the press missed the central project of *Him*. That is, they missed the poet's attempt to reconstruct New York little theatre as simultaneously avant-garde and carnivalesque.

NOTES

1 Kiesler's first name is spelled both Frederick and Friedrich; I have opted for the former, following the Vienna-based Frederick and Lillian Kiesler Private Foundation.

2 Conference Program for the International Theatre Exposition, New York (1926); qtd. in Cummings, "The Theatre" 146.

3 In capitalizing E.E. Cummings's name, I follow the suggestion of his principal biographer, Richard Kennedy (xi–xii).

4 I am particularly indebted to the work of Robert C. Allen, David Chinitz, Michael North, and Rachel Shteir for my conception of popular entertainment during this era and of circus and burlesque theatre in particular.

5 Notable examples of poems that employ the vernacular of burlesque comedians and comic strip characters and emulate the style of variety shows, circus acts, and roller coasters include "Buffalo Bill" and "in Just" (*100 Selected Poems* 7, 5).

6 As Guy Rotella explains in his bibliographic study, even as critics "express high praise" for Cummings's "themes," his "'eccentric' typography is the despair of some reviewers," and most voice "serious doubts about the legitimacy of his technical experiments" (1).

7 Bakhtin has suggested that we understand the complex relationship between avant-garde modernism and popular culture as a form of the carnivalesque. For example, he cites Alfred Jarry and Bertold Brecht as contemporary exemplars of the carnivalesque, arguing that such playwrights' uses of folk culture revive the grotesque and destructive as well as the regenerative aspects of carnival time (46). I would also note here that the carnivalesque projects of Cummings and Kiesler are avant-garde in Peter Bürger's terms, in that they critique the "bourgeois institution of art" by directing aesthetic work toward lived and embodied experience (Berman 253n4).

8 Consider the following polemic that Cummings uses to explain the importance of drama to his artistic identity:

> [T]he question "who am I?" is answered by what I write – in other words, I become my writing; and my autobiography becomes the exploration of my stance as a writer. Two questions now make their appearance. The first – what constitutes this writing of mine? – can be readily answered: my writing consists of a pair of miscalled novels; a brace of plays, one in prose, the other in blank verse; nine books of poems; an indeterminate number of essays; an untitled volume of satire; and a ballet scenario. The second question – where, in all this material, do I find my stance as a writer most clearly expressed? – can be answered almost as readily: I find it expressed most clearly in the later miscalled novel, the two plays, perhaps twenty poems, and a half a dozen of the essays. (4)

On this point, Cummings opens the lectures by stressing his dual identity as painter and writer.

9   About circus nudes and striptease performers, for example, Davis argues that "showmen were keenly aware of circus women's transgressive potential. As a result, they repositioned these strong, athletic, traveling women into traditional gender categories: as models of domestic womanliness, and as objects of titillation" (83). With respect to race, while performers of colour were billed as "pre-industrial 'primitives,'" Davis shows that such representations were the work of circus marketers and were aimed at middle-class white audiences. The case of Krao Farini – a Southeast Asian native fluent in seven languages and a library tutor in Bridgeport, Connecticut, but billed as the "missing link" – Davis suggests is typical of many sideshow performers (128–29).

10 See the opening three lines of Eliot's lyric: "Let us go then, you and I, / When the evening is spread out against the sky/Like a patient etherized upon a table" (lines 1–3).

11 For access to Cummings's manuscripts and notes for *Him*, I am grateful to the Houghton Library at Harvard and the Berg Collection of English and American Literature at the New York Public Library, where I conducted archival research in the summer of 2005.

12 The project entailed a conversion of two adjacent tailor shops into a gallery space inspired by the surrealist, Cubist, and abstract expressionist art it would house. The surrealist gallery was both industrial and earthy: a dimly lit, asymmetrical room with curved walls on one side, whose coldness of material and light was unsettled by its concave and exagerrated forms. The gallery produced fifty-five exhibitions between 1942 and 1947, including a solo show for Mark Rothko in 1945; see Davidson and Rylands; "Peggy and Kiesler."

13 For analogues to Art of This Century, we might turn to nineteenth-century dime museums. For example, the galleries at PT Barnum's American Museum shared space with freak shows and variety acts, and museum visitors were less heavily policed than they are today. As Lawrence Levine's research shows, American art museums, along with theatres, symphony halls, and opera houses, became increasingly segregated and "sacralized" by the 1870s and 1880s.

14 Recognizing that a small art gallery and a major museum are subject to different conditions of security and access, we might compare the Duchamp wheel to Michelangelo's *Pietà* at St. Peter's or to Da Vinci's *Mona Lisa*, both of which are housed behind a wall of glass.

15 The space stage was later compared to the Total Theatre. Gropius's theatre, designed for Piscator, was a spherical structure in which mobile aerial stages were surrounded on all sides by seating.

16 Here we might compare Kiesler's space stage to the marionette-style of Maurice Maeterlinck or to the later sculptural theatre of Robert Wilson; see Worthen 103–06.

17 As Kiesler describes it, the set

> had a big, square panel window in the middle of the stage drop which could be opened by remote control. When the director of the human factory in the play pushed a button at his desk, the panel opened and the audience saw two human beings ... a foot-and-a-half tall, casually moving and talking,

> heard through a hidden loudspeaker. ... a minute later you saw the same
> actors appear on stage full size. (qtd. in Pringle)

18   However, this machine is a roller coaster with a difference – not a closed circuit,
     but rather an open loop. The audience's own energy becomes one of the
     "funnel's" constitutive "components."

19   The Exposition was covered widely in the popular press, especially *The Nation*
     and *The New York Times*. Shortly after, Kiesler founded the International
     Theatre Arts Institute as a laboratory and production centre for new theatre. The
     institute was organized into three departments: pantomime and expression,
     stagecraft, and ballet.

20   Referencing Aristotelian catharsis, Cummings argues that the theatre should
     arouse elemental emotions of "pity and terror" as well as "mirth and amaze-
     ment" in the actors and the audience. That said, Cummings may be misreading
     Aristotle in that the *Poetics* defines "catharsis" as an emotional response located
     in the mind, rather than the body, a response that allows the spectator to
     make ethical judgments about mimetic actions (Halliwell 90). In this sense,
     catharsis is a "normative" theatrical effect, regulating the spectator's cognitive
     response to a performance to promote social stability (Halliwell 83). In the
     Poetics, mimesis is pleasurable to the spectator precisely because of his or her
     distance from the events. In contrast, Cummings – admiring the "alive-ness,"
     "actuality," and awesome sensations of the big top, the coaster, and the space
     stage – eschews the mimetic distance of normative theatre. Further, while
     Aristotle accords spectacle itself a slight role in the theatre because "visual
     effects" belong to designers rather than authors, Cummings assigns spectacle,
     and carnivalesque spectacle specifically, a vital role. In chapter six of the
     Poetics, Aristotle argues that "spectacle is emotionally powerful but is the least
     integral of all to the poet's art: for the potential of tragedy does not depend
     upon public performance and actors; ... the art of the mask-maker carries more
     weight than the poet as regards the elaboration of visual effects" (38–39).

21   For reproductions of those drawings see Cummings, "Line Drawings" at <http://
     www.gvsu.edu/english/cummings/Cohen1.htm>.

22   Cummings certainly privileges "precision" in both burlesque and avant-garde
     theatre. Like *Parade*, a ballet composed by modernist Eric Satie, whose work
     Cummings championed in his essays, Cummings's own theatrical projects aim
     for both technical precision and performative excess. Cummings attended the
     debut performance of Satie's 1917 ballet in Paris. One reviewer captures the
     significance of the show as both an international avant-garde collaboration
     and a circus-inspired romp:

> Satie's ballet *Parade* received its infamous debut in Paris in May, 1917. It was
> a star-studded show: Picasso designed the curtain and costumes, Diaghilev
> supplied his Ballets Russe, Massine did the choreography, and Cocteau
> contributed the plot, such as it was. The story line involves three "man-
> agers," trying to hustle up an audience for three circus acts, the Chinese
> Conjurer, the acrobats, and the young American girl, the only problem being
> that no audience ever appears. (Kautsky)

23 In a letter to friend William Slater Brown, Cummings explicitly depicts their social circle in New York as a circus; see Cummings, "Letter to William Slater Brown."
24 The new stage was the site of Mae Dix's "accidental" strip – reportedly the first public undressing act in American culture – later that year.

WORKS CITED

Aristotle. *The Poetics of Aristotle*. Trans. and commentary Stephen Halliwell. Chapel Hill: U of North Carolina P, 1987.

Allen, Robert C. *Horrible Prettiness: Burlesque and American Culture*. Chapel Hill: U of North Carolina P, 1990.

Artaud, Antonin. "The Theatre of Cruelty: First Manifesto." 1931–37. Rpt. in *Artaud on Theatre*. Ed. and trans. Claude Schumacher. London: Metheun, 2001. 112–18.

Bakhtin, Mikhail. *Rabelais and His World*. Trans. Helen Iswolsky. Bloomington: Indiana UP, 1984.

Berman, Russell A. *Modern Culture and Critical Theory: Art, Politics, and the Legacy of the Frankfurt School*. Madison: U of Wisconsin P, 1989.

Bürger, Peter. *Theory of the Avant-Garde*. 1984. Trans. Michael Shaw. Theory and History of Literature Series, Vol. 4. Minneapolis: U of Minnesota P, 2002.

Chinitz, David. *T.S. Eliot and the Cultural Divide*. Chicago: U of Chicago P, 2003.

"Circus Guided Tour." *People Play UK: Theatre History Online*. Theatre Museum: National Museum of the Performing Arts. 25 Apr. 2006. 9 Sept. 2008 <http://www.peopleplayuk.org.uk>.

Conference Program. International Theatre Exposition. 1926. New York Public Library.

Cummings, E.E. "The Adult, the Artist, and the Circus." *Vanity Fair* October 1925. Rpt. in Firmage 45–49.

———. "Burlesque, I Love It." *Stage* March 1936. Rpt. in Firmage 292–95.

———. "Coney Island: A Slightly Exuberant Appreciation of New York's Famous Pleasure Park." *Vanity Fair* (June 1926). Rpt. in Firmage 149–53.

———. *Him*. 1927. New York: Boni and Liveright, 1970.

———. *i: six nonlectures*. 1953. Cambridge, MA: Harvard UP, 2000.

———. Letter to William Slater Brown. 12 Aug. 1923. Rpt. in *The Selected Letters of E.E. Cummings*. Ed. F.W. Dupee and George Stade. New York: Harcourt, 1969. 100–01.

———. Line drawings. *Dial* 1920–21. Rpt. in "The *Dial*'s 'White-Haired Boy': E.E. Cummings as *Dial* Artist, Poet, and Essayist." By Milton A. Cohen. *Spring* (1992): 8–27. 8 Sept. 2008 <http://www.gvsu.edu/english/cummings/Cohen1.htm>.

———. *100 Selected Poems*. 1923. New York: Grove, 1954.

———. "The Theatre." Parts 1 and 2. *Dial* 80.5 May 1926. Rpt in Firmage 141–48.

———. "You Aren't Mad, Am I?" *Vanity Fair* Dec. 1925. Rpt. in Firmage 126–31.

Davidson, Susan and Philip, Rylands eds. *Peggy Guggenheim and Frederick Kiesler: The Story of Art of This Century*. New York: Guggenheim, 2005.

Davis, Janet. *The Circus Age: Culture and Society under the American Big Top.* Chapel Hill: U of North Carolina P, 2002.

Eliot, T.S. "The Love Song of J. Alfred Prufrock." 1917. 8 Sept. 2008 <http://www.cs. amherst.edu/ccm/prufrock.html>.

Firmage, George, ed. *E.E. Cummings: A Miscellany.* 2nd ed. New York: October House, 1965.

Gundrum, Jeff. "A Catalyst of the Avant-Garde." *New York Times* 19 Jan. 1989: C10. Rpt. in ProQuest Historical Newspapers Database. 14 October 2008 <http://pro-quest.umi.com/>.

Halliwell, Stephen. Commentary. *Aristotle* 69–184.

Huhtamo, Erkki. "On the Origins of the Virtual Museum." Virtual Museums and Public Understanding of Science and Culture. Nobel Foundation, Stockholm, Sweden. 26–29 May 2002.

Kautsky, Catherine. "Paris in Performance: Music, Ballet, Poetry, Lectures, and Art Recreating French Political and Artistic Visions from 1870–1920." Introduction to Concert Series. The Arts Institute, U of Wisconsin at Madison. 5 Jan. 2007 <http://www.music.wisc.edu/uploads/media/kautsky-parisinperf.html>.

Kennedy, Richard S. *Cummings Revisited.* New York: Twayne, 1994.

Kiesler, Frederick. "Address at the International Theatre Exposition." 1926. Rpt. in Firmage 145–48.

Levine, Lawrence. *Highbrow/Lowbrow: The Emergence of Cultural Hierarchy in America.* Cambridge, MA: Harvard UP, 1988.

"Modern Art in a Modern Setting." *New York Times* 1 Nov. 1942: SM16. Rpt. in ProQuest Historical Newspapers Database. 14 October 2008 <http://proquest. umi.com/>.

North, Michael. *Reading 1922: A Return to the Scene of the Modern.* New York: Oxford UP, 1999.

"Peggy and Kiesler: The Collector and the Visionary." Exhibition Press Release, Peggy Guggenheim Collection. Guggenheim Venice. Oct. 2003. 8 Sept. 2008 <http:// www.guggenheim-venice.it/img/pdf_press/84pdf2_143.pdf>.

Pringle, Patricia. "Seeing Impossible Bodies: Fascination as a Spatial Experience." *Scan: An Online Journal of Media Arts Culture.* 2004. 8 Sept. 2008 <http://scan. net.au/scan/journal/display.php?journal_id=34>.

Puchner, Martin. "The Theatre in Modernist Thought." *New Literary History* 33.3 (2002): 521–32.

Rotella, Guy. Introduction. *Critical Essays on E.E. Cummings.* Ed. Guy Rotella. Boston: Hall, 1984. 1–27.

Seldes, Gilbert. "A Tribute to Florenz Ziegfeld." *The Seven Lively Arts.* New York: Harper, 1924. 127–46.

Shteir, Rachel. *Striptease: The Untold History of the Girlie Show.* New York: Oxford UP, 2004.

Smith, Matthew Wilson. *The Total Work of Art: From Bayreuth to Cyberspace.* London: Routledge, 2007.

Spender, Matthew. *From a High Place: A Life of Arshile Gorky.* New York: Farrar, 2003.

Turner, Victor. *From Ritual to Theatre: The Human Seriousness of Play.* New York: PAJ, 1982.

Williams, Williams Carlos. "Lower Case Cummings." *The William Carlos Williams Reader.* Ed. and intro. M.L. Rosenthal. New York: New Directions, 1966. 401–05.

Worthen, W.B. *Modern Drama and the Rhetoric of Theatre.* Berkeley: U of California P, 1992.

APPENDIX 1: CAST OF *HIM* (1928)

E.E. Cummings, *Him*
Provincetown Players Production, 18 Apr. 1928
Director James Light; Settings and Costumes Eugene Fitsch

Actor	Part
Bergman, Herbert	Second Passenger
Bergman, Herbert	Fourth Fairy
Bolton, Lawrence	Doctor
Bolton, Lawrence	Third Drunk
Bolton, Lawrence	Soap-Box Orator
Bolton, Lawrence	Intruder
Bolton, Lawrence	Personage (John Rutter)
Bolton, Lawrence	Plainclothesman
Bolton, Lawrence	Mussolini
Bolton, Lawrence	A Gentleman
Bolton, Lawrence	A Barker
Bradley, Louise	Virgo
Bradley, Louise	Black Figure
Bradley, Louise	First Shape
Bradley, Louise	Vestiare
Bratt, George	Second Drunk
Bratt, George	Black Figure
Bratt, George	Englishman
Bratt, George	Second Fairy
Bratt, George	Fourth Shape
Bratt, George	Headwaiter
Chorpenning, Ruth	Older Woman
Cooper, Christine	Frankie
Cooper, Christine	Elderly Woman
Dale, Virginia	Woman
Dale, Virginia	Fairly Young Woman
Dale, Virginia	18-inch lady
Daniels, Jack	Bill
Daniels, Jack	Third Shape

Continued

APPENDIX 1: *Continued*

E.E. Cummings, *Him*
Provincetown Players Production, 18 Apr. 1928
Director James Light; Settings and Costumes Eugene Fitsch

Actor	*Part*
Floyd, Sara	Second Weird
Frank, Philip	Will
Frank, Philip	Second Centurion
Frisbie, Edith	Mother w/ child
Frisbie, Edith	Queen of Serpents
Gilbert, Adele	Black Figure
Hill, Evelyn	Black Figure
Hill, Evelyn	Blond Gonzesse
Ismena, Ida	Black Figure
Johnson, Marion	Youthful Woman
Johnstone, William	Him
Johnstone, William	Interlocutor
Jones, Mary	Six Hundred Pounds of Pulchritude
Laddon, Ora	Whore (Act 2.3)
Mounts, Della	First Weird
O'Brien-Moore, Erin	Me
Ray, Madeleine	18-inch lady
Rose, Virginia	Third Weird
Rose, Virginia	Old Woman
Rosenberg, Henry	Black Figure
Rosenberg, Henry	Fascist
Rosenberg, Henry	Missing Link
Row, Arthur William	Policeman (Act 2.9)
Row, Arthur William	Waiter
Russell, Morton	First Centurion
Russell, Morton	Tattooed Man
Ruttle, Leo Francis	Messenger
Ruttle, Leo Francis	Chasseur
Spelvin, George	Nine Foot Giant
Stander, Lionel	Cop (Act 2.6)
Stander, Lionel	First Fairy
Steiner, Goldye	Female Black Figure
Swanson, Alice	Whore (Act 2.9)
Vorse, Heaton	Human Needles
Winfield, Hemsley	Porter
Winfield, Hemsley	Male Black Figure
Winfield, Hemsley	Ethiopian
Winfield, Hemsley	King of Borneo

Continued

APPENDIX 1: *Continued*

E.E. Cummings, *Him*
Provincetown Players Production, 18 Apr. 1928
Director James Light; Settings and Costumes Eugene Fitsch

Actor	*Part*
Zipser, Stanley	First Drunk
Zipser, Stanley	Black Figure
Zipser, Stanley	Third Fairy
Zipser, Stanley	Second Shape
Ensemble	9 jazz players
Crowds	Act 3.4
Cripples	Act 3.4
Beggars	Act 3.4
Black Figures	Act 3.4
Jazz Dancers	Act 3.4
Shapes	Act 3.4

Source: *Him* Playbill, Provincetown Players Archive, Fales Collection, New York Public Library

APPENDIX 2: PARTS PER ACTOR, *HIM* (1928)

Actor	Parts
Bolton, Lawrence	9
Bratt, George	6
Zipser, Stanley	4
Bradley, Louise	4
Winfield, Hemsley	4
Rosenberg, Henry	3
Dale, Virginia	3
Bergman, Herbert	2
Daniels, Jack	2
Stander, Lionel	2
Frank, Philip	2
Frisbie, Edith	2
Ruttle, Leo Francis	2
Hill, Evelyn	2
Russell, Morton	2
Row, Arthur William	2
Johnstone, William	2

Continued

APPENDIX 2: *Continued*

Actor	Parts
Cooper, Christine	2
Rose, Virginia	2
Floyd, Sara	1
O'Brien-Moore, Erin	1
Ray, Madeleine	1
Mounts, Della	1
Laddon, Ora	1
Jones, Mary	1
Johnson, Marion	1
Ismena, Ida	1
Spelvin, George	1
Gilbert, Adele	1
Steiner, Goldye	1
Swanson, Alice	1
Vorse, Heaton	1
Chorpenning, Ruth	1
Grand Total	71

Source: author's analysis

6

How to Do Nothing with Words, or *Waiting for Godot* as Performativity

RICHARD BEGAM

Que nous propose *En attendant Godot*? C'est peu de dire qu'il ne s'y passe rien. Qu'il n'y ait ni engrenages ni intrigue d'aucune sorte, cela d'ailleurs s'est déjà vu sur d'autres scènes. Ici, c'est *moins que rien* qu'il faudrait écrire: comme si nous assistons à une espèce de régression au-delà du rien.

[What does *Waiting for Godot* offer us? It is hardly enough to say that nothing happens in it. That there should be neither complications nor plot of any kind has already been the case on other stages. Here, it is *less than nothing*, we should say: as if we were watching the kind of regression *beyond* nothing.]

– Alain Robbe-Grillet

[Beckett] has achieved a theoretical impossibility – a play in which nothing happens . . . What's more, since the second act is a subtly different reprise of the first, he has written a play in which nothing happens, twice.

– Vivian Mercier

Nothing is more real than nothing.

– Democritus

I

Over the past generation, performance studies has largely transformed how we think about the contemporary stage, expanding our idea of serious theatre to include such "lowbrow" forms as mixed media, vaudeville, and monologue.[1] The "happenings" of the 1960s and 1970s serve as the immediate precursor to much contemporary art, as more distantly do the Dadaist and surrealist exhibitions of the 1910s and 1920s. These avant-garde beginnings are notable because, like the performance artists of today, the Dadaists and surrealists challenged the idea that life and art are distinct and autonomous spheres, unambiguously separated by a stage proscenium.[2] Yet, as we consider the genealogy of theatrical performativity, there is another source worth examining. For if mixed media, monologue, and vaudeville are among the defining elements of performance art, they are also among the defining elements of Samuel Beckett's theatre. *Krapp's Last Tape* (1958)[3] represents one of the earliest dramatic ventures in mixing live and taped performance, while Beckett's forays into radio (*All That Fall*, 1957; *Embers*, 1959; *Words and Music*, 1962; *Cascando*, 1963; *Rough for Radio I*, 1976; *Rough for Radio II*, 1976), television (*Eh Joe*, 1966; *Ghost Trio*, 1977; . . . *but the clouds* . . ., 1977; *Quad*, 1982; *Nacht und Träume*, 1983) and cinema (*Film*, 1965) enabled him to experiment with a variety of audio-visual technologies.[4] At the same time, he constructed entire plays around individual characters speaking directly to the audience (*Not I*, 1972; *A Piece of Monologue*, 1980; *Rockaby*, 1981) or wordlessly enacting vaudeville stunts and routines (*Act without Words I*, 1957; *Act without Words II*, 1959). More generally, the effect of Beckett's theatre, like that of Dadaism and surrealism, has been to interrogate the assumptions of Ibsenian realism, particularly insofar as the latter depends on the ontological separation of the aesthetic from the real.

In what follows, I propose to examine the relation between Beckett's first published play, *Waiting for Godot*, and the tradition of performativity that has defined so much of his own theatre, as well as the contemporary stage. While there are various approaches one might take to this subject, I will focus on the theoretical and philosophical dimension of performativity. Along the way, I will consider how a writer whose principal influences had been Proust and Joyce and whose composition up to the late 1940s was devoted entirely to poetry and fiction, suddenly decided to write for the theatre. It is my view that we can only begin to understand *Waiting for Godot* not by treating it in generic and genetic isolation – as though it represented a radical break with Beckett's earlier career – but by reading it through the problems of language and representation that so dominated Beckett's short stories and novels during the 1930s and 1940s. In other words, performativity, as it is philosophically conceived, provides the logical bridge that connects Beckett's fiction to his drama. For his idea of language was essentially performative, and the only way he could test such an idea was through the aesthetics of performance.

Beckett's intensive reading and thinking about language and philosophy occurred in the 1930s and centred around Fritz Mauthner, but it was in the early 1950s that his work strikingly aligned itself with what are arguably the two most important contributions to language philosophy of the last century.[5] Between 1952 and 1954, J.L. Austin delivered a series of lectures at Oxford under the title "Words and Deeds." Then, in 1953, Beckett inaugurated his theatrical career in Paris with a richly worded but strangely deedless play entitled *En Attendant Godot*.[6] That same year Ludwig Wittgenstein published *Philosophical Investigations*, which radically transformed how philosophers understand language and performativity. By 1955, Austin was delivering a revised version of his Oxford lectures at Harvard under the title, *How to Do Things with Words*, and *Waiting for Godot* was having its English premiere in London. That Austin's speech-act theory, Wittgenstein's language philosophy, and Beckett's revolutionary theatre – three of the most memorable developments in mid-twentieth culture – all burst upon the scene at the same moment is a matter of coincidence. Austin had not seen Beckett's play – or, as far as we know, read any of the Irishman's work – when he began to contemplate locutions, illocutions and perlocutions; Wittgenstein had developed his notions of "language games," "family resemblances," and "forms of life" in the 1940s; and Beckett was unacquainted with Austin and Wittgenstein when he first imagined how he might do nothing with words not once but twice.[7] Yet, as with many cultural phenomena, the absence of a direct connection does not mean the absence of any connection. For Austin, Wittgenstein, and Beckett were all shaped to a lesser or greater degree by a common intellectual tradition, one that questioned the idea that the primary function of philosophy, and more generally of language, is to give us a picture or representation of the world. This anti-representationalist tradition, especially as it relates to ordinary language, had its origins in the so-called Vienna Circle.[8] One of the early thinkers associated with the Circle was Fritz Mauthner, whose "language critique" profoundly influenced Beckett's writings. Another key figure – indeed, the most famous member of the group – was Ludwig Wittgenstein, whose "language games" anticipated and complemented Austin's performatives.[9]

As I have indicated, the move from page to stage that *Godot* brought about was crucial for Beckett, not only because it opened up a new genre to him, but also because it posed a special challenge to his linguistic pragmatism. After all, how does one dramatize – actually bring to the boards – a functionalist as opposed to a representationalist view of language? How, in effect, does one perform linguistic performativity? This, I believe, is a central concern of *Waiting for Godot*, and one of the reasons Beckett was so fascinated with the relation between what Austin calls constatives and performatives – between language that is used descriptively and language that is used instrumentally.

II

Toward the beginning of *How to Do Things with Words*, Austin observes, "It was for too long the assumption of philosophers that the business of a 'statement' can only be to 'describe' some state of affairs, or to 'state some fact,' which it must do either truly or falsely" (1). In contesting this assumption, Austin develops his famous distinction between what he calls "constatives" and "performatives."[10]"Constatives" are statements, usually descriptive, that may be judged to be true or false. To take a classic example from modern philosophy, the utterance "The cat is on the mat" is a constative. It describes a state of affairs and is verifiable or falsifiable according to the empirical test of looking at the mat. "Performatives," on the other hand, "do not 'describe' or 'report' or constate anything" and – here is the crux of the matter – "the uttering of the [performative] sentence is, or is a part of, the doing of the action" (5). Examples Austin gives of performatives are " 'I do' . . . as uttered in the course of the marriage ceremony"; " 'I name this ship the *Queen Elizabeth*' – as uttered when smashing the bottle against the [stern]"; " 'I give and bequeath my watch to my brother' – as occurring in a will" (5). Performatives are, in other words, specialized uses of language where to say is to do, or as Austin puts it, where "saying makes it so" (7). Because performatives, unlike constatives, do not describe anything, they cannot be true or false, any more than marrying, christening, or bequeathing can be true or false. Rather, if a performative conforms to certain conditions – Austin refers to these as "felicity" conditions – then it will be properly executed and achieve its desired effect; but, if it fails to meet these conditions, then saying will not be translated into doing. For instance, "for naming the ship, it is essential that I should be the person appointed to name her, for (Christian) marrying, it is essential that I should not be already married" (8). When felicity conditions are met and a performative succeeds, we call it "happy"; when these conditions are not met and the intended action fails to occur, we call it "unhappy."

For Austin, performatives may be analysed according to three categories. First, there is the *locution*, which focuses on the utterance itself, on the words and their meaning; second, there is the *illocution*, which focuses on the force of the utterance, such as warning, promising, urging, commanding, and so on; third there is the *perlocution*, which focuses on the material effect that the utterance produces; for example, someone ducks, after having been warned; someone pays five dollars, after having promised to do so. Austin gives two examples of his tripartite distinction:

Act (A) or Locution
He said to me "Shoot her!" meaning by "shoot" shoot and referring by "*her*" to her.
Act (B) or Illocution
He urged (or advised, ordered, &c.) me to shoot her.
Act (C.*a*) or Perlocution
He persuaded me to shoot her.
Act (C.*b*) He got me to (or made me, &c.) shoot her. (101–2; emphasis in original)

Austin later schematizes his tripartite distinction as follows: locution is *meaning*, illocution is *force*, and perlocution is *effect* (109).

So far my presentation of speech-act theory has emphasized classificatory rigour, the unambiguous boundaries that separate constatives from performatives. Austin's lectures are, however, exploratory and experimental, and the further he advances into them the more he comes to believe that virtually every statement has an assertive and therefore a performative dimension. Indeed, by the conclusion of his lectures, he has largely rejected the bright-line distinction between constatives and performatives, preferring instead to affiliate the former with the locutionary function of a statement (its "meaning") and the latter with the perlocutionary function (its "force").[11] But, even here, he introduces qualifications, acknowledging that "we have here not really two poles" (146) but a range of descriptive possibilities that change through time ("a historical development" [146]). In the place of a simple "dichotomy [between] performatives and constatives" (150), he proposes "more general *families* of related and overlapping speech acts" (150), evoking a Wittgensteinian notion of "family resemblance."[12]

The larger effect of Austin's analysis is to align him with a post-foundational view of philosophy. By deconstructing the distinction between constatives and performatives, by shifting attention away from linguistic mimesis and toward linguistic praxis, Austin participates in the post-Nietzschean tradition according to which language is a series of metaphors designed to help us manage and control reality, as opposed to a series of descriptors designed to represent the essential nature or structure of reality.[13] As we shall see, Beckett takes a similar approach to constatives and performatives: he, too, is interested in a functional as opposed to a descriptive understanding of language, and he, too, wishes to show how the former inevitably contaminates and subverts the latter.

Yet if Austin and Beckett share the view that constatives inevitably give way to performatives – that effectively all language is performative – matters become more complicated with respect to the role played by "aesthetic" or "fictional" uses of language. Of special interest in this regard is a passage in lecture two of *How to Do Things with Words*, where Austin speaks about the status of performatives in works of art. He writes,

> [A] performative utterance will, for example, be in *a peculiar way* hollow or void if said by an actor on the stage, or if introduced in a poem, or spoken in soliloquy . . . Language in such circumstances is in special ways – intelligibly – used not seriously, but in ways *parasitic* upon its normal use . . . All this we are *excluding* from consideration. (22)

For Austin, when a performative is not "seriously" intended – I deliberately use his language – when it occurs in a play, for instance, it loses its "illocutionary force." In other words, the actors pretend, when uttering a performative, that saying leads to doing, but the audience knows this is a sham.

Hence, when Othello tells his riotous soldiers to "[k]eep up [sheathe] thy bright swords, for the dew will rust them" (1.2.59), the utterance has no genuine performative or illocutionary power, because we know that if the actors refuse to obey, they will not be court-martialed. They put away their swords in obedience not to an order but to a stage direction.

On the face of it, Austin's commonsense approach to distinguishing between theatrical and ordinary-language performatives seems incontestable, but the issue – as I hope to demonstrate presently – is a good deal more complicated than Austin's straightforward presentation suggests. The issue is consequential for Beckett because it raises the larger question of the division of life from art, of whether there is an aesthetically privileged space where words do not translate into deeds. Precisely how Beckett responds to this question is a matter I will take up toward the end of this chapter. Meanwhile, I would like to turn to *Waiting for Godot* and consider in detail how constatives and performatives function in the play's ending and beginning.

III

Endings and beginnings are structurally important in any work of art, but they take on special significance in *Waiting for Godot* because it is preoccupied with the suspension of time, with narrative rendered shapeless and directionless by its non-eventuality. While critics have long recognized the open-endedness of the play's conclusion, what they have not noticed is that Beckett achieves this effect through the elaborate interplay of constatives and performatives.[14] Here are the last nine lines of the play, delivered as Estragon stands with his trousers around his ankles:

> ESTRAGON Well? Shall we go?
> VLADIMIR Pull on your trousers.
> ESTRAGON What?
> VLADIMIR Pull on your trousers.
> ESTRAGON You want me to pull off my trousers?
> VLADIMIR Pull ON your trousers.
> ESTRAGON (*realizing his trousers are down*). True. *He pulls on his trousers.*
> VLADIMIR Well? Shall we go?
> ESTRAGON Yes, let's go.
> *They do not move. Curtain.* (109)

In the present context, Estragon's "Shall we go" is a variation on "Let's go" and functions as a hortatory, a performative of urging.[15] Vladimir responds not with action but with words, in this case an imperative, a performative of command ("Pull on your trousers").[16] Although Vladimir's utterance is as direct and straightforward as it can be, it must be repeated three times before Estragon understands and acts upon it, which is to say, before it achieves perlocutionary effect. But notice, when Estragon finally grasps what has been said, how he replies: "True." It should be remembered that performatives can be happy or unhappy, but they cannot be "true" or "false," making his response inappropriate, if not infelicitous. What is more, Estragon appears to read Vladimir's performative ("Pull on your trousers") as a constative ("Your trousers are down"), raising the possibility that, in pulling on his trousers, he is motivated not by his friend's command but by his own modesty. The second act of the play famously concludes in precisely the same way as the first act. A proposal to act ("Shall we go"), followed by an agreement to act ("Yes, let's go"), followed by inaction ("*They do not move*"). In this scene, it as though the vaudeville material of the clown, with his pants around his ankles, has been used to deconstruct the traditional antinomies of speech-act theory. Unambiguous imperatives are misheard, performatives are interpreted as constatives, and the two actors prove incapable of executing the fundamentals of stagecraft – in this case of "performing" the action known as "making an exit."

We find even richer opportunities for Austinian analysis if we turn to the beginning of the play, which consists of a simple piece of stage business and a single line of dialogue:

> *Estragon, sitting on a low mound, is trying to take off his boot. He pulls at it with both hands, panting. He gives up, exhausted, rests, tries again. As before. Enter Vladimir.*

ESTRAGON (*giving up again*). Nothing to be done. (2)

Estragon's utterance invites a variety of interpretations, but I will limit myself to three, beginning with what I call the "futility reading": the boots won't come off and Estragon finds himself powerless before an intransigent reality. His locution functions as a simple constative designed to express his frustration and hopelessness. But the matter is more complicated than such a bare-boned account would indicate. Estragon's struggle with his boots – in particular, his inability to find a pair that fits – acquires existential resonance when considered within the larger context of the play. For these words tell us that, in a chaotic and indifferent universe, human endeavour is useless, or, as Beckett's pun would have it, "bootless." *Waiting for Godot* commences, then, not with a personal complaint but with a cosmic pronouncement: humankind is without agency, without hope, without meaning. Yet, as the object of Estragon's utterance changes from his feet to his fate, something else changes as well: the locution is transformed not only in its meaning but also in its force, shifting from a description to an assertion – shifting, that is, from a constative to a performative. After all, "My feet hurt" is a statement that can be true or false, whereas "Man is without meaning" is a declaration, along the lines of "We hold these truths to be self-evident" and as such is not subject to verification.[17]

The second interpretation I will propose, the "intransitive reading," treats Estragon's words as a complex constative. Viewed from the perspective of speech-act theory, his observation may be understood as a self-reflective statement about the nature of art and agency. Remember that, for Austin, locutions lose their illocutionary force in drama, so that a speech act uttered on stage functions intransitively – that is, it makes nothing happen. Austin's notion of aesthetic intransitivity owes an obvious debt to Kant's notion of aesthetic autonomy, the idea that life and art are ontologically distinct spheres.[18] On this reading, Estragon's "Nothing to be done" describes his own situation, since, from an illocutionary standpoint, he can *utter* words, but he cannot make them *do* anything. He is an actor who has, performatively speaking, been rendered actionless. But this line of analysis produces some surprising consequences. For, if Estragon's words are *genuinely* self-reflective, if at the moment of their utterance he has stopped playing a role and actually perceives himself not as a character but as an actor who speaks *in propria persona*, then he no longer inhabits the privileged space of the purely aesthetic. Having breached the wall separating life and art, the actor is restored to the realm of "ordinary language," and his words consequently recover their performative power. Paradoxically, to utter the constative that describes his intransitivity has the effect of releasing him from that intransitivity, which means that the constative has acquired illocutionary force and therefore has become a performative.

And this brings us to my third interpretation, the "imperative reading," which treats Estragon's words not as a complex constative but as a self-reflexive performative. Seen from this perspective, "Nothing to be done" functions as a global directive in a play that might be entitled "How to Do Nothing with Words." Here, we must distinguish between two notions: on the one hand, a failure of action, a lack of eventuality, a state in which "there is not anything to be done"; on the other hand, a command to make the nothing palpable, to give shape to the suspension of time and event. In shifting from the intransitive to the imperative reading, we move from a privative to an affirmative condition, from the inability to enact an action to the obligation to enact an inaction. To put the matter more concretely, here Estragon appears to say, "Yes, there is something to be done and that something consists of staging the intransitive nothing that is a theatrical performance, so let's get on with doing it; let's get on with making nothing happen twice."

IV

It would seem that *Waiting for Godot* participates in the kind of performativity that is crucial to Austin's analysis of speech acts. But how representative of the play as a whole is this performativity? And how fully does the deconstructive trend we have observed – that is, constatives being undone by performatives – extend to the rest of *Waiting for Godot*? In pursuing these questions, I will examine Acts One and Two, focusing first on Austinian illocutions and Wittgensteinian language games and then on the performance of performativity. We might begin our discussion of Act One by considering the dialogue between Vladimir and Estragon. It is revealing that, in a play celebrated for its non-action, their exchanges consist almost entirely of performatives or discussions about performatives. Thus, excluding simple imperatives, which occur throughout the play, we discover performatives of repenting (5), damning and saving (6–7), forgiving (12), praying and supplicating (14), begging (24–5), denouncing (25–6), inviting to depart (27), comforting (31), insulting (33), asking for forgiveness (34), inviting to sit down (36), bidding farewell (50), interrogating (53), promising (55) and exhorting (59). The magnitude and variety of this catalogue – and what I have offered here is by no means exhaustive – suggests that Beckett was as interested in exploring performatives in *Waiting for Godot* as Joyce was in exploring rhetorical figures in *Ulysses*.[19]

At the centre of performativity in Act One is the character of Pozzo, and, through him, we begin to observe connections between rhetorical performativity and theatrical performativity. Hence, Pozzo's entrance is announced by two performatives of command ("On!" and "Back!" [18]), followed by performatives of warning ("Be careful!" [18]), introduction ("I present myself: Pozzo" [19]), interrogation ("Who is Godot?" [20]), and threatening ("So you were waiting for him . . . Here? On my land?" [20]). Indeed, Pozzo's simple act of seating himself is one of the most elaborate exercises in rhetorical illocution in all of theatre, involving no fewer than twenty performatives, which run over the space of three pages: "Up pig!" "Up hog!" "Back!" "Stop!" "Turn!" "Closer!" "Stop!" "Coat!" "Hold that!" "Coat!" "Whip!" "Stool!" "Closer!" "Back!" "Further!" "Stop!" "Basket!" "Basket!" "Further!" "Happy Days!" (20–2). Aside from its obvious comic effect, what significance, if any, does this scene have? We might approach this question by thinking of Pozzo's performatives as a Wittgensteinian language game designed to establish his position not only socially but also epistemologically. Of course, here it must be remembered that Wittgenstein invents the language game as an alternative to Augustine's model of communication.

Philosophical Investigations famously begins with a quotation from the *Confessions*, where Augustine presents his "ostensive" theory of language in which words signify by pointing to things:

> When they (my elders) named some object, and accordingly moved toward something, I saw this and I grasped that the thing was called by the sound they uttered when they meant to point it out . . . Thus, as I heard words repeatedly used in

their proper places in various sentences, I gradually learnt to understand what objects they signified. (qtd. in *Investigations* 2)

Augustine conceives of language as a form of nomenclature, which consists almost exclusively, as Wittgenstein observes, of "nouns like 'table,' 'chair,' 'bread,' and of people's names, and only secondarily of the names of certain actions and properties; and of the remaining kinds of word[s] as something that will take care of itself" (2). In order to gain critical distance from Augustine's notion of language, Wittgenstein invents a primitive language – what he calls a "language game" – that appears to operate according to protocols of nomenclature and ostentation:

> The language is meant to serve for communication between a builder A and an assistant B. A is building with building-stones: there are blocks, pillars, slabs and beams. B has to pass the stones, and in the order in which A needs them. For this purpose they use a language consisting of the words "block," "pillar," "slab," "beam." A calls them out; – B brings the stone which he has learnt to bring at such-and-such a call. – Conceive this as a complete primitive language. (3)

It is difficult to imagine a more rudimentary system of communication. It consists of four words, each of which is a noun, and one "plays" the game by uttering the words and then receiving the objects to which they refer. But as Wittgenstein's analysis unfolds, we come to realize just how complex this apparently simple language game is. How many building blocks should B bring A? What will be their colour, size, and dimension? And where should B place them? From our perspective, what is most telling is that, although the building-block game is supposed to illustrate Augustine's "ostensive" or "nomenclatural" theory of language – a language based entirely on a descriptive model – the game consists of nothing but imperatives, in which "block" is short for "Bring me the block!" In other words, what we imagined was a series of constatives turns out to be a series of performatives.

But if the form of Wittgenstein's language game is not innocent – all those performatives in constatives' clothing – neither is its content, for the latter serves to expose the philosophical "foundationalism" that stands behind a constative or descriptive model of language.[20] That foundationalism assumes that one can only establish a philosophy of truth and certainty by fully examining the "premises" and "grounds" of one's thought, thereby establishing philosophy on a "firm foundation," as Descartes argued in the *Discourse on Method.*[21] Wittgenstein parodies this idea by, as it were, putting on his philosophical hard hat and turning his language game into a travestied construction site ("block," "pillar," "slab," "beam"). Yet, in the process, we discover that one "lays the foundations" of philosophy not by accurately describing reality – not through an act of linguistic or empirical intuition – but by acknowledging the instrumental function of language. As Wittgenstein puts it,

> Now what do the words of this language signify? – What is supposed to shew what they signify, if not the kind of use they have? . . . Think of tools in a toolbox: there is a hammer, pliers, a saw, a screw-driver, a rule, a glue-pot, glue, nails and screws. – The functions of words are as diverse as the functions of these objects. (6)

How does Wittgenstein's building-block game operate? What is its performative as opposed to its constative effect? It proposes that we think of language not as a blueprint for discovering the deep structure of reality but as a set of tools, games, or procedures for negotiating the day-to-day problems of life. The "foundations" of philosophy are performative rather than constative, operational rather than descriptive.[22]

Now, if we return to the scene of Pozzo's seating himself, we find that Beckett, like Wittgenstein, uses a language game to deconstruct philosophical foundationalism. Beckett's deconstruction is specifically directed at Descartes and the celebrated moment in the heated closet when the latter discovers the first principles of his philosophy during an act of sedentary meditation.[23] It is no accident that in Descartes' account, the *cogito* is pictured as sitting and thinking.[24] By rendering the subject static and stationary, by throwing under it ("sub-ject" literally means "thrown under") an unshakeable foundation, the philosopher symbolically enacts the mental operation that will provide the "basis" or "ground" of his apodeictic philosophy.[25] Of course, it is revealing that Pozzo establishes his "subject position" – just as Wittgenstein plays the building-block game – through a series of performatives, indicating that the subject is not the "foundation" of language and knowledge, so much as the operational after-effect of these things. At the same time, the fact that Cartesian sedentariness has been re-imagined as a camp stool – a collapsible and transportable "foundation" – shows just how fully (and humorously) Beckett has undermined the idea of a Cartesian first principle or "premise." What is more, when we are finally given an example of Pozzo's thinking – Cartesian dualism here consists of linking Pozzo to Lucky by a rope – the discourse that emerges does not affirm man as the measure of all things so much as elegize his demise.[26]

I have been arguing that Pozzo's mobile sedentariness and the illocutionary gestures attached to it parody the philosophical foundationalism that Wittgenstein and Austin challenge with their performative conception of language. But the character of Pozzo does much more, for he also enables Beckett to engage in an extended meditation on drama as genre. So it is that virtually all Pozzo's rhetorical performatives translate into theatrical performances. We have already seen how his language game of commands produces the ceremony of sitting down, of "establishing" him as both *cogito* and character. The same kinds of performatives define much of what happens when Pozzo is on stage. Thus, when he orders Lucky to think, he assumes the role of a stage director blocking the scene: he situates Vladimir and Estragon as bystanders ("Stand back!" [44]), positions Lucky for his monologue ("Stop!" "Forward!" "Stop!" "Think!" [44]), and finally returns the latter to his feet after his collapse. ("Forward!" "Back!" "Turn!" "Done it!" [49]). Similarly, Pozzo's departure, consisting of a number of shouted commands ("On! On!" [51]) – echoed by Estragon and Vladimir ("On!" "On!" [51]) and repeated by Pozzo ("On! On!" [51]) – lays bare the essential conditions of theatre, which involve locating bodies in space and time, whether on the horizontal plane of coming and going, entering and exiting, or on the vertical plane of falling and rising, sitting and standing. Even the more discrete actions specified by "Forward!" "Back!" and "Turn!" have the effect of adjusting temporal and spatial relations, of reducing blocking and stage-business – much as a language game might – to its most basic elements: stasis and kinesis, location and dimension, speed and vector. And again, it is crucial that the constituents of performance are achieved through a series of performatives.

But it is not enough to say that Pozzo's performatives make the performance happen. More than this, he is the principle of theatricality itself. First, there is his elaborately choreographed entrance: the terrible cry, the offstage crack of the whip and the shouted commands, followed by the appearance of the roped slave and the imperious master. Surely, so dramatic an arrival can mean only one thing: at last the evening has been saved – at last Godot has come. It is not only Estragon and Vladimir but also the audience who are disappointed by the revelation that they are dealing not with the title character but with a minor landowner named Pozzo ("You're not Mr. Godot, sir?" [19]). Still, if Pozzo does not represent the authorizing presence of Godot, he nevertheless fills the stage with his larger-than-life personality, epitomizing the ham actor of the company, with his bellowing voice and importunate demands for attention. We soon learn that, like all good performers, Pozzo keeps in reserve a set piece, a highly elaborate speech that he brings out when the dialogue flags or the action fails. Yet, despite its rhetorical flourishes and gestural effects, the substance of Pozzo's high-flying oratory – an explanation of the twilight – could not be more mundane:

POZZO   Ah yes! The night. (*He raises his head.*) But be a little more attentive, for pity's sake, otherwise we'll never get anywhere. (*He looks at the sky.*) Look! (*All look at the sky except Lucky who is dozing off again. Pozzo jerks the rope.*) Will you look at the sky, pig! (*Lucky looks at the sky.*) Good, that's enough. (*They stop looking at the sky.*) What is there so extraordinary about it? Qua sky. It is pale and luminous like any sky at this hour of the day. (*Pause.*) In these latitudes. (*Pause.*) When the weather is fine. (*Lyrical.*) An hour ago (he *looks at his watch, prosaic*) roughly (*lyrical*) after having poured forth ever since (*he hesitates, prosaic*) say ten o'clock in the morning (*lyrical*) tirelessly torrents of red and white light it begins to lose its effulgence, to grow pale (*gesture of the two hands lapsing by stages*) pale, ever a little paler, a little paler until (*dramatic pause, ample gesture of the two hands flung wide apart*) pppfff! finished! it comes to rest. But – (*hand raised in admonition*) – but behind this veil of gentleness and peace night is charging (*vibrantly*) and will burst upon us (*snaps his fingers*) pop! like that! (*his inspiration leaves him*) just when we least expect it. (*Silence. Gloomily.*) That's how it is on this bitch of an earth. (38–9)

The monologue is pure theatre.[27] Pozzo begins by establishing his presence, opens with a rhetorical question, introduces several dramatic pauses, builds interest by shifting stylistic registers ("lyrical," "prosaic"), reaches his first climax by enacting the end of day ("pppfff!") and then, undiminished, drives to a second climax with the fall of night. Of course, the consummation proves hollow ("pop!") and the denouement leaves him taciturn and gloomy, with nothing to cheer him but the consolation of philosophy ("That's how it is on this bitch of an earth"). Rhetorically, Pozzo's speech consists mostly of constatives, but these function performatively, since he is deliberately playing to an audience, seeking not to describe but to divert. So it is that he immediately asks for his notices ("How did you find me . . . Good? Fair? Middling?" [39]) and, after receiving the praise he has begged for, concedes that the entire speech was a performance, something prepared in advance and committed to memory:

POZZO . . . I weakened a little towards the end, you didn't notice?
VLADIMIR Oh perhaps just a teeny weeny little bit.
ESTRAGON I thought it was intentional.
POZZO You see my memory is defective. (39)

The subject of the speech is inspired by Vladimir's comment, "[T]ime has stopped" (37), which provokes Pozzo's rejoinder, "Don't you believe it . . . Whatever you like, but not that" (37). The explanation of the twilight that follows functions as a critique of the play itself, a critique of duration without pattern or coherence. Pozzo's own preference is for a more traditional handling of dramatic event, one in which time functions as *kairos* rather than *chronos*, and words serve as the vehicles for deeds.[28] And yet, insofar as Pozzo's speech makes nothing happen, is about nothing but the passage of time, it epitomizes the play itself, aptly summed up by Didi and Gogo:

VLADIMIR That passed the time.
ESTRAGON It would have passed in any case.
VLADIMIR Yes, but not so rapidly. (51)

Indeed, if, in waiting for Godot, Vladimir and Estragon are waiting for eventuality, happening, action – in a word, theatricality – then it is crucial that Godot does not come. Yet if, as I have claimed, the play is about performativity, then why is it that nothing happens? That Godot fails to appear? That Pozzo is the palest substitute – trace, simulacrum – for the title character? As should be obvious by now, *Waiting for Godot* is obsessively concerned with the rhetoric of performativity, but it seems to be a peculiarly ineffectual performativity, one in which nothing happens. Here we cannot help but recall what Austin says about the onstage speech act: "a performative utterance will, for example, be *in a peculiar way* hollow or void if said by an actor on the stage" (22). Is Beckett in agreement with Austin? Does *Waiting for Godot* demonstrate that performatives lose their effect once they enter into the realm of aesthetic discourse?

V

At this point, we must pause and consider in greater depth Austin's claim that a performative utterance is "hollow" or "void" when delivered onstage. Admittedly, the special case of the work of art is introduced towards the beginning of Austin's lectures, where he is establishing definitional boundaries and laying down clear-cut distinctions. But while he later qualifies or modifies a number of his earlier assertions, he offers no such revision on the subject of "fictional" discourse, suggesting that he stands by his original statement. Probably the best-known critique of Austin's position on fictional discourse occurs in Jacques Derrida's "Signature Event Context."[29] In that essay, Derrida focuses on the passage from lecture two, where Austin seeks to separate the citational language of the stage from the ordinary language of everyday life. This passage is of special interest to Derrida because it goes to the heart of his own analysis of speech-act theory:

> Austin has not taken account of what – in the structure of *locution* (thus before any illocutory or perlocutory determination) – already entails that system of predicates I call *graphematic in general* and consequently blurs [*brouille*] all the oppositions which follow, oppositions whose pertinence, purity and rigor Austin has unsuccessfully attempted to establish. ("Signature Event" 14)

For Derrida, conventionality and iterability are the enabling attributes of a performative – what makes it possible for a performative to function in the first place – and these attributes extend not simply to speech acts but more generally to the whole of language. Hence, when Austin attempts to separate from ordinary language instances of citationality – language that is quoted "on stage, in a poem, or a soliloquy" ("Signature Event" 17) – he is excluding that "without which there would not even be a 'successful'

performative" ("Signature Event" 17). As Derrida puts it, "would a performative utterance be possible if a citational doubling [*doublure*] did not
come to split and dissociate from itself the pure singularity of the event?"
("Signature Event" 17).[30] In other words, performatives must mark themselves as performatives – otherwise they could not be recognized as such –
and this introduces into them a "split" that "dissociates" them from the
event itself. So it is that performatives often have a theatrical character, de-
pending upon a ceremonial or ritualistic action (such as kissing the bride
or breaking the bottle over the ship) that helps to authorize the utterance,
even to make it happen. Of course, Derrida acknowledges that "citationality" or "iterability" must be distinguished from the counterfactual or hy-
pothetical nature of a stage play,[31] but he argues that this distinction

> does not emerge *in opposition to* citationality or iterability, but in opposition to
> other kinds of iteration within a general iterability which constitutes a violation of
> the allegedly rigorous purity of every event of discourse or every *speech act*. Rather
> than oppose citation or iteration to the noniteration of an event, one ought to con-
> struct a differential typology of forms of iteration, assuming that such a project is
> tenable and can result in an exhaustive program . . . Above all, at this point, we will
> be dealing with different kinds of marks or chains of iterable marks and not with an
> opposition between citational utterances, on the one hand, and singular and orig-
> inal event-utterances, on the other . . . ("Signature Event" 18; emphasis original)

In the final analysis, Derrida does not so much disagree with Austin as
push the latter to his own logical conclusion: a functional as opposed to
descriptive conception of language begins by acknowledging that words
are, in the Nietzschean sense, nothing more than a "movable host of metaphors, metonymies, and anthropomorphisms" (Nietzsche, "On Truth and
Lies" 84). As a result, there are no instances of "pure" or "originary" forms
of discourse that escape the conventionality of language – which is to say
meanings are generated not ostensively by words pointing to things but
systemically by words referring to other words. It follows that "ordinary"
language does not establish a standard or criterion for the "real," against
which "aesthetic" language is judged to be deficient or parasitic, since
from a philosophical standpoint words are not representations of the thing
itself but tools or instruments for negotiating with reality.[32] Admittedly,
one can, as a matter of everyday life, differentiate between utterances that
purport to "state the case" and those that engage in "make believe," but
this is a matter of *practical* as opposed to *theoretical* knowledge.

With Derrida's analysis in mind, I would like to return to *Waiting for
Godot* and examine more closely how Beckett employs performativity. The
idea of *enacting* the play, of *making* the nothing happen, is largely the
theme of Act Two. First, much of this act is concerned with performing

performativity, with commands that direct actors to carry out specific actions. In one such instance, Vladimir exhorts Estragon, "Say something!" (69) and Estragon exhorts Vladimir "Sing something!" (70). There follows a series of hortatory locutions that amusingly produce precisely what the characters say they cannot produce:

ESTRAGON That's the idea, let's contradict each other.
VLADIMIR Impossible.
ESTRAGON You think so?
VLADIMIR We're in no danger of ever thinking any more.
ESTRAGON Then what are we complaining about?
VLADIMIR Thinking is not the worst.
ESTRAGON Perhaps not. But at least there's that.
VLADIMIR That what?
ESTRAGON That's the idea, let's ask each other questions.
VLADIMIR What do you mean, there's that?
ESTRAGON That much less misery.
VLADIMIR True.
ESTRAGON Well? If we gave thanks for our mercies? (70–1)

Estragon and Vladimir appear to be playing a game – a language game – in which, by denying ("Impossible") or questioning ("What do you mean?") the capacity of language to function transitively, they succeed in translating words into deeds, succeed in achieving a kind of transitivity. Nevertheless, we are left wondering to what extent the characters are themselves conscious of the game they are playing, aware of how their exchange exposes its own performative logic.

At other points, however, it is clear that Estragon and Vladimir understand that they are performing performativity, as they deliberately work through ceremonies designed to make the time pass more quickly. To achieve this goal, they must convert *chronos* to *kairos*, invest otherwise insignificant actions with broader meaning and larger import. Hence time-killing – if not time-filling – activities enact rituals of cursing and forgiving, rituals that play out in humorously reduced forms eschatological narratives of damnation and salvation:

ESTRAGON That's the idea, let's abuse each other.
They turn, move apart, turn again and face each other.
VLADIMIR Moron!
ESTRAGON Vermin!
VLADIMIR Abortion!
ESTRAGON Morpion!
VLADIMIR Sewer-rat!

ESTRAGON Curate!
VLADIMIR Cretin!
ESTRAGON (*with finality*).
  Crritic! (85)

. . .

ESTRAGON Now let's make it up.
VLADIMIR Gogo!
ESTRAGON Didi!
VLADIMIR Your hand!
ESTRAGON Take it!
VLADIMIR Come to my arms!
ESTRAGON Your arms?
VLADIMIR My breast!
ESTRAGON Off we go!
They embrace. They separate. Silence. (85–6)

Of course, Vladimir recognizes that he and Estragon are simply beguiling the hours: "How time flies when one has fun!" (86). The empty and mechanical nature of such exchanges is fully revealed when, having exhausted their stock of routines and uncertain of what to do next, they are reduced to mere exercises:

ESTRAGON What do we do now?
VLADIMIR While waiting.
ESTRAGON While waiting.
Silence.
VLADIMIR We could do our exercises.
ESTRAGON Our movements.
VLADIMIR Our elevations.
ESTRAGON Our relaxations.
VLADIMIR Our elongations.
ESTRAGON Our relaxations.
VLADIMIR To warm us up.
ESTRAGON To calm us down.
VLADIMIR Off we go. (86)

The use of stichomythia in these exchanges, along with the repetitions, rhymes, and alliterations, confers upon them a stylized quality, further underscoring the extent to which they are self-conscious theatrical performances, aesthetic artefacts meant to divert rather than inform. It also adds to the poignancy of Vladimir and Estragon's situation that they fully comprehend the significance – or more precisely the insignificance – of their diversions.[33] Thus, after the exchange in which they contradict each other and then ask each other questions, Vladimir remarks, "That wasn't such a bad little canter," and Estragon replies, "Yes, but now we'll have to find something else" (72). Later, Estragon remarks, "We don't manage too badly, eh Didi, between the two us . . . We always find something, eh Didi, to give us the impression we exist?" (77).

Indeed, the performance of performativity in Act Two is ultimately directed at the play itself. Hence, the larger narrative shape of the second act duplicates that of the first act: Vladimir and Estragon wait for Godot; Pozzo and Lucky arrive and depart; Vladimir and Estragon wait for Godot; the Boy informs them Godot will not come; Vladimir and Estragon consider going, but they "do not move." The circularity and repetition of this structure are represented by the Round Song at the beginning of Act Two (62–3).

> A dog came in the kitchen
> And stole a crust of bread.
> Then cook up with a ladle
> And beat him till he was dead.
> Then all the dogs came running
> And dug the dog a tomb—
> *He stops, broods, resumes:*
> Then all the dogs came running
> And dug the dog a tomb
> And wrote upon the tombstone
> For the eyes of dogs to come
> A dog came in the kitchen
> And stole a crust of bread [etc.] . . . (62)

It is significant that the song functions in ways that are both iterative and abyssal, that it not only *repeats* but also *reproduces* itself, beginning after a certain point to perform itself as a piece of performativity. In a similar vein, Vladimir seeks to restage Act One, mimicking Pozzo as he inspects the wound on Estragon's leg ("Pull up your trousers . . . The other, pig!" 74), or helps him on with a boot ("Come on, give me your foot . . . The other, hog!" 77). Later still, Vladimir suggests that the two of them actually take over the parts of the other two characters:

> VLADIMIR Will you not play?
> ESTRAGON Play at what?
> VLADIMIR We could play at Pozzo and Lucky
> ESTRAGON Never heard of it.
> VLADIMIR I'll do Lucky, you do Pozzo. (*He imitates Lucky sagging under the weight of his baggage. Estragon looks at him with stupefaction.*)

Go on.
ESTRAGON What am I to do?
VLADIMIR Curse me! (82)

The larger argument I am advancing – that increasingly the play is about its own performance as a play – appears to support a widely accepted interpretation of *Waiting for Godot*, what we might call the aesthetic reading.[34] On this view, the play makes nothing happen in the sense that art makes nothing happen, thereby exemplifying the Kantian idea that aesthetic experience is autonomous and the Austinian idea that aesthetic discourse is intransitive. But I want to argue precisely the opposite. The power of *Waiting for Godot* – its capacity to engage, disturb, enchant, compel – results not from a retreat into autonomy and intransitivity but from the subversion of these aesthetic strategies. Yes, the play makes nothing happen, and it accomplishes this through the rhetoric of performativity. Yet in the process it undoes the logic not only of traditional mimeticism but also – and here we discover the play's real seditious force – of traditional aesthetics. I might illustrate how this deconstruction operates by focusing on a passage that is repeated so often that it effectively becomes the play's refrain:

ESTRAGON Let's go.
VLADIMIR We can't.
ESTRAGON Why not?
VLADIMIR We're waiting for Godot.
ESTRAGON Ah! (*Pause. Despairing.*) What'll we do, what'll we do!
VLADIMIR There's nothing we can do. (76)

Earlier, we considered the beginning and ending of the play, but this passage, which occurs on six separate occasions, can be seen as representing the play's middle, a crucial position in a piece of theatre that eschews the outer boundaries of narrative, that aspires to be all medial duration without start or finish.[35] Indeed, one might push matters further and argue that this passage stands as a metonym for the play itself, distilling the essence of its plot, while displaying and replaying its endlessly iterative form. Now if we accept the proposition that the "Let's go" exchange is a key passage in the play, even that it is arguably *the* key to the play, then how do we read it?

We might approach this passage by treating it as an extension of what I earlier called the imperative reading of "Nothing to be done." As we have observed, Estragon's "Let's go" carries hortatory force, operating as a performative of urging. Vladimir responds with what appears to be a straightforward constative, saying in effect: We have an appointment with Godot, which prevents us from leaving. Yet how can we fail to notice that this famous refrain contains as its punch line the title of the play? Indeed, construed at the most literal level, the answer to Estragon's question is disarmingly obvious. Estragon and Vladimir cannot go because they are "Waiting for Godot," which is to say, because they are in a play called *Waiting for Godot*.[36] The title of the play guarantees their detention on two levels. First, it summarizes the plot, whose "inaction" consists precisely in doing nothing, in suspending activity, in waiting. Second, the title serves as a speech act that has illocutionary and perlocutionary consequences. Titling a play is part of the legal performative known as registering a copyright. In this sense, the reason Estragon and Vladimir cannot go is because they are legally bound to stay. Just as the author or his estate can sue to block a production of the play that changes the gender of the characters, so too the author or his estate can withhold copyright permission from a production in which Estragon's "Let's go" elicits an "All right" from Vladimir, followed by the direction, "*They exit stage left.*" Here it is also worth returning to the "intransitive" reading of "Nothing to be done" and Austin's claim that speech acts lose their illocutionary and perlocutionary force when performed in a play. In citing his own title, in engaging in what Derrida calls "citationality," it is as though Beckett is producing a counter-example with Austin in mind. The "action" of the play is guaranteed by the performative that is the script of *Waiting for Godot*. The title is, by literary convention and legal sanction, the part that we use to refer to the dramatic whole. When he cites his title, Beckett reminds us that the *entire* play – which consists of a series of imperatives telling the actors how to move and what to say – functions not descriptively but instrumentally, functions not as a constative but as a performative.

Of course, we must not forget that, in the passage I have been analysing, Estragon's "Let's go" fails to produce its intended perlocutionary effect and that this failure may be said to extend to the play as a whole: Godot does not come; Vladimir and Estragon do not leave. From the standpoint of action, the result is a stalemate, in which it appears that Beckett is doing *nothing* with words. But so bald a statement misses the point, for it fails to recognize that Estragon's utterance does have an effect. The dialectical temporizing that follows from it ("We can't," "Why not," "We're waiting for Godot") not only constitutes the performative outcome of Estragon's words – its unforeseen perlocutionary effect – but also generates the performance of the play itself. And this, I want to suggest, is the larger logic of *Waiting for Godot*, the sense in which it is *doing* nothing with words. In all those passages in which constatives become performatives, in which language games expose foundationalist conceptions of subjectivity and representation, in which the play begins to cannibalize itself and perform its own performativity, Beckett shows how a functionalist or performative idea of language radically alters our understanding of theatrical performance.

Critical consensus has generally held that Beckett's radical innovation in the theatre consisted in laying bare the artifice of representation, in de-realizing the theatre by exposing its illusion-making devices. But rather than merely unmask the ceremonies and protocols of the stage, forcing us to see their unreality, Beckett goes a step further: he insists that we understand these ceremonies and protocols as a function not of art but of life. His performative view of language recognizes that citationality, iterability, ceremony, and protocol – in short, the paraphernalia of stage artifice – necessarily define our everyday relation to words and things. Consequently, there is no transcendent realm that stands beyond language, that escapes the conventional and constructed categories of discourse. And it is here that we discover the genuine shock of Beckett's theatre: not that it reveals the artificiality of art, but that it affirms the artificiality of life. Yet, in doing so, it makes the life we observe on the stage all the more real. For in stripping away the veneer of mimeticism, in dismantling the fourth-wall conventions of Ibsenian realism, *Waiting for Godot* restores ontological presence to its actors and their actions. This is not to say that Beckett invests his characters with a "metaphysics of presence," a position against which I have argued elsewhere (see Begam). On the contrary, Beckett shares the Heideggerian view that "being-there" is not a philosophical problem, something we need to submit to Cartesian proof, whether the "there" is in life or art.[37] Of course, Beckett concedes that, in watching *Waiting for Godot*, we are witnessing a performance, a series of performatives. But if *everything* functions performatively, if all those descriptive uses of language are, in fact, instrumental uses, then the larger effect is to return illocutionary or transitive force to the theatre, to recover for the actors an ontology that transcends the proscenium. As a result, Beckett's theatre breaks through the wall not only of Ibsenian realism but also of Kantian aestheticism, reclaiming for the dramatic event the kind of "there-ness" that Robbe-Grillet discovered in the first performances of *Godot* (see Robbe-Grillet).

My larger argument in this paper has been that *Waiting for Godot* uses performativity to challenge the Kantian idea that there is a strict boundary between art and life. In this sense, Beckett shares common ground with the Dadaist and surrealist exhibitions of the period from 1910 to the 1930s, with the "happenings" of the 1960s and 1970s, and with much contemporary performance art.[38] But here two qualifications are important. First, in the twentieth century, the avant-garde's challenge to aestheticism was largely motivated by its political commitments: the belief that art should speak directly to the social and economic issues of the day. If, in *Waiting for Godot*, performativity frees the play from intransitivity and restores the actors to "being-there," it nevertheless does not make things happen in the sense of Brechtian intervention or Sartrean engagement.[39] Beckett's theatre, which is more philosophical than political, is dedicated to rethinking the boundaries between words and deeds, between representation and performativity.

And this brings me to my second and more general qualification. The avant-garde has tended to take a levelling approach in deconstructing the separation between art and life. The predictable, indeed intended, result was the validation of the everyday: the artefacts of quotidian life became as valuable, if not more so, as traditional works of art. Beckett's own approach is markedly different. Unlike much of the avant-garde, he is not hostile to the idea of aesthetic canonicity, nor does he reject the tradition that canonicity has generated.[40] What is more, Beckett does not *entirely* dispense with such notions as aesthetic distance or aesthetic autonomy. For him, the boundary between art and life is more porous – more liminal[41] – than that envisioned by Kant, but there is a boundary; and while he insists that art not be cut off from life, he nevertheless recognizes, as does Derrida, that on a practical level art is not the same as life. On a philosophical level, however, Beckett's perspective is, like Derrida's, more radical. For Beckett shares with Nietzsche the view that the world is a "movable host of metaphors," which means that, ultimately, life is, in the Nietzschean sense, a work of art.[42] As such, words function not as pictures but as tools or instruments through which we generate the world and accomplish all the things we associate with living in it. Among those things is showing that to do nothing with words – even twice – is to do a great deal with words.

NOTES

1 For some discussions of performance studies, see Carlson; Parker and Kosofsky Sedgwick; Pelias; Reinelt and Roach; Schechner.

2 In Bürger, see especially "On the Problem of Autonomy in Bourgeois Society" and "Avant-Garde and Engagement."

3 Beckett later mixed live and taped performance in *That Time* (1976) and *Rockaby* (1981).

4 Dates given are for performance, transmission, or theatrical release.

5 See Ben-Zvi "Limits"; "Fritz Mauthner." Beckett copied out a lengthy passage from Mauthner's Beiträge in notes he took on German philosophy in the 1930s; see ms. 10951/5 at the Trinity College Library in Dublin.

6 *En Attendant Godot* premiered on 5 January 1953 at the Théâtre de Babylone in Paris in a production directed by Roger Blin. Blin also played the role of Pozzo.

7 Austin is not mentioned in any of the Beckett biographies (Bair, Cronin, Knowlson), and I have found no indication that Austin knew of Beckett's work in the 1950s. Obviously, the concurrent publication of *Philosophical Investigations* and premiere of *Godot* means that Beckett could not have read the former before writing the latter. For an excellent discussion of Beckett and Wittgenstein, see Perloff.

8 Obviously, both Nietzsche and Heidegger were profoundly interested in the problem of language as it relates to the representation of reality, but their emphasis did not fall on "ordinary language."

9 See Janik and Toulmin. Mauthner's *Beiträge zu einer Kritik der Sprache* [*Contributions to a Critique of Language*] was published in 1901; as Mauthner observes in volume I of the *Beiträge*, "Language is only a convention, like a rule of a game: the more participants the more compelling it will be. However it is neither going to grasp nor alter the real world" (qtd. in Janik and Toulmin 126).

10 Austin later comments, "This topic is one development – there are many others – in the recent movement towards questioning an age-old assumption in philosophy – the assumption that to say something, at least in all cases worth considering, i.e. all cases considered, is always and simply to *state* something. This assumption is no doubt unconscious, no doubt is precipitate, but it is wholly natural in philosophy apparently" (12).

11 Austin observes, "What then finally is left of the distinction of the performative and constative utterance? Really we may say that what we had in mind here was this: (*a*) With the constative utterance, we abstract from the illocutionary (let alone perlocutionary) aspects of the speech act, and we concentrate on the locutionary . . . (*b*) With the performative utterance, we attend as much as possible to the illocutionary force of the utterance, and abstract from the dimension of correspondence with facts" (145–6).

12 Scholars and admirers of Austin are understandably hesitant to view him as unduly influenced by Wittgenstein. Still Isaiah Berlin, while defending his fellow Oxonian's originality, concedes that Wittgenstein's then unpublished "Blue" and "Brown" Books had circulated at Oxford in the late 1930s (11) or early 1940s (15), while acknowledging that "[Austin's] implicit rejection of the doctrine of a logically perfect language, which was capable of reflecting the structure of reality, sprang from a philosophical system not dissimilar to that of Wittgenstein" (15). For further discussion of the relation of Austin to Wittgenstein, see Furberg; DiGiovanna.

13 For a discussion of Austin's deconstruction of his own categories, see Culler: "Austin's investigation of the qualities of the marginal case leads to a deconstruction and inversion of the hierarchy: the performative is not a flawed constative: rather, the constative is a special case of the performative" (113).

14 There is little criticism on *Waiting for Godot* and performativity, especially of the Austinian kind. Some relevant articles include Brewer; Corfariu and Roventa-Frumusani; Levy's "Notions"; "On and Offstage."

15 In lecture twelve, Austin categorizes hortatories as "exercitives"; see his sample list, which includes "urge" (156).

16 "Command" is also an exercitive (156)

17 For Austin, "declarations" are "commisives" when they "commit" someone to a course of action and are "expositives" when they expound a particular view (157–63).

18 According to Kant, the art work's autonomy is guaranteed by the doctrines of aesthetic disinterestedness ["*ohne alles Interesse*" (*Kritik* 116)] and purposiveness without a purpose ["*Zweckmässigkeit . . . ohne Zweck*" (Kritik 135)]; see the "Analytic of the Beautiful" in *The Critique of Judgment*.

19   See the "Aeolus" chapter of *Ulysses*.

20   Remember what Austin says at the beginning of *How to Do Things with Words*: "It was for too long the assumption of philosophers that the business of a 'statement' can only be to 'describe' some state of affairs, or to 'state some fact,' which it must do either truly or falsely" (1). The idea that philosophy is dedicated to the examination of those logical and empirical conditions that make a statement true or false derives from Cartesian rationalism and British empiricism. Standing behind these philosophical traditions and animating both is the foundationalism I describe above, which attempts to confer upon philosophy the "certainty" that the Enlightenment associated with science.

21   Descartes repeatedly uses the architectural metaphor of "foundations [*fonde-ments*] as a way of explaining his idea of a philosophy of certainty that would rival mathematics and the sciences. There are numerous instances of this meta-phor in the *Discours*. Here are just two examples: "[t]hus, as regards the other sciences, in so far as they borrow their principles from philosophy, I judged that it was impossible that anything solid could have been built on foundations [*fondements*] that were so weak" (10); "[t]hose nine years passed by, however, before I had made up my mind about the questions that are usually debated among educated people or had begun to look for foundations [*fondements*] for a philosophy that would be more certain than what is generally accepted" (23). It is also noteworthy that Descartes uses metaphors of "firmness" and "unshak-ability" in establishing the "groundwork" of his philosophy: "[w]hen I noticed that this truth 'I think, therefore I am' was so firm [*si ferme*] and certain that all the most extravagant assumptions of the sceptics were unable to shake it [*l'éb-ranler*], I judged that I could accept it without scruple as the first principle of the philosophy for which I was searching" (25).

22   For an example of such a performative or operational approach to language, see Richard Rorty's discussion of Donald Davidson's "passing theory" (14).

23   The second part of the *Discours* opens with the well-known scene of Descartes withdrawing to his *poêle* [stove-heated chamber], where by sitting quietly and thinking he discovers his "method."

24   In Beckett's *oeuvre*, the classic statement of this trope is "*Sedendo et quiescendo anima efficitur prudens* [By sitting and remaining quiet the soul gains wis-dom]." Beckett uses this idea at various points to deconstruct Cartesian founda-tionalism, from Murphy's anything-but-static chair to Belcqua's highly mobile cab ride in the short story, "Sedendo et Quiescendo."

25   As Heidegger writes, "For up to Descartes . . . that which is, insofar as it is a par-ticular being, a particular *sub-iectum* (*hypo-keimenon*), is something lying be-fore from out of itself, which, as such, simultaneously lies at the foundation of its own fixed qualities and changing circumstances. The superiority of the *sub-iectum* (as ground lying at the foundation) that is preeminent because it is in an essential respect unconditional arises out of the claim of man to a *fundamen-tum absolutum inconcussum veritatis* (self-supported, unshakable foundation of truth, in the sense of certainty)" ("Age" 148; italics original).

26   The larger argument of Lucky's monologue is as follows: the academy of anthropometry has determined that, despite advances made in human nutri-tion ("alimentation and defecation" 46) and exercise ("physical culture" 46),

the size of man's head has actually diminished over time ("wastes and pines" 46), the exact loss being "one inch four ounce per head" (46). Notably Lucky connects man's diminished capacities with the Enlightenment – i.e., he dates the loss as having occurred "since the death of Bishop Berkeley [*depuis la mort de Voltaire*]" (46/61). A useful point of comparison is Foucault's discussion of the "end of man" at the conclusion of *Les mots et les choses*, a work that, like Austin's, meditates on the relation of words to things.

27 Does Beckett's portrayal of Pozzo participate in "anti-theatricality"? On the one hand, it certainly parodies the bourgeois theatre's desire for sensationalism, baroque gesture, and exaggerated affect. On the other hand, Pozzo's theatricality is one of the means by which the play finally performs its own performativity, thereby deconstructing an aesthetics of intransitivity. Although I cannot develop the argument here, I do not believe that Beckett shares the "anti-theatrical" prejudice that Martin Puchner's *Stage Fright* identifies with "a number of obsessions: the immorality of public display, of arousing the audience, and, most importantly of those who professionally practice the art of deception" (1). The moralizing Platonism that stands behind anti-theatricality (*Stage Fright*, 22–8) could not be farther from Beckett's own sensibility, and his objection is not to "arousing the audience" (as *Krapp's Last Tape* demonstrates) but to doing so through devices that are emotionally shallow or cheap.

28 For a classic discussion of the distinction between *chronos* and *kairos*, see Kermode: "*chronos* is 'passing time' or 'waiting time' – that which, according to Revelation, 'shall be no more' – and *kairos* is the season, a point in time filled with significance, charged with a meaning derived from its relation to the end" (47; italics original).

29 The paper, originally presented in Montreal in 1971, was published in French in *Marges de la philosophie* in 1972 and then published in English in *Glyph* 1 in 1977. The latter inspired John Searle's "Reiterating the Differences: A Reply to Derrida" published in *Glyph* 2 in 1977, a volume which also included Derrida's response to Searle, "Limited Inc. a b c . . . " Derrida subsequently published his two essays together in a book entitled *Limited Inc*. My own quotations from "Signature Event Context" are drawn from *Limited Inc*.

30 By way of elaboration, Derrida asks, "Could a performative utterance succeed if its formulation did not repeat a 'coded' or iterable utterance . . . if the formula I pronounce in order to open a meeting, launch a ship or a marriage were not identifiable as *conforming* with an iterable model, if it were not then identifiable in some way as a 'citation'?" ("Signature Event" 18).

31 "Not that citationality in this case is of the same sort as in a theatrical play, a philosophical reference, or the recitation of a poem" ("Signature Event" 18), which is "why there is a relative specificity, as Austin says, a 'relative purity' of performatives" ("Signature Event" 18).

32 "The 'thing in itself' (which is precisely what the pure truth, apart from any of its consequences, would be) is likewise something quite incomprehensible to the creator of language and something not in the least worth striving for. This creator only designates the relations of things to men, and for expressing these relations he lays hold of the boldest metaphors" (Nietzsche, "Truth and Lies" 82).

33　At least Vladimir appears to comprehend their situation; Estragon grasps it only intermittently.

34　For the best account of this approach to Beckett, see Daniel Albright's splendid study, *Beckett and Aesthetics*.

35　The four-line exchange, culminating in "We're waiting for Godot," occurs twice in Act One (8, 51) and four times in Act Two (76, 78, 88, 96). It is also repeated twice more in varied forms at 100 and 107.

36　In the original French, Beckett cannot reproduce the title as the punch line of this passage, but he comes fairly close, "*On attend Godot*" being a fair approximation of *En attendant Godot*.

37　As Heidegger writes in *Being and Time*, "When Dasein directs itself towards something and grasps it, it does not somehow first get out of an inner sphere in which it has been proximally encapsulated, but its primary kind of Being is such that it is always 'outside' alongside entities which it encounters and which belong to a world already discovered . . . [F]urthermore, the perceiving of what is known is not a process of returning with one's booty to the 'cabinet' of consciousness after one has gone out and grasped it; even in perceiving, retaining, and preserving, the Dasein which knows *remains outside*, and does so *as Dasein*" (89; italics original).

38　Beckett was familiar with the work of the Dadaists and surrealists and, around 1930, translated a number of poems by André Breton, René Creval, and Tristan Tzara (see Knowlson 137).

39　This is not to say that one cannot discover political significance in *Waiting for Godot* in particular or in Beckett's theatre more generally, but Beckett's deconstruction of the Kantian division between art and life is not principally motivated by a commitment to intervention or engagement.

40　This alone sets Beckett apart from much of the avant-garde, whose anti-aestheticism consisted not merely in painting a moustache on the Mona Lisa but in jettisoning the very idea of the museum – i.e., the idea that certain works have become classics and as such are worthy of preservation.

41　See Turner's use of "liminal."

42　"Only by forgetting this primitive world of metaphor can one live with any repose, security and consistency: only by means of the petrification and coagulation of a mass of images which originally streamed from the primal faculty of human imagination like a fiery liquid, only in the invincible faith that *this* sun, *this* window, *this* table is a truth in itself, in short, only by forgetting that he himself is an *artistically*, *creating* subject, does man live with any repose, security, and consistency" (Nietzsche, "Truth and Lies" 86).

WORKS CITED

Albright, Daniel. *Beckett and Aesthetics*. Cambridge: Cambridge UP, 2003.

Austin, J.L. *How to Do Things with Words*. Eds. J.O. Ursmon and Marina Sibsà. Harvard UP, 1977.

Bair, Deirdre. *Samuel Beckett: A Biography*. New York: Harcourt, 1978.

Beckett, Samuel. *En Attendant Godot*. Paris: Minuit, 1952.

———. "Notes on Fritz Mauthner." Ms. 10971/5, Trinity College Dublin Library.

———. *Waiting for Godot*. New York: Grove, 1954.

Begam, Richard. "Beckett and Postfoundationalism, or, How Fundamental Are Those Fundamental Sounds." *Beckett and Philosophy*. Ed. Richard Lane. Houndsmills, UK: Palgrave, 2002.

Ben-Zvi, Linda. "Fritz Mauthner for Company." *Journal of Beckett Studies* 9 (1984): 65–88.

———. "Samuel Beckett, Fritz Mauthner, and the Limits of Language." *PMLA* 95 (1980): 183–200.

Berlin, Isaiah *et al. Essays on J.L. Austin*. Clarendon: Oxford UP, 1973.

Brewer, Maria Minich. "Performing Theory." *Theatre Journal* 37.1 (1985): 12–30.

Bürger, Peter. *Theory of the Avant-Garde*. Trans. Jochen SchulteSasse. Minneapolis: U of Minnesota P, 1984.

Carlson, Marvin. *Performance: A Critical Introduction*. London: Routledge, 1996.

Corfariu, Manuela, and Daniela Roventa-Frumusani. "Absurd Dialogue and Speech Acts – Beckett's *En Attendant Godot*." *Poetics* 13 (1984): 119–33.

Cronin, Anthony. *Samuel Beckett: The Last Modernist*. New York: HarperCollins, 1996.

Culler, Jonathan. *On Deconstruction: Theory and Criticism after Structuralism*. Ithaca: Cornell UP, 1982.

Derrida, Jacques. "Signature Event Context." Trans. Samuel Weber and Jeffrey Mehlman. *Limited Inc*. Evanston: Northwestern UP, 1988.

———. *Marges de la philosophie*. Paris: Minuit, 1972.

Descartes, René. *Discourse on Method and Related Writings*. Trans. Desmond M. Clarke. London: Penguin, 1999.

DiGiovanna, Joseph J. *Linguistic Phenomenology: Philosophical Method in J.L. Austin*. New York: Peter Lang, 1989.

Foucault, Michel. *Les mots et les choses*. Paris: Gallimard, 1966.

Furberg, Mats. *Saying and Meaning: A Main Theme in J.L. Austin's Philosophy*. Oxford: Blackwell, 1971.

Heidegger, Martin. *Being and Time*. Trans. John Macquarrie and Edward Robinson. New York: Harper, 1962.

———. "The Age of the World Picture." *The Question Concerning Technology and Other Essays*. Trans. William Lovitt. New York: Harper, 1977. 115–54.

Janik, Allan, and Stephen Toulmin. *Wittgenstein's Vienna*. Chicago: Elephant, 1996.

Kant, Immanuel. *The Critique of Judgment*. Trans. J.H. Bernard. Amherts, NY: Prometheus, 2000.

———. *Kritik der Urteilskraft*. Frankfurt: Suhrkamp, 1974.

Kermode, Frank. *The Sense of an Ending: Studies in the Theory of Fiction*. London: Oxford UP, 1981.

Knowlson, James. *Damned to Fame: The Life of Samuel Beckett*. New York: Simon & Schuster, 1996.

Levy, Shimon. "Notions of Audience in Beckett's Plays." *Assaph: Studies in the Theatre* 61 (1984): 71–81.

———. "On and Offstage: Spiritual Performatives in Beckett's Drama." *Samuel Beckett Today* 9 (2000): 17–29.

Nietzsche, Friedrich. "On Truth and Lies in a Nonmoral Sense." *Philosophy and Truth: Selections from Nietzsche's Notebooks of the Early 1870s.* Ed. and trans. Daniel Breazeale. Atlantic Highlands, N.J.: Humanities, 1979. 77–97.

Parker, Andrew, and Eve Kosofsky Sedgwick, eds. *Performativity and Performance.* London: Routledge, 1995.

Pelias, Ronald J. *Performance Studies: The Interpretation of Aesthetic Texts.* New York: St. Martin's, 1992.

Perloff, Marjorie. "Witt-Watt: The Language of Resistance/The Resistance of Language." *Wittgenstein's Ladder: Poetic Language and the Strangeness of the Ordinary.* Chicago: U of Chicago P, 1996. 115–43.

Puchner, Martin. *Stage Fright: Modernism, Anti-Theatricality, and Drama.* Baltimore: Johns Hopkins UP, 2002.

Reinelt, Janelle G., and Joseph R. Roach, eds. *Critical Theory and Performance.* Ann Arbor, MI: U of Michigan P, 1992.

Robbe-Grillet, Alain. "Samuel Beckett, or Presence on the Stage." *For a New Novel: Essays on Fiction.* Trans. Richard Howard. New York: Grove, 1965. 111–25.

Rorty, Richard. *Contingency, Irony, and Solidarity.* Cambridge: Cambridge UP, 1989.

Schechner, Richard. *Performance Studies: An Introduction.* London: Routledge, 2002.

Turner, Victor. *The Ritual Process: Structure and Anti-Structure.* Chicago: Aldine, 1969.

Wittgenstein, Ludwig. *Philosophical Investigations.* Trans. G.E.M. Anscombe. New York: Macmillan, 1968.

7

Reinventing Beckett[*]

S.E. GONTARSKI

I don't know whether the theater is the right place for me anymore.

– Samuel Beckett

[T]he bourgeoisie will recuperate [the avant-garde] altogether, ultimately putting on splendid evenings of Beckett and Audiberti (and tomorrow Ionesco, already acclaimed by humanist criticism).

– Roland Barthes

Samuel Beckett's creative life (and personal life, for that matter) was marked by a series of transformations and reinventions. In the process of remaking himself, over and again, from donnish academic to avant-garde poet, from Joycean acolyte to post-Joycean minimalist, from humanist to post-humanist, perhaps, most certainly from poet to novelist to playwright to theatre director, Beckett was simultaneously reinventing every literary genre he turned his attention to. In the midst of remaking narrative in the wake of World War II, for example, he began simultaneously the reinvention of theatre, writing the ground-breaking (but still unproduced) *Eleutheria* between *Molloy* and *Malone meurt [Malone Dies]* and *En attendant Godot [Waiting for Godot]* between *Malone meurt* and *L'Innommable [The Unnamable]*. Almost as soon as he began to experience some recognition, most notably in the theatre, however, he began to recoil from it as well, as if it represented a threat, the desired attention he had struggled so hard to achieve barbed with threats to his art (and even perhaps to his self-image). Enthusiastic about his anti-boulevard play *Eleutheria* and eager for its publication and performance, for example, he quickly repudiated it, withdrawing it from scheduled publication after the staging of *Godot*, finding it in later years impossible to translate even for his long-time publisher, Barney Rosset, refusing again to have it published,[1] at least in his lifetime, and finally, if fundamentally by proxy, prohibiting any staging, apparently in perpetuity. It was, however, a play central to Beckett's theatrical reinvention as it, almost literally, swept the stage clear of both boulevard and naturalistic debris and so bared the stage for what would become, in English, *Waiting for Godot*. British critic and staunch Beckett advocate Harold Hobson may have privileged Beckett's second full-length play in the following description, but his comments are equally apposite to *Eleutheria*, the restriction to "the English theatre" excepted. *Godot*, he noted,

> ... knocked the shackles of plot from off the English drama. It destroyed the notion that the dramatist is God, knowing everything about his characters and master of a complete philosophy answerable to all of our problems. It showed that Archer's dictum that a good play imitates the audible and visible surface of life is not necessarily true. It revealed that the drama approximates or can approximate the condition of music, touching chords deeper than can be reached by reason and saying things beyond the grasp of logic. It renewed the English theatre in a single night. (11)

Joyce may have celebrated "Ibsen's New Drama," noting that "the long roll of drama, ancient or modern, has few things better to show" (49), and Shaw accepted the role of heir in "The Quintessence of Ibsenism," but for Beckett, no such lineage; Ibsen's new theatre smacked of didacticism and "explicitation" from which Beckett recoiled: "All I know is in the text." He wrote to his American director, Alan Schneider, on 16 October 1972 in relation to the staging of *Not I*, " 'She' [Mouth in this case] is purely a stage entity, part of a stage image and purveyor of stage text. The rest is Ibsen" (Harmon 283).

Godot would not, of course, be Beckett's sole or final theatrical reinvention. At the dawn of a new century, it has become the most "recuperated" of Beckett's plays, its fiftieth anniversary in 2003 celebrated by waves of bourgeois nostalgia. By 1963, however, a decade after the French premiere of *Godot*, Beckett would repudiate the character-based drama on which he had, thus far, made his theatrical reputation and focus instead on shaping and reshaping, as author and stage director, an iconic theatre of sculpted images. The composition and performance history of *Play*, beginning in 1963, not only moved stage space to the interior, it triggered an increase in Beckett's direct involvement in stagecraft as well, since it demanded a level of technical sophistication and precision unknown in his earlier work, and the demands of staging *Play* finally forced a reluctant and private Samuel Beckett to assume full, public, directorial responsibility for his own works. With *Play*, then, Beckett reinvented the theatre again, moving it yet further from Ibsen, if not more broadly from humanism itself, as his art moved beyond, even denied, character, the mainstay of traditional theatre, and shifted the theatrical (and theoretical) ground from corporeality to the incorporeality of what we call (perhaps too glibly) Beckett's late theatre – a shift from the body, say, to the voice or consciousness, from "matter to memory" (to echo Henri Bergson), often detached from any ground; that is, memory ungrounded and with no discernable reservoir. After 1963, Beckett's became a theatre of immateriality, of ghosts, his work itself the ghost or after-image, not only of the commercial theatre, but of his own earlier work. It became more overtly a theatre of images and the enigmas of perceiving them. His theatre would become, in many respects, a recuperation of the Bergson he had lectured on in his short unhappy career as a university don. Moreover, as a man of the theatre, he not only began directing most of his new work but also began revising, and thereby reinventing, his previous oeuvre, his own canon, even those works firmly established within the theatrical repertory.

Beckett's transformation from playwright to theatrical artist was thus a seminal development, a final blow perhaps to modernist or Ibsenist theatre, a shift beyond textuality, since most of the late works are unreadable, and yet that transformation is slighted in the critical and historical discourse that continues to privilege print over performance, the apparent stability of text over the vicissitudes of theatre. Such neglect of the impact of Beckett's direct staging of his plays distorts the arc of his creative evolution (to coin a phrase) as it undervalues his emergence as an artist committed to the performance of his drama as its creation and continual re-creation. Beckett would finally embrace theatre not just as a medium through which a preconception was given its accurate completion but as *the* process through which the work of art was realized. As Beckett evolved from being a playwright offering advice to directors and actors to taking full charge of staging his plays, practical theatre offered him the opportunity for self-collaboration, through which he might reinvent himself as an artist yet again, as he found the means to subvert his own texts. Not only does denial of the evolutionary vitality of performance mark most Beckett criticism today, as it delimits a dynamic process of becoming (or creation) at an arbitrary point – publication; such emphasis on stability, arbitrary as it might be, has become the core ideology of the protectors of Beckett's reputation into the after-Beckett. The Beckett estate, the legal extension of the author, remains committed to the decidedly untheatrical ideology of invariant texts, in the face of overwhelming evidence to the contrary. The estate seems determined to stop the process of self-subversion that is the hallmark of vanguard art, blunting its political edge and domesticating Samuel Beckett and his work into bourgeois acceptability. Theirs is an argument for a homogeneous Beckett. Such recuperation of the revolutionary has, of course, become the hallmark of late capitalism, as patronage of even our most radical art has come from global corporatism, and the Beckett estate is following suit if only by insisting on its property rights. What grates is the exercise of those rights under the banner of an aesthetic purity and authorial protection designed to save Beckett from his own self-subversions.

EMBRACING THE PERFORMATIVE

Reluctant as he may have been at the onset, Beckett embraced the volatility of performance as *the* theatrical art. The transition was gradual, growing from his involvement in staging *En attendant Godot* [*Waiting for Godot*] between 1950 and its opening in January of 1953. Jean Martin, who was the first Lucky, recalls Beckett's being passive at rehearsals in the closing weeks of 1952:

> I rehearsed for only about three weeks in all. Sam said practically nothing while we were putting it on. You see he was extremely shy and very, very discreet ... He relied entirely on Roger Blin [his French director, who also played the role of Pozzo]. But he came to rehearsals every day. And Suzanne came very often too. But they didn't offer any advice. (qtd. in Knowlson and Knowlson 117)

Beckett's letters to Roger Blin belie Martin's observations, however. As early as 19 December 1950, Beckett wrote Blin, "I have an idea for the set. We must get together. Could you pass by our house one day this week?" (qtd. in Oppenheim 295). In spirit, though, Martin's observation represents at least Beckett's public posture, his advice almost always rendered privately. What diffidence or reluctance existed began to be assuaged in 1957 with the staging of Beckett's next play, *Fin de partie* [*Endgame*], but the year of near-total transformation from author to director committed to performance was 1966. Beckett was preparing (with Mariu Karmitz and Jean Ravel) a film version of Jean-Marie Serreau's June 1964 Paris staging of *Comédie* [*Play*]. He rushed off to London to oversee the taping of *Eh Joe*, with Jack MacGowran and Siân Phillips, his first teleplay (nominally directed by Alan Gibson and broadcast on BBC 2 on 4 July 1966). He supervised two vinyl recordings for Claddagh records: *MacGowran Speaking Beckett* and *MacGowran Reading Beckett's Poetry*, the former accompanied by music – Schubert's Quartet in D minor – Beckett himself playing gong in a family trio that included John and nephew Edward. He then rushed back to Paris to oversee Jean-Marie Serreau's series of one-acts at the Odéon, Théâtre de France, including a reprise of *Comédie*, *Va et vient* [*Come and Go*], and his own staging of Robert Pinget's *Hypothèse*, with actor Pierre Chabert. Beckett wound up taking over full responsibility for staging this theatrical evening at the Odéon, but without program credit. The first of his works for which Beckett received full directorial billing was the 1966 Stuttgart telecast of *He Joe*, broadcast by SDR on Beckett's sixtieth birthday, 13 April 1966.

By 7 April 1966, Beckett would lament to his American director, "Very tired. Nonstop theatre, film (*Play*), TV and Radio since before Xmas ... Forget what writing is about" (qtd. in Harmon 202); but he soon went on to accept an invitation from the Schiller Theatre to direct a play. He chose *Endspiel* [*Endgame*]. The decision was monumental and would commence a systematic reinvention of nearly all of his theatre works over the next two decades. He prepared a *Regiebuk* [director's notebook] for each production, and those notebooks, with their meticulous outlines of the play's actions and internal parallels, would characterize his approach to directing.[2] In February 1969, Theodor Adorno wrote to relay an offer for Beckett to direct *Waiting for Godot* in Hamburg. In his reply to Adorno on 15 February 1969, Beckett politely declined, citing the amount of work it would take: "it is a very big job and health is not grand." But he noted as well, "I have promised to do *Das letzte Band* [*Krapp's Last Tape*] with Martin Held at the Schiller (Werkstatt) this summer."[3]

As crucial as Beckett's re-intervention in his published texts is the almost simultaneous development of his radical minimalism, an imagistic aesthetics that would come to dominate his theatrical work. That minimalism may be most evident, of course, in the thirty-five-second playlet called *Breath*. When Ruby Cohn asked Beckett in the summer of 1968 whether or not he had a *new play* in the offing, "He answered, almost angrily, 'New? What could be new? Man is born – vagitus. Then he breathes for a few seconds, before the death rattle intervenes" ' (qtd. in Knowlson and Knowlson, 129). He then wrote out the entire play called *Breath* for Cohn on the paper table cover of a café.[4] That spirit of abstraction and contraction, captured most succinctly and fully in *Breath*, would inform the whole of his directing career.

Beckett's directorial changes, then, represented – and still do for that matter – his "latest word" on his plays, yet that latest word has, more often than not, been ignored – by theatre directors, scholars, and most importantly, by his guardians and heirs. Theatre directors and some scholars have themselves often been suspicious of the implications of Beckett's own productions, fearing that Beckett's "latest word" might freeze text and performance possibilities. The pressing issue for these scholars and theatre practitioners quickly became, what relationship existed between Beckett's creative interventions, his self-subversions in his own meticulously directed works, and future performances? Are Beckett's productions now the standard from which no deviation should obtain? This is roughly the position of the estate that sanctions, in both senses of that self-contradictory term, performances. Oddly, the estate also rejects the texts that are the products of that final intervention. That is, they have rejected the revised texts, arguing that they are localized variations on an invariant text as originally published (with minor subsequent corrections). The revised texts are thus merely versions of a published original, but all texts, reaching back to the earliest drafts, are merely versions – and each was deemed a stage that the author considered final, until the next version. The revised texts are then that next version. Whether or not the creative process comes to a halt at publication is a much-debated point, especially in theatre and theory, but even conservative Beckett critics do not accept a doctrine of textual invariance. Yet that, essentially, is the position of the Beckett estate, and it has caused something of a crisis in the theatrical community. More than a few directors have refused to work with Beckett's material (Herbert Blau and Lee Breuer, chief among them), while others have been prohibited from doing so (Deborah Warner and JoAnne Akalaitis, among them).

Admittedly, some of the tensions between Beckett's theatre and the international community of directors were created and aggravated during Beckett's lifetime. Beckett was less than happy with André Gregory's 1973 *Endgame*, for which the audience was seated within wire-meshed chicken coops.[5] In Robert Brustein's 1999 review of the Beckett/Schneider letters, he identified Beckett's American director, Alan Schneider, as a self-interested conspirator, quoting Schneider's condemnation of his competitor:

> The André Gregory troupe ... was "inclined to use text for own purposes," later reporting, in a long letter, on how "the production takes such liberties with your text ... and with your directions," calling it a "self-indulgent travesty, determined to be 'different' for the sake of being 'different.' "

Beckett intervened to stop a European tour of Gregory's production, on Schneider's advice and request. But it was JoAnne Akalaitis's staging of *Endgame* at the American Repertory Theater in December 1984 that prompted Beckett to intervene fully and forcefully to try to halt the performance. Hours before the opening, lawyers were still negotiating the textual alterations. Akalaitis's crimes were that she had set her production in a subway station with an abandoned subway car as backdrop, adding music by her ex-husband, Philip Glass. Beckett was convinced, with much encouragement from Schneider, that the production was an unacceptable alteration of the text, particularly the stage directions, which for Beckett, as we know, are not ancillary but integral to the text. He further objected to the increasingly common American theatrical practice of colour-blind casting, black actors here in two of the four roles. A final compromise allowed the production to open but with Beckett's disclaimer printed in the playbill: "A complete parody of the play. Anybody who cares for the work couldn't fail to be disgusted" (qtd. in Brustein 13).

In addition to Akalaitis's 1984 *Endgame*, high-profile conflicts surrounded De Haarlemse Toneelschuur's all-female *Waiting for Godot* in 1988. Through the Société des Auteurs et Compositeurs Dramatiques, Beckett took legal action to prevent the Dutch company from staging its all female production. Gildas Bourdet's "pink" *Fin de partie* [*Endgame*] for the venerable Comédie-Française also in 1988 met overwhelming resistance as well. Beckett and his French publisher, Jérôme Lindon, forced the Comédie-Française to withdraw certain alterations of, and additions to, the prescribed setting and costumes for the production, leading to Bourdet's decision to remove his name from the credits. The Beckett estate, then controlled by the French publisher, saw as its duty such continued enforcement. Susan Sontag's radical *Godot* in war-torn Sarajevo in 1993 erred by the introduction of multiple cast members,[6] but Sarajevo was evidently beyond the reach of western European law; Deborah Warner did not fare as well with her 1994 London production of *Footfalls* at the Garrick Theatre, which was denied permission to tour Europe after being viewed by Edward Beckett. But Katie Mitchell's "peripatetic" evening called *Beckett Shorts*, for the Royal Shakespeare Company at the Other Place in 1997, where several productions were shown simultaneously, was ignored by the estate's lawyers. Unsurprisingly, Akalaitis and Warner have directed no Beckett since their 1984 *Endgame* and 1994 *Footfalls*, respectively. As Akalaitis has noted, "I don't think I'd be allowed the rights" (qtd. in Fanger).

Some theatre artists with personal connections to Beckett received the dispensation of benign neglect, however – the itinerant Hungarian theatrical director George Tabori, for one, who studied in Germany until 1933, before emigrating to England, where he was a journalist for the BBC. He then worked with Brecht in America, returning to Germany after World War II. Fascinated by Beckett's work, Tabori directed many of the plays, situating himself within the debate between directorial originality and fidelity to Beckett's vision. His search for a subtext in Beckett's theatre assumed radical forms in a series of productions of what he called "dangerous theatre" in the 1980s. *Beckett Evening 1* in 1980 took place in the Atlas Circus in Munich, with circus artists and animals representing the state of being captured and tamed, whips and whistles suggesting the Holocaust. The actors were to take Beckett's work literally, find their personal subtexts, and pursue the concrete experience behind the image. His production of *Breath* was simply recited, stage directions and all; *Not I* presented a young actress tied to a wooden wall with knives fixed all around her by a knife-thrower. The Auditor was an elephant on which the woman, set free by the elocutionary act, rode triumphantly from the arena. *Play* was performed by three actors walking about restlessly, *seeking* the limelight to tell their part of the story.

Beckett's reaction to Tabori's excesses was restrained. When Tabori staged *Le Dépeupleur* [*The Lost Ones*], Beckett wished him "the best of agonies" but did not restrict a bizarre interpretation that combined Auschwitz with being improperly born, naked bodies, black plastic pipes, a carp in a large aquarium, and the subtext of the human condition in a scorched landscape bereft of love. Tabori's 1984 *Waiting for Godot* was much acclaimed, but it horrified Beckett. The characters were refugees, intellectuals, foregrounding Beckett's activities in the Resistance during the war. The play was set in the round, with production crew onstage to suggest the evolution of an imaginary rehearsal, with scenes of hatred and compassion, despair and tenderness, played out as interludes in the ritual of waiting. His *Happy Days* of 1986 was even more *outré*, with Winnie's mound replaced by a bed and Beckett's "woman about fifty" acted by the attractive, young Ursula Höpfner, in plunging décolletage. The subtext was to imbue the metaphysical with concrete human experience, that of a tense human relationship; but casting the physically disabled Peter Radtke as Willie, in a performance incorporating Karl Böhm's rehearsal comments about *Tristan und Iseult* and groans and whistles of whales to accompany Willie's agonized craving for Winnie, was a curious mix (see Feinberg-Jütte 95–115). Through it all, Tabori's hope was to liberate Beckett's texts from dogmatic models, a hope shared by many subsequent directors, Gildas Bourdet and Deborah Warner among them.

Beckett, himself, thus assumed an exigent approach during his lifetime, modulating such antinomies of production. He was far from consistent in this respect, of course. For all that he believed in authorial control, in practice, when it came to "alternative" productions, "it made a tremendous difference if he liked and respected the persons involved," as biographer James Knowlson notes (*Damned* 608). On the issue of gender change, however, he remained steadfast. Writing to his American publisher and theatrical agent, Barney Rosset on 11 July 1973, he noted,

> I am against women playing *Godot* and wrote Miss [Estelle] Parsons to that effect. Theatre sex is not interchangeable and *Godot* by women would sound as spurious as *Happy Days* or *Not I* played by men. It was performed once in Israel, without our authorization, by an all-female cast, with disastrous effect.[7]

The position that Beckett himself took with regard to Akalaitis's 1984 ART *Endgame* is the one currently holding sway internationally. Simply stated, it is that the author is the sole authority on and arbiter of the theatrical works, a position accepted and extended by his estate and buttressed by international law. In other words, the process of reinvention that had been the hallmark of Beckett's creative life has apparently come to an end, Beckett's theatre rapidly becoming part of the quid pro quo of bourgeois commerce, a system he struggled so hard to unmask. One consequence of such a repositioning is that the climate in which scholars and theatre practitioners investigate the complexities of Beckett's theatrical oeuvre and his theatrical career has been chilled.

The inevitable question that arises in the early years of the twenty-first century, fifty-plus years after the premiere of *En attendant Godot*

[*Waiting for Godot*], in the seventeenth year of the after-Beckett, is whether Beckett is thus rapidly becoming theatrically irrelevant. Put another way, will the year of celebrations of Samuel Beckett's work in the centenary year of 2006, including innumerable productions, presumably all authorized, be its headstone as well? Put yet another way, is there a future for Beckettian performance? Can it be reinvented again? And if so, what might such reinvention look like, given the restrictions on performance imposed by the legal heirs to the work, heirs who function with all the *droits d'auteur*, but none of his flexibility? Must the avant-garde, already "the parasite and property of the bourgeoisie," accept its own impotence, as Roland Barthes has asked, or worse bring about its own death? (69). In addition to their most publicized interventions into performance, the executors have all but kept from the public the principal work of the final two decades of Beckett's creative life, his continuation of the creative process, his full revisions of his dramatic texts. These revisions are, of course, available in a limited capacity, in the very expensive editions of *The Theatrical Notebooks of Samuel Beckett*, which Beckett himself not only authorized but financed as well, but their cost severely restricts their availability. Even university libraries resist such an expenditure under current budgets. The estate has refused permission to publish the revised or acting texts separately as alternative editions or to re-issue the *Notebooks* in affordable, paperback editions.

Admittedly, part of the reason for the position of the estate is the difficulty of determining authorial intent off the page. Which of the revisions in Beckett's productions are meant for the local contingencies of particular actors or a particular stage? As Beckett wrote to Polish director Marek Kędzierski on 15 November 1981, "Herewith corrected copy of *Fin de partie*. The cuts and simplifications are the result of my work on the play as director and a function of the players at my disposal. To another director they may not seem desirable."[8] What Beckett sent Kędzierski, however, is simply not readily available to other directors, except in *The Theatrical Notebooks.*[9] Moreover, Beckett did not direct and revise each of his plays, and so not every text has been systematically reinvented. That is, Beckett's work on productions did not always result in permanent changes to a printed text. Occasionally, local revisions were made by Beckett to respond to the process of collaboration and to the nature of a particular theatrical space, or changes were contemplated that were never formally incorporated into any text or production. In his notebook for *Damals*, the German translation of *That Time*, which he directed along with *Tritte [Footfalls]* at the Schiller Theatre in 1976, for instance, Beckett offered an alternate staging of the play, one that might increase its verisimilitude. If Listener's hand were to be *seen* at full light, it should be clutching a sheet around his neck. The tension of that grip should then increase during the silences.

That detail added to the play's limited frame suggests that *That Time* is something of an experiment in perspective. We perceive the Figure as if we were watching him from above as he lay in a bed.

In addition, for his television production of *What Where* Beckett revised the German text extensively, but he never fully revised the stage directions of the original English text. This was due in part to the fact that Beckett continued to work on the visual imagery of the play all through rehearsals. By this stage of his directing career, he had developed more confidence in or grown more trusting of the creative collaborations that theatre entails, and he was creating his theatre work in rehearsals, directly onstage (or in this case on the set), although he made his usual pre-production notebook for the performance as well. As his technical assistant, Jim Lewis, recalls,

> If you want to compare this production [of *Was Wo*] with the others for television, there's one major difference. And that is his concept was not set. He changed and changed and changed ... I've never experienced that with him before. You know how concrete he is, how precise he is. Other times we could usually follow through on that with minor, minor changes; but this time there were several basic changes and he still wasn't sure. Many things, different things. (qtd. in Fehsenfeld 236)

Lewis's observation suggests the single most salient element in Beckett's evolution into a theatre artist: his commitment to the idea of performance and his acceptance of a variety of possible creative outcomes. In practical and literary terms, such a commitment meant that nothing like a final text of his work could be established before he worked with it directly onstage. Writing to Alan Schneider in response to his American director's queries about staging *Play*, Beckett expressed what had become obvious to him: "I realize that no final script is possible until I work on rehearsals."[10]

Almost simultaneously, after Beckett had just seen a rough cut of *Film* in 1964, he argued quite clearly against a slavish fidelity to the script. Beckett wrote to Schneider on 29 September 1964, shortly after viewing *Film*:

> [G]enerally speaking, from having been troubled by a certain failure to communicate fully by purely visual means the basic intention [as outlined in the script, presumably], I now begin to feel that this is unimportant and that the images obtained probably gain in force what they lose as ideograms ... It does I suppose in a sense fail with reference to a purely intellectual schema ... but in so doing has acquired a dimension and a validity of its own that are worth far more than any merely efficient translation of intention. (qtd. in Harmon 166)

Moreover, textual variants among the published texts testify to the fact that Beckett's plays do not exist in a uniform, static state. Legally, a director can follow any of these various published texts and still conflict with Beckett's recorded intentions. Most English editions of *Krapp's Last Tape*, for instance, still depict Krapp with a clown's nose and wearing white boots, and the play is often performed thus. Arguments about staging a *Godot* respectful of Beckett's wishes are frequently based on the assumption that a single authoritative script exists. In the general editor's note to *The Theatrical Notebooks*, James Knowlson has observed that "in the case of *Waiting for Godot* ... whole sections of text have *never* been played as printed in the original editions" (vii). And I myself have noted in the *Endgame* volume of *The Theatrical Notebooks*, "[C]ritics and directors [are] forced into a position of building interpretations and mounting productions of Samuel Beckett's work not so much on corrupt texts such as almost all English versions of *Waiting for Godot*, but on those the author himself found unsatisfactory, unfinished" (xxv).

The response of the estate has its own compelling logic and its standard contract calls for adherence to "the integrity of the text and stage directions" in order to create "the image of universality that the author sought." In a letter to the *Guardian*, Edward Beckett continues his defence with an analogy:

> There are more than fifteen recordings of Beethoven's late string quartets in the catalogue, every interpretation different, one from the next, but they are all based on the same notes, tonalities, dynamic and tempo markings. We feel justified in asking the same measure of respect for Samuel Beckett's plays. (25)

He suggests that since musicians, however freely they may "interpret" a piece of music, do not deviate from the composer's notes, why should a director depart from Beckett's dialogue or directions? The analogy is intriguing. What we know of a score is that it is not music, as a playtext is likewise not theatre. Both printed versions are approximations. But, of course, Edward's analogy is imperfect in other respects. Theatre, as Beckett spent much of his career demonstrating, is as much a visual as an aural art form, at least as much gesture and plastic imagery as poetry. Theatre is not a music CD. The more apposite analogy might be with opera, and there the analogy breaks down. Most operas have been staged in a myriad of what strict interpreters might consider outlandish versions, and the music has survived, as would Beckett's unique music. But the estate seems adamant and so Beckettian performance in the twenty-first century may be at an impasse.

KENNETH TYNAN'S *BREATH*

> The power of tragedy, we may be sure, is felt even apart from representation and actors.
>
> – Aristotle

Perhaps the most egregious violation of Beckettian law, the sort of thing that Beckett's works apparently need protection from in the after-Beckett, according to those in the business of such protection, occurred during Beckett's lifetime. The result was both a travesty of Beckett's intention, and, ironically, Samuel Beckett's most successful, at least most popular, theatre piece. *Breath* has been problematic since its conception. For many a director, the problem of mounting Samuel Beckett's shortest (but not slightest, I will insist) play, has been less how to stage so short a piece (the options for this characterless, thirty-five-second playlet are really quite limited) than in what context to offer it. Although Beckett called it a "farce in five acts" (qtd. in Cohn 298), it is something less than an evening's theatre. The play is simplicity itself, an anonymous life cycle reduced to its fundamental sounds – birth cry and death groan, which, according to what text there is, sound identical. A debris-littered stage with "[n]o verticals," a brief cry and inspiration as lights fade up for ten seconds; a hold for five more; then expiration, "immediately cry as before," and slow fade down of light. The recorded voices and lighting fades, up and down, are identical and have the simple symmetry of Pozzo's poignant observation: "They give birth astride of a grave, the light gleams an instant, then it's night once more" (*Godot* 58). There seems very little a director can do to muck it up. Its most memorable performance was its first,[11] as the opener, called "Prelude," to the Jacques Levy–directed and Kenneth Tynan–conceived sextravaganza, *Oh! Calcutta!*, the image and title adapted from the painting of Camille Clovis Trouille's posterior odalisque, with its pun on the French "*O quel cul t'as* [*O what a lovely ass you have*]," said "*cul*" being prominently displayed. As an opener to an evening of shorts, by Beckett or a variety of artists, as was the case with the Tynan–Levy production and as it is most frequently performed, the play is inevitably lost. Tynan drew attention to the playlet by adding three words to the opening tableau. To Beckett's "Faint light on stage littered with miscellaneous rubbish," Tynan added, "including naked people" (Calder 6).

Leading off with Beckett, *Oh! Calcutta!* premiered at the Eden Theatre in New York City on 17 June 1969. After a cautious thirty-nine previews, it opened, moving to Broadway on 26 February 1971, where it ran, and ran, and ran, with only slight interruption, until 6 August 1989. Finally, 85 million people saw the 1,314 performances, making it, uncontestedly, the most viewed Beckett play ever, a record unlikely to be broken. Top ticket prices were an astounding US$25.00, "unprecedented even *on* Broadway," according to Bruce Williamson, who introduced the work for a "pictorial essay" in *Playboy* billed as "A Front-Row-Center Look at *Oh! Calcutta!*". *Calcutta!* (known by some wags [so to speak] as Jingle Balls), was "the only show in town that has customers piling into front row-center seats armed, by God, with opera glasses," according to Williamson. But Tynan was called a literary pimp, and his stable of authors, Beckett included, "a pack of whores" (Williamson 167).

As the *Playboy* feature suggests, the musical spawned something of an industry, reflecting the era's sexual revolution and its commodification of sex. A book version of the play was issued by Beckett's American publisher, Barney Rosset of Grove Press, who published the play *as performed* in an illustrated edition in 1969, attributing to Beckett alone the playlet – with Tynan's erotic alterations. While only the earliest playbills identified authors,[12] Rosset's volume listed them under a traditional Table of Contents. The musical was subsequently issued as an LP, was made into a Hollywood film, and is still currently available in CD, VHS, and DVD formats. The enterprise may have been Beckett's sole entry into the Age of Aquarius, certainly his only appearance in *Playboy*. Despite such phenomenal success and unprecedented exposure, drama reduced to its bare necessities, one might say, most respectable critics have generally joined Beckett in the condemnation of at least his contribution to the production. John Calder has argued that "the American edition of *Oh! Calcutta!* has completely changed the atmosphere of sterility and indeed the message itself by changing the stage directions ..."(6). And, indeed, Tynan's revision makes explicit the possibility of regeneration amid the brief seconds between life and death, a possibility already implicit in Beckett's text, since the opening "vagitus" is identical to the closing "cry as before," hence another "vagitus." Moreover, Beckett's characterless drama is never completely so, as the stage is always inhabited at least by the ghosts of actors, afterimages of performances, even in their absence. When actors are not present, memory provides their images, in *Breath* no less than *Godot* or *Hamlet*. Tynan's production merely re-projected, re-directed that implicit image onto the stage.

Breath's association with the infamous *Oh! Calcutta!* has, however, been ignored in early publications, particularly in Grove Press's catchall volume, *First Love and Other Shorts*, published in 1974. The production was finally acknowledged in the *Collected Shorter Plays* of 1984 and the *Complete Dramatic Works* of 1986. Like Calder, Beckett was appalled by Tynan's alterations, but his contract forbade immediate interference, and so the play continued as re-written – at least in the United States. Beckett successfully suppressed his contribution in British productions and moved to halt all future productions. He wrote to agent Jenny Sheridan on 27 April 1972: "I have come to the conclusion it is almost impossible to do *Breath* correctly in the theatre so I must ask you to decline this request and *all future ones for the play*" (emphasis added).[13] But Tynan's production uncovers a haunting subtext, and as such it is a production worthy of re-examination, especially if we accept the necessity of periodic reinvention of Beckett's *oeuvre* that Beckett himself seems to have embraced.

GONTARSKI'S *BREATH,* OR AFTER TYNAN

It was the clamour over Tynan's excesses that kept me thinking about how a director might solve the problems of staging *Breath.* My solution was not to "stage" it at all – that is, not to perform it in a theatrical space – but I also wanted a performance closer to Beckett's than to Tynan's *Breath* and to present it as an independent entity not as part of an evening's theatrical sequence. Moreover, I wanted to foreground what I still consider the play's avant-garde potential, its power to subvert or defy conventions and expectations, to foreground the play of memory, and to shock its audience into thinking, at very least, about performance itself. That was what Deborah Warner wanted with her *Footfalls* that so provoked the ire of the Beckett estate, after all. I needed something other than a theatrical venue for the sort of performance I had envisioned. I kept in mind as well Beckett's comments to his favourite actress, Billie Whitelaw, while they were rehearsing *Footfalls*: "I don't know whether the theatre is the right place for me anymore," Beckett told her. "He was getting further and further away from writing conventional plays," Whitelaw observed. "And I know what he meant. I thought, well perhaps he should be in an art gallery or something. Perhaps I should be pacing up and down in the Tate Gallery . . ." (qtd. in Kalb 235).

My opportunity presented itself in December of 1992, when I was invited to participate in an evening of visual art and performance at Florida State University Gallery and Museum. The evening would be built around the electronic satellite reception of a piece of hypertext, *Agrippa (A Book of the Dead),* from novelist William Gibson. *Agrippa* was scheduled for simultaneous broadcast to nine sites around the world, immediately after which, the piece would be distorted and destroyed by its own viruses. It was in such a fragile and ephemeral artistic environment that I wanted to present *Breath.* The overall plan for the evening was to use the gallery as a decentred theatre space. Events would be performed in several venues of the gallery, and the audience would roam or drift from one to the other with only the slightest prompting. Rather than adopt the structure of an outdoor fair, where simultaneous performances are offered to a roaming audience, the gallery evening would feature sequential performances without overlap. The evening, then, would comprise readings and other theatrical performances and environments among the gallery's various nooks and rooms. My offering was, then, in keeping with the hypertext theme, or rather would present versions of digital or telereality. I decided that *Breath,* like all of Beckett's short plays needed a frame, and since the traditional proscenium arch was unavailable in the gallery, I would create my own. Rather than construct a proscenium, however, I built an oversized prop television, through the absent screen of which *Breath* would be performed "live," if that's the word, or at least the pile of "miscellaneous rubbish" would be physically present in the gallery. In the printed program, I called the performance "A Simulated Television Production," but the heap of "miscellaneous rubbish" was of a piece with other installations in the gallery, so that Beckett's "play" was, for many, indistinguishable from the other art objects on display (or from the gallery's refuse outside the service entrance, for that matter). Mine, or rather Beckett's, was simply framed by an almost clownish simulated television screen. To my mind, this was the continued development of the hybrid art that I take to be Beckett's late theatre, an art of icons, images and afterimages, ghosts of memories – as closely related to sculpture as to what we have traditionally called theatre.

The performance of *Breath*, as opposed to the gallery's other sculptures, was "announced" by the light's fading up on the set, that is, on the heap of rubbish some ten feet behind the television screen, as the gallery lights simultaneously (but only slightly) dimmed. The brief cry (vagitus) and amplified inspiration would sound for some ten seconds, and after the prescribed five-second pause, the expiration and identical cry for some ten seconds. Fade down the stage; fade up the gallery.

Breath was repeated several times during the evening, interspersed amid other performances. I had hoped that such repetition might suggest the regenerative element I saw as implicit in the play (which the theatre-savvy Tynan made explicit). Since I had deliberately chosen to associate Beckett's "play" with sculpture by the very fact of offering the performance in an art gallery, I was not surprised that the audience never seemed to understand that it was watching what I would consider live theatre, since the performance lacked what had heretofore been deemed an essential ingredient of theatre, actors. The audience, deprived of its standard ambience and cultural cues, failed to applaud at the fade down, but neither did they applaud the viewing of other sculptures as they departed, even when the gallery lights dimmed as they did to announce another *Breath*. And, of course, there was no curtain and so no curtain call – whom would we have called, after all? I took that lack of response as a measure of the success of this production, which had blurred the distinction among artistic forms and became, almost, invisible theatre, but while I may have saved the play from being lost amid a sequence of other plays as planned, I may also have lost it to a neo-Dadaist revival of found sculpture.

ATOM EGOYAN: *STEENBECKETT*

One dynamic possibility for the future of performance is that offered by Egyptian-born Canadian film maker Atom Egoyan, who directed a traditional production of *Krapp's Last Tape*, starring John Hurt, for the Beckett on Film series, the ambitious attempt in 2000 to record the Gate Theatre's much toured and touted Beckett festival, during which all nineteen stage plays were performed. Egoyan subsequently used the completed film as a centre-piece for his own personal artwork, an installation at London's Museum of Mankind, the entry dominated by massive marble pillars. The installation folded continuous showings of the film, in altered, antithetical perspectives, into a larger environmental exhibit of recorded memory that Egoyan called *Steenbeckett*. Egoyan's work – like Beckett's – focused on memory, its pres-ervation and evocation. Participants entered the now all-but-deserted Museum of Mankind, walked past stacks of nineteenth-century diaries that obsessionally documented a diarist's every meal, say, or every journey, every bed slept in, every partner slept with. These were the obsessive record-ing of what unrecorded might be deemed incidental, and it seemed to be the exhaustiveness of such documentation that appealed to Egoyan, as it did to Krapp and presumably Beckett. Spectators walked through a darkened warren of passages, up stairs, through tunnels, past discarded typewriters, phonographs, disks, "spoooools," photographs, to a makeshift projection room, where the commercial film of *Krapp's Last Tape* was screened for a restricted audience, 10–12 at a time, sitting on a makeshift bench no more than six feet from the film projected on the opposite wall. The film's grainy images were a massive twelve- to eighteen-feet high, and so they dwarfed the spectators, who had discovered or stumbled upon what seemed to be another discarded cultural object. From there spectators ambled or stumbled to another room, some not waiting for the film to end, others sitting through it more than once. In the next room, a mass of film – two-thousand feet of it, according to the program – ran continuously and noisily along rollers, up and down, back and forth, in and around the room, floor to ceiling, wall to wall, over and over again, and finally through an antique Steenbeck editing table at the far end of the room, where the film was visible in miniature and seen through the cat's cradle of noisily rolling film. Obsolete, the Steenbeck editing machine was the equipment that Egoyan deemed right for editing his film of *Krapp's Last Tape*. The ana-logue device had all the look of a clumsy antique, the look Egoyan was appar-ently trying to achieve in his film. As important as the film itself, both its materiality and the giganticized and miniaturized images it provided, was the material editing machine itself, central to Egoyan's reinvention of *Krapp's Last Tape* and the centrepiece of his installation, as the material tape recorder might be to Beckett's. The play *Krapp's Last Tape* was thus another deteriorating relic, a museum piece, say – Beckett frozen in time – and simultaneously a stunningly fresh work of art (see also Barfield).

ADRIANO AND FERNANDO GUIMARÃES: *TODOS OS QUE CAEM*

The treatment of a Beckett text or performance as a found object, as in Egoyan's *Steenbeckett*, is central to the aesthetics of the Guimarães brothers, visual artists based in Brasilia, Brazil, who have maintained an ongoing and evolving dialogue with Beckett's work since their first show, *Happily Ever After* [*Felizes Para Sempre*], which included various versions of *Happy Days, Come and Go, Play*, and *Rockaby* and which ran, in a variety of venues, almost all in Brazil, from 1998 to 2001. The approach of Adriano and Fernando Guimarães is to combine theatre, performance pieces, music, visual arts, and literature into a hybrid, composite art form and to collaborate with major contemporary artists. For *Happily Ever After*, they worked with plastic artist Ana Miguel, who designed costumes and stage props; with photographer and lighting designer Dalton Camargos; with museum curator Marília Panitz; and with guest actresses Vera Holtz as Winnie in *Happy Days* and Nathalia Thimberg as the "Woman in chair," W, in *Rockaby*. A second instalment of their work *We Were Not Long ... Together*, which ran in a variety of configurations during 2002–03, was built around *Breath* and featured four other pieces: *Catastrophe, Act without Words II, What Where*, and *Play*. The third incarnation of their dialogue with Beckett was built around *All That Fall*, again interspersed with their own videos, photographs, objects, and performance pieces, and featuring as well *Rockaby, Not I, Rough for Theater II*, and *A Piece of Monologue*. These three anthologies, performed over a six-year period, constituted a multimedia trilogy of spectacles in a variety of manifestations that connected Beckett's theatre works to larger public spaces beyond theatre. It was thus, in conception and execution, the very opposite of the Beckett on Film project taking shape at almost the exact same time in Europe. No two manifestations of the Guimarães brothers project were ever the same. Theirs was an art that resisted being reduced to homage, the goal of the film project, presumably.

As art critic Vitória Daniela Bousso writes, "The transition between the visual and the theatrical constitutes a hybrid space, a territory of complexities ruled by experimentation in the work of Adriano and Fernando Guimarães" (97). As their work focuses on the human body, they engage directly the cultural games of regulation and control that are played upon it. For the Guimarães brothers, the body is less ancillary than it might generally be in Beckett, say, and instead becomes the seat of the struggle of power relationships – if not overtly expressed, certainly a subtext of Beckett's work as well. The body is here foregrounded, according to art historian Nicholas Oliveira:

> The body interprets or plays the part of a character but simultaneously represents itself, affirms itself as a recipient of the unconscious, in other words, the body interprets that role, in the installation, that gives access to what is unstable and ephemeral. The body's unpredictable action always offers a condition for rupture or destabilization in the postmodern work. (qtd. in Bousso 98)

Beckett's works are thus treated as ready-mades by the Guimarães brothers and hence in no need of serious revision or renovation, since they are already – preceded and followed, as they are, by images of the Guimarães brothers' re-imagining of Beckett – afterimages of Beckett's texts. The Guimarães' performances are, thus, less critiques of Beckett's work, than reinventions of it, its afterimages. What is elicited from Beckett is as much the result of the Guimarães brothers' installed environments as it is an intrinsic part of the works themselves, and thus Beckett's works move, unadulterated, into a new poetic space – become part of a new poetics. The Guimarães brothers create something like their own Beckett archive, Beckett in or as a cabinet of curiosities, a Beckett made up of cultural shards.

Their antiphonal use of Beckett's works and words is a case in point. Their treatment of the play *Breath*, for example, is presented in conjunction with an installation that they call *Breath +*. Although performed along with other, better known plays, *Breath* here takes on the role of a central work, one version of which features a live, naked actor in an embryonic sack that harkens back to Tynan's *Breath*. Their image, then, foregrounds the regenerative potential of the embryo. Corollary productions, the *Breath +*, feature an actor (or actors) submerged in water who responds to an authoritarian and apparently arbitrary bell that commands and controls his (or their) submersions and resurfacings; hence it controls his (or their) breath. In one version, actors immerse their heads in buckets of water at the bell's command. In another, a single fully clothed actor is submerged in a massive fish tank, the duration of his submersion regulated by the bell. In a third image, submerged actors, again fully clothed, are grotesquely contorted in a bathtub and viewed from above. In each case, the actor's breathing appears subject to or regulated by an arbitrary, external force, in this case a bell or buzzer, but it might be as well the whistle or prod in the two *Acts without Words* or the piercing bell in *Happy Days*, works that the brothers staged as part of this ongoing dialogue. Much of their work, then, spills out of the theatre into gallery space (or out of the gallery back into the theatre). The extension of the playing space emphasizes the idea of expressive space, something other than theatrical space used as a backdrop.

Another performance is called *Light –*. Here, power (much of it in the form of electrical power) is transferred to a participating audience, where spectators turn light switches on and off to control the pace of action in performance. In this case, the light switches are often dummies, the light controlled by a remote switch; so the regulatory system of control is itself diffused, often mysterious, frustrating both actors and audience; thus, the body of the audience (or the audience's bodies) is folded into the performance and into the power struggle. *Double Exposure* is an installation composed of four environments, with the words of several of Beckett's short plays projected onto walls, windows, and transparent boxes. Beckett's words themselves are presented within boxes, as cabinets of curiosities, the eighteenth-century forerunners of what we, today, call museums:

> Along the whole length of the gallery's entrance glass doors there are texts by Samuel Beckett. Upon entering, the spectator finds himself in the first environment: an almost dark rectangular foreroom, outlined by glass panes, on which fragments from texts have also been written. At each end of this room there are life-size pictures of the character that appear throughout the exhibition. The photographs are almost identical, but they reveal the character under the action of two contrasting lights: one that is excessively bright and one that is too dark. Both make its image evanescent. (103)

That is, what we see as apparently life-like is decidedly an image (as Bergson has been reminding us at least since his *Matter and Memory*) or afterimage, its appearance or disappearance regulated by light, which in turn is regulated by (electrical) power, which in turn is regulated (apparently) by spectators. If *Breath+* emphasized the materiality and machinery of the body, *Light –* foregrounded its ethereality. The focus is, thus, on the fact that all perception is imagistic if not imag(e)inary. The second environment is a house, a rectangular prism made of exposed brick, along which Beckett's texts continue. Along its outer walls spectators can look through peepholes and see real-time videos (again images) of the gallery taken by a set of security cameras from a variety of angles. An interior lined with dark panes is the third environment. Here, the audience watches black-and-white video of a character closing windows to stop a flood of light entering that threatens to extinguish his own image, since he is only a projection of light. When vapour lamps are turned on in the room the character's image disappears and the spectator "encounter[s] his or her own reflection on the walls." They (the subjects) have thus *replaced* what appeared to be the "character" (object).

The fourth environment consists of a glass scale model of the house, sitting on a table. Projected images are then reflected on the model's glass and on the room's walls. In another section of the installation, the audience is encouraged to deposit objects, usually, but not exclusively, photographs of sentimental value – but, of course, only to themselves. The audience moves through the installation, lingers, examines, and reads those images on the walls or Beckett's words on or in boxes as a preface or postlude to the performances of those plays that are on display; so that the play itself, once performed, is already an echo, a double, an afterimage.

THE FUTURE OF BECKETT STUDIES AND BECKETT PERFORMANCE

Amid the restrictions on performance imposed by the Beckett estate, its attempts to restrain if not subdue the recalcitrant artwork by its insistence on faithful and accurate performances, a faith and accuracy no one seems able to define, a resilient and imaginative set of theatrical directors and artists continues to re-invent Beckett by developing a third way, through radical acts of the imagination, by folding the authorized, legally owned object, like a ready-made in a gallery, into another context, such as store-fronts, disused or abandoned buildings, or museum installations. They thus assert the heterogeneity of Beckettian performance without violating the dictates of an estate-issued performance contract. "Here, precisely, is the Beckett that will hold the stage in the new century," notes Fintan O'Toole, discussing the issue of fidelity to Beckett's texts in another context (45). "The merely efficient translations of what are thought to be the great man's intentions will fade into dull obscurity. The productions that allow their audiences to feel the spirit of suffering and survival in our times will enter the afterlife of endless re-imaginings" (45). The Guimarães brothers, Atom Egoyan, and others offer one approach to the re-imaginings necessary to a living art. The alternative is that Beckett work be presented as what it may, indeed, have already become, a curio in a box of curiosities, a museum piece preserved, without deviation (except perhaps for deterio-ration), exactly as written (at least in some hypothesized version); but, even so, as I have been suggesting, even such a presentation could be re-imagined and altered radically in a new environment, an alternative space. If the Beckettian stage space has become a battleground for political and legal contention, the squabble one over property rights more than artistic integrity or aesthetic values, those directors who have taken their cue from Beckett's own comments on theatre and the developing aesthetics of his late plays have found their freedom of expression, a liberation of their imaginations, by abandoning or spilling out of that contested space we call theatre into a more expressive one. They have developed a hybrid art, sweeping Beckett along with them, moving theatre to where he always thought it belonged, among the plastic arts, and accomplishing yet another reinvention of Beckett.

NOTES

* This chapter was presented as a contribution to the "Samuel Beckett at 100" Distinguished Lecture Series at the University of Toronto, 10 March 2006.
1 The full details are available in my "Introduction" to *Eleutheria*.
2 The notebooks, transcribed, translated, and annotated, have been published as *The Theatrical Notebooks of Samuel Beckett*.
3 *Das letzte Band* opened at the Schiller Werkstatt on 5 October 1969, on a twin bill with Ionesco's *Der neue Mieter*. Beckett's own direction of *Godot* would not take place until March 1975 at the Schiller-Theater in Berlin.
4 For holograph, see Harmon 219.

5 Gregory's production opened at New York University School of the Arts on 8 February 1973.
6 Good discussions of these productions appear in Oppenheim; for Sontag's *Godot*, see Bradby 164–68.
7 Cited with the permission of Grove Press and the Beckett estate.
8 Cited with permission.
9 Most of these changes are also outlined in Beckett's letter to Blin of 3 April 1968; as Beckett notes, "I strongly recommend to you the following simplifications" (qtd. in Oppenheim 299).
10 For details, see "De-theatricalizing Theatre."
11 The British premiere was given at the Close Theatre Club in Glasgow in October 1969, produced by Geoffrey Gilham, according to John Calder's note in *Gambit*, where the play was first published in its unadulterated form (7).
12 Those for productions at the Eden Theatre and published at first by Evergreen Showcard, a division of Grove Press, and then by Playfare.
13 Cited with the permission of Faber and Faber.

WORKS CITED

Aristotle. "The Definition of Tragedy." *The Poetics of Aristotle*. Trans. S.H. Butcher. New York: Hill, 1961. sec VI.

Barfield, Steve. "In Ghostly Archives Keener Sounds." *The Beckett Circle / Le Cercle de Beckett: Newsletter of the Samuel Beckett Society* 25.1 (2002): 1–2.

Barthes, Roland. "Whose Theater? Whose Avant-Garde?" *Critical Essays*. Trans. Richard Howard. Evanston, IL: Northwestern UP, 1972. 67–70.

Beckett, Edward. "The Wrong Route to the Heart of Beckett." Letter. *Guardian* 24 Mar. 1994: 25.

Beckett, Samuel. "Prologue" [*Breath*]. *Oh! Calcutta!* New York: Grove Press, 1969.

———. Letter to Barney Rosset. 11 July 1973. Rosset Archive. Boston College.

———. Letter to Jenny Sheridan. 27 Apr. 1972. Faber and Faber archive.

———. Letter to Marek Kędzierski. 15 Nov. 1981. Copy in the possession of the author.

———. Letter to Theodor Adorno. 15 Feb. 1969. Frankfurter Adorno Blätter 3/Herausgegeben vom Theodor W. Adorno Archiv. Munchen: edition text + Kritik, 1992. 59.

———. *The Theatrical Notebooks of Samuel Beckett*, Vols. I–IV. General Ed. James Knowlson. New York: Grove Press, 1993–99.

———. *Waiting for Godot* New York: Grove, 1954.

Bousso, Vitória Daniela. "Interstice Zone." Guimarães and Guimarães, *Todos Os Que Caem* 97–99.

Bradby, David. *Beckett: Waiting for Godot*. Cambridge: Cambridge UP, 2001.

Brustein, Robert. "I Can't Go On, Alan. I'll Go On." *New York Times Sunday Book Review*. 31 Jan. 1999. 13–14.

Calder, John. "Samuel Beckett's New Play." *Gambit: An International Theater Review*. 4.16 (1969): 6–7.

Cohn, Ruby. *A Beckett Canon*. Ann Arbor: U of Michigan P, 2001.

Fanger, Iris. "After *Endgame*: JoAnne Akalaitis Throws a *Birthday Party*." *Boston Phoenix* 5–11 Mar. 2004. 6 July 2006, http://www.bostonphoenix.com/boston/events/theater/documents/03644284.asp.

Fehsenfeld, Martha. "Beckett's Reshaping of *What Where* for Television." *Modern Drama*. 29.2 (1986): 229–40.

Feinberg-Jütte, Anat. "'The Task Is Not to Reproduce the External Form, But to Find the Subtext': George Tabori's Productions of Samuel Beckett's Texts." *Journal of Beckett Studies*. 1.1 & 2 (1992) 95–116.

Gontarski, S.E. "Introduction." *Eleutheria*. By Samuel Beckett. Trans. Michael Brodsky. New York: Foxrock, 1995. vii–xxii.

———. "De-theatricalizing Theatre: The Post-*Play* Plays." *The Shorter Plays*. Vol. 4 of Beckett, *Theatrical Notebooks* xv–xxix.

———. "The No against the Nothingness." Introduction. *Endgame*. Vol. 2 of Beckett, *Theatrical Notebooks*. xiii–xxiv.

Guimarães, Adriano, and Fernando Guimarães. "Double Exposure: Multimedia Installations Composed of Four Environments." Guimarães and Guimarães, *Todos Os Que Caem [All That Fall]*. Catalogue. Rio de Janeiro: Centro Cultural Banco do Brasil, 2004. 103–05.

———. *Happily Ever After / Felizes Para Sempre*. Catalogue. Rio de Janeiro: Centro Cultural Banco do Brasil, 2001.

Harmon, Maurice, ed. *No Author Better Served: The Correspondence of Samuel Beckett and Alan Schneider*. Cambridge, MA: Harvard UP, 1998.

Hobson, Harold. "The First Night of *Waiting for Godot*." *Beckett at Sixty: A Festschrift*. London: Calder, 1967, 25–28.

Joyce, James, *Occasional Critical, and Political Writing*. Ed. and notes Kevin Barry. Oxford: Oxford UP, 2000>

Kalb, Jonathan. *Beckett in Performance*. Cambridge: Cambridge UP, 1989.

Knowlson, James. *Damned to Fame: The Life of Samuel Beckett*. New York: Simon, 1996.

———. General Editor's Note. *Waiting for Godot*. Vol. 1 of Beckett, *Theatrical Notebooks* vii–viii.

Knowlson, James, and Elizabeth Knowlson, eds. *Beckett Remembering Remembering Becket: A Centenary Celebration*. New York: Arcade, 2006.

Oppenheim, Lois. *Directing Beckett*. Ann Arbor: U of Michigan P, 1994.

Oliveira, Nicholas. "The Space of Memory: Installation Plays by the Brothers Guimarães." Guimarães and Guimarães, *Happily* 11–17.

O'Toole, Fintan. "Game without End." *New York Review of Books*. 20 Jan. 2000: 43–45.

Williamson, Bruce. "A Front-Row-Center Look at *Oh! Calcutta!*" *Playboy* 10 Oct. 1969: 166–71, 242–43.

8
Uncloseting Drama: Gertrude Stein and the Wooster Group

NICK SALVATO

UNCLOSETING DRAMA

In the late winter and early spring of 2005, the New York theatre troupe the Wooster Group staged, both in Brooklyn and Manhattan, a limited return engagement of their 1999 piece *House/Lights*, an "adaptation" of Gertrude Stein's 1938 play *Doctor Faustus Lights the Lights*. The word "adaptation" belongs firmly in scare quotes, not only because it is a methodological description that the members of the Wooster Group would themselves resist, but also because it simultaneously over- and underrepresents the terms of the group's engagement with Stein's text. If an adaptation is a modified version of a work that nevertheless retains the integrity of and an obvious resemblance to the original, then *House/Lights* falls short of the mark; it is, rather, an eccentric pastiche of many source materials, among which *Doctor Faustus* comprises only one elliptically integrated element. Yet, at the same time as *House/Lights* fails to meet the requirements of an adaptation – and precisely on account of the manner in which it does so – the piece also exceeds the constraints of mere modification and offers instead a rigorous and sophisticated *interpretation* of Stein's text. Of course, every theatrical presentation of a play is an act of interpretation, but the singular nature of the Wooster Group's approach constitutes a mode of analysis more akin to the work of literary criticism than it is to the goals of traditional dramaturgy. In short, the Wooster Group highlights the potential of performance to embody a way of reading, and *House/Lights* highlights, in particular, a way of reading the notoriously difficult Stein. In turn, I propose a reading of Stein alongside – and through the lens of – the Wooster Group, in order to underscore the ways in which the group's complex performance amplifies shades of meaning already at play in Stein's correspondingly complex writing.

Such a project, while potentially useful as a methodological model, would nevertheless remain firmly in the realm of close reading (although not traditional close reading) were it not for the broader cultural and performative phenomenon represented by the Wooster Group's negotiation with Stein: the contemporary "uncloseting" of modernist closet drama – a class of drama that deliberately (and paradoxically) resists performance. Indeed, Stein's plays are best understood alongside the work of other major American modernists (among whom Djuna Barnes, T.S. Eliot, Mina Loy, Ezra Pound, William Carlos Williams, and Louis Zukofsky might be named) who also turned, in the early and mid-twentieth century, to the writing of closet drama, a genre that had last fully flowered roughly one hundred years earlier. Likewise, the Wooster Group is only one among many important professional companies to stage such modernist closet drama in the last thirty or so years.

Why this twentieth-century interest in and resuscitation of closet drama? I contend that the queer potential of the genre belongs prominently among the reasons for its modernist renewal. In his own recent work on modernist closet drama, Martin Puchner suggests that closet drama has always been marked by what he calls "various forms of ambiguity and deviance" (17). And it is true that the "ambiguity and deviance" that he identifies as symptomatic of closet drama as such inform plays like Byron's *Manfred* and Shelley's *The Cenci*, both of which explore homoerotic and incestuous subjects. Nevertheless, only in the twentieth century, when sexual discourses are ubiquitous and sexual identities are codified, does the queering of closet drama become a truly significant phenomenon.

In describing modernist closet drama as distinctly queer closet drama, I revert, perhaps unfashionably, to the formulation of queerness most popularly espoused by academics in the early and mid-1990s. As I intend it, the word "queer" designates not so much a category as a border-crossing between categories, if not the contestation of categorization altogether. I use the concept of queerness not to designate a static site of lesbian and gay identity but to gesture toward transgressive *movements* between and among different positions of sex, gender, and desire. Queerness has come under fire for precisely the definitional disruptions that I describe here and that I take to be a methodological strength. Indeed, such a method is required to attend to the nuanced works of modernist authors because the authors themselves resisted or rejected certain conceptions of sexual identity taking hold in the late nineteenth and early twentieth centuries. Most notoriously (and oft cited) among them, Djuna Barnes declared about her relationship with her long-time female lover, "I'm not a lesbian. I just loved Thelma" (qtd. in Michel 53); but in myriad and arguably more subtle ways, Barnes and her modernist peers all used their dramatic work to interrogate received notions about sexuality. Nor is it an accident that the work in question should take the form of closet drama. Just as closet drama approaches the stage (if it does so at all) ambivalently and ambiguously, so does the queer refuse to fit neatly into stable sexual roles. Thus, queerness produces confusions and contortions akin to those of closet drama, and closet drama provides a uniquely suitable space for the expression of queer sensibilities. Modernist authors exploit this suitability as they seek simultaneously to challenge sexual normativities and dramatic conventions.

Both the sexual and dramatic challenges of modernist closet drama have a specifically temporal dimension. As early twentieth-century authors look backward for models – to the plays of ancient Greece, Rome, and Japan, or to romantic verse drama – so too do they look forward and imagine sometimes utopian possibilities for theatrical and erotic representation that have yet to come into being. Following the critic Kenneth Cox's conjecture that closet drama seeks the theatre – or, more broadly, the *polis* – of the future (43), I argue that modernist closet drama remained closeted until the end of the twentieth century because the conditions of the theatre had not yet caught up to the drama's vision. After the efflorescence of performance art in the 1960s, new generations of theatre practitioners (such as the Wooster Group) could bring to bear techniques and styles of staging – indeed, perverse media – uniquely suited to the adaptation of notoriously difficult modernist works. Modernist closet drama required (and, in a sense, anticipated) the advent of innovations in postmodern performance.

To be sure, modernist dramatic experiments reward close – if not closet – reading, and many of their opaque meanings only begin to become clear to the industrious student who pores over their words. Yet the most industrious students have often been the actors, directors, and other performance artists who have paid attention to these challenging texts, many of which have been almost entirely overlooked by the academy – and the proof of their non-academic but serious and rigorous "reading" is in the traces of their performances. Reading modernist drama through the lens of performance, as I do in this paper, offers a corrective to those literary scholars who would privilege the former over the latter – to the detriment, in my view, of richer understanding. Our understanding of the queer textures of modernist closet drama is, in particular, enriched by a consideration of such drama's performance history. In performance, sexed and gendered "embodiment" – and, at times, embodiment that calls into question the categories of sex and gender – constitutes an interpretive dimension that mere reading (or at least our fantasy of disembodied reading) does not usually accommodate.

Where reading Stein, in particular, is concerned, calling her plays closet dramas requires some qualification and justification, and the term "closet drama" needs to be situated among various critical perspectives. In the most recent book-length study of Stein's drama, *Mama Dada: Gertrude Stein's Avant-Garde Theater*, Sarah Bay-Cheng rejects the idea that Stein's plays ought to be construed as closet dramas. Bay-Cheng, who wants to tell a developmental narrative about Stein's dramatic writing and who is interested in the connections between experimental writing and the cinematic revolution, suggests that "the cinema made a profound impression on [Stein's] dramatic writing after 1929" and "helped her to understand how to manipulate time and meaning on stage." As a consequence of Stein's confrontation with film, Bay-Cheng argues, "Stein's best dramatic writing emerges only after her second, more adventurous film experiment [a screenplay] in 1929." Although "[t]he methods of making movies and staging plays are obviously different," Bay-Cheng believes that Stein eventually wrote with an eye to performance precisely because of her exposure to cinematic methods of representation (35).

Several significant issues call into question the validity of Bay-Cheng's account. Chiefly, the strength of her argument rests on the credibility of the idea that cinema made, in Bay-Cheng's words, "a profound impression" on Stein, but there is scant evidence to support this claim, and, in fact, no compelling reason to distrust Stein's own claim in the essay "Plays" that "I myself never go to the cinema or hardly ever practically never and the cinema has never read my work or hardly ever" (xxxv).[1] Moreover, Bay-Cheng's interest in the relationship between cinema and Stein's drama motivates her to ignore the many writings that Stein labelled "plays" before 1929, as though these dramatic efforts do not count as such because they do not serve her argument. A closer look than Bay-Cheng allows at the similarities between Stein's early and late plays suggests that an uncomplicated story of Stein's so-called growth and maturity as a dramatist is untenable. Many of Stein's late plays, not mentioned by Bay-Cheng, continue to resemble early efforts in their lack of discernible plot, character, or dialogue. And even the late plays that do attract her attention – what she calls "Stein's best dramatic writing" – disrupt dramaturgical conventions in ways that Bay-Cheng fails to consider out of a desire, it would seem, to uphold a notion of Stein as a dramatist who ultimately learned how to write a "good" play. I finally view with suspicion Bay-Cheng's preserving traditional notions of theatricality and her having recourse to taste to camouflage (or at least to suspend contention with) the conservatism of her point of view. Though Bay-Cheng applauds, early in her book, Stein's moving away from Freytag's schema of dramatic structure (19), Stein, in fact, in the most radical of her dramatic experiments, goes far beyond dismissing rising and falling action. Indeed, I would cite her extreme radicality – the at times complete abandonment of theatrical method and principle in her plays – as the signal factor that makes Stein such a compelling figure in the history of modern drama.

I would also cite this extreme radicality as the basis on which to understand Stein as a closet dramatist. We need not suppose that Stein only intended her plays to be read – or indeed suppose any programmatic intention at all – to call the work "closet drama." Rather, the term closet drama may be assigned to Stein's work simply because of her refusal to follow the rules – anyone's rules – of how to write a play. As an essay such as "Plays" makes clear, Stein was not ignorant of the mechanics of staging a play. Far from it, she had thought deeply about – and was dissatisfied and frustrated with – the disjunction between what she called one's "emotional time as an audience" and "the emotional time of the play" ("Plays" xxix). At the same time, her plays do not, in any obvious or immediate way, propose an alternative mechanics to compensate for the "syncopated time" of the theatre (xxix); they simply do away with the mechanics altogether by blurring beyond recognition the distinctions among dialogue, *didascalia*, and other diegetic language that seems to belong to the province of neither dialogue nor *didascalia*. Puchner, who also views Stein as a closet dramatist, attributes such perverse playwriting strategies to Stein's "conflicted form of resistance [to the theatre], a resistance that entails a simultaneous attachment to the theater" (111). While I appreciate the finesse with which Puchner identifies Stein's ambivalence toward the theatre, I would finally characterize the form that this ambivalence takes less as a resistance to theatricality than as a taunting provocation to theatre practitioners. Stein's plays so aggressively violate theatrical norms that they constitute an implicit challenge. "Stage *this*," they seem egotistically to dare, beckoning an ingenious director to top Stein's own ingenuity. Elizabeth LeCompte, the perhaps equally aggressive director of the Wooster Group, took up just such a challenge in *House/Lights*, and the result is a kinky homage to Stein's *Doctor Faustus* that pays special attention to the ways in which Stein's violation of theatrical norms dovetails with her more general interest in violation, violence, and sadism.

Imagine the following cinematic scene. In the middle of the woods, a woman holds one end of a rope, the other end of which is tied around another woman. The first woman, anchored on one spot of muddy ground, whips the second woman and forces the bound woman to run in circles around her. Because of the way in which the shots are framed, we never see the whip touch the skin of the second woman. Rather, the camera cuts back and forth, repetitively, between dizzying shots of the woman running in circles and equally dizzying shots of the trees and the sky, also whirring by in a series of circles. The viewer identifies with the woman's torture not because the torture is imaged directly, but because the cinematography makes him or her feel as disoriented as the victim of the whipping. Similarly, in Stein's 1938 play *Doctor Faustus Lights the Lights*, a reader understands the heroine's pain and confusion when she is stung by a viper not because the viper sting is graphically depicted, but because the heroine's repetitive and obsessive language in the aftermath of the sting makes the wound unforgettable, invests the sting with indelible importance, and, in effect, *stings* the reader.

Like the scene from Stein's *Doctor Faustus*, the cinematic scene that I have just described is neither imaginary nor incidental. Indeed, it is the penultimate scene of *Olga's House of Shame*, the 1964 film that the Wooster Group juxtaposed with portions of Stein's text in *House/Lights*. As I offer a reading of both Stein's play and the Wooster Group's production, I will explain more fully both Stein's investment in sexual domination and the Wooster Group's understanding of and sensitivity to that investment. I will also stay attuned to the queer dynamics of Stein's drama, which have been all but ignored by critics of her plays (a surprisingly small concentric loop within the otherwise large circle of Stein scholars).[2] Though the "queerness" of Stein's writing is evident everywhere throughout her corpus, I find in the particular nexus of sex, violence, and dramatic experimentation toward which I have gestured here one of the most fruitful areas for a queer inquiry into her work.

A ROSE (IS A ROSE IS A ROSE IS A ROSE) BY ANY OTHER NAME?

In the same perverse spirit with which Stein wrote *Doctor Faustus*, I want to begin my discussion of the play not with its eponymous protagonist but with a seemingly unrelated figure: Lord Berners, a British aristocrat and composer who hosted and befriended Stein during a visit to England and who later wrote the music for the 1937 production of *A Wedding Banquet*, a balletic adaptation of Stein's play *They Must. Be Wedded. To Their Wife.* Berners's professional association with Stein did not end with his musical composition for *A Wedding Banquet*. Stein, who attended and was delighted by a performance of the ballet at Sadler's Wells, approached Berners as a potential collaborator on a new project that she had in mind: an opera of the Faust story. Originally conceived with no reference to Faust and as a novel called *Ida* (a version of which was later completed and published), the project mutated into *Doctor Faustus Lights the Lights* in early 1938.[3] Sarah Bay-Cheng convincingly dates this turn to Stein's attendance of a performance of *Don Giovanni*:

> Apparently, Stein decided to shift from novel to drama during the performance of Mozart's *Don Giovanni* on February 23, 1938 at the Académie Nationale de Musique et de Danse. Among the notes she scribbled in her production program that evening were an opening stage direction for *Doctor Faustus* ... The program notes themselves for *Don Giovanni* may have also influenced Stein's decision to combine the woman from *Ida* with the Faust myth. An announcement of upcoming productions listed the performance of Charles-François Gounod's *Faust* ... Also included in the program was a photograph from the Académie's

production of Hector Berlioz's *The Damnation of Faust* (1846) presented earlier in 1938. (74–76)

Stein began writing *Faustus* shortly after this performance, and two months later, she had already seduced Berners into providing the music to accompany her words. On 28 April 1938, Berners wrote to Stein, "Please send me the first act of Doctor Faustus. I was very thrilled by what you showed me [on a visit to Stein's home in Paris] and read to me – and I want to have it by me and as soon as I've finished my present business I'll start on it." Between May and October of 1938, Stein sent Berners drafts of the opening acts of *Faustus* and modified them according to his suggestions: "I think that perhaps in the 1st act the sentences ought to be a little longer at the opening. Doctor Faustus ought to start off with an aria – this is from a musical point of view – but we can discuss all this when we meet" (May/June 1938). "Perhaps I may ask you to alter one or two words here and there that are difficult vocally. Words like 'miserable' are sometimes awkward – but we can easily fix that together when I start the music" (15 Oct. 1938).

How much music Berners ever wrote for *Faustus* – or whether he really started at all – is unclear, but in December 1939, by which point Stein had long before completed the libretto, Berners announced, in a very moving letter, his inability to continue work on the project:

My dear Gertrude
I was delighted to get your letter and to hear that things are not too bad with you. What I want to say is, and it makes me very sad to say it – that all inspirational sources seem to have dried up: I can't write a note of music or do any kind of creative work whatever and it's not for want of trying and I don't believe I shall be able to as long as this war lasts. I feel confronted with the break-down of all the things that meant anything to me and the thought of it has got into my subconscious and filled it up to the exclusion of anything else. Not being able to find a note of music is driving me mad. I don't know when I shall be able to go on with Faust. That is why I very reluctantly suggest that you give it to someone else. Virgil Thompson [sic] perhaps. It makes me miserable to think of anyone else doing it. But it is unfair to you if I keep hold of it when I can't do it. And I really feel at present that I shall never be able to write music again. I had a letter from Francis he is in Cornwall. He stayed for a long time with Cecil and I gather they ended by getting on each others [sic] nerves. Give my love to Alice and bless you both.
Love from Gerald

Honouring her friendship to Berners, Stein never did send *Faustus* to Thomson or to anyone else – and so, with Berners's retreat from the music, *Faustus* retreated into the closet. Though Stein began and revised the play, unlike almost any of her other dramatic works, with an assumption of and an eye toward eventual performance, I would nevertheless argue that *Faustus* was always a sort of closet drama. Stein writes stage directions and assigns dialogue to specific characters in *Faustus* more obviously than she does in other plays, but she is not consistent in her approach. At times, she lapses into explanatory prose that reads more like a novel than a play ("As she went she began to sing"; "The dog sighs and says"), and she renders so poetically lines that could be construed simply as stage directions that they, too, demand to be set to music: "Faustus gives him an awful kick, and Mephisto moves away and the electric lights just then begin to get very gay" (*Doctor Faustus* 91–99). As with *Four Saints in Three Acts*, Stein must have assumed that others (Berners, for instance) would worry about the details of adapting her words and making them suitable for the stage.

One particularly difficult decision for performance concerns the character Marguerite Ida and Helena Annabel. Though she has two (compound) names, she is one woman[4] – but ought that necessarily to mean that one actress should play the role? Two actresses speaking or singing her lines in unison might allow for interesting physical choreography and vocal harmonies. Moreover, Marguerite Ida and Helena Annabel speaks at times to "herself" in such a way that she seems to divide into Marguerite Ida, on the one hand, and Helena Annabel, on the other. Consider the pivotal moment at which she is stung by a viper:

> There is a rustling under the leaves and Marguerite Ida and Helena Annabel makes a quick turn and she sees that a viper has stung her, she sees it and she says and what is it. There is no answer. Does it hurt she says and then she says no not really and she says was it a viper and she says how can I tell I never saw one before but is it she says and she stands up again and sits down and pulls down her stocking and says well it was not a bee not a busy bee no not, nor a mosquito nor a sting it was a bite and serpents bite yes they do perhaps it was one. (96–97)

Practically, Marguerite Ida and Helena Annabel's dialogue with herself, posed as a series of questions and answers, suggests the possibility that one actress could ask about the viper and another could respond to her. At the same time, the scene's comic potential might best be mined by one actress speaking all the lines. "Was it a viper," she would ask, no doubt earning a laugh when she replied to herself with exasperation, "[H]ow can I tell I never saw one before." Yet, for all of its humour, the scene is also full of menace; and Marguerite Ida and Helena Annabel's division from herself, as a result of the viper sting, has important thematic and theatrical implications.

When she first appears onstage, Marguerite Ida and Helena Annabel is stably two in one, and this paradoxical status represents her erotic communion with herself. Something like Luce Irigaray's famous "two lips" touching each other (24), her simultaneous singularity and duality represent a woman's desire not simply or narcissistically for herself but for her self's other, in a complex constellation that escapes any sort of phallic economy – until the viper sting, that is. Suggesting, at least in part, some sort of sexual violation, if not an outright rape, the sting threatens Marguerite Ida and Helena Annabel's autoerotic completeness and plunges her into an existential confusion about her singly multiple (or multiply single) identity: "And I am I Marguerite Ida or am I Helena Annabel/Oh well/Am I Marguerite Ida or Helena Annabel/Very well oh very well/Am I Marguerite Ida very well am I Helena Annabel." This doubt about her own nature is mirrored by a doubt about the nature of her injury: "She stops she remembers the viper and in a whisper she says was it a sting was it a bite am I all right; was it a sting was it a bite, all right was it a sting, oh or was it a bite" (97). Ironically, her desire to continue to resist easy categorization or classification – to be both Marguerite Ida and Helena Annabel – gives way here to a desire, repetitively expressed, to categorize her hurt as either one (a sting) or the other (a bite). Indeed, the "poison" that runs now through her veins and for which she eventually seeks a cure from Doctor Faustus, seems to be the poisonous impulse toward overly schematic classification. The dominion that comes with (misrepresentative) linguistic mastery and fixity – and for which Marguerite Ida and Helena Annabel earns "an artificial viper there beside her and a halo ... around her" – comes at the price of her own eventual domination (104). Prefigured by the viper sting, a "man from ... over the seas" called Mr. Viper comes to subjugate Marguerite Ida and Helena Annabel sexually and to make her his "[p]retty pretty pretty dear ... all my love and always here" (107). He is egged on by a little boy and girl who insist repetitively and creepily on the heteronormativity of their gender assignments (and who, through a slippage of language, admit inadvertently that they are "annoying"): "Mr. Viper dear Mr. Viper, he is a boy I am a girl she is a girl I am a boy we do not want to annoy but we do oh we do oh Mr. Viper yes we do we want you to know that she is a girl that I am a boy" (109). Through a sinister tautology that provides the scaffolding for an even more sinister logic, boys are boys, girls are girls, and women belong with and to men – certainly not with or by themselves. Following this verbal assault by Mr. Viper and the children and further, repeated threats from Faustus, Marguerite Ida and Helena Annabel makes one last valiant effort to defend her sexual autonomy – "I am Marguerite Ida and Helena Annabel and I know no man or devil no viper and no light and I can be anything and everything and it is always always all right" – but as she says these words "she falls back," like the swooning heroine of a nineteenth-century melodrama, "fainting into the arms of the man from over the seas" (118).

Before Marguerite Ida and Helena Annabel comes to this tragic end, it is none other than Faustus who recognizes the power of her name and who denies her a cure to the viper sting. As he insists to the little dog that is his companion, "She will not be ... never never never, never will her name be Marguerite Ida and Helena Annabel" (95). No doubt the doctor would prefer to inhabit an earlier and simpler version of his legend, in which he could identify without complication Marguerite and Helena as a modern woman and an ancient Greek adulteress, respectively – and Ida and Annabel wouldn't even enter the picture. Nor is Faustus the only one to be troubled by or puzzle over Marguerite Ida and Helena Annabel's name(s).[5] Critics have expended a great deal of energy tracing the various mythological, classical, literary, and historical allusions embedded in the quadruplicate; and while I applaud this effort and assent largely to the findings, I want to suggest an alternative inspiration and genesis for the character. Consider the following list of names: Bella, Anna; Black, Ida; Griffin, Marguerite; McCoy, Helen. These four names are culled from the thousands of entries (among whom many other Marguerites, Idas, Helens, Annas, and Bellas might be cited) in a Storyville *Blue Book* preserved among Stein's papers in the Yale Collection of American Literature. Storyville was a red-light district of New Orleans where, between 1898 and 1917, prostitution was legal, and the blue books were directories of the women who worked there. Based on information provided by Al Rose in *Storyville, New Orleans: Being an Authentic, Illustrated Account of the Notorious Red-Light District*, Stein's edition of the *Blue Book* (the fifth and final) can be dated to a period between 1912 and 1915 (146).[6] Whether Stein received the *Blue Book* from a friend who had been to New Orleans during that period, or whether she acquired it belatedly and as a curio during her own visit to the city in the 1930s, remains unclear. Indeed, it is unclear whether Stein would have known anything, beyond the information that the *Blue Book* itself provides, about the women who lived in New Orleans's self-proclaimed "Queer Zone" – and just how queer some of them were.[7] Perhaps Stein could not have known, for instance, of Norma and Diana, the proprietresses of the "French House," that "[b]oth women were reportedly lesbians" (Rose 77), but her imagination could certainly have been piqued by the innuendo of the following *Blue Book* advertisement: "Why visit the playhouses to see the famous Parisian models portrayed, when one can see the French damsels, Norma and Diana? Their names have become known on both continents, because everything goes as it will, and those that cannot be satisfied there must surely be of a queer nature" (n. pag.). As Stein wrote *Doctor Faustus* in her own French house, might not these "model-quality" prostitutes have provided the models for Marguerite Ida and Helena Annabel? It is certainly no stretch of imagination to suppose that Stein could have had enough interest in the *Blue Book* for it to influence the composition of *Faustus*. Stein loved names and also loved to list them; her play *Short Sentences*, which she wrote just six years before *Faustus* and in which she names a long series of characters who each speak one line, reads less like a play than a directory – and at times like a directory of prostitutes (consider the sequence of "Frederika Holding," "Marguerite Line," and "Madge Cotton") (329).

In proposing the *Blue Book* as a background for and subtextual current in *Doctor Faustus*, I do not mean to underestimate the importance to Stein of such precursors as Marlowe and Shakespeare or even to diminish the fruitful connections to be drawn between *Faustus* and Stein's novel *Ida*, an early draft of which became the basis for the play. Rather, I wish only to underscore further a point that I have also tried to develop through a strictly intra-textual reading: Marguerite Ida and Helena Annabel's story, like many stories that emerge from Storyville, concerns a queer woman who is bought (metaphorically, at least) by a man. She finally has as much in common with Goethe's Gretchen as she does with Emma Johnson, described by Al Rose as a "wench ... [e]arly drawn to lesbianism, [who] exercised a strange power over many of her sex and took great pride in the fact" (50).[8] This description could apply equally well to Marguerite Ida and Helena Annabel, whose viper sting grants her a similarly strange power over an ever-growing audience of followers. Stein writes of her heroine's adoring female fans: "See how they come/See how they come/To see her./See how they come" (106). It is only a matter of time before the man from over the seas joins the country women to admire her, and then she, like Emma Johnson before her, must stage a show for his benefit. Just as the play's electric lights thematize technological anxiety, and its eponymous protagonist points us toward religious conundrums, so too is *Doctor Faustus* a queer meditation on shifting sexual power relations.

No readers of the play have understood these power relations better than the Wooster Group.

"GOING THE LIMIT"

In a foreword to David Savran's book *Breaking the Rules: The Wooster Group*, Peter Sellars (then director at the American National Theater) offered the following prognostication about the Wooster Group:

> Anyone with an interest in theater in the United States of America in 1986 owes it to themselves to know what some of the latest developments are. If theater in the United States is to become large again, the Wooster Group is out there, up ahead,

scouting the way. They are inventing theatrical vocabulary that ten and twenty years from now will become the lingua franca of a revivified American Theater. For my money, they are the most important theater company in our country today. (xvi)

Despite the controversy that some of the Wooster Group's productions have provoked and the distaste that certain critics have for their methods, at least some parties would still assent to Sellars's claim that "they are the most important theater company in our country today." And now that the ten and twenty years that he projected have elapsed, even more would concur that Sellars's prediction has come true and that the Wooster Group's theatrical language has become American theatre's "lingua franca"; as Nick Kaye attested in 1996, "Through its challenging and innovative nature, the Wooster Group's work has become the focal point around which much contemporary practice as well as performance theory and criticism positions itself" (253). In his description of the "challenging and innovative nature" of the Wooster Group's work, David Savran identifies five common, salient "objects" or elements in such diverse early productions as *Rumstick Road, Nayatt School*, and *L.S.D.* – elements that persist in such later pieces as *Brace Up!, To You, the Birdie!*, and *Poor Theater*: "recordings of private interviews or public events"; "previously written dramatic material"; "prerecorded sound, music, film and video"; the use of "various architectonic elements" of the performance space of one piece "in the development of a new piece"; and "improvised action-texts: gesture, dance and language to be used either as an independent strand in the work or as an elaboration of material from one of the other categories" (51). As the Wooster Group synthesizes these various elements of performance in the manner of a collage, no hierarchical relationship is established in advance among the different elements. Perhaps more importantly, no idea or theme is explicitly sought outside a persistent emphasis on the forms, patterns, rhythms, and movements that inhere necessarily in their structurally complex performances. As Elizabeth LeCompte, the group's director, explains,

> The most important thing in all of this is that ... I don't have any thematic ideas – I don't even have a theme. I don't have anything except the literal objects – some flowers, some images, some television sets, a chair, some costumes I like ... And then the ideas come after the fact. It's a total reversal of most of the processes. (260)

The "object" with which the group's 1999 piece *House/Lights* began was a 1964 film, *Olga's House of Shame*, directed by Joseph Mawra and now considered to be a camp classic. *Olga's House of Shame* was a sequel to the popular *White Slaves of Chinatown*, a film with an auspicious pedigree as the cinema's first "nudie-kinkie," "a subgenre obsessed with sadistic bondage and fetish situations" and distinct from "the 'nudie-roughie,' which primarily dealt with rape themes, and the 'nudie-ghoulie,' which threw graphic violence and horror elements into the mix" (Firsching). Both films concern the escapades of Olga Petroff (Audrey Campbell), a sadistic procuress with lesbian inclinations and a high-ranking member of a nebulously defined crime syndicate. Olga taunts, whips, burns, stockades, racks, and otherwise brutalizes young women until they agree to her demands, which usually amount to prostituting themselves to her "business associates," peddling drugs, or smuggling jewels. *Olga's House of Shame*, like its predecessor, is a grainy, black-and-white film with low production values, sparse dialogue, and a heavy reliance on sleazily and melodramatically intoned narratorial voice-overs, such as the following gem:

> Olga was still playing her cat-and-mouse game with Nadja. She would tie her to a tree and leave her there as long as a day at a time without doing anything else. This method eventually disturbed Nadja and slowly began working on her nervous system. Nadja never knew what to expect. Did Olga really know what to do with her? Was Olga stalling for time? What was Olga up to?

After several years and incarnations of pieces that deconstructed the work of Eugene O'Neill, the Wooster Group decided in 1996 that *Olga's House of Shame* would be a crucial element in their next project, though they, perhaps like Olga, didn't "really know what to do with it" or "what they were up to" yet. As Clay Hapaz, the assistant director of *House/ Lights*, explained to me, *Olga* first came to the attention of the group when it was privately screened for him, Elizabeth LeCompte, and the actress Kate Valk (the "star" of *House/Lights*) by friend and film critic Dennis Dermody. Immediately upon seeing the film, LeCompte and Valk exclaimed that they had found "it"; shortly thereafter, the company began doing improvisational work with and around the film during rehearsals at the Performing Garage on Wooster Street, the Manhattan performance space that the group has inhabited since its formation in the 1970s. Along the way, the decision to juxtapose pieces of the film with excerpts of Stein's *Faustus* was something of a fortuitous accident. In an interview that I conducted with LeCompte and Valk, LeCompte explained that she had long been encouraged by friends and colleagues to work with a Stein text and specifically with *Faustus*. She had been reading Stein for some time, but she had shied away from undertaking *Faustus* because she feared the overdetermining influence of the play's many earlier incarnations in the hands of other avant-garde directors and luminaries: Judith Malina at the Living Theater; Lawrence Kornfeld at Judson Church; Richard Foreman at the Festival d'Automne; and, most recently, Robert

Wilson at a variety of international theatres. Nevertheless, as she worked with *Olga* and continued to read Stein, she realized that she couldn't avoid the "perfect fit" that *Olga* and *Faustus* made with one another, and so the play joined the growing brew of rehearsal elements. In a slow and repetitive process that wrought small changes over the course of many months, some members of the group would read Stein aloud as others acted out scenes from the film, and the two began to converge.

When I first viewed *Olga's House of Shame*, my knee-jerk, academic response was an objection to what I perceived as an improbable male fantasy of lesbian S/M. But it was precisely the *fantastic* elements of the film – the strange camera angles and stylized acting, which *Olga* shares with contemporaneous 1960s "art" films – that struck the Wooster Group. I asked LeCompte and Valk whether their initial enthusiasm for *Olga* stemmed from attraction or revulsion, and they responded without hesitation that theirs was an unalloyed attraction to the film. In addition to the aesthetic appeal that *Olga* held for them, as a piece that could call into question the boundary between highbrow art and lowbrow entertainment, they must also have been intimately interested in the film's exploration of power dynamics between women. LeCompte and Valk described *House/Lights* as, in part, a reflection upon and assessment of their own working and personal relationship (Personal interview). This observation invites a measured comparison between Olga and LeCompte, who has responded with ambivalence and even self-contradiction to the suggestion that she is an "autocratic director." She has said,

> I think I have an autocratic style. I don't think that the way I work is autocratic. I like to run a tight ship. I like to have the final say, not so much because I want the power of it, but because otherwise, I lose my way. These workers bring this material to me, and I sift and siphon through it ... It's a slow process, and it's not democratic in any way. But autocratic is the wrong word for it. (Savran 115–16)

In Olga's syndicate, there is no question that she is an autocrat and a successful one – until, that is, her power is challenged by the upstart Elaine, whose relationship with Olga is at the centre of the film and who double-crosses Olga in a jewel-smuggling operation. Elaine says, as she subsequently cuts a deal with her boss, "I think it would be nice to be the hunter this time instead of the hunted." Olga grants Elaine more and more power in the organization, and the film ends with the narrator's description of a newly forged, unholy alliance between them:

> This day marked another triumph for Olga. The day that her protégé took over the reins as second in command. This was a day that Elaine had been waiting for, and she wasn't going to let anything or anyone stop her now.

Yes, this was a proud day for Olga. She had created Elaine in her own image and likeness. Now there were two of them. Two vicious minds working as one. Set upon the destruction of all who stood in their way, by whatever means possible.

References to viciousness and destruction aside, this passage must have conjured for LeCompte and Valk a sense of the evolution of their own collaboration. Though earlier pieces by the Wooster Group focused chiefly on performances by male members of the company, including Spalding Gray, Willem Dafoe, and Ron Vawter, *House/Lights* places the reins firmly in Valk's hands.

With Valk at centre stage, and given *Olga*'s emphasis on the "twinning" of Olga and Elaine, whom Olga creates "in her own image and likeness," we might expect the collision in *House/Lights* of *Olga's House of Shame* with *Doctor Faustus Lights the Lights* to focus on the patently queer figure of Marguerite Ida and Helena Annabel. Indeed, Kate Valk exclaimed to me with an almost childlike glee, "This is our lesbian piece!" – but the seeming innocence of this declaration belies the complex ways in which *House/Lights* construes and constructs lesbianism as such (Personal interview). In the "final" version of the piece (if any performance of the Wooster Group's endlessly retooled works can be called final), Valk plays the role of "Elaine/Faustus," and Suzzy Roche joins her onstage as "Olga/Mephistopheles." Much of the piece's minutely detailed choreography focuses on longing glances and slow caresses between Valk and Roche – that is, when Roche is not cracking the whip at Valk or holding Valk aloft and upside down to mime a bite of her inner thigh (Figure 1). This last moment, placed at the end of the first act of *House/Lights*, comes as Valk delivers the line, "A viper has bitten her she knows it too a viper has bitten her believe it or not it is true, a viper has bitten her and if Doctor Faustus does not cure her it will be all through her a viper has bitten her a viper a viper." Like nearly all of the Stein text incorporated into *House/Lights*, this account of the viper sting figures as part of one long (though frequently interrupted) monologue, assigned to Elaine/Faustus and delivered by Valk in an electronically modified, "dewdrop Betty Boop voice" (Sebastian). Marguerite Ida and Helena Annabel's sexual plight is subsumed under Faustus's presiding consciousness, as Faustus in turn morphs into Elaine and embodies aspects of her alternation between masochistic victimization and sadistic domination.

As Marguerite Ida and Helena Annabel says of Faustus in Stein's play, "Doctor Faustus a queer name" (98), and LeCompte certainly mines the latent queer potential of the character in her cross-gender casting and her fusion of Faustus with Elaine. Just as Faustus resists and denies his pact with Mephistopheles, to whom he has sold his soul "to make white electric light and day-light and night light," but without whom, he

Figure 1: *House/Lights*. (l-r) Suzzy Roche, Ari Fliakos, and (upside down) Kate Valk
Photo © Mary Gearhart.

claims, he can still "do everything" (89), so too does Elaine chafe at her ser-
vitude to Olga ("I think it would be nice to be the hunter this time instead
of the hunted"). In the end, neither Faustus nor Elaine can escape their alli-
ances with Mephistopheles and Olga, respectively. Elaine joins Olga in her
torture of the other girls, and Faustus, who cannot resist Mephistopheles's
"will of iron," "sinks into the darkness" with the devil (118). As *Olga's House
of Shame* plays almost continuously on television monitors placed at the
front and back of the stage (Figure 2), and as the actors shift between imitative recreations of the film's action and impressionistic riffs on Stein's text,
the parallels between *Faustus* and *Olga* become clear – just as they are distorted and reconfigured. Faustus's spiritual indenture to Mephistopheles
becomes an erotic indenture to a sexually appetitive, lesbian devil; as Olga
says when she stumbles upon one of her girls, Marianna, performing a
belly dance for some of the others, "These kids were ready to go the limit.
All that they needed was a little push in the right direction. And that's just
what I was going to do."

For the Wooster Group, "going the limit" meant more than simply staging
a confrontation between *Faustus* and *Olga*. As the piece developed gradually
over a two-year-long period of rehearsals, other elements were also woven
into the fabric of the production, either as video or sound: clips from

Figure 2: *House/Lights.* (l-r) Peyton Smith, Kate Valk, and Roy Faudree
Photo © Mary Gearhart.

various Hollywood musicals of the 1930s and from the Mel Brooks spoof *Young Frankenstein* (1974); a musical number from an episode of the television series *I Love Lucy*, whose integration into the piece invites a comparison between Cuban band leader Ricky Ricardo (Desi Arnaz) and Stein's "man from over the seas"; and the Johnny Cash song "Ring of Fire" ("I fell into a burning ring of fire"), played in the first act after Valk describes the viper sting. In addition, the piece's second act, a loose rendering of the song and ballet from *Faustus*'s own second act, interpolates a comic routine between Valk and "Mr. Viper," represented here as a microphone "puppet" with a viper's head (Figure 3). The viper, who "speaks back to [Valk] in the hilarious, ventriloquist-dummy voice of John Collins," mouths lines that allude parodically to the act of Señor Wences, a Spanish ventriloquist and regular guest on American variety shows of the 1950s and 1960s (Sebastian). A detailed analysis of these various aspects of production is too complicated for the present discussion, but I do want, in closing, to focus on one element in particular: the Powerbook sound improvisations provided by Tanya Selvaratnam (Christine & Nadja), who used a Mac laptop computer to generate a series of disruptive "bings," "bongs," "quacks," "bip-bips," "blips," "crows," "waa-woos," "beeps," "klinks," and musical notes (piano, organ, and flute) throughout the course of the piece. As Elizabeth LeCompte recalls, Selvaratnam, who was an intern with the group, clashed heatedly during the development of *House/Lights* with the male sound designers and operators, who felt that her "intrusions" marred the effect of their carefully calculated score (Personal interview). LeCompte defended the young woman, however, in what she perceived as a sort of battle of the sexes, and the Powerbook improvisations stayed, ultimately becoming a fixed and precisely timed group of sounds in the piece. In this victory for Selvaratnam, something of Marguerite Ida and Helena Annabel's spirit persists in the work, despite her otherwise complete integration, if not evaporation, into the role of Elaine/Faustus. Valk may say, at the end of the third and final act of *House/Lights*, that "you Marguerite Ida and Helena Annabel ... you know I can go to hell and I can take some one too and that some one will be you," but the "klink" orchestrated to come fast on the heels of this line, as though "spoken" by the absent woman, derides and deflates it. Stein's text may air a grave suspicion of technology in the form of electric lights that "get brighter and nothing comes" (92), but I think that she would have been pleased to see that something *could* come from technological innovation. In this case, it preserves her heroine's voice and transmutes it into the idiom of another power(ful) book.

Ultimately, Selveratnam's discordant noise making serves as a figure in miniature for the discordant pulses of *House/Lights* as a whole. By describing *House/Lights* as "discordant," I do not mean simply to suggest (though it is certainly true) that the piece's kaleidoscopic fusion of *Faustus, Olga,*

Figure 3: *House/Lights*. Kate Valk
Photo © Paula Court.

Frankenstein, Lucy, et al. creates a sense of discomfort and dis-ease, as the constituent parts of the work crash into and bounce off each other like bumper cars. Rather, what *House/Lights* "illuminates" for us, ironically, is just how discordant and *dark* Stein's play about blinding electric lights has been all along. Reading in tandem with the Wooster Group's interpretation, we want to say with LeCompte of Stein's play, "Of *course* Faustus is a sadomasochist." Indeed, how better to describe a man whose self-punishing desire to suffer hell's torments fuels his violent designs on Marguerite

Ida and Helena Annabel, the boy, and the dog? As Faustus says in the play's third act, "[H]ow can I be I again all right and go to hell ... I will kill I will I will" (116). Significantly, Faustus's murderous impulse is linked here not only to his wish to go to hell but also to a hope that "I [can] be I again." In a highly disturbing translation, Stein re-imagines her famous line, "I am I because my little dog knows me" ("Identity" 588) as "I am I because I kill my little dog." Human subjectivity may depend in part on the little dog's recognition, but Stein recognizes in turn and in her meditation on caninicide that the subjectivity thus constituted is nasty, brutish, and not as short in the duration of its bloodthirstiness as we might like.

Gertrude Stein is not a pre-eminently moral or ethical writer. She does not ask with, through, or of the figures in her fictions and dramas, "Who is right and who is wrong?" but rather, "Who is weak and who is strong? Who has the power?" And almost invariably, Stein's own identification is with the strong. Consider not just her personal reputation as something of a bully to the artists and friends who surrounded her but, more importantly, her by-and-large positive depictions of soldiers and sovereigns, like Napoleon. If Stein is, as she reports in lectures and essays, a great fan of detective fiction, she comes to the genre from the perspective of the hard-boiled, hard-nosed, flat-footed cop, not the victim. In "What Are Master-Pieces and Why Are There So Few of Them," Stein applauds detective stories, which she considers the "only really modern novel form":

> In real life people are interested in the crime more than they are in detection ... but in the story it is the detection that holds the interest and that is natural enough because the necessity as far as action is concerned is the dead man, it is another function that has very little to do with human nature that makes the detection interesting. And so always it is true that the master-piece has nothing to do with human nature or with identity, it has to do with the human mind and the entity that is with a thing in itself and not in relation. (149)

Stein makes a crucial distinction here, as elsewhere, between human nature and the human mind. If she presents human nature at all, as she does in *Doctor Faustus*, she will present it in all of its ugliness. But how preferable, in her view, to do away with human nature altogether and focus scrutiny on the cold, calculating human mind. As for the human body, so much the better if it should appear, as it does in detective fiction, as an outright *dead* body. "The hero is dead to begin with," she writes approvingly, "and so you have so to speak got rid of the event before the book begins" (149).

Conversely, in the theatre, the human body is arguably the one indispensable element, the *sine qua non*, of live performance. Indeed, it is perhaps just this intractable body that Stein resists when she writes plays that resist performance. The Wooster Group understands this impulse, and they account for it in their production of *House/Lights*. If the human body must appear, then it will appear disfigured. Costumes contain weird bulges that prohibit graceful movement, and LeCompte describes the corseted actors onstage as "lumpy women" (Personal interview). And if the *lumpy* body must appear, and speak, then it will appear only to be flagellated and speak only through electronic mediation – or, even more ideally, it will speak as a corpse. In *Doctor Faustus*, the final line of the play is given to the little boy who has suddenly and unceremoniously died a page earlier. From beyond the grave and presumably disembodied in Stein's imagination, he says, "Please Mr. Viper listen to me ... please Mr. Viper listen to me" (118). This is also the final line of *House/Lights*, which Kate Valk delivers as the eponymous houselights go down and, in the darkened theatre, her voice temporarily achieves the disembodiment that Stein imagines.

But only temporarily. When the lights come back up, Valk takes her bow, and the assembled viewers applaud, we are reminded of the *other* intractable human bodies constituted in and by the theatre: the audience. Yet exactly what sort of an audience is interpellated by such a performance? In thinking through this question, I am reminded of Judith Butler's description of coming out:

> Conventionally, one comes out *of* the closet ... so we are out of the closet, but into what? what new unbounded spatiality? the room, the den, the attic, the basement, the house, the bar, the university, some new enclosure whose door, like Kafka's door, produces the expectation of a fresh air and a light of illumination that never arrives? (16)

Similarly, could directors like LeCompte really be said to "un-closet" modernist drama, when the New York audiences for her productions are circumscribed and elite? What of the secondary definition of closet drama as drama meant for private, (s)elect performance? Is *House/Lights*, for instance, just a "coterie" production that takes place in a space more similar to the closet than to other, larger stages? What are the stakes, purchase, and relevance of the performance of closet drama?

One preliminary answer to these questions relates to the very technological advances of which Stein was so suspicious and to which the Wooster Group's productions are so heavily indebted. Increasingly, our spectatorial habits make of us *closet viewers*, as our computers allow us to consume culture in "the room, the den, the house, the university" and to participate in virtual rather than "fresh air" communities. The scripts of closet drama govern myriad aspects of our lives and our interactions (or non-interactions) with others. Thinking about modernist closet drama may give us a rhetoric and methodology with which to discuss and analyse the broader subjective positions that we and others take when we are not assuming the scholarly mask.

NOTES

1 Bay-Cheng locates Stein's handful of references to the cinema in an effort to contravert this claim, but she fails to realize the extent to which, occasionally, cinema provided Stein with a handy *metaphor* for certain ideas about time, space, and movement rather than a practical model for dramatic writing. As Stein says earlier in the same essay of the "thing[s] heard" and the "thing[s] seen" in the theatre, "I suppose one *might* have gotten to know a good deal about these things from the cinema ..." (xxxiv–xxxv; emphasis added). The fact remains that Stein was not indebted to the cinema for her ideas about theatricality; she simply recognized the usefulness of the cinematic metaphor as a way to make her ideas more readily understandable and accessible to her readers.

2 Though Bay-Cheng promises to reckon with the queer dimensions of Stein's drama in *Mama Dada*, the book almost invariably gestures toward queer readings without actually positing them. I also consider short-sighted the principles according to which Bay-Cheng designates aspects of Stein's writing "queer," her account being largely limited to Stein's attitude toward gender roles.

3 As Stein wrote in a letter to Thornton Wilder on 11 May 1938, "Ida has become an opera, and it is a beauty, really is, an opera about Faust ... some day she will be a novel too, she is getting ready for that, but as an opera she is a wonder ..." (Stein and Wilder 217–18).

4 It would be tempting to view Marguerite Ida and Helena Annabel as a figure who undermines the notion of singular identity even more radically than I indicate here. The compositional origins of Stein's play in her work on the novel *Ida*, in which one woman divides into twin halves, suggest strongly, however, that Stein is not engaging in so wholly deconstructive a manoeuvre.

5 See, for instance, Neuman.

6 The different editions of the *Blue Book* can be easily distinguished from one another based on variations in their prefatory material.

7 As the preface to the *Blue Book* states, "This Directory and Guide of the Sporting District has ... proven its authority as to what is doing in the 'Queer Zone'" (n pag.).

8 Emma Johnson is just one prostitute and proprietress among many described in Al Rose's *Storyville* who invite a greater or lesser degree of comparison with Marguerite Ida and Helena Annabel. Take, for instance, Fanny Sweet, a "thief, lesbian, Confederate spy, poisoner, procuress, and brawler" (14); or Marie Rodrigues, "whom the police had arrested in a vile den of infamy ... where she was consorting with the worst characters – male and female – in the city" (18).

WORKS CITED

Bay-Cheng, Sarah. *Mama Dada: Gertrude Stein's Avant-Garde Theater*. New York: Routledge, 2004.

Berners, Gerald. Letters to Gertrude Stein. Yale Collection of American Literature. New Haven.

Blue Book. Yale Collection of American Literature. New Haven.

Butler, Judith. "Imitation and Gender Insubordination." *Inside/Out: Lesbian Theories, Gay Theories*. Ed. Diana Fuss. New York: Routledge, 1991. 13–31.

Cox, Kenneth. *In the Shadows of Romance: Romantic Tragic Drama in Germany, England, and France*. Athens: Ohio UP, 1987.

Firsching, Robert. Rev. of *White Slaves of Chinatown.msn.movies*. 3 Nov 2006 <http://movies.msn.com/Movies/movie.aspx?m=103966&stab=1>.

Hapaz, Clay. Personal interview. 17 June 2004.

Irigaray, Luce. *This Sex Which Is Not One*. Trans. Catherine Porter with Carolyn Burke. Ithaca: Cornell UP, 1985.

Kaye, Nick. *Art into Theatre: Performance Interviews and Documents*. Amsterdam: Harwood Academic, 1996.

LeCompte, Elizabeth. Interview with Nick Kaye. *Art into Theatre*.

LeCompte, Elizabeth, and Kate Valk. Personal interview. 1 July 2004.

Michel, Frann. "'I Just Loved Thelma': Djuna Barnes and the Construction of Bisexuality." *Review of Contemporary Fiction* 13.3 (September 1993): 53–61.

Neuman, Shirley. "'Would a Viper Have Stung Her If She Had Only Had One Name?' *Doctor Faustus Lights the Lights*." *Gertrude Stein and the Making of Literature*. Ed. Shirley Neuman and Ira B. Nadel. Houndmills, UK: Macmillan, 1988. 168–93.

Olga's House of Shame. Dir. Joseph Mawra. 1964. Something Weird Video, 2003.

Puchner, Martin. *Stage Fright: Modernism, Anti-Theatricality, and Drama*. Baltimore Johns Hopkins UP 2002.

Rose, Al. *Storyville, New Orleans: Being an Authentic, Illustrated Account of the Notorious Red-Light District*. Tuscaloosa: U of Alabama P, 1974.

Savran, David. *The Wooster Group, 1975–1985: Breaking the Rules*. New York: Theatre Communications, 1988.

Sebastian, Cyrus. "Stein Soup." 2003 *HotReviews.org*. 24 Sep. 2004 <http://www.hotreview.org/articles/stein-soup.htm>.

Sellars, Peter. Foreword. *The Wooster Group, 1975–1985: Breaking the Rules*. xv–xvii.

Stein, Gertrude. *Doctor Faustus Lights the Lights*. Stein, *Last Operas and Plays*, 89–118.

———. *Last Operas and Plays*. Baltimore: John Hopkins UP, 1995.

———. "Plays." Last Operas and Plays. xxix–lii.

———. *Short Sentences*. Stein, *Last Operas and Plays*, 317–32.

———. "What Are Master-pieces and Why Are There So Few of Them" *Writings and Lectures: 1911–1945*. Ed. London: Peter Owen, 1967. 146–54.

———. "Identity: A Poem." *A Stein Reader*. Ed. Ulla Dydo. Evanston, IL: Northwestern UP, 1993. 588–94.

Stein, Gertrude, and Thornton, Wilder. *The Letters of Gertrude Stein and Thornton Wilder*. Ed. Edward Burns and Ulla Dydo with William Rice. New Haven: Yale UP, 1996.

9

Synge's *Playboy* and the Eugenics of Language

NICHOLAS CRAWFORD

The Playboy of the Western World (1907)[1] has received much critical
attention for its unlikely blending of genres, its ethnographic elements,
and its striking language. The play's dramatic mode is a puzzling hybrid,
drawing as it does upon traditions of tragedy, comedy, and romance.
Although the plot is marginally predicated on an anecdote familiar to
Synge about "a man from Connaught who killed his father with the blow
of a spade" and then sought refuge on the Western islands (*Aran*,
Collected 2: 95), the drama's development distinguishes itself more by its
departures from this local account than by its faithfulness to it.[2] The
play's speech proves most vexing of all, as it deploys English words with
Gaelic rhythms and inflections, along with locutions particular to the
Aran Islanders who inspired its distinctive diction. The play's originality
and its apparent lack of indebtedness to any single dramatic tradition
extend to the character of Christy Mahon himself, prompting Patricia
Meyer Spacks to announce that the play "presents essentially the vision
of a man constructing himself before our eyes" (16). Also typical of this
approach is Bruce Bigley's contention that we should read the play not
as a comedy "but as a *Bildungsdrama* in which Christy grows from a
timid lad, dominated by his father [into] ... master of his circumstances,
chiefly through his mastery of language" (98). The emphasis these and
other critics put on Christy's self-actualization through language is a
natural response to the freshness of Synge's dialogue and to Christy's
increasing rhetorical powers.[3]

What is lost in these discussions is the kind of engagement with the
relationship between language and heritage, both biological and cultural,
that we would expect from commentary on one of the Irish Literary
Revival's centerpieces. Recent critics, however, have begun to address
The Playboy's preoccupation with the past in productive ways. This
chapter seeks to link such discussions to the play's language. Susan
Cannon Harris, for example, has pointed out the play's connection to

contemporaneous debates on biological heredity and eugenics, while Gregory Castle has called attention to Synge's ambivalent preoccupations with things folklorist and anthropological. "The self-critical mode of Synge's anthropological modernism" (144), explains Castle, "derives from his ability to create a performative context in which the social authority of the ethnographic text is contested by the subjects of it"(145). The ameliorative imperative implicit in such a dialectic notwithstanding, it is, perhaps, through the text itself – the social authority and subversiveness of its imagined language rather than its subjects – that Synge negotiates his critique of heritage and, more pointedly, his critique of literary and linguistic evolution. What I propose in this chapter, then, is reading the language of the play through its attitudes toward culture and heritage rather than the other way around. *The Playboy* both insists upon and resists its own evolutionary fantasy of language; it mocks its own legitimation of the idea of linguistic eugenics.

The biologically eugenic component that this discourse of heredity implies is revealed in the overarching objective of the main character, which is to kill his father and reinvigorate his lineage by marrying the beautiful and vital Pegeen Mike.[4] The cultural work that the dramatic action embeds is the playwright's invention of a hybrid language, a linguistic negotiation between the colonizers' English and the land's native Gaelic. Inseparable from the idea of a newly bred language is the promise of an incipient Irishness able to draw from its split traditions and capable of informing a new sense of personal and national identity. *The Playboy* performs a kind of cultural aikido, triumphing over heritage by accepting and redirecting its energy. The "message" of the play is that, much as one might want to, one cannot deny the force of heritage by attempting to eradicate the past, an attempt that is symbolically enacted in the play by Christy's repeated assaults on his "da." The only way, in fact, to gain ascendancy over one's unwanted heritage is to accept its inexorable authority and then subvert it by an act of imagination. This is exactly how Synge negotiates the writing of Irish drama in English.[5]

If we examine Christy's relation to language, acknowledging that he becomes more and more confident and poetical through the rehearsal of his da-killing story, we cannot help but notice not only how special his language is but how singular is the speech of all the characters. The initial debate when the play was first staged, about whether, as Synge seemed to claim, his language was an accurate transcription of Aran Island dialect, or whether, as some in the audience claimed, no Irish peasant ever spoke like that, has been largely resolved in the audience's favour. The dialogue of the play is Synge-speak, not Irish, not standard English, not Aran Island dialect. The curious diction employed by the inhabitants of *The Playboy of the Western World* is a kind of de-Anglicized English that has been imaginatively wrought by its author to seem at once poetic and mimetic. Synge has taken the rich history of Gaelic, its incorporation into the English speech of some Irish, as well as certain properties of English itself, and he has created a hybrid language that is both an idiolect beholden to heritage and an imaginative and wilful departure from that heritage. By paying attention to Synge's relationship to the heritage of his medium, we can begin to understand Christy's relationship to his heritage. In essence, Christy finally arrives with his father where Synge arrives with the dominant English tongue: he capitulates to its inevitable presence, while imaginatively redefining its authority.

Since language is the great carrier of culture, of memory, of the past, it is also the great constructor of identity. When Synge "invents" a language, he also redefines Irish identity and Irish history. In the strictest sense, *The Playboy*, through the invention of its linguistic particularity, engages the discourse of national identity and cultural heritage. To speak of cultural heritage is, of course, to speak also of that culture's literary heritage. At the outset, however, I claimed that *The Playboy* is a drama of heritage in the ordinary biological sense as well, a story of fathers and sons, of impending marriages, of widows and orphans. Pursuing a discussion of the role of cultural and biological heritage in the play entails identifying and presumably separating these two components of the drama; however, in certain respects, they are inseparable. If we look to the play's literary antecedents, not only do we find the amorphous linguistic and cultural parents of the drama; we also find a legacy of the discourse of lineage, of both personal and national identity configured along the lines of a genetic, biological model – not literally, of course, but certainly metaphorically. The transgressive nature of a play that does not legitimately descend from any one genre, or even a set of parent genres, and that seems to attempt metaphorically to destroy its dramatic "*das*" while at the same time holding out a new future for its (theatrical) community, is mirrored in the vitality and questionable parentage of Christy Mahon himself.

While a number of critics have approached the play's relationship to the past and to heritage, what has been often overlooked in discussions of *The Playboy* – and at this point essential to mention – is the mystery of Christy's maternal line. Although we know the identity of Christy's father, we never know the identity of his mother. Her physical absence and the absence of any mention of who she is maintain in the audience a sense that Christy's origins are indeterminate. We are told that the Widow Casey – who also never appears in the play – suckled the boy as an infant, which implies either that the Widow Casey is his biological mother or that she functioned simply as a surrogate mother, widow as wet nurse, as it were. Either way, Christy's mother is never named, and so we are never asked to see Christy as the child of a particular father *and* mother. If the play essentially depicts a negotiation with biological and cultural heritage, then the enigma of the protagonist's parentage, the incomplete information about his biological heritage, and the compromised nature of his cultural standing should undoubtedly figure importantly into the dramatic equation. Just as the lineage of the protagonist is cloaked in mystery, the heritage of the play itself (its possible literary antecedents) also confounds our desire to ascribe origin.

The attempt to view *The Playboy* as originating from a particular genre has never been a very fruitful approach. The play famously defies categorization. *The Playboy* clearly has affinities with the traditions of tragedy, comedy, romance, and even folk tales, and just as clearly belongs to none of these genres. Because assigning *The Playboy* to a genre seems a hopeless undertaking, finding specific and convincing literary sources and analogues poses significant problems as well. The play's literary antecedents, however, are highly pertinent to a discussion of linguistic heritage and cultural identity and memory. As Edward Hirsch rightly points out, "the play creates a variety of different mythologies and anti-mythologies; thus Christy has been considered a mock Cuchulain, a mock Oedipus, a Christ figure, a mock Christ figure, a self-actualizing romantic poet, and a parody of a romantic poet" (114).[6]

We can easily understand the commentary on Christ, Oedipus, and even Odysseus, but the connection to Cuchulain is at first less evident as it is certainly less familiar. As both Toni O'Brien Johnson and Walter S. Phelan make clear, the link lies chiefly between Christy's attacks on his father's head (which do not lead to his demise but rather to repeat encounters) and Cuchulain's – and later Sir Gawain's – beheading contest, which also serves, in the case of Sir Gawain, as prologue to a medieval rematch.[7] These critics see a second parallel between Christy's athletic competitions for Mayo supremacy and the nationalistic iconography of the medieval tournament. Phelan explains:

> [T]he beheading contest has a purely nationalistic motive, indeed involves a national championship. It is at this point that J.M. Synge's *Playboy of the Western World* (1907) becomes instructive. Not coincidentally the modern play and the medieval romance share the same heroic ancestor in the Cuchulain of Irish folklore who became Champion of Ireland by answering the beheading challenge. (554)

When Synge reviewed Lady Gregory's book of *Cuchulain of Muirthemne* (1902), he noted reservations, along with his praise, about her omission of some of Cuchulain's more unsavoury character traits (see Synge, "An Epic"). Heidi J. Holder has speculated that some of these details were apparently an uncomfortable fit with a program whose aim was the reinvigoration of national pride (147). She points out that, as Synge well knew, "[t]he great hero Cuchulain ... was given to spasms of bloody rage and had, in fact slain his own son" (147). Thus the Cuchulain legend would seem to be an inversion of the Oedipus myth rather than its analogue. Such contradictions are, of course, what make *The Playboy* the enigmatic, genre-defying work that it is. Quite likely, Synge is satirizing not only Celtic myth-making and hero worship but the values upon which all such idolatry is based. Even though these two related predecessors seem to point in opposite directions and their relation to the drama is ambiguous and complex, the events of the play nevertheless allude unmistakeably to both of them. What the Greek drama and the Celtic myth have in common is their central concern with father–son conflict and thus with the whole rubric of heritage and the degree of determinism it exerts. Here the discourses of literary, cultural, and biological heredity are tightly intertwined.

Harris has pointed out a more immediate connection between the action of *The Playboy*, its reception, and concurrent ideas of biological heredity. In her compelling analysis, she calls attention to the early eugenics movement in England and the currency of the debate it generated in both England and Ireland at the turn of the century. The Eugenics Education Society in England was founded in 1907, the same year that *The Playboy* had its premiere. Additionally, the Irish nationalist newspaper *Sinn Féin* was aware of and engaged in the discourse of eugenics even during the weeks just preceding the opening of the play. Harris concludes that an important reason for the play's unfriendly reception was that audiences were

> profoundly disturbed by the fact that so many of the Irish bodies he put on stage were diseased, decrepit, or dead. Synge's play was dangerous because it mobilized the discourse of infection, filth, and degeneracy promoted by eugenicists in England–a vocabulary that both the play's defenders and its detractors recognized. (73)

The controversy over the play's accuracy of representation, its mimetic objectivity,[8] is crucial, Harris contends, "because Synge's treatment of the human body seems to these audience members to coincide with the construction of the Irish as a degenerating race. To admit that his portrait was accurate would be to agree that the story that British medicine has been telling about Ireland and the Irish is correct" (73–74).[9]

Harris's insistence, like my own, that the play revolves around issues of heredity may seem off the mark at first because the play's dialogue does not call particular attention to this topic. Although Harris's argument concerning eugenics and the parallel Phelan draws to the beheading game are enlightening, we actually need not go beyond the basics of the drama to understand that heritage – biological, cultural, theatrical, and linguistic – is its central subject. *The Playboy of the Western World* is, after all, the story of a young man caught between, on the one hand, trying to "kill" his powerful but troglodytic father (the embodiment of an oppressive and backward heritage) and, on the other hand, trying to create a union of mutual vitality that will reanimate the lifeless race of Mayo. Christy discovers that his most effective means for ensuring a future of vital procreation lies in telling his prospective mate the story of his da-destroying. By poetically and rhetorically transforming the past in order to ensure his romantic future, he figuratively "kills" the real past and literally creates for himself a real future. In brief, he uses the cultural coinage of storytelling to transact the business of biology.

To state that Christy's father embodies heritage is not to fish for symbolism but rather to articulate the obvious. This heritage, however, is carried and shared by all the characters in the language they speak, and it is through their linguistic negotiations that these parties construct an imaginative cultural identity. The cultural issues, particularly the linguistic ones, extend beyond the characters of the play to the author's attempt to revive Irish culture while evolving a stage language through the marriage of Irish and English tongues. Commenting on Synge's own attitude toward Darwinian ideas and their relation to language, Sinéad Garrigan Mattar explains that "[f]or Synge, a return to the Irish language on a national level was an attempt to defy the most basic laws of evolution" (154). The biological or evolutionary issues raised are thus really cultural issues as well, based as they are not in scientific discourse but in the author's deployment of linguistic and tropological analogues to evolutionary discourse and in the popular beliefs reflected in the play by the characters' whimsical convictions. Christy attempts to legitimate his line by legitimating his voice, just as Synge attempts to legitimate a new Irish literature by legitimating a Gaelicized English.

To better understand *The Playboy*'s discourse of cultural and biological heredity, mediated by and mirrored in linguistic legitimation, we need to examine the specific figurations the drama deploys. The play opens with Pegeen ordering goods in preparation for a wedding. Though we are catching our first glimpse of this "*wild coast of Mayo*" (*Collected* 4: 55) and of Pegeen, the "*wild-looking but fine girl*" (4: 57), the scene is anything but wild. She is writing a mundane list of provisions that serves to associate prospective marriages with eternal tedium, with a kind of living death. If there is any question about whether death and marriage are conflated in this scene, it is dispelled only a few moments later. The subject of both Kate Cassidy's wake and the possibility of Pegeen's marrying Shawn Keogh – a man who inspires in her indifference, at best – are broached

and then held at arm's length. Pegeen laments the absence of the Daneen
Sullivans and the Marcus Quins, presumably men more suited to the "wildness" for which the region is known. The death-in-life motif is relentlessly
developed in this opening scene, as Shawn relates that he spied "a kind of
fellow [Christy] above in the furzy ditch, groaning wicked like a maddening
dog" (4: 61); and Pegeen will ask "if they find his corpse stretched above in
the dews of dawn, what'll you say then to the peelers … ?" (4: 61). Much of
what is pertinent to a discussion of the play is introduced in these first few
moments.

The idea of a procreative union introduced as a kind of death-in-life and
the image of a living man groaning in a ditch as though he were dying and
already in his makeshift grave evoke the liminal world these characters
inhabit. Clearly, despite the lovely poetry of even the initial dialogue, we
are in a land that is wasting and wanting, where the spectre of real death
and the metaphor of a living death are both powerfully and immediately
brought to bear on the proceedings. We have, right from the start, the suggestion of the marriage that would end (not begin) the traditional comedy
and the death(s) that would end (not begin) the prototypical tragedy. In
other words, even at the outset of the play, the tone, the action, and the
characterization mix and simultaneously mock elements of comedy,
tragedy, and romance. More importantly, however, the motif of death-in-
life, of deathly marriages, of the veritable walking dead underscores the
need for the renewal and regeneration of once "wild" – now stale –
Mayo. "The queer dying fellow's beyond looking over the ditch," says
Shawn, "He's come up … he's following me now" (4: 67). This is Christy,
who seems to rise from the dead, just as his father will in the next act.
The mock resurrections do not signal godly immortality but rather the
smell of death that clings all too often to the living.

The physical presence of the past in the form of the dead and of those
playing at being dead highlights Synge's insistence on the presentness of
the past and on the living influence of a heritage one might presume
defunct.[10] The figure of the corpse, and often only a seeming corpse, loiter-
ing on the stage amidst the doings of the living is a recurring motif in
Synge's work. Not only does the supposedly dead Old Mahon of *The
Playboy* appear and reappear, in *Riders to the Sea* (1904) one of the dead
sons is dragged onto the stage and left there to exert his dumb immutabil-
ity. Though that play catalogues the drowning of a series of sons and seems
to emphasize the inevitability of death and the transience of life, the inert,
palpable body of the boy reminds all that, although people die, their deaths
do not. They linger on as memories, as a force in the family, as a piece of
identity present even in its absence: "They're carrying a thing among
them and there's water dripping out of it and leaving a track by the big
stones," says Nora as the men approach (*Collected* 3: 23). And the arresting

stage directions recount the action: "*Then the men carry in the body of Bartley, laid on a plank, with a bit of a sail over it, and lay it on the table*" (3: 23). Needless to say, the "track" of water will evaporate, but the trace of the dead as memory will remain as surely as the stones and will reinscribe itself as often as they sit down at the table.

In *The Shadow of the Glen* (1903), a tramp (an early analogue for the wandering Christy Mahon) woos a woman while her husband, Dan Burke, lies stretched out with a sheet drawn up over him. All presume he is dead. Dan's first words are, "Don't be afeard, stranger; a man that's dead can do no hurt" (*Collected* 3: 41). Nothing less true was ever said, and Synge knows it well. After some conversation, the tramp asks, "Is it not dead you are?" (3: 43), as though his interlocutor's obvious pulse and voice were not enough to convince entirely. Even in Synge's short story, "An Autumn Night in the Hills," the hurt and abandoned dog "dragged himself along like a Christian till he got too weak with the bleeding" (*Collected* 2: 190); meanwhile, there is a wake for Mary Kinsella in the offing. The line between the living and the dead is not a sharp one in Synge's world. The dead may still be living and the living may be as good as dead.

Synge is not always content simply to show the past symbolically embodied in a deathly being or to figure it in the tyranny of daily drone. On occasion, *The Playboy*'s dialogue directly takes up the issue of heritage and even its relation to language. As Pegeen begins to fall for Christy, she fantasizes about his ancestors:

PEGEEN ... You should have had great people in your family, I'm thinking, with the little small feet you have, and you with a kind of a quality name, the like of what you'd find on the great powers and potentates of France and Spain.

CHRISTY (*with pride*) We were great surely, with wide and windy acres of rich Munster land. (*Collected* 4: 79)

The sense here for both is that Christy is the bearer of some lost or diluted vitality worth recovering. Later, Pegeen connects strength directly to a facility with language, to poetic powers, as she speculates that if Christy were not so tired from his travels, he would "have as much talk ... as Owen Roe O'Sullivan or the poets of the Dingle Bay, and I've heard all times it's the poets are your like, fine fiery fellows with great rages when their temper's roused" (4: 81). Pegeen weighs his suitability as a mate not only on the scale of transgressive "wildness" but by the yardstick of his imagined lineage and the wattage of his linguistic power: "Aye. Wouldn't it be a bitter thing for a girl to go marrying the like of Shaneen ... with no savagery or fine words in him at all?" (4: 153). And her father concurs:

I'm a decent man of Ireland, and I'd liefer face the grave untimely and I seeing
a score of grandsons growing up little gallant swearers by the name of God, than
go peopling my bedside with puny weeds the like of what you'd breed, I'm
thinking, out of Shaneen Keogh. (*He joins their hands.*) A daring fellow is the jewel
of the world, and a man did split his father's middle with a single clout, should
have the bravery of ten, so may God and Mary and St. Patrick bless you, and
increase you from this mortal day. (4: 157)

The evolutionary discourse is comical, but the father's investment is
serious. Donald J. Childs wonders "[h]ow much of Michael Flaherty's positive eugenics is Synge's" and concludes that this "is impossible to determine because of Synge's pervasive irony" (10). The Darwinian overtones
of Pegeen's and Michael Flaherty's assessment of Christy become even
clearer when Christy is presented with an evolutionary choice of his own
in the figure of Widow Quin, who offers herself to him as mate and
mother of dead children. The question she raises by her interference at
the end of the first act is, "Which of the two women is the more desirable
for Christy's line?" Widow Quin, as killer of her children, sees herself as
Christy's natural complement, suitably similar in her proud murderous-
ness. "There's a great temptation in a man did slay his da," she says by
way of recognition (4: 89). Holder sees a debate about national identity,
and implicitly heritage, in Christy's choice between Pegeen Mike and the
Widow Quin, the latter representing "shameful lowliness" and the former
"lyric heroism." Holder construes these as "the very options the cultural
nationalists routinely offered to Ireland" (145). She sees, in the choice of
Pegeen, a pattern typical in Synge's work, one in which the imagination
is endowed with the agency actually to make history and construct identity:
"[T]he central figures invariably face ... [the] same imperative that faced
Ireland: to make their own histories, often from a kind of void, to the
best possible ends. Synge's characters are notable for their rejection of a
known present, a joyless reality, for a better – if fictional – world" (144).

The consequences of Christy's choice are not merely symbolic, however.
They are biological as well. We should notice that, although the Widow
Quin shares with Christy a common bond in terms of deeds done,
Pegeen seems to have motherlessness in common with the younger
Mahon. Widow Quin lets it be know that Father Reilly feels that "[i]t isn't
fitting ... to have his likeness [Christy's] lodging with an orphaned girl"
(*Playboy, Collected* 4: 87). Later we learn that Shawn too claims himself
an orphan. With a world populated by widows and priests, orphans, poss-
ible illegitimates, and despised fathers, one has the distinct sense not just of
a culture in crisis but of a lineage in crisis. The ramifications of Christy's
possible pairing with Widow Quin have not been sufficiently appreciated.
Her proposal to Christy is even more radically transgressive than it might

first appear. The highly oedipal overtones of Christy's near-marriage to the Widow Casey, who, Christy tells us, "did suckle me for six weeks when I came into the world, and she a hag," are echoed in the possibility of a marriage with the Widow Quin (4: 103). If the Widow Casey is not actually Christy's mother, she was clearly a substitute mother to Christy.

Moreover, the Widow Quin suggests that, if Christy marries her, she will give him free rein as an adulterer: "Come on, I tell you, and I'll find you finer sweethearts [than Pegeen] at each waning moon" (4: 165). This promise is supposed to prompt Christy to utter the line most associated with *The Playboy*'s opening night riot: "[W]hat'd I care if you brought me a drift of chosen females, standing in their shifts itself maybe, from this place to the Eastern World?" (4: 167). But as Christopher Morash explains, on opening night the actor playing Christy, Willie Fay, mistakenly said, "a drift of Mayo girls standing in their shifts itself," thus rendering the line considerably more provocative and personal than the scripted one (132).[11] Lady Gregory's famous telegram to W.B. Yeats in Scotland, "Audience broke up in disorder at the word shift," then, does not tell all of what she presumably knew (qtd. in Kenner 20). Nicholas Grene points out that this is not the first time in the play that the word "shift" is uttered (*Politics* 80). Grene speculates elsewhere that the real reason for the opening night pandemonium may have been the reappearance of Christy onstage just after he has seemingly murdered his father and just before he utters the famous line (*Synge: A Critical Study* 145).[12] It does stand to reason that such a strong reaction from an audience would be the result of a cumulative and complex impression rather than of one galling moment or utterance. I would like to suggest that one of the true sources of moral outrage is to be found in the depiction of an Irish widow who offers herself as a virtual bawd to a roving parricide. Her proposal not only outrages the institution of marriage but also suggests the creation of a slew of illegitimates spawned from Christy and a "drift of" Irish women. This point seems to give weight to a eugenic reading that locates the source of the audience's outrage not just in the depiction of debilitated Irish bodies but in the portrayal of Irish degeneracy and in the threat of runaway illegitimacy tainting the legacy of Ireland.

Though Synge routinely evokes the past as death's presence, curiously he figures the presence of the past as an animate force. The play negotiates the power of the past by insisting upon the present, even as that present is weighed upon by the past, and even as the future is implicit in the every incipient moment. The attempt to eradicate both the past and the future finds its representatives in Christy and the Widow Quin, respectively. Christy attempts to kill the past by doing in his father and abandoning his birthplace, and the Widow Quin attempts to kill the future by doing in her children and husband and by intervening in the salutary union of

Pegeen and Christy, thus quashing the best attempt at regeneration. Synge employs various strategies for evoking time in a drama that seeks to deny the past before reconciling to negotiate with it. As George Watson notes, Synge has a "fondness for the continuous form of the verb ... Synge's syntax largely creates what may be called the time-sense of his dramatic universe: that of a static continuum" (52). Synge uses gerunds and progressive tenses as the most prominent verb forms. This lends immediacy and movement to the present and serves to move the past into the present.

Both the playwright's propensity to depict the force of the past and his attempts to eradicate it manifest themselves in a number of throw-away metaphors throughout the play. Jimmy, for example, tells the story of "a party [who] was kicked in the head by a red mare, and he went killing horses a great while till he eat the insides of a clock and died after" (4: 137). Similarly, Michael, fed up with Christy, tells him to "[g]o on to the foreshore if it's fighting you want, where the rising tide will wash all traces from the memory of man" (4: 155). He and Shawn decline to fight Christy because Christy's imagined heritage exerts too great a force on the present, making him unapproachably fearsome: "Is it me fight him, when it's father-slaying he's bred to now?" (4: 155). Such is Michael's explanation for his own cowardice. This negotiation or tension between the power of the past and the desire to overcome its force not only is enacted in Christy's attempts to kill his father but is epitomized in his missing mother. The spectre of uncertain parentage raises the issue of compromised lineage, of the absence of societal sanction and the need for legitimation, not only in the arena of biology but in the field of identity and on the map of language that inscribes consciousness. The complex proprietary considerations of national culture and identity – including ideas of parentage and seemliness, of provenance, and of all that attends upon heritage – are temporarily neutralized and then suspended for examination by Synge's special language, a language that holds fast to the present and slowly stretches the limits of the now.

The ending of *The Playboy* is a vivid demonstration of Synge's subtle deal making with the undead. Most critics have seen the ending of this play as Christy's triumph. He has now reversed roles with his father; he has established his self-confidence and his mastery over both his father and himself. Alan Price, for example, writes, "Father and son ... stare at each other for a moment while the truth sinks in that Christy is now master – as his first words show: 'Are you coming to be killed a third time ... ?'" (174). Similarly, Seamus Deane reads the final scenes as "Christy Mahon's transformation from a stuttering lout into the playboy poet who is finally master of his da and of himself" (*Short History* 152). More recently, George Cusack has suggested that "[b]y taking command of the patriarch who once dominated him, he [Christy] creates his own legendary persona" (586–87). These critics see Christy at the very least as budding poet, the plot as a dramatized *Küntslerroman*, wherein the protagonist achieves not just maturity and independence but artistic self-actualization. Many commentators on the play have seen not just Christy's own development but the application of his new powers in his dominating and essentially reversing the previous father–son dynamic.[13] These readings, in my view, fail to see the irony of the ending. In the simplest sense, the father not the son triumphs in the end.[14]

To understand this, we need to recognize not just what is being said but what is happening onstage. What we find is another manifestation of "the great gap" between word and deed (4: 169).[15] Not only does the father leave happy and satisfied, "*with a broad smile*" (4: 173), rather than dejectedly, but he leads the way back home, as Christy trails after him. Although Christy pushes him, it is Old Mahon who is "*walking out and looking back at CHRISTY over his shoulder*" (4: 173). If Christy will be, as he proclaims, "like a gallant captain with his heathen slave" (4: 173), then why does he not take his father in tow and behave like the master he purports to be? The father exclaims, "I am crazy again!" and Christy follows him off, spouting empty vows that he will "go romancing through a romping lifetime from this hour to the dawning of the judgment day" (4: 173). If Christy's future were really to be, from that day forth, a series of independent exploits of derring-do and satyric triumphs, he would surely be striking forth into the wild and not following his da home to the bleak and dreary Kerry farm from whence they came.

Figuring the authority of the past as patriarch, Rob Doggett sees

> Father Reilly as the pillar of the Church, Michael Flaherty as the pillar of the Irish state, and most importantly, old Mahon as ... the "bogland father" – the wet soil in which both pillars are grounded and the suffocating force which controls the present by denying the possibility of social freedom. (286)

The last scene of the play is then a "final reassertion of the past" (293). Where Doggett reads here a bleak sociological message meant to convey the peasant's true situation as being far from a mythopoeic fairyland – he is locked in a gritty and backward past, "trapped in stagnation" (293) – I read the assertion of an undying past as being mitigated as much by the spirit of comedy and romance as by that of tragedy. Although Pegeen Mike and Christy's romance dies, the father and son are reunited, as are the less-than-ideal lovers Pegeen and Shaun. In fact, the ending is a double marriage of sorts. More importantly, however, the triumph of the da is leavened by Christy's complete denial of the defeat of his agency, a denial he achieves through an imaginative act of language. In other words, even though Christy has, in fact, lost the battle with his father and consequently with his hated heritage, he vociferously denies that loss. In doing so, he transforms his defeat into an imaginative triumph, one mediated by the inventiveness of his language, by words that defy the reality to which he is subjected.

Christy's only "triumph" is that he accepts "the lie of a pipe dream," as it is memorably called in O'Neill's *The Iceman Cometh* (569). His newly found poetic powers, his imaginative ability, constitute a kind of liberation from the social and historical circumstances that he cannot transcend. When he returns to live with Old Mahon, there is really no reason to think that the dynamic of their relationship will be any different from what it was before, in spite of what Christy proclaims. We know that Old Mahon will lord it over his son just as before, and that Christy will be rising up on occasion to chase the codger 'round the potato patch with his loy being riz and the old man calling to the Easter moon and cursing the stars for his eternal salvation.

As Gérard Leblanc helpfully explains, the ending "vouches for the ultimate triumph of the story over the real" but not of the son over the father (40). "For the *mariage raté* of Christy and Pegeen, that is of the hero and the community, Synge substitutes the final union of the son and the father" (40). So that even though "the murder or overthrow of a father-figure by a hero whom the community recognizes as its regenerator and saviour" is recognizable as an archetypal pattern, the biological imperative of the young replacing the old (40), Synge does not entirely conform to this model. Rather, he "neutralizes in advance possible analogies with archetypal myths" by having the father survive and by having the community laud the tale and not the act (40). The play ends not with the autonomous self-actualization of Christy through his successful unfettering from the past but rather with the imaginative subversion of the past through the invention of a hybridized language grounded in heritage but simultaneously defiant of its dominion.

The intersections of culture, biology, and language in the play are characterized by the combination of determinism and agency implicit in the incomplete picture we are given of Christy's parentage. If we return to *The Playboy*'s cultural and literary heritage, we can better understand the role of biological, cultural, and linguistic legitimacy:

> The mutant in medieval literature and in *Sir Gawain* especially, is not a biological accident or an artificial, mechanical creation of mankind inventing the future (as in the modern Frankenstein myth), but rather a retrogression to the pure stock of a cultural ancestry. In *Sir Gawain* the outrageous retrogression involves the axebearing (pre-courtly) Celtic playboy who in the end, like Christy Mahon, turns out to be the champion impostor, an interloper sent by Morgan le Fay to play a game on Camelot. (Phelan 547)

Note that the Celtic playboy of "pure stock" is in fact an impostor. The figure of the illegitimate, the counterfeit, the "champion impostor" employs a language that recuperates and reinvigorates the authenticity of the Irish language. It does so by creating a mutant tongue, born of the combination of a bona-fide heritage and the relatively strong, ahistorical agency implicit in one whose immediate lineage is partially shrouded in mystery.

The same could be said of Synge, who, though Irish, was no peasant and was, in fact, an imposter as an Aran Island rustic. Though he knew and loved Gaelic, it was only as an imposter that he could claim it as his native tongue. Though his work is indebted to the traditions of Celtic mythology, as is much of the literary output of the Irish Literary Revival, these myths had been recuperated by an "outrageous retrogression" and used to produce a new strain of literature neither wholly modern nor wholly retrograde. Synge was well aware of the bold blending of languages and genres he was attempting. In 1904, he indicated in a letter his reservations about the wholesale adoption of anachronistic forms: "I do not believe in the possibility of 'a purely fantastic unmodern, ideal, breezy, springdayish, Cuchulanoid National Theatre'" (qtd. in Watson 60). The playboy is the play-boy, the pretender who paradoxically is more alive than the real but deadened inhabitants of Kerry and Mayo because part of him and his heritage is either unknown to the community and to himself or is simply left unsaid. Christy plays out dramatically the oedipal metaphor of Synge's linguistic tribulations, in which he tries to "kill" English (the tyrannical father tongue) and marry the local tongue of the motherland. But he knows he is doomed to failure in such an absolutist quest, and so he negotiates a settlement between the two, wherein he stays with the father (stale English) but keeps the heart of his vital lover Pegeen–Gaelic.

To complement Phelan's cultural perspective on *The Playboy*'s literary ancestors, we have seen Harris's reading of the biologic implications of the drama. She writes that "[b]y turning the sacrificial narrative into a story about racial redemption through better breeding, the eugenist reading implies that in Synge's Ireland, degeneration is already far advanced – that the Irish have already been polluted by 'foreign-borne diseases'" (85). These two readings which place the theme of heritage front and centre differ in that the first sees national identity masked as domestic drama and the second sees genetics masked as archetypal myth. All readers, however, acknowledge that it is the uniqueness of Synge's poetics that is responsible for much of the play's force and for whatever masking effects are to be found in its action. Just as it is Christy's role as storytelling poet–imposter that defines him, it is the linguistic flavour that largely defines the achievement of the play. *The Playboy of the Western World* is a drama not primarily of genetics or identity, but of language, of linguistic eugenics, masked in various tropes of heredity.

Phelan begins to approach this view when he writes that

> the central question at stake for both poets [Synge and the Gawain poet] in this
> discussion is evolutionary. Does the human race survive and thrive ... by purity or
> by mixture? ... For Synge and the Gawain-poet, however, the highest national
> value is the language ... which despite the most outrageous marriages and
> intrusions, remains pure and intact. (557)

That language ever remains pure and intact is patently untrue, and it is particularly untrue for Synge, whose drama comments on the idea of linguistic
evolution by playing with the purity and mixture of languages. Synge's
central question is perhaps evolutionary, but his answer is to contribute
his own mutation of language, and only by implication to influence cultural
evolution and the reformation of national identity. Language is, in one
certain sense, a kind of living memory, the temporal trace of cultural life.
As Christy increasingly proclaims his destruction of his father, along with
his consequent independence from his past, his heritage, and his community, he gains powers as poet and performer, as a shaper of a dramatic
language. But if we look closely at the language of *The Playboy* itself, we
see that it is a triumph over its linguistic heritage exactly in proportion to
its imagined mutation from all its mother tongues and its "*das*" of dramatic
dialogue. Synge neither writes plain English nor faithfully repeats the local
speech of the Aran Islands; nor does he attempt to invent a stage language
out of whole cloth. The peculiar power and originality of Synge's dialogue
derives from both his love of Irish poetic rhythms and the assertion of his
own quirky mastery over them in English. His relation to English is much
like Christy's relation to his father at the close of the play.[16] And, perhaps
to overextend the simile, Synge's relation to Gaelic is much like Christy's
relation to Pegeen – ultimately, it does not portend a viable future. The playwright successfully subverts English authority and the program of linguistic
eugenics associated with that authority by apparently submitting to them
while sneaking in the muse of Gaelic poetry and Aran Island speech to generate a unique stage dialect that is, in fact, no living language at all, but rather
a theatrical imposture. As Irish as Synge's language sounds, it is finally a form
of dramatic English, albeit a gloriously syncretic one. *The Playboy* flaunts its
linguistic hybridity and its whimsical provenance, just as it thumbs its nose
at its literary and theatrical antecedents; all the while, however, it plays slyly
with multiple traditions and with evolutionary expectations.

NOTES

1 Parenthetical dates for plays refer to the year of their first theatrical production.
2 See Castle 153–54; Kiberd 425 for recent discussions of Synge's use of the
   story, which Castle calls "translating ethnographic knowledge into a dramatic

context" (153). Most critics, however, readily acknowledge that *The Playboy* engages numerous sources and traditions. For example, Declan Kiberd, among others, connects the drama's storyline to a number of Cuchulain legends as well (413–14). Seamus Deane seeks, on the other hand, to demonstrate the play's indebtedness to the work of nineteenth-century Irish playwright, Dion Boucicault (*Strange Country* 142).

3   A slight variant of the self-actualization view is the traditional idea of self-recognition through drama: "The major action of the play, the recognition of self, demands the second 'murder' of the old man by the son" (Gerstenberger 44).

4   See Levitas for the suggestion that the killing of the father might also have been seen "as a symbol of national rebellion" (*Theatre* 117).

5   As Kiberd puts it, "he [Synge] opted to write in an English as Irish as it is possible for that language to be, re-creating Gaelic syntax, rhythms, images" (603–04).

6   See Roll-Hansen for an exploration of the parallels between Christy and Peer Gynt. Roll-Hansen notes that "Ibsen and Synge have this much in common that they have chosen a liar for their main character" (156). Oddly, the author ultimately rejects his own theory.

7   W.B. Yeats's interest in Cuchulain is well known. His play, *The Green Helmet* (1910), stages a Cuchulainoid version of the beheading game.

8   See Hirsch and also Spacks on the relative realism of the play versus its fantastical or folkloric qualities. The actor Cyril Cusack, after performing the part of Christy for many years, felt that finally "reality disappears in a balloon-burst of disillusionment and the person of Christopher Mahon suddenly resolves itself into a dew" (qtd. in Fallis 108).

9   The degree to which Synge was aware of the effect his drama would have is a point of disagreement among critics. Ben Levitas, for example, argues that Synge was finely attuned to audience and critical reception ("Mirror" esp. 575–76), whereas Nicholas Grene finds Synge strangely innocent of how his plays might be received (*Politics* 77–109).

10 See King 82–83; she points out that the insistence of the past is of course a theme Ibsen made great use of (e.g. *Ghosts*) and that its echoes are to be found in Synge's work.

11 Padraic Colum remembers the line as, "A drift of the finest women in the County Mayo standing in their shifts around me" (368).

12 In 1926, Padraic Colum suggested that it was the entrance of the realistically bloodied Old Mahon (just previous to Christy's chasing him off to "kill" him again) that incited the crowd, rather than the utterance of any particular word (368).

13 Often this attitude is taken in articles that have little to do with this question. For example, Pierce, writing on the Widow Quin, throws in "although youth does triumph over age" (122).

14 See Synge, *Collected Works*, vol. 4, for earlier drafts of *The Playboy*'s ending, in which Christy does not finish by even verbally dominating his father.

15 Another way of articulating "the great gap" is to say that "[t]he drama relies upon this interplay of correspondences and incongruities between

language and the facts it purports to describe. The onus is on language" (Maxwell 50).

16 See Castle, who credits Synge with "the creation of a Hiberno–English dialect that aspires to avoid the assimilative impulses of anthropology, colonialism, and nationalist groups like the Gaelic league" (148). In other words, Synge seems to reject both a status-quo English and an entrenched Gaelic.

WORKS CITED

Bigley, Bruce. "*The Playboy* as Antidrama." Bloom 89–99.

Bloom, Harold, ed. and intro. *John Millington Synge's* The Playboy of the Western World. New York: Chelsea House, 1988.

Castle, Gregory. *Modernism and the Celtic Revival.* Cambridge: Cambridge UP, 2001.

Childs, Donald J. *Modernism and Eugenics: Woolf, Eliot, Yeats, and the Culture of Degeneration.* Cambridge: Cambridge UP, 2001.

Colum, Padraic. *The Road Round Ireland.* New York: Macmillan, 1926.

Cusack, George. "'In the Gripe of the Ditch': Nationalism, Famine, and *The Playboy of the Western World.*" *Modern Drama* 45.4 (2002): 567–92.

Deane, Seamus. *A Short History of Irish Literature.* London: Hutchinson, 1986.

———. *Strange Country: Modernity and Nationhood in Irish Writing since 1790.* Oxford: Clarendon Press, 1997.

Doggett, Rob. "The Three Fathers of the Past: A Sociological Reading of *The Playboy of the Western World* and the Playboy Riots." *Colby Quarterly* 33.4 (1997): 281–94.

Fallis, Richard. *The Irish Renaissance.* Syracuse: Syracuse UP, 1977.

Gerstenberger, Donna. "A Hard Birth." Bloom 39–56.

Grene, Nicholas. *Synge: A Critical Study of the Plays.* London: Macmillan, 1975.

———. *The Politics of Irish Drama: Plays in Context from Boucicault to Friel.* Cambridge: Cambridge UP, 1999.

Harris, Susan Cannon. "More than a Morbid, Unhealthy Mind: Public Health and the *Playboy* Riots." *A Century of Irish Drama: Widening the Stage.* Ed. Stephen Watt et al. Bloomington: Indiana UP, 2000. 72–94.

Hirsch, Edward. "The Gallous Story and the Dirty Deed: The Two *Playboys.*" Bloom 101–16.

Holder, Heidi. "'Stimulating Stories of Our Own Land': 'History Making' and the Work of J.M. Synge." *Assessing the Achievement of J.M. Synge.* Ed. Alexander G. Gonzalez. Westport: Greenwood Press, 1996. 139–50.

Johnson, Toni O'Brien. *Synge: The Medieval and the Grotesque.* Buckinghamshire, UK: Colin Smythe, 1982.

Kenner, Hugh. *A Colder Eye: The Modern Irish Writers.* New York: Knopf, 1983.

Kiberd, Declan. *Irish Classics.* Cambridge, MA: Harvard UP, 2001.

King, Mary C. "J.M. Synge, 'National' Drama and the Post-Protestant Imagination." *The Cambridge Companion to Twentieth-Century Irish Drama.* Ed. Shaun Richards. Cambridge: Cambridge UP, 2004. 79–92.

Leblanc, Gérard. "The Three Deaths of the Father in *The Playboy of the Western World.*" *Cahiers du Centre d'études irlandaises* 2 (1977): 33–42.

Levitas, Ben. "Mirror up to Nurture: J.M. Synge and His Critics." *Modern Drama* 47.4 (2004): 572–84.

———. *The Theatre of Nation: Irish Drama and Cultural Nationalism 1890–1916.* Oxford: Clarendon Press, 2002.

Mattar, Sinéad Garrigan. *Primitivism, Science, and the Irish Literary Revival.* Oxford: Clarendon Press, 2004.

Maxwell, D.E.S. *A Critical History of Modern Irish Drama 1891–1980.* Cambridge: Cambridge UP, 1984.

Morash, Christopher. *A History of Irish Theatre: 1601–2000.* Cambridge: Cambridge UP, 2002.

O'Neill, Eugene. *Complete Plays: 1932–1943.* New York: Library of America, 1988.

Phelan, Walter S. "The Playboy of the Medieval World: Nationalism and Internationalism in *Sir Gawain and the Green Knight.*" *The Literary Review* 23.4 (1980): 542–58.

Pierce, James C. "Synge's Widow Quin: Touchstone to the *Playboy*'s Irony." *Eire-Ireland* 16.2 (1981): 122–33.

Price, Alan. *Synge and Anglo-Irish Drama.* London: Methuen, 1961.

Roll-Hansen, Diderik. "*The Playboy of the Western World*: An Irish *Peer Gynt?*" *Studies in Anglo-Irish Literature.* Ed. Heinz Kosok. Bonn: Bouvier Verlag/Herbert Grundmann, 1982. 148–54.

Spacks, Patricia Meyer. "The Making of the *Playboy.*" Bloom 7–17.

Synge, John Millington. *The Aran Islands.* Synge, *Collected Works* 2: 47–184.

———. "An Autumn Night in the Hills." Synge, *Collected Works* 2: 187–92.

———. "An Epic in Ulster." Rev. of *Cuchulain of Muirthemne*, by Lady Augusta Gregory. Synge, *Collected Works* 2: 367–70.

———. *J.M. Synge: Collected Works.* 4 Vols. Gen. ed. Robin Skelton. London: Oxford UP, 1962–68.

———. *The Playboy of the Western World.* Synge, *Collected Works* 4: 51–175.

———. *Riders to the Sea.* Synge, *Collected Works* 3: 1–27.

———. *The Shadow of the Glen.* Synge, *Collected Works* 3: 29–59.

Watson, George J. *Irish Identity and the Literary Revival: Synge, Yeats, Joyce and O'Casey.* London: Croom Helm, 1979.

Yeats, W.B. *The Green Helmet. The Variorum Edition of the Plays of W.B. Yeats.* Ed. Russell K. Alspach. New York: Macmillan, 1966. 420–53.

10

The Pillowman and
the Ethics of Allegory

HANA WORTHEN AND W.B. WORTHEN

Allegories are, in the realm of thoughts, what ruins are in the realm
of things.
                    – Walter Benjamin, *Origin of German Tragic Drama*

Martin McDonagh's 2003 play *The Pillowman* allegorizes a key question
about the meaning and purpose of art: what are its consequences in the
world beyond the stage? Set in an interrogation room in an unnamed, apparently eastern-European totalitarian state, the play centres on the writer
Katurian Katurian, whose violent short stories seem to have inspired a
local wave of copy-cat crimes. As children, Katurian and his brother Michal
had been the subject of a bizarre educational/artistic experiment. Their
parents systematically tortured Michal to inspire their younger son's storytelling skills. Katurian has become a writer and discovers that Michal has
committed the brutal crimes inspired by his stories. As the play proceeds,
it's now Katurian who is tortured, as Detective Tupolski struggles to get the
confession that will justify the inevitable execution. In this essay, we explore McDonagh's meditation on the purpose and consequences of art,
not by framing a dialogue between *The Pillowman* and McDonagh's other
plays, but by considering the principal trope that *The Pillowman* offers for
art's implication in the world: allegory.

   Applying the term "allegory" to *The Pillowman*, we may seem already to
have consigned the play to that deepest pit of modern opprobrium, the dry
and dogmatic rationalism of the thesis play.[1] But, in many respects, *The
Pillowman*'s strategic deployment of violent stories not only reframes the
uses of theatrical violence animating recent British drama – plays like
Sarah Kane's *Blasted*, Mark Ravenhill's *Shopping and Fucking*, and Mc-
Donagh's earlier work in the "comedy-horror genre," *The Lieutenant of In-
ishmore* (Benedict) – but engages with the structure of interpretation and
assessment informing their reception as well. For these plays have proven

Modern Drama, 49:2 (Summer 2006)

controversial, not merely because they're bloody (after all, *Titus Androni-cus* is violent, too), but because, in their excess (cannibalism in *Blasted*) and in their tone (the funny dismemberment scene in *Lieutenant of Inish-more*), such plays seem to deny us a clear perspective on the dramatic and theatrical purposes of violent representation. As the history of Kane's *Blasted* shows, the question of the ethics of such violence cannot be answered by the work itself. The meaning of violent representation de-pends on how we make it mean, usually by claiming the play's metonymic, *allegorical*, relation to the world beyond the stage. In 1995, for instance, the play seemed at best to evince a "numbing amorality" (Jeremy King-ston), "its pointless violence just comes over as pointless" (Sarah Hem-ming), making "you question values: yours, the playwright's, the world's. We need these moral ordeals even if we have to pay for them" (John Peter).[2] By the 2001 revival, Michael Billington was only one of many critics to say that "[f]ive years ago I was rudely dismissive" about the play, "stunned by the play's excesses. Now it is easier to see their dramatic pur-pose. Kane is trying to shock us into an awareness of the emotional conti-nuum between domestic brutality and the rape-camps of Bosnia and to dispel the notion of the remote otherness of civil war" (Rev. of *Blasted*).

The critical reception of *Blasted* enacts a fundamentally allegorical per-spective on the ethics of art: the violence of the play can be redeemed from pornographic gratuitousness only if it can be assimilated to an ethical cri-tique of the world beyond the stage (even if that critique consists in repre-senting the horrors of a violent and arbitrary world in a violent and arbitrary way). Beyond that, though, allegorical reading becomes the means of claiming the play's implication in the world at large, as the play not only interprets offstage reality but, in so doing, enables a new kind of reality to come into being. As Edward Bond put it, "*Blasted* changed reality because it changed the means we have of understanding ourselves. It showed us a new way in which to see reality, and when we do that reality is changed" (190). We should not dismiss this way of valuing Kane or Mc-Donagh – whose violence is similarly described as "meretricious tosh," tart-ing up an otherwise "superficial drama" (Spencer) – in part, because *The Pillowman* specifically uses allegory to interrogate the relationship between artistic intention and the consequences of art.[3]

From the beginning of its career on the stage, *The Pillowman* has drawn a surprisingly allegorical line of criticism from reviewers, substantiating al-legory's centrality to the play's thematics. "Can art (including McDonagh's own) corrupt and cause damage? Is it parasitic on suffering and does its survival count for more than human life (including the artist's own)?" (Tay-lor). "Should writers be brought to task for dealing in violence, child abuse and blasphemy?" (Coveney, Rev. of *The Pillowman*). "Does art reflect or influence life? Is that the business of the writer or the reader?" (Benedict).

Yet again and again, the critics, in their readings of the play, hesitate to accept the conclusions seemingly suggested by the play's allegory. Jane Edwardes's review is a perfect example; to Edwardes, McDonagh "seems to overstate the importance of art, bind it too closely to pain," and so "fail." But what seems to fail – and to motivate all the critics' questions – is a basic hesitation about allegory itself. Allegorized violence seems to assert an unacceptable relationship between art and the world, either by failing as art (allegory is too driven by meaning, concept) or by failing to reflect our commitments to (or illusions about) a liveable world. As Charles Spencer suggests, "[I]f you took the nastiness out" of the play, and the world it embodies, "there would be almost nothing left."

But while many reviews dismiss *The Pillowman* as using "shock tactics" (Young) arising from the playwright's "disturbingly defective moral sense" (Taylor), their comments respond to the crisis of allegory that connects us to our eighteenth-century predecessors. As Theresa M. Kelley asks, "[W]hy does allegory survive modernity and what does modernity (still) have against it" (2)? In her extensive reading of allegory's transmission and adaptation to modernity (to which we will return), Kelley remarks how the mechanistic, abstract character of allegory conveys "a violence that looks as though it might be real and material, not figural," insofar as "allegorical abstractions are fundamentally hostile to human particularity." Summarizing Gordon Teskey, Kelley suggests that, as "a figure that both names and abstracts, allegory is prone to 'forms of violence' akin to those imposed by a tribe or community on a victim who is punished in the name of, or instead of, everyone else" (8). Resisting the temptation that so often seduces contemporary theory – where, as Kelley continues, "this violence takes the form of a temptation to invent abstract schemas" (8) – Victoria Segal responds to McDonagh's allegory with an allegory of her own.

The play's "sheer beauty and power of storytelling" offer "a great truth that will leap out of the curious on-stage events like grandmother from the wolf's stomach, but ultimately it's more mysterious than that." Setting McDonagh's play in the context of European folklore, Segal implies that allegory is not merely a means of mapping abstract ideas onto the material world, a map that other critics either dismiss as mere abstraction or fear to read. Instead, she suggests that the play evokes allegory's fundamental commitment to *meaning*, to a metonymic, worldly truth that involves a violent encounter between representation and the represented, even when that truth is veiled in the mysterious assertions of metaphor. That is, while we tend to regard allegory as a relatively straightforward, even simplistic figure – one that plots a direct connection between art and the world – a more dynamic sense of the violence of allegory itself would be considerably more challenging. "[I]f this was just a play about the pre-eminence of art and the responsibility of the artist, it would be a slight and slightly petulant play, a mirror-gazing love letter from the playwright to himself. Instead, McDonagh's interest in storytelling is dramatised, the strange, magical and nightmarish events onstage embodying his belief in art" (Segal).

Narrating "Katurian's stories and his terrifying childhood," *The Pillowman* veers between "queasily beautiful tableaux in the poisoned-apple colours of Disney's *Snow White and the Seven Dwarfs*" (Segal), illustrating Kelley's sense that the force of modern allegory "depends on its capacity to animate and thereby particularize its figures" (10). Allegory operates in several registers simultaneously, its tone consistently infusing and complicating what may seem at first a merely metonymic rhetoric connecting art to the world.

It is, perhaps, not surprising that theatrical journalism veers between dismissing plays as too allegorical and dismissing them as not allegorical enough, all the while enacting a fundamentally allegorizing practice of interpretation. For, as Walter Benjamin argued in *The Origin of German Tragic Drama*, allegory has been regarded with suspicion at least since the late eighteenth century precisely because of its ways of implicating art in the world. As Benjamin suggests, German classicism depends for its defining notion of the symbol on demonizing "its speculative counterpart," the "allegorical"; while a "genuine theory of the allegory did not, it is true, arise at that time," it is "nevertheless legitimate to describe the new concept of the allegorical as speculative because it was in fact adapted so as to provide the dark background against which the bright world of the symbol might stand out" (161).

Taken out of its context, the following statement by Goethe may be described as a negative, *a posteriori* construction of allegory: "There is a great difference between a poet's seeking of the particular from the general and his seeing the general in the particular. The former gives rise to allegory, where the particular serves only as an instance or example of the general; the latter, however, is the true nature of poetry: the expression of the particular without any thought of, or reference to, the general. Whoever grasps the particular in all its vitality also grasps the general, without being aware of it, or only becoming aware of it at a late stage." (161)

Romantic writers were troubled by two elements of allegory: its sublimation of the concrete particulars of material experience into an abstract realm of ideas and the relatively conventional ways in which this assimilation of the particular to the general takes place. "Even great artists and exceptional theoreticians, such as Yeats, still assume that allegory is a conventional relationship between an illustrative image and its abstract meaning" (Benjamin 162). The alternative to allegory is symbolic representation, in which, as Benjamin puts it, paraphrasing Friedrich Creuzer, the particular does not signify " 'merely a general concept, or an idea which is different from itself,' " but " 'is the very incarnation and embodiment of the idea' " (164). The symbolic meaning of the poem should be organic, innate, and original; its vitality arises from its rejection both of a preceding order of abstract ideas and of the particulars of the material world beyond the poem. As Paul de Man puts it, the "supremacy of the symbol" has become a "commonplace that underlies literary taste, literary criticism, and literary history"; allegory "appears as dryly rational and dogmatic in its reference to a meaning that it does not itself constitute, whereas the symbol is founded on an intimate unity between the image that rises up before the senses and the supersensory totality that the image suggests" ("Rhetoric" 189).

Yet, as the reception of *The Pillowman* and other plays suggests, we can't do without allegory. Like de Man, Benjamin works to rehabilitate allegory, in part because its use of "substitution" places allegorical representation in a characteristically dialectical relationship to time and human experience. While the "measure of time for the experience of the symbol is the mystical instant in which the symbol assumes the meaning into its hidden and, if one might say so, wooded interior," allegory has a corresponding dialectic that separates "visual being from meaning" (Benjamin 165). The symbol annihilates history, but allegory depends on it, on the melancholy principle of separation, on what de Man calls "the unveiling of an authentically temporal destiny" ("Rhetoric" 206). For Benjamin, the symbol idealizes nature "in the light of redemption," while allegory confronts the observer with history, "history as a petrified, primordial landscape" (Benjamin 166). For Benjamin, allegory guarantees art's engagement with the material world of temporal experience, even while that engagement is always dialectically mediated by the sign. If, as de Man elaborates, allegory foregrounds its dependence on the "*repetition* . . . of a previous sign with which it can never coincide," it is, at the same time, this principle of metonymic deferral, of "duration as the illusion of a continuity that it knows to be illusionary," that articulates allegory and irony as the figures of worldly experience ("Rhetoric" 207, 226). Benjamin argues,

> Any person, any object, any relationship can mean absolutely anything else. With this possibility a destructive, but just verdict is passed on the profane world: it is characterized as a world in which the detail is of no great importance. But it will be unmistakably apparent, especially to anyone who is familiar with allegorical textual exegesis, that all of the things which are used to signify derive, from the very fact of their pointing to something else, a power which makes them appear no longer commensurable with profane things, which raises them onto a higher plane, and which can, indeed, sanctify them. (175)

What allegory makes possible is a poetry that can respond to truths outside itself, to the temporal order of human history. Allegory enables poetry to speak to the world.[4]

As Goethe's heirs, modern readers habitually deploy allegorical means of interpreting art works – "[q]uestions about art and morality are kicking around" in *The Pillowman* (Gross) – while typically finding allegory embarrassing, too insistent on idea, meaning, at the expense of the particularities of experience. Yet a conception of allegory, of the capacity for the particularities of art to represent more general claims about the temporal ruins in which we live, is essential to any critique of the ethics of art, its implication in the social world of human action. And allegory is crucial to *The Pillowman*: Katurian's stories are parables in the mould of Kafka or Borges, and they are interpreted in a rigorously allegorical manner both by Michal and by Detective Tupolski. If the ethics of art are at stake in *The Pillowman*, they are inseparable from the ethics of allegory.

Allegory is the trope for art's engagement with time, experience, and history, and so allegory is always potentially political in its implications. As Gordon Teskey has argued, to the extent that allegories "engage us in the practice of ritual interpretation" by which ideologies "are reproduced in bodies," allegory acts as "a substitute for genuine political speaking" and so elicits "the ritual repetition of an ideologically significant world" (132). McDonagh enlarges and complicates this perception by pointedly – if somewhat artificially – setting the play in an unnamed police state. Like many contemporary advocates for greater censorship of both popular and élite culture, Detective Tupolski understands Katurian's writing both as elevating the "profane world" into art and, at the same time, as altering that world, bringing a kind of violence into being in the world. As he charges, Katurian's stories all have a "theme" connecting them with the crimes: " '[s]ome poor little kid gets fucked up.' Your theme" (McDonagh 15). Despite his sense of possible ambiguity, Tupolski deftly rephrases Benjamin's sense that the power of allegory derives from "the very fact of [its] pointing to something else" (Benjamin 175). To Tupolski, Katurian's narrative typically works like "a pointer" – "on the surface I am saying this, but underneath the surface I am saying this other thing" (McDonagh 18–19) – that points both beneath the fictional surface and to murderous action in the world.

McDonagh may seem to stack the deck here. Even political art's most avowed adherents rarely urge such a simplistic vision of the politics of art. At the same time, our distaste for Tupolski's politics, his violence, or even his forensic purposes should not obscure McDonagh's irony. The critical understanding that "all art is political" is not a view unique to the critique from the political left. It is a view deeply engrained in a totalitarian vision of social control, in which the state has the authority to enforce its own allegories of reading: "[a]ny person, any object, any relationship can mean absolutely anything else" (Benjamin 175). If the police are responsible for articulating a vision of the real-world consequences of art, Katurian – admittedly, trying to avoid the execution that seems inevitably to await him –

takes the opposing view, describing his writing from a purely formalist, "art for art's sake" perspective that attempts to sidestep Tupolski's instrumental allegory by claiming a merely "symbolic" disinterestedness. "A great man once said, 'The first duty of a storyteller is to tell a story,' " which to Katurian means, "No axe to grind, no anything to grind. No social anything whatsoever. And that's why, I can't see, if that's why you've brought me in here, I can't see what the reason would be, unless something political came in by accident, or something that *seemed* political came in, in which case show me where it is" (7–8). If Tupolski can find political content, Katurian says, "Show me where the bastard is. I'll take it straight out. Fucking burn it. You know?" (8). Although Katurian's stories – "The Little Apple Men," "The Tale of the Town on the River," "The Little Jesus" – are all about tortured or murdered children, when Tuposki asks, "Are you trying to say, 'Go out and murder children?' " Katurian protests, "No! No bloody way! Are you kidding? I'm not trying to say anything at all! That's my whole thing . . . If there are children in them, it's incidental. If there is politics in them, it's incidental. It's *accidental*" (16).

Katurian and Tupolski represent two opposed views of the ethics of representation, the "recurrent debate opposing intrinsic to extrinsic criticism" (de Man, *Allegories* 5). Tupolski reads allegorically but not dialectically: to Tupolski, the particulars of Katurian's stories are not mediated by narrative form and seem hardly to achieve the status of artistic *signs* at all; the stories are merely irritating murder manuals. Katurian, on the other hand, refuses allegory altogether and so refuses its generalizing potentiality, denying that his work has anything other than symbolic value – the meaning of its "hidden and . . . wooded interior" stands apart from the world of action.

Yet, as de Man argues in *Allegories of Reading*, the literal and figural capacities of language are not so readily distinguishable. Deconstructing the ostensible opposition between intrinsic and extrinsic critique, the poetic "inside" and the "outside" to which it gestures, de Man argues that the distinction between rhetoric and grammar, the distinction that would enable us to separate and assess the figural and the literal elements of allegory, inevitably collapses, so that it can only be "cleared up by the intervention of an extra-textual intention" (de Man, *Allegories* 10). Katurian's stories similarly complicate the relationship between inside and outside by enacting a strangely blank, but nonetheless palpable, moral complexity; at the very least, they enact a formal irony that seems to evoke the ruins of a world of moral choice. The two stories that seem to have inspired crimes – "The Little Apple Men" and "The Tale of the Town on the River" – are fundamentally about justice, even while they are elliptical, "fashionably downbeat" parables (McDonagh 104). In "The Little Apple Men," a girl who is abused by her father carves apples into several little men, telling her father not to eat them but to keep them as a memory of her childhood. Needless to say, he gobbles them up, finding only too late that she has hidden razor blades inside. As Katurian says, "[T]hat's kind of like the end of the story, that should be like the end of the story, the father gets his comeuppance"; but the story "goes on" (13). One night, the girl awakens to find "[a] number of applemen . . . walking up her chest. They hold her mouth open. They say to her . . . [. . .] 'You killed our little brothers,'" and climb down her throat choking her to death (13). (The first crime victim, a little girl, had been forced to swallow little applemen concealing razor blades.) In "The Tale of the Town on the River," another abused child, a boy, flees from his parents and is shivering under a bridge when a dark stranger approaches in a cart filled with small, empty animal cages. The boy shares his sandwich with the driver, who repays him, surprisingly, by snatching up his meat cleaver and chopping off the boy's toes, tossing them to the rats in the gutter. The story concludes, "[He] got back onto his cart, and quietly rode on over the bridge, leaving the boy, the rats, the river and the darkening town of *Hamelin* far behind him" (22). As Katurian explains, it's "the children the Pied Piper was after. To begin with. My idea was he *brought* the rats . . . It was the children he was after in the first place," and so he saved the little boy by crippling him (22–23). (The second victim was a little boy who bled to death when his toes were cut off.)

While Katurian's stories do have the "theme" of children getting "fucked up," they also insist on ending with a surprising narrative "twist" (McDonagh 22); the apparent closure of the narrative is, through the "*staccato* of irony," extended in a second, nonetheless formal, peripeteia (de Man, "Rhetoric" 228). In "The Little Apple Men," the justice of the girl's revenge on her father doesn't take into account her sacrifice of the applemen; in the second story, the dark stranger's savage mutilation of the little boy turns out to be an act of kindness, as it saves him from being drawn to his death by the dark stranger himself, the Pied Piper of Hamelin. In "The Little Jesus," a little girl – whose desire to imitate Jesus becomes a kind of torment when her foster parents crucify and bury her alive – would have risen from the grave had the beggar walking through the forest been able to hear her cries. Katurian's "something – esque" (18) stories all depend on an ironic twist, in which "good" acts have "bad" consequences ("Little Apple Men"), "bad" acts have "good" consequences ("Tale of the Town"), and the "good," Jesus-like girl suffers just like Jesus and almost rises like him, too, but not quite. Katurian's stories repeatedly substitute this formal "twist" for moral or ethical decision; the enactment of allegory's violent formal symmetry displaces moral judgment. In this sense, Katurian is only partly right when he says that his stories don't "say anything." It would be fairer to say that his stories represent a world subject to the meaningless artifice of aesthetic form. Like the little girl's voice in "The Little Jesus," fading away in the "black, black gloom of the empty, empty, empty forest" (72), the stories insistently subject ethical concern to the shaping priorities of formal allegory.

Katurian's stories have the structure of parables, yet like Kafka's or Borges's, Katurian's allegories refuse to assimilate narrative "particulars" to a given pre-text, in the way Christian allegorical drama is sustained by its reference to and dependence on an antecedent "text" of scripture. In this sense, Katurian's stories represent more than merely "fashionable" experiment. They dramatize the ways that genre functions as a structure of assertion, a kind of rhetoric; as blank allegories – what we might take to be the allegorical equivalent to Fredric Jameson's blank parody – Katurian's stories insist on their transformation of the "profane world," while at the same time withholding the terms of that transformation (see Jameson 17). But while we may be alarmed or irritated by the way Katurian's fictional world displaces ethical claims with irony, we may also wonder whether there is really any alternative. For allegory and irony resemble one another in this respect: "[b]oth modes are fully de-mystified when they remain within the realm of their respective languages but are totally vulnerable to renewed blindness as soon as they leave it for the empirical world" (de Man, "Rhetoric" 226). Both allegory and irony insist on and are sustained by their metonymy of the world of action; all the same, a figural "rightness" may be the only justice we can expect them to deliver.

Katurian's allegorical parables and Michal's enactment of them are also framed within larger historical narratives, within both personal and social histories that serve to qualify the implication of allegory in the human world of action. Katurian's only autobiographical story, "The Writer and the Writer's Brother," describes the genesis of his career as a writer. In the story, two brothers a year apart in age are raised in separate rooms; beginning at the age of seven, the younger brother begins to have nightmares, when he hears the sounds of a child being tortured in the next room, part of the parents' plan, it turns out, to raise the younger child as a writer. The horrific sounds of torture continue until the younger child's fourteenth birthday, when he submits a story to a writing competition and also finds a bloody note slipped under the door of the next room: " 'They have loved you and tortured me for seven straight years for no reason other than as an artistic experiment, an artistic experiment which has worked. You don't write about little green pigs any more, do you?' The note was signed 'Your brother,' and the note was written in blood" (32–33). The child breaks down the door to find the parents playing with pig's blood and tools; they say that it was all an educational hoax and show him the back of the bloody note, the prize in the writing competition. The boy is satisfied, but when he later returns to the torture room and pokes around, he finds the corpse of a tortured child, and "a story that could only have been written under the most sickening of circumstances, and it was the sweetest, gentlest thing, he'd ever come across, but, what was even worse, it was better than anything he himself had ever written. Or ever would" (34). So he burned the story, hid the brother's corpse, and never said a word.

Yet while "The Writer and the Writer's Brother" externalizes Katurian's guilt, it also dramatizes something else about art's implication in the world: art always lies. For Katurian, in fact, found his brother Michal alive but "brain-damaged beyond repair," and on the night of his fourteenth birthday, suffocated his father with a pillow and, "after waking her a moment just to let her see her dead blue husband . . . held a pillow over his mother's head for a little while, too" (34–35). Katurian's formal "twist" – Katurian's only the brother of the *real* writer – here stands in for the truth, replacing the messiness of events with a neat sense of completion. Just because allegory provides a means of implicating art in the temporal world of things, it doesn't mean that it must or even *can* tell the truth – or that we would be able to tell when it did. As Archie Bunker asks in de Man's celebrated discussion of the interplay between the figural and the literal, "What's the difference?"[5]

As it happens, Michal has also been arrested and seems – from his screams from an adjoining room – to be being tortured in another part of the prison, replicating "The Writer and the Writer's Brother" as theatre. We soon discover, though, that Michal isn't being tortured at all but is bribed to feign torture so that Katurian will confess. Michal has already confessed to killing the children according to the "directions" of Katurian's stories. "I was just testing out how far-fetched they were. 'Cos I always thought some of 'em were a bit far-fetched. (*Pause.*) D'you know what? They ain't all that far-fetched" (50). After nearly a decade of torture, Michal is unable to tell the difference between the real and the fictional and seems not to have developed empathy for others' suffering. At the same time, though, it's not clear that his horrific history is the cause of his moral anomie. Michal's scripture has been neither the Bible nor the book of nature; his moral sense has been formed by reading Katurian's stories.

> The little boy was just like you said it'd be. I chopped his toes off and he didn't scream at all. He just sat there looking at them. He seemed very surprised. I suppose you would be at that age. His name was Aaron. He had a funny little hat on, kept going on about his mum. God, he bled a lot. You wouldn't've thought there'd be that much blood in such a little boy. Then he stopped bleeding and went blue. Poor thing. I feel quite bad now, he seemed quite nice . . . But the girl was a pain in the arse. Kept bawling her eyes out. And she wouldn't eat them. She wouldn't eat the applemen, and I'd spent *ages* making them. It's really hard to get the razor blades inside. You don't say how to make them in the story, do ya? (48–49)

Michal's actions shape less a critique of the artist's responsibility for his work than an image of the violence that allegorical abstraction invariably brings to the world of things. Katurian's downbeat irony is echoed in Michal's chilly disconnection from the reality of his victims' suffering. Recalling *Macbeth* (Duncan held a surprising amount of blood, too), Michal is nonetheless fascinated by the details as he works to extend and realize Katurian's scripture. After all, Michal actually has to figure out how to *make* the little applemen. Allegory may be a strategy of assertion, a way to map the literal into the figural that invariably does violence to the literal's particularity. But allegory is also a mode of interpretation and so raises the reciprocal problems of the violence of interpretation.

Despite Katurian's sense that he is not saying anything, his works make sense in the world or are made into sense in the world, only as allegories of worldly action. Indeed, while Katurian's stories dramatize the tension between pathos and mechanization in modern allegory, *The Pillowman* tends to blur the distinction between allegory and *allegoresis*, or allegorical *interpretation*. Kelley reminds us that the work of *allegoresis* is to conduct "the work of allegorical interpretation" and so "to specify the outward shape for allegory's 'other speech.' Few recognitions are as prescient for modern allegory, where putative distinctions between narrators, readers or theorists, and allegory tend to dissolve" (7).[6] Like that of all censors, Tupolski's reading is a form of *allegoresis*: he legislates a single interpretation as the licensed "reading" of the work, finding the "other speech" of Katurian's stories in the crimes that afflict the city. Michal reads allegorically too, taking Katurian's writing to provide equipment for living. We might want to distance ourselves from both kinds of reading, but it's finally hard to do so. The alternative to this kind of reading seems to be the vacuous position, enunciated by Katurian, that art is nothing, says nothing, does nothing. Moreover, it's not merely a question of violence; Katurian's only non-violent story has its application too. Michal's favourite of Katurian's stories, "The Little Green Pig," is about a green pig, tormented by the other pigs but happy being "a little bit different, a little bit peculiar" (65). One night the farmers take him and paint him pink, like the other pigs. When the Little Green Pig prays to be peculiar again, a green rain falls, painting all the other pigs green but leaving the Little Green Pig a bit peculiarly pink. From the outset of *The Pillowman*, detectives are searching for a third missing child, fearing that she has been murdered according to one of Katurian's stories. Although Michal leads Katurian to think that the child has been subjected to the events of "The Little Jesus" and buried alive, at the end of the play the police discover the third victim, a little deaf girl. She is alive and well, happily playing with some piglets, and has been painted an astonishing shade of green. Perhaps both Tupolski and Michal are inured to the pathos of Katurian's stories; responding to the formal symmetry of the stories with a merely mechanistic process of *allegoresis*, they model not so much the "wrong" reading as the kind of reading that haunts modern allegory itself, the fear that the imprimatur of the violent, abstract, mechanical cannot be escaped.

The Pillowman frames the rhetoric of allegory in political terms, as necessarily implicated in the material world and its ways of understanding itself, of representing itself to itself. Yet while Nicholas de Jongh draws a lucid parallel between Katurian's parents' experiment and state terrorism – "Can profoundly abusive parents, products of a totalitarian regime, ironically foster the creative spirit in some victims of their cruelty, while for others they do irretrievable damage?" – *The Pillowman* is less interested in anatomizing the "totalitarian fucking dictatorship" (McDonagh 23) than in using the totalitarian frame to interrogate the ethics of allegory.[7] Much as there is symmetry between Michal and Tupolski, on the one hand, and readers of allegory, on the other, so, too, McDonagh emphasizes the likeness between Katurian and Tupolski by underscoring the artistry of interrogation. In the first scene of the play, Tupolski and his sidekick Ariel show themselves as fully versed in the narrative conventions of the "interrogation scene"; as the brutal Ariel puts it, "Oh, I almost forgot to mention . . . I'm the good cop, he's the bad cop" (12). More to the point, the detectives are sensitive to the aesthetics of Katurian's testimony and frequently absorb Katurian's language into their own "story." Tupolski, for example, catches Katurian glancing at the papers on his desk and wants to know if he has been "reading" them.

KATURIAN My eyes caught the titles, just glancing.
TUPOLSKI Oh, like your peripheral vision?
KATURIAN Yes.
TUPOLSKI But, hang on, for it to be your peripheral vision, you'd have to be turned around this way . . . (*TUPOLSKI turns sideways on, glancing down at papers.*) See, like this way. Like sidewards, like this way . . .
KATURIAN I meant . . .
TUPOLSKI See? Like this way. Like sidewards.
KATURIAN I meant my peripheral vision at the bottom of my eyes.
TUPOLSKI Ohh, the peripheral vision at the *bottom* of your eyes.
KATURIAN I don't know if there's a word for that.
TUPOLSKI There isn't. (6)

Tupolski uses this exchange about "peripheral vision" artfully to establish his relationship with Katurian. He insists on his power to define the relationship (who will decide the meaning of Katurian's "glance"), in part by examining and defining the words that Katurian uses. After all, it's Tupolski who says there isn't a word for "peripheral vision at the *bottom* of your eyes." Again and again, Ariel and Tupolski insist on their control of the narrative structure of the interrogation, on its aesthetic protocol: "[w]e

know we can draw our own fucking conclusions" (11); " 'Should I have?'
Good answer. 'Should I have?' Kind of lily-livered and subservient on the
one hand, yet vaguely sarcastic and provocative on the other" (14).

Moreover, much as Katurian insists that his stories are just stories, Tupolski asks, "I am a high-ranking police officer in a totalitarian fucking dictatorship. What are you doing taking my word about anything?" (23).
Artists lie, policemen lie. As Katurian points out, there's a striking similarity
between the ways the detectives use narrative (lying to Katurian that they
are torturing Michal, for example, when they have only bribed him to
scream) and the more formal processes of storytelling. "Why are we believing everything they're telling us," Katurian asks. "This is just like storytelling . . . A man comes into a room, says to another man, 'Your mother's
dead.' What do we know? Do we know that the second man's mother is
dead?" (39). While Katurian insists that his stories don't "say anything," in
an odd "twist," the detectives believe that violent, abusive, deceptive
"storytelling" can nonetheless be an instrument for the discovery of the
truth, even when the stories they tell are lies.

We might expect that a detective story like *The Pillowman* would come
down to "the facts," but the world of *The Pillowman* is troped by competing fictions. Everyone's a writer, and Tupolski tells his own allegorical tale
of police work, a tale that illustrates the somewhat peculiar understanding
of the relationship between writer and reader that animates Tupolski's understanding of interrogation. Tupolski "wrote this little story once," a story
that "if it doesn't sum up my world view, it sums up my view of detective
work and the relation of that detective work to the world at large" (85).
"The Story of the Little Deaf Boy on the Big Long Railroad Tracks. In
China" is much like Katurian's stories, a kind of "puzzle without a solution"
(17) that seems at once allegorical and mysterious. In the story, a deaf
child is walking along a railroad track while a locomotive bears down on
him from many miles away. About a mile down the tracks, a mathematician is working in a tower and sees the situation; but rather than warn the
boy, he begins to calculate when the train will "plough straight through the
poor little deaf boy's little fucking back" (88). The boy is about thirty yards
away when the mathematician figures out that the train will hit him when
he is ten yards from the tower. But the mathematician seems only interested in his calculations, not the child, and folds the paper into an airplane
and tosses it out the window. Eleven yards from the tower, the boy sees the
airplane, leaps from the tracks to catch it, and is saved.

Tupolski's story illustrates the fundamental problem with allegory: how
do we relate the pre-text, the "general," to the "particular" of the story's
events, in which "[a]ny person, any object, any relationship can mean
absolutely anything else" (Benjamin 175)? Tupolski insists on the propriety
of authorial intention and insists that the story sums up his "view of

detective work, or whatever" (89). Yet Katurian assumes that the mathematician is absorbed in his calculations and that he saves the little boy only by accident, while, for Tupolski, "the old wise man, see, he represents *me*," calculating from day to day without "much affinity with his fellow man" (represented by the little boy) (89). "He comes along, oblivious to every fucking thing, doesn't even know there's a fucking train coming, but *I* know there's a train coming, and by the brilliance of my calculations, and by the brilliance of throwing that paper plane at that very moment, I shall save that idiot from that train, I shall save my fellow man from those criminals, and I won't even get a word of thanks for it" (90). Unlike most artists, Tupolski is unusually well placed to insist on the force of his intentions, but he shares his understanding of the proprieties of interpretation with his captive audience, for both Tupolski and Katurian insist on the author's intention as the final point of appeal in matters of interpretation.

Katurian's stories may not say anything, but their subjecting an ethical to a formal resolution produces real consequences; Tupolski insists on what his story is saying, yet his audience – on- and offstage – finds it to say something else. For all that Tupolski's story seems to dramatize his callous indifference both to justice and to the suffering of his "fellow man" and Katurian's stories seem at best to enact the illusion of moral choice, in the end, *The Pillowman* locates the ethics of allegory less in the "work itself" than in the "intervention of extra-textual intention" – here, the ability of author or audience to enforce interpretation, to enforce *how* the work will be imbricated in the world (de Man, *Allegories* 10).

To the extent that we take Tupolski to be a kind of artist in the play, then *The Pillowman* finally articulates a deeply sceptical vision of the relationship between narrative and truth. After all, while Tupolski seems to be searching for the truth – who is the murderer of the children? – he has already determined to execute Katurian and Michal. Like Katurian, Tupolski insists on the proprieties of form: what's important to him is have a good "story" to tell, to make it look like the writer and his brother are guilty, at least guilty enough to execute. As the play progresses, Katurian kills Michal and confesses to all of the crimes – killing his parents, killing Michal, killing the first two children, and killing the deaf girl, according to the instructions in his story "The Little Jesus" – so that his stories will be saved in his criminal file and not be destroyed. But when the deaf girl is discovered green and alive, Katurian's confession and Tupolski's execution begin to unravel. As Ariel points out, Katurian is hazy on the details of how the first two children were really killed: "[t]he only killing we can definitely pin on you is the killing of your brother. In light of the extenuating circumstances, I doubt it highly that you would be executed for it" (98). But in the end, the confession is not really necessary. Much as Katurian chose the ending to "The Writer and the Writer's Brother," Tupolski will choose the ending to the tale of Katurian and his brother. He tells Katurian to kneel, says he will give him ten seconds to think, and begins counting backward from ten, shooting Katurian on "Four." The detective is a storyteller who always gets the ending he wants and always lies.

The Pillowman frames allegory's series of violent dialectics, between the intention of the artist and the consequences of art, between inscription and reception, between allegory's representation of a world and the world's use of allegory. And since *The Pillowman* is full of pillowmen – Katurian killed his parents with a pillow, he kills Michal with a pillow, Ariel also suffocated his brutal father with a pillow – we might expect Katurian's story, "The Pillowman," to provide a final point of repair. In the story, the Pillowman (yes, he's made of pillows) is a kind of saviour. When someone has had "a dreadful and hard life and they just wanted to end it all, they just wanted to take their own lives and take all the pain away," the Pillowman appears and takes the suicide back to that moment in childhood when all the torment began and attempts to persuade the child to take his or her own life "and so avoid the years of pain that would just end up in the same place for them anyway: facing an oven, facing a shotgun, facing a lake" (44). Of course, a child suicide is another kind of horror and would be an endless torment for the child's parents, so the Pillowman always makes the suicide look like an accident. Eventually, though, his work takes its toll on the Pillowman, who comes to see suicide as *his* only way out of a life of suffering. The moment he contemplates suicide, the Pillowboy (the Pillowman as a boy) appears and the Pillowman persuades him to immolate himself. But as the Pillowboy burns, and the Pillowman fades away,

> [t]he last thing he heard was something he hadn't even contemplated. The last thing he heard was the screams of the hundred thousand children he'd helped to commit suicide coming back to life and going on to lead the cold, wretched lives that were destined to them because he hadn't been around to prevent them, right on up to the screams of their sad self-inflicted deaths, which this time, of course, would be conducted entirely alone. (47)

In one sense, "The Pillowman" is a story relating allegory to history. If the Pillowman can successfully tell the story of the child's coming suffering, then the child's suicide will erase it. Allegorizing history as narrative provides the means at once to engage, understand, and even, perhaps, change it. Yet the final moments of the play give "The Pillowman" a final, perhaps vertiginous, spin. Having just been executed by Tupolski, Katurian rises to speak to the audience, telling a new story about Michal and the Pillowman. In this story, the Pillowman visits Michal on the evening before his years of torture begin, and gives him a choice between killing himself now and so avoiding torture, mental instability, his own crimes, and being murdered by his brother on a cold prison floor, on the one hand; or staying alive so that his brother hears his screams and becomes a writer, on the other. Michal decides to live, and Katurian's final story heads toward its usual "fashionably downbeat" ending. Michal chooses torture so as to inspire Katurian's art, but in the end, Ariel is about to burn the stories rather than placing them in the criminal records. Yet, "for reasons known only to himself, the bulldog of a policeman chose not to put the stories in the burning trash, but placed them carefully with Katurian's case file, which he then sealed away to remain unopened for fifty-odd years" (103–04).

As Katurian notes, this fact "would have ruined the writer's fashionably downbeat ending," but was nonetheless "somehow . . . somehow . . . more in keeping with the spirit of the thing" (104). Katurian's final story ends with its typical "twist," the irony that Michal's sacrifice is finally pointless. In McDonagh's play, the world enacts a final, ironic, lightly utopian twist on Katurian's tale: the brutal policeman saves the stories and so seems to provide a different kind of closure. For Benjamin, allegory provides a way to engage with and interpret the world of experience and history; for de Man, the irony of believing that with "the internal law and order of literature well policed, we can now confidently devote ourselves to the foreign affairs, the external politics of literature" (de Man, *Allegories* 3) is ineffably complicated by the inherent unreliability of language itself, in which metaphor and metonymy are mutually deconstructive, a state which rather than producing the illusion of political, interpretive certainty should bring us to recognize our "state of suspended ignorance" (19). In the final moments of *The Pillowman*, we see the world of experience responding to and revising Katurian's allegory, perhaps in a way somehow "more in keeping with the spirit of the thing." How should we take this epiphany? While *The Pillowman*'s final tale is more reminiscent of the logic of "The Tale of the Town on the River" and "The Little Green Pig" than of that of "The Little Apple Men" or "The Little Jesus," all five stories are formally identical and seem to imply that the fateful logic of narrative "rightness" has little to do with ethical or moral value. There's always a twist: sometimes you win, sometimes you lose. What's the difference?

Yet, at the same time, in the final moments of *The Pillowman*, the formal logic of Katurian's stories seems to extend from the tales into the world itself. Whatever their value as allegory, their structure as allegory is replicated in the world beyond the tale. Katurian's blank allegories do, finally, affect the world of action, but not in the tendentious way assumed by Michal and Tupolski. Instead, the ethical neutrality of Katurian's formal "twists" provides a trope that emplots a momentarily utopian possibility in the world of action. In a world of moral uncertainty, perhaps the tension between narrative closure and moral choice can, sometimes, result in a closure that not only feels right but that is, ironically enough, through some kind of insistently arty and arbitrary twist, *right*. Insofar as "the real is necessary to allegory, not antithetical to it," *The Pillowman*'s anatomy of allegory arrives, finally, at its own "twist"; that is, for all that allegory asserts its worldliness, an assertion that subjects the order of the world to the violence of representation, it is finally the world that determines the meaning and purpose of allegory (Kelley 260). McDonagh's play refuses to answer the critics – is the artist responsible for the consequences of art? what is the relation between art and politics? – but it does not refuse their questions. Instead, in taking allegory as the mode of the play's inquiry, as the instance and the instrument for its inquiry into the worldliness of art, *The Pillowman* is finally limited by the dynamics of allegory, where assertions about the world are invariably qualified by the artifice of the assertion. It's up to us to decide, as Ariel decides, how to use the work of art.

In this sense, Segal's suggestion that *The Pillowman* stages the appeal of the "words 'once upon a time' " while withholding "definitive meaning" responds to the character of allegory's revival in contemporary literature (Segal). As Kelley argues, allegory "prospers now precisely because it is inventive, endlessly adaptive, and open to a calculus of time and change as more stable systems of representation are not," even if such allegories finally stage "the impossibility of moral and logical absolutes" (269). But withholding "moral and logical absolutes" is not the same as not "saying anything." *The Pillowman* frames the work of art in the often-violent dialectic between intention and execution, between the formalities of the art work and the forms of work it can be made to accomplish in the world. To this extent, McDonagh's analysis of the ethics of allegory in *The Pillowman* seems less reminiscent of the opaque horrors of *Blasted* or *Shopping and Fucking* than of the work of a writer pointedly engaged in the problems of art in the world of political struggle, Seamus Heaney. For, as Heaney also recognizes, the slippage between metaphor and metonymy, rhetoric and grammar makes it hard to insist on the specific ethical efficacy of art. Sometimes, the best we can do is to be alert to the moments when "hope and history rhyme" (Heaney 77).

NOTES

1   We allude here to Paul de Man's sense that "[a]llegory appears . . . dryly rational and dogmatic in its reference to a meaning that it does not itself constitute" ("Rhetoric" 189).

2   While reviews of the play were famously disgusted, Michael Coveney did remark,

> At once cool and classical, this atmospheric essay in the end-of-millennium violence of Tarantino and the not-so-new apocalyptic brand in Bond's "War Plays" (recently acclaimed in Paris) posed a simple question: how do you feel

about having the *News at Ten* made real in the front room? A tense and gripping first hour was followed by horrors, sexual explicitness apart, no worse than in Shakespeare's *Titus* or Seneca's *Thyestes*. The performances were stunning. I can hardly wait to see what Ms Kane does next. (Rev. of *Blasted*)

3   *The Pillowman* premiered at the Cottesloe Theatre, Royal National Theatre, London, November 13, 2003. It has since been produced throughout Europe and the Americas.

4   Kelley's fine reading of the work of allegory throughout Benjamin's writing notes that Benjamin is the "modern writer whose tragic understanding of allegory initiates the modern reinvention of allegory" (251), particularly insofar as Benjamin understands an "allegory more cognizant of its necessary, transient factitiousness and for this reason as free as it ever can be from fixed, inflexible codes and receptive to the productive, material decay of its modern figures" (258).

5   We refer here to de Man's arresting account of the television show *All in the Family*. When Archie Bunker's wife Edith asks whether he would like his bowling shoes "laced over or laced under, Archie Bunker answers with a question: 'What's the difference?' " To de Man (who seems not to know what lacing over or under means), this question operates in two self-cancelling registers: the question grammatically insists on the fact of difference by asking what the difference is; at the same time, the question rhetorically insists on the absence of difference, asserting that the difference is immaterial, that there is no difference. "Confronted with the question of the difference between grammar and rhetoric, grammar allows us to ask the question, but the sentence by means of which we ask it may deny the very possibility of asking. For what is the use of asking, I ask, when we cannot even authoritatively decide whether a question asks or doesn't ask?" (*Allegories of Reading* 9, 10).

6   Kelley argues that "[t]he role of pathos in modern allegory is one warrant for taking this risk"; that is, risking the temptation to mechanistic abstraction. "For without pathos, allegory might otherwise constantly reproduce the mechanization that Neoclassical critics hoped for (a mechanical allegory is at least safely dead), but which Romantic and post-Romantic readers have despised" (8).

7   Katurian's address is "Kamenice 4443" and he works at the "Kamenice abattoir" (9). "Kamenice" is a common name for villages throughout eastern Europe, particularly in the Czech Republic; with the alternate spelling "Kamenica," it's also common in Poland, Slovakia, and Serbia, and in Serbia, a "Kamenica" was recently the site of ethnic political struggle leading to ethnic cleansing. Michael Billington, among others, suggests that McDonagh is "playing with big issues to do with literature's power to outlast tyranny rather than writing from any kind of experience" (Rev. of *The Pillowman*).

WORKS CITED

Benedict, David. Rev. of *The Pillowman. Independent on Sunday* 23 Nov. 2003. Rpt. in *Theatre Record* 23 (2003): 1553–54.

Benjamin, Walter. *The Origin of German Tragic Drama.* Trans. John Osborne. London: Verso, 1990.

Billington, Michael. Rev. of *Blasted. Guardian* 4 Apr. 2001. Rpt. in *Theatre Record* 21 (2001): 421.

———. Rev. of *The Pillowman. Guardian* 14 Nov. 2003. Rpt. in *Theatre Record* 23 (2003): 1551.

Bond, Edward. "Afterword: Sarah Kane and Theatre." *Love Me or Kill Me: Sarah Kane and the Theatre of Extremes* by Graham Saunders. Manchester: Manchester UP, 2002. 189–91.

Coveney, Michael. Rev. of *Blasted. Observer* 5 Feb. 1995. Rpt. in *Theatre Record* 15 (1995): 42.

———. Rev. of *The Pillowman. Daily Mail* 14 Nov. 2003. Rpt. in *Theatre Record* 23 (2003): 1552.

de Jongh, Nicholas. Rev. of *The Pillowman. Evening Standard* 14 Nov. 2003. Rpt. in *Theatre Record* 23 (2003): 1551.

de Man, Paul. *Allegories of Reading: Figural Language in Rousseau, Nietzsche, Rilke, and Proust.* New Haven: Yale UP, 1979.

———. "The Rhetoric of Temporality." *Blindness and Insight: Essays in the Rhetoric of Contemporary Criticism.* 2nd ed. Minneapolis: U of Minnesota P, 1983. 187–228.

Edwardes, Jane. Rev of *The Pillowman. Time Out* 19 Nov. 2003. Rpt. in *Theatre Record* 23 (2003): 1553.

Gross, John. Rev. of *The Pillowman. Sunday Telegraph* 16 Nov. 2003. Rpt. in *Theatre Record* 23 (2003): 1550.

Heaney, Seamus. *The Cure at Troy: A Version of Sophocles'* Philoctetes. New York: Farrar, 1991.

Hemming, Sarah. Rev. of *Blasted. Financial Times* 23 Jan. 1993. Rpt. in *Theatre Record* 15 (1995): 40.

Jameson, Fredric. *Postmodernism, or, The Cultural Logic of Late Capitalism.* Durham: Duke UP, 1991.

Kelley, Theresa M. *Reinventing Allegory.* Cambridge: Cambridge UP, 1997.

Kingston, Jeremy. Rev. of *Blasted. Times* 20 Jan. 1995. Rpt. in *Theatre Record* 15 (1995): 39.

McDonagh, Martin. *The Pillowman.* London: Faber, 2003.

Peter, John. Rev. of *Blasted. Sunday Times* 29 Jan. 1995. Rpt. in *Theatre Record* 15 (1995): 41.

Segal, Victoria. Rev. of *The Pillowman. Sunday Times* 23 Nov. 2003. Rpt. in *Theatre Record* 23 (2003): 1554–55.

Spencer, Charles. Rev. of *The Pillowman. Daily Telegraph* 14 Nov. 2003. Rpt. in *Theatre Record* 23 (2003): 1550.

Taylor, Paul. Rev. of *The Pillowman. Independent* 17 Nov. 2003. Rpt. in *Theatre Record* 23 (2003): 1551–52.

Teskey, Gordon. *Allegory and Violence.* Ithaca: Cornell UP, 1996.

Young, Toby. Rev. of *The Pillowman. Spectator* 22 Nov. 2003. Rpt. in *Theatre Record* 23 (2003): 1553.

11

Cognitive Catharsis in *The Caucasian Chalk Circle*[1]

R. DARREN GOBERT

In Bertolt Brecht's 1930 *Lehrstück* [learning play] *The Measures Taken*, the Four Agitators relate to the Control Chorus (and their offstage audience) the events leading up to their killing of the Young Comrade, whose violation of the teachings of Communism has endangered their cause and justified his sacrifice. During their propaganda efforts, they explain,

> [W]e went down into the lower section of the city. Coolies were dragging a barge with a rope. But the ground on the bank was slippery. So when one of them slipped, and the overseer hit him, we said to the Young Comrade: "Go after them, make propaganda among them after work. But don't give way to pity!" And we asked: "Do you agree to it?" And he agreed to it and hurried away and at once gave way to pity. (*Measures* 84)[2]

The Young Comrade's first misstep – significantly, an acquiescence to pity – figures as a moment of peripeteia, demarcating, in Aristotle's terms, the end of the play's involvement. The Agitators' denunciation of pity (which constitutes one pillar of their juridical defense) is upheld in the play's unraveling, in which the Control Chorus adjudges the killing justified: "We agree to what you have done" (*Measures* 108). Thus, *The Measures Taken*, which has been called the "classic tragedy of Communism," seems to make susceptibility to pity the Young Comrade's hamartia, reversing his fortunes and leading to his expulsion from the collective (Sokel 133).[3]

Brecht here employs his customary sly irony, echoing the tragic form while signaling the *Lehrstück*'s militancy against Aristotle by castigating pity, one of the constituent elements of katharsis as well as its enabling precondition. More generally, the Agitators' disdain for the Young Comrade's pity (a disdain they describe but do not display for the Control Chorus) enacts Brecht's contempt for theatrical emotion in his early career. "I don't let my feelings intrude in my dramatic work," he declared in a 1926 statement that John Willett calls "the first expression of his doctrine of the 'epic theatre'" ("Conversation" 14; qtd. in Brecht, "Conversation" 16): "Contrary to present custom [figures] ought to be presented quite coldly, classically and objectively. For they are not a matter for empathy; they are there to be understood. Feelings are private and limited. Against that the reason is fairly comprehensive and to be relied on" ("Conversation" 15).[4] This binary distinction between "feelings" and "reason" is often taken as Brecht's position on theatrical emotion in general, an assumption with justification in Brecht's writings of the period. Indeed, his notorious 1930 table itemizing axes of distinction between "dramatic" and "epic" theatres climaxes in "feeling [*Gefühl*]" versus "reason [*Ratio*]" ("Modern Theatre" 37; "Anmerkungen zur Oper" 79). This stance toward "feeling" is borne out in his early plays, with their reluctance either to represent emotion or to incite it. As Brecht instructs his spectators in his prologue to his 1927 play *In the Jungle of the Cities*: "Judge impartially the technique of the contenders, and keep your eyes fixed on the finish" (118).

Brecht's hostility toward emotional effects in this period is rooted in his refusal to view spectators as objects to be conditioned in the manner proposed by some of his Soviet counterparts. But Brecht's equation of spectatorial emotion with group passivity recedes in his theoretical writings, as his resistance to theatrical emotion softens. This softening, complete by the 1953 version of the "Short Organum for the Theatre,"[5] does not represent a "theoretical compromise" on the issue of emotion – the judgment is John Willett's – but rather a gradual rejection of the behaviorist paradigm relied upon by Eisenstein, Meyerhold, and like-minded theorists (qtd. in Brecht, "On Experimental Theatre" 135).[6] Brecht's 1944 declaration that "the orthodox theatre . . . sins by dividing reason [*Vernunft*] and emotion [*Gefühl*]" suggests a prescient view of emotions that challenges the orthodoxies of 1940s psychology and philosophy whose cultural dominance would not slip for many years ("Little Private" 162; "Kleine Liste" 315–16). In this chapter, I locate the plays and theoretical writings that led up to *The Caucasian Chalk Circle* within a history of "emotion," a concept that has undergone significant upheaval in the last century. More specifically, I trace how Brecht's evolving view of emotion foretells the displacement in this history of one paradigm of the emotions by another: their wholesale rejection in *The Measures Taken* and its onstage Control Chorus emblematizes Brecht's response to behaviorist emotion, while his nuanced treatment of emotion in *The Caucasian Chalk Circle* highlights the integral role that emotions, differently understood, might play in ethical decision making. But while Brecht's later texts prefigure cognitivist dramatic theory such as that of Martha Nussbaum, they also offer a nuanced corrective *avant la lettre* to its excesses. His description of and indulgence in emotive clarification help to elucidate and evaluate the ways in which a cognitive katharsis might function. To speak of Brechtian catharsis may seem counterintuitive. Yet, as Dickson notes, Brecht "devotes more space [to catharsis] in his critical writings than to any other single aspect of traditional theatre" and "came to regard it as the cardinal principle of dramatic tradition" (233). As we will see, all of Brecht's writings on emotion are relevant to the question of catharsis in general and to the interpretation of katharsis in the *Poetics* in particular.[7] That is, in an irony that he would no doubt appreciate, Brecht insightfully glosses his theoretical adversary, Aristotle.

Brecht had complained in 1931 that American comedies, like Soviet didactic art, treated the human being as an "object" and the audience as if it were "made up of Pavlovians [*Reflexologen*]," an inert mass to be acted upon by emotional stimuli ("Film" 50; *Der Dreigroschenprozeß* 478).[8] That Brecht's rejection of emotion equates to a rejection of behaviorist emotion is made equally clear in a 1935 article. Discussing "aristotelian theatre," he writes,

> It is a common truism among the producers and writers of [this] type of play that the audience, once it is in the theatre, is not a number of individuals but a collective individual, a mob, which must be and can be reached only through its emotions; that it has the mental immaturity and the high emotional suggestibility of a mob ... The latter theatre [*Lehrstücke*] holds that the audience is a collection of individuals, capable of thinking and of reasoning, of making judgments even in the theatre; it treats it as individuals of mental and emotional maturity, and believes it wishes to be so regarded.[9] ("German Drama" 79)

Brecht's description of the mob in the "Aristotelian" tradition echoes Eisenstein's description of the proletarian audience whose consciousness he proposed to forge as one forges iron, by "concentrating the audience's emotions in any direction dictated by the production's purpose" ("Montage" 41).[10] And in so writing, Brecht distinguished himself from various Soviet artists whose work had been influential on him and whose interest in various kinds of anti-realistic defamiliarization he continued to share.[11] Eisenstein's view and others like it rely on a collectivist view of spectatorship that erases distinctions between individuals in the audience; for the early Brecht, such a view follows logically from a model of theatrical and film emotion as reflexive and conditioned. Brecht had written in 1936 that "[a]cceptance or rejection of [characters'] actions and utterances was meant to take place on a conscious plane, instead of, as hitherto, in the audience's subconscious" ("Alienation" 91); his seemingly interchangeable usage of "psychological" and "subconscious" in this period betrays his assumption that emotions reside outside reason or consciousness – an assumption that reflects the cultural currency of psychoanalysis and behaviorism in the 1930s.

Therefore, Brecht's program required him to refigure the audience as a "collection of individuals" instead of a "collective individual," finding in a model of individual spectatorship a basis for individual agency. To do so, Brecht had both to disentangle individual spectators from a collective audience and to distance them from emotional effects such as identification and catharsis. As he wrote in 1935,

> non-aristotelian . . . dramaturgy does not make use of the "identification" of the spectator with the play, as does the aristotelian, and has a different point of view also towards other psychological effects a play may have on an audience, as, for example, towards the "catharsis." Catharsis is not the main object of this dramaturgy . . . [I]t has as a purpose the "teaching" of the spectator a certain quite practical attitude . . .[12] ("German Drama" 78)

Brecht asserts that the empathetic identification of spectators with a hero concentrates their collective emotion in a single direction, ensnaring them in a somatic, uncritical experience; his theatre, on the other hand, "teaches" its individual spectators by avoiding the emotional. "Conscious" understanding thus requires an assiduous avoidance of emotional effects; in a theatre based on alienation effects, "the audience [is] hindered from simply identifying itself with the characters in the play" – that is, prevented from being constructed as a collective ("Alienation" 91). Similarly, for the early Brecht, hindering such an identification requires an acting style different from that proposed by Stanislavsky or, for that matter, Eisenstein:[13]

> it is simpler [for the actor] to exhibit the outer signs which accompany these emotions and identify them. In this case . . . there is not the same automatic transfer of emotions to the spectator, the same emotional infection. The alienation effect intervenes, not in the form of absence of emotion, but in the form of emotions which need not correspond to those of the character portrayed. On seeing worry the spectator may feel a sensation of joy; on seeing anger, one of disgust. ("Alienation" 94)[14]

But Brecht's experiments in this period with "A-effects," which sought precisely to preclude emotional identification, led to a reappraisal of the role of emotion in theatrical representation and reception. By 1940, he had conceded the resilience of emotional effects: "As for the emotions, the experimental use of the A-effect in the epic theatre's German productions indicated that this way of acting too can stimulate them, though possibly a different class of emotion is involved from those of the orthodox theatre" ("Short Description" 140). Indeed, Brecht even allows in his appendices to this essay that "emotions [*Emotionen*]" can work alongside "reason [*Ratio*]," an observation, he claims, that "will surprise no one who has not got a completely conventional idea of the emotions" ("Short Description" 145; "Über rationellen" 501). In other words, Brecht imagines a space within which "emotions" can aid the pedagogical function of theatre, which imagining requires him to separate the "emotional" from the still-stigmatized realm of the "subconscious" or the "psychological." In order to understand how "emotion" could be reintroduced to "reason," Brecht's 1940 readers would, indeed, have needed a less than "completely conventional" idea of the emotions; signaling his own increasingly unconventional understanding, he writes, "All the modern theatre is doing is to discard an outworn, decrepit, subjective sphere of the emotions and pave the way for the new, manifold, socially productive emotions of a new age" ("Little Private" 161). As he articulates in 1940, in this modern theatre, "emotions are only clarified [*geklärt*] . . . steering clear of subconscious origins and carrying nobody away" ("On the Use" 88; "Über die Verwendung" 162).

In a remarkable coincidence, in the same year, the Liddell-Scott-Jones *Greek-English Lexicon* entry for "katharsis [καθάρσις]" was updated, its editors adding the denotation "clarification" to the word's other meanings, including "purging" and "purification." The new definition heralded an entirely new interpretation of Aristotle's notoriously vague clause *(Poetics* 1449b), an interpretation first articulated in Leon Golden's 1962 article "Catharsis" and elaborated in his 1969 and 1976 articles.[15] These texts set the foundation for more detailed versions of kathartic clarification in Stephen Halliwell's *Aristotle's Poetics* and Martha Nussbaum's *The Fragility of Goodness* (both 1986).[16] Certain features of these accounts emerge as central. First, pleasure derives from (seemingly unpleasurable) pitiable and fearful experience because this experience is accompanied by intellectual insight.[17] Second, the insight drawn from the particular, historical scene represented is general or even universal—that is, the emotion is intellectual insofar as it facilitates an inductive judgment from a particular case.[18] Third, this clarifying katharsis in the audience is rooted in the playwright's mimesis, uniting the apparent telos of tragedy with tragedy's general function in society. The audience's understanding derives not from intellectual argumentation, as in some neoclassical tragedies, but rather from an emotionally engaged spectatorship that leads spectators to a judgment about the causes of the protagonist's suffering. Emotions are clarified in the manner that Brecht had proposed for his "non-Aristotelian" theatre, enabling rather than obfuscating understanding.

Golden's emphasis on the audience's "judgment" is foregrounded in Nussbaum's account of katharsis, which stresses spectators' emotional pleasure in seeing representations because, as Aristotle argues in Book 4 of the *Poetics,* we draw conclusions about the images that we see (7; Nussbaum, *Fragility* 388). Significantly, though, in *Fragility,* Nussbaum bristles at Golden's translation of *Poetics* 1449b: "*[k]atharsis* does not *mean* 'intellectual clarification.' It means 'clarification,' " she writes (390; emphasis in original). Clarification derives from emotions, Nussbaum argues, because emotions themselves are cognitive. As she writes elsewhere, "Once we notice their cognitive dimension, as Golden did not, we can see how they can, in and of themselves, be genuinely illuminating" ("Tragedy" 281). Having adumbrated a cognitivist view of emotions that she would fully articulate in 2001's *Upheavals of Thought*, Nussbaum's argument in *Fragility* can reach a sublimely Aristotelian telos: "we might try to summarize our results by saying on Aristotle's behalf that the function of a tragedy is to accomplish, through pity and fear, a clarification (or illumination) concerning experiences of the pitiable and fearful kind. But that is, by a surprising piece of good luck, exactly what Aristotle has already said" (391).

Precepts of the cognitivist paradigm on which Nussbaum relies might be summarized as follows:[19]

1 physiological changes are signs that an emotion is occurring; they do not constitute the emotion as (most strikingly) in the behaviorist model;[20]
2 emotions are intentional – that is, directed by an agent toward an object;
3 emotions are rational or predicated upon beliefs;
4 emotions are evaluative, necessarily involving judgments or appraisals; and
5 emotions give rise to, rather than being constituted by, behaviors.

Each of these features, we will see, has a role to play in tragic practice as Nussbaum has theorized it and – surprisingly – as Brecht has metatheatrically glossed it.

Cognitivism arose out of the same disenchantment with behaviorism that Brecht had articulated in the 1930s, specifically behaviorism's inability to explain the extraordinary complexity of individual behaviors[21] – and Brecht's journey provides an excellent analogue for cognitivism's ascent and its integration of "emotion" into "reason." Not incidentally, the shift in Brecht's position correlates with a change in his view of Aristotle; as M.S. Silk notes, looking to the later Brecht, we find explicit "evidence of a compromise with the *Poetics*, as part of a series of shifts in Brecht's overall theoretical position" (189). While Silk claims that "the relative tolerance and restraint of [Brecht's] later compromise seems unimpressive in comparison to the verve and the intellectual edge of the earlier formulations" (189), in fact, Brecht's "compromise" articulates a more sophisticated position than did his earlier declarations of "anti-Aristotelianism," one that derives from the more nuanced understanding of emotion that his "compromise" reveals. Emotion, or at least a behaviorist understanding of emotion, drove Brecht away from Aristotle – but emotion, on Brecht's new understanding, would also help reconcile him to the *Poetics*.

Tellingly, Brecht's "Short Organum" begins by acknowledging the correctness of Aristotle's dictum that poetry is first and foremost pleasurable ("Kleines Organon" 66–67).[22] It connects this pleasure explicitly to katharsis: "Thus what the ancients, following Aristotle, demanded of tragedy is nothing higher or lower than that it should entertain people . . . And the catharsis of which Aristotle writes – cleansing by pity and fear, or from pity and fear – is a purification [*Waschung*] which is performed not only in a pleasurable way, but precisely for the purpose of pleasure" ("Short Organum" 181; "Kleines Organon" 67). Without embracing catharsis, Brecht concedes that the emotional response of the spectator is fundamental to the spectacle – a concession sharpened in a posthumously published appendix in which he acknowledges that he had been "too inflexibly opposed" to the "dramatic," his long-time synonym for "Aristotelian" ("Appendices" 276). Unlike the *Lehrstücke*, then, the modern theatre permits the spectator's emotional involvement and even encourages the role of emotions in ethical action. Through its emotional pleasures, the theatre can facilitate the audience's "unceasing transformation [*Verwandlung*]," Gotthold Lessing's term for catharsis that Brecht uses in a strikingly different way ("Short Organum" 205; "Kleines Organon" 97).

A year after finishing the "Short Organum" – his lengthiest treatment of, and his most sustained and internally coherent theoretical statement on, theatrical emotion – Brecht similarly defended his new position to Friedrich Wolf:

> It is not true, though it is sometimes suggested, that epic theatre (which is not simply undramatic theatre, as is also sometimes suggested) proclaims the slogan: "Reason this side, Emotion (feeling) that." It by no means renounces emotion, least of all the sense of justice [*Gerechtigkeitsgefühl*], the urge to freedom, and righteous anger; it is so far from renouncing these that it does not even assume their presence, but tries to arouse or to reinforce them. The "attitude of criticism" which it tries to awaken in its audience cannot be passionate enough for it.
> ("Formal Problems" 227; "Formprobleme" 110)

More than merely connecting "justice" to "emotion" in this passage, Brecht equates the two, describing "justice" and "anger" as parallel emotion-terms and expressing the former with a compound: *Gerechtigkeitsgefühl*. Brecht thus anticipates the cognitivist notion that emotions are based on beliefs and are experienced as part of appraisals: the theatre, he claims, "reinforces" such evaluative emotions in the spectators, presumably by setting before them objects for appraisal and emotional agents whose judgments can be shown to be sound or unsound. Reaching back to the Greeks, then, Brecht adapted *Antigone* that same year, noting that it was chosen for the "topicality of [its] subject matter" – a subject matter that not coincidentally emphasizes the soundness of Antigone's inductively and emotionally motivated actions over Creon's deductive and dogmatic ones ("Masterful Treatment" 210). As Brecht writes in his verse précis of the plot, the play shows us "how, as

Antigone was brought in and questioned as to why / she broke the law, she looked around and turned to the Elders / and saw that they were appalled and said: 'To set an example' " (*Sophocles' Antigone* 2).[23] Aristotle had linked poetry's aims of bringing pleasure and conferring insight, noting that men "enjoy the sight of images because they learn as they look" (*Poetics* 1448b). Brecht, in choosing *Antigone* and defending its "topicality," thus concurs with Aristotle about the pleasure – and insight-bearing qualities – of tragedy.

However, Brecht, who had declared in 1935 the necessity for the director to have a historian's eye, disagrees with Aristotle's understanding of universal, transhistorical truth – for Aristotle insists that the insights of poetry are universal and not (like those of history) particular ("Anmerkungen zur 'Mutter' " 172). Adopting a Marx-inflected model of history instead, Brecht writes in the "Short Organum" that "[w]e need a type of theatre which not only releases the feelings, insights and impulses possible within the particular historical field of human relations in which the action takes place, but employs and encourages those thoughts and feelings which help transform the field itself" (190). The ethical soundness of Antigone's emotional actions, then, would be historically bound, and their relevance to the 1948 audience could not be taken for granted – hence Brecht's addition of a prologue to the play, set in modern times. In it, two sisters in post-war Berlin discover first, to their joy, that their beloved brother has deserted the Nazi army and second, to their sorrow, that he has been hanged for so doing. The prologue ends abruptly with a Nazi officer questioning one sister, who is preparing to cut down her brother's corpse from the hook on which it hangs. Brecht exposes laws operative in Sophocles' tragedy (as Aristotle envisioned[24]) – the ethical dilemma a totalitarian state causes a loving sister – but locates these laws within two different historical frames. He writes that "there can be no question of using the Antigone story as a means or pretext for 'conjuring up the spirit of antiquity' ": "Even if we felt obliged to do something for a work like *Antigone* we could only do so by letting the play do something for us" ("Masterful Treatment" 210–11). These simultaneous gestures of embracing Sophocles' text and rendering it strange are encapsulated in Brecht's title, *Sophocles' Antigone* [*Antigone des Sophokles*].

The prologue invites us analogically to draw a conclusion about the as-yet-unmade judgment of the sisters in the prologue from the wisdom gained from Antigone and Ismene in Sophocles' plot. This process is similar to the one that (according to Golden's account) Aristotle proposes, where the spectator apprehends a general insight from the particular scene represented – with the crucial difference that, in Brecht's case, we are compelled to draw a historically located, not universal, conclusion. As he wrote in "Short Organum," "If art reflects life it does so with special mirrors. Art does not become unrealistic by changing the proportions but by changing them in such a way that if the audience took its representations as a

practical guide to insights and impulses it would go astray in real life"
(204). As if to ensure that the play is not misconstrued as offering a transhistorical "moral," Brecht leaves this structure open: although the prologue
ends on a note of suspense, with the sisters questioned about their brother
by a Nazi officer, the play never returns to its initial setting.

A similar framing device contextualizes the insights into emotional judgment provided by *The Caucasian Chalk Circle*, Brecht's strongest reconci-
liation between the demands of his political theatre and the shadow cast
over it by Aristotle. The judgment in the central action (the validity of
Grusha's claims on the infant) is analogically paralleled with the judgment
in the prologue (the validity of the fruit-growing kolkhoz's claim on the valley). Grusha's story, set "[o]nce upon a time," thus fulfills the role of the
"general" or "poetry" in Aristotle's schema, while the story of the dueling
kolkhozes intends explicitly to reintroduce the particular or "history," as
suggested by Brecht's revisions: he had originally situated the play in 1934,
emphasizing the agricultural restructuring that was happening in the Soviet Union, but later updated the action to highlight the theme of post-war
reconstruction (*Caucasian* 9;[25] Ritchie 18).

These two levels of action are mediated by the Singer, who thus fulfils
the role of the Greek chorus. Just as he had lauded the Greeks' use of
masks in "Short Organum," Brecht notes in his foreword to *Antigone* that
the use of the chorus in classical tragedy was an A-effect (*Antigonemodell*
75). However, the Singer's presence in the prologue also stifles the impulse
to generate a universal moral, not alienating the spectators so much as
framing the presentation of reality before them so that it can be seen more
clearly. The Singer chorically mediates between the represented action and
his onstage (instead of offstage) audience; in this way, the onstage kolkhozes presumably refract or deflect the offstage audience's impulse to
identification with the spectacle. For Azdak's judgment may not be relevant to the specific historical field offstage; rather, it announces its relevance only to the context of post–World War II Soviet Georgia. As Brecht
wrote to his publisher in 1954,

Die Fragestellung des parabelhaften Stücks muß ja aus Notwendigkeiten der
Wirklichkeit hergeleitet werden und ich denke, es geschah in heiterer und leichter
Weise. Ohne das Vorspiel ist weder ersichtlich, warum das Stück nicht der chine-
sische Kreidekreis geblieben ist (mit der alten Richterentscheidung), noch, warum
es der kaukasische heißt. Zuerst schrieb ich die kleine Geschichte (in den „Kalendergeschichten" gedruckt). Aber bei der Dramatisierung fehlte mir eben ein his-
torischer und erklärender Hintergrund. (*Briefe* 3: 256–57)

[The question posed by the parable-like play must be seen to derive from the
necessities of reality, and I think that this has been done in a cheerful and light

way. Without the prologue it is neither evident why the play has not remained the Chinese chalk circle (with the old verdict) nor why it is called Caucasian. First I wrote the little story (that was printed in *Kalendergeschichten*). But for the dramatization I felt I needed a historical, explanatory background.]

Publicly, however, Brecht had been squeamish about the appellation "parable." Presumably fearing that a text so described might be taken to offer universal insight, he had written in 1944 that

Der „Kaukasische Kreidekreis" ist keine Parabel. Das Vorspiel könnte darüber einen Irrtum erzeugen, da äußerlich tatsächlich die ganze Fabel zur Klärung des Streitfalls wegen des Besitzes des Tals erzählt wird. Genauer besehen aber enthüllt sich die Fabel als eine wirkliche Erzählung, die in sich selbst nichts beweist, lediglich eine bestimmte Art von Weisheit zeigt, eine Haltung, die für den aktuellen Streitfall beispielhaft sein kann. ("Zu 'Der kaukasische' " 342)

[The *Caucasian Chalk Circle* is no parable. The prologue could possibly produce such a mistaken impression, since superficially the whole fable will be told to clarify the argument over the valley's ownership. More precisely observed, the fable is seen as a real story that in itself proves nothing, but merely shows a certain kind of wisdom, an attitude, that can be an example for the present argument.]

The framed story of the chalk circle test, he claims, demonstrates for the kolkhozes not a just verdict but "a certain kind of wisdom" – "an attitude" that might help produce a verdict in the still-undecided argument over the valley's ownership.

The Measures Taken had also used a chorus to direct the action – "Step forward!" they declare at the top – as well as to "enlighte[n] the spectator about facts unknown to him" (*Measures* 77; "Theatre for Pleasure" 72). In that play, the chorus recapitulates and endorses the clear-headed "rational" judgment of the Agitators, which proceeds deductively from the precept that communist utility trumps individual desire – that "[a] single man can be wiped out" in the interests of the Party (*Measures* 101). In *The Caucasian Chalk Circle*, by contrast, the Singer's mediation supports the position that ethical actions ought to proceed inductively from emotional assessments instead of from categorical precepts like those that govern in *The Measures Taken*. As the Expert in the prologue says, "It's true that we have to consider a piece of land as a tool with which one produces something useful. But it's also true that we must recognize the love for a particular piece of land" (*Caucasian* 5). Sound law in *The Caucasian Chalk Circle* not only replaces capitalist precedents with Marxist ones; it also formally integrates the social and individual emotional concerns that undergird decisions – like Grusha's decision to save Michael or later to fight for his custody – into the process that regulates ethical correctness and guarantees social harmony.

To do so Brecht demonstrates, *pace* behaviorist psychology and in advance of cognitivist theory like that of Nussbaum's *Upheavals*, that emotions are a valid source of illumination. His commitment to this demonstration reveals itself in a choice to represent emotions more fully onstage. Brecht notes in the "Short Organum" that *The Caucasian Chalk Circle* relies on presentational methods, as when the Singer uses an "unemotional way of singing to describe the servant-girl's rescue of the child" (203). But elsewhere, the play contains more conventional representations of emotion that seem designed, as clearly as Kattrin's death scene in *Mother Courage*, to incite a sympathetic emotional response. These scenes uphold Brecht's comment in his notes for "Der Messingkauf" that "[n]either the public nor the actor must be stopped from taking part emotionally; the representation of emotions must not be hampered, nor must the actor's use of emotions be frustrated" (173). For example, Grusha's heartbreaking, post-war reunion with Simon is mimetically, even realistically, rendered: she confronts him – "*with tears in her eyes*" and "*in despair, her face streaming with tears*" – with the news that she has married during their separation (*Caucasian* 58; 59). Her inability to explain the circumstances of her strategic union with Yussup augments the scene's pity-inducing effect. Moreover, Grusha's emotional development during her absence from Simon is marked by this scene's difference from the couple's engagement scene before she left with Michael; the earlier scene's avoidance of emotion – as well as its "objective" emphasis on social utility – seems parodic of the early Brecht:

SIMON   May I ask if the young lady still has parents?

GRUSHA   No, only a brother.

SIMON   As time is short – the second question would be: Is the young lady as healthy as a fish in water?

GRUSHA   Perhaps once in a while a pain in the right shoulder; but otherwise strong enough for any work. So far no one has complained.

SIMON   . . . The third question is this: Is the young lady impatient? Does she want cherries [i.e., *Äpfel*] in winter?

GRUSHA   Impatient, no. But if a man goes to war without any reason, and no message comes, that's bad.

SIMON   A message will come . . . And finally the main question . . .

GRUSHA   Simon Chachava, because I've got to go to the third courtyard and I'm in a hurry, the answer is "Yes." (*Caucasian* 18; *Der kaukasische* 109)

Of course, the play's most emotional scene is its climactic custody trial, and the difference between it and Brecht's earlier representations of legal proceedings, like the differences between the Singer and earlier choric figures, is deeply resonant. Brecht had used trial scenes previously – in *The Measures Taken* but also in *The Exception and the Rule* and *The Good Person of Szechuan*, for example – but *The Caucasian Chalk Circle*'s trial importantly foregrounds, in both its pleadings and just judgment, the importance of emotion in jurisprudence. Natella Abashvili's lawyers note her "fear" of losing her child, but the plaintiff herself falls short in describing this claim in emotional terms: "It's not for me to describe to you the tortures of a bereaved mother's soul, the anxiety, the sleepless nights," she testifies (*Caucasian* 89). The banality of her emotional plea – which her lawyer equally tritely recapitulates as the "moving statement" of "the human tragedy of a mother" (89) – contrasts vividly with the palpable rage that Grusha rains down on the judge at the thought of being separated from her adopted charge: "Aren't you ashamed of yourself when you see how afraid I am of you? . . . You can take the child away from me, a hundred against one, but I tell you one thing: for a profession like yours, they ought to choose only bloodsuckers and men who rape children" (92). Grusha's screed not only foregrounds her own emotions; it presumes that Azdak is heartless and dares him to feel "ashamed." She is as yet unaware that Azdak's wisdom stems precisely from his emotional sensitivity: his chalk circle test seeks to evaluate the sincerity of Grusha's and Natella's emotional rhetoric by gauging their willingness to do Michael harm. His judgment awards the child to the mother whose emotional claim is most strongly substantiated in context-specific action. (Unlike in Brecht's sources, she is not the child's birth mother.[26]) We might say that Azdak exposes the particular inadequacy of the lawyer's generalizing "human tragedy of a mother."

But the chalk circle test happens late in the play. In contrast to his advice, in *In the Jungle of the Cities*, to focus on the finish, Brecht's proactive defense against directors who would cut scenes from *The Caucasian Chalk Circle*[27] validates the centrality of the emotionally complex journeys that precede the trial. ("Couldn't you make it shorter?" the Expert asks the Singer at the end of the prologue, and the Singer answers "No" [8]. The "moral" – a helpful analogue for the problem of the prologue but not a precept for its resolution – is not as simple as some commentators have suggested: despite stock characters such as the "Girl Tractor Driver," Brecht's project is considerably more complicated than social realist propaganda.) First, the intertwined plots of Grusha and Azdak emphasize the cognitive basis of emotions. William James had proposed a causal relationship – "we feel sorry because we cry" – that helped structure the behaviorist paradigm (1066); Brecht reverses this causality, as the Singer makes clear while presenting Grusha's conflicted state when she temporarily abandons Michael:

THE SINGER Why so gay, you, making for home?
THE MUSICIANS Because with a smile the child
                Has won new parents for himself, that's why I'm gay.
                Because I am rid of the loved one
                That's why I'm happy.
THE SINGER And why are you sad?
THE MUSICIANS I'm sad because I'm single and free
                Of the little burden in whom a heart was beating:
                Like one robbed, like one impoverished I'm going.

                                          (*Caucasian* 35)

The Singer expresses the "aboutness," in Nussbaum's terminology, of the emotions felt by Grusha, who assesses the happiness she feels at being relieved of the burden Michael had represented against the sorrow that she feels in his absence (*Upheavals* 33). Emotions, the later Brecht tells us, are object-directed states motivated by evaluations.

These evaluations are derived from beliefs. Emotions occur within the context of an agent's viewpoint; they are based on his or her "scheme of goals and projects, the things to which [he or she] attach[es] value in a conception of what it is . . . to live well," as Nussbaum puts it (*Upheavals* 49). Thus, just as the beliefs that underlie emotional motivations and emotional object-choice can be refined, so too can emotional responses be developed. The initiating event of Grusha's journey (taking Michael) is a choice clearly unwise from the viewpoint of "rational" deduction, as The Stableman correctly recognizes: "I'd rather not think what'd happen to the person seen with that child" (*Caucasian* 23). However, despite its happy ending, the play is equally clear that it does not valorize Grusha's " 'abnormal' humanist action," in Darko Suvin's wonderful coinage (165). Rather, it demonstrates that she earns wisdom (or more constructive beliefs) during the journey from her initial mistake. Grusha's emotional response toward the infant at the beginning of the play is predicated on a humanist impulse that is expressed, significantly, alongside some unpragmatic dithering to no one's benefit. As the Singer narrates, Grusha delays her escape from Grusinia for an entire night, watching the infant's "soft breathing" and "little fists" in spite of the dangers of a city "full of flame and grief" (*Caucasian* 25; 25; 24). It is no accident that her action clearly hinges on the one emotion, empathy, for which Brecht never abandoned his contempt.[28] As the Singer relates,

[S]he heard
Or thought she heard, a low voice. The child
Called to her, not whining but calling quite sensibly
At least so it seemed to her: "Woman," it said, "Help me."
Went on calling not whining but calling quite sensibly:

"Don't you know, woman, that she who does not listen to a cry for help
But passes by shutting her ears, will never hear
The gentle call of a lover
Nor the blackbird at dawn, nor the happy
Sigh of the exhausted grape-picker at the sound of the Angelus."
Hearing this . . .
she went back to the child
Just for one more look, just to sit with it
For a moment or two till someone should come . . . (*Caucasian* 24)

Moreover, Grusha's empathetic response, which is neatly yoked to her self-delusion (just "one more look," she promises) and lack of sense, inheres in an impulse to Aristotelian identification that Brecht consistently scorns. She misreads the child's cries as a "sensible" argument not for quick flight (with or without him) but rather about her own relationship with her lover. (Tellingly, the Singer describes Grusha's act of empathy in erotic terms: "*Verführung* [seduction]" [*Der kaukasische* 116].) Grusha has herself just been abandoned by Simon Chachava, and her attraction to the child, the playwright implies, is narcissistic. She thus reads the child's cries in the context of universal "love" instead of within the specific context in which, according to Brecht, ethical choices ought to be made. Her emotion is predicated on inappropriate beliefs. Indeed, the vague humanistic impulse she feels – an apparent "maternal instinct" that is revealed to be a projection of her own unhappiness and that Brecht called a "suicidal weakness" – is no firmer a foundation for an emotional response than Natella's "human tragedy of a mother" ("Short Organon" 203; *Caucasian* 89). Grusha, in her "humane" action, in fact ignores important personal (and class) values and, in so doing, endangers her own life as surely as revolutionary war endangers the aristocratic infant's.

One condition for Azdak's decision to award her custody of Michael, then, is Grusha's admission of error, made possible by her grueling journey out of Grusinia: "I ought to have walked away quickly on that Easter Sunday," she eventually concedes (*Caucasian* 48). While it is still emotional, Grusha's claim to the infant gains validity only after the development of her emotional ethos. During the trial, it stands on objectively better ground: importantly, it resides not in general love but in particular love – the bond of social utility and responsibility – that the two have developed during their journey together. "He's mine," Grusha declares, "I've brought him up according to my best knowledge and conscience. I always found him something to eat. Most of the time he had a roof over his head. And I went to all sorts of trouble for him. I had expenses, too. I didn't think of my own comfort. I brought up the child to be friendly with everyone. And from the beginning I taught him to work as well as he could" (88; 88–89). The trial's assessment is that her feeling of "love" in relation to its object, Michael, has been clarified, a clarification that Azdak's sound judgment confirms. (If the Cook – who, it is implied, has not left Grusinia during the insurrection – fails to understand Grusha's decision to fight for Michael, this failure must then reflect her own need for emotional refinement: "What I can't understand is why you want to hold on to it at any price, if it's not yours," she declares [83]). Grusha's action (mothering the child), then, does not change during the play. However, the emotion that motivates this action changes, as does the foundational belief that grounds the emotion.

The other necessary condition for Azdak's judgment is, of course, his own emotional development, which is initiated (with dramaturgical neatness) by an abnormal humanist action of his own: harboring the Grand Duke. The Singer ties his action to Grusha's explicitly: "On the Easter Sunday of the great revolt, when the Grand Duke was overthrown / And his Governor Abashvili, father of our child, lost his head / The village clerk Azdak found a fugitive in the woods and hid him in his hut" (*Caucasian* 61). Azdak must repent his "compassionate" decision, which like Grusha's is deductively based on a categorical imperative instead of inductively derived from particular circumstances. Significantly, once Azdak realizes the fugitive's identity, his appropriate emotion – shame, the emotion that Grusha later accuses him of lacking – incites him to surrender. "In the name of Justice, I demand to be judged severely in a public trial!" Azdak declares (64). But a comment that Azdak makes during this scene – "I *don't* have a good heart! How often am I to tell you I'm a man of intellect?" – hints at the distance that he must still travel in his emotional development (62). A good heart is not the problem; indiscriminate good-heartedness that jeopardizes class interests is.

Azdak's development into judicious good-heartedness is thematized in the convolutions of his two years as judge during the civil war, during which time he makes problematic rulings (including the acquittal of an alleged rapist – in an overcorrection that misapplies emotional logic – on the grounds that he was aroused by the victim's beauty [*Der kaukasische* 164–66]). Brecht parallels these convolutions to the geographic distance that Grusha must travel to earn custodial rights to Michael, a distance that literalizes her own emotional development. Brecht sets the many strategic errors each makes in the context of a carnivalesque period of misrule – "*die Zeit der Unordnung*" – that makes possible the sober wisdom into which each is initiated (*Der kaukasische* 169): Azdak after his second appointment as judge (following the civil war), and Grusha after she passes the chalk circle test and is reunited with Simon (*Der kaukasische* 169). This reunion, of course, is facilitated by Azdak's decision "accidentally" to divorce her from Yussup: "Have I divorced the wrong ones? I'm sorry, but it'll have to stand. I never retract anything. If I did, there'd be no law and order" (*Caucasian* 96).

Ending the play with Azdak's divorce of the "wrong" couple, Brecht highlights several of the play's themes: the significance of Azdak's errors,

which have made possible his evolved *ethos* and also the happy resolution
of Grusha's plot; the importance of emotional concerns in upholding ethical "law and order"; and the difficulty (relative to categorical deduction) of
adequately doing justice to those concerns. More generally, by foregrounding the importance of error, Brecht privileges an attitude of provisionality
for a society whose concept of law is to be founded on individual and social
desires – desires, Brecht stresses, to be continually reassessed. As he writes
in the "Short Organum," "[t]he laws of motion of a society are not to be
demonstrated by 'perfect examples,' for 'imperfection' (inconsistency) is
an essential part of motion and of the thing moved" (195). These demonstrated laws of motion, moreover, are to be understood by the spectator in
his or her cognizance of the play's complex analogical relationships.

Importantly, here too Brecht leaves open the space for interpretive error
whose importance in emotional and ethical evolution he has repeatedly
stressed. In assessing the play's structure, Suvin himself errs in asserting
that Brecht ties an emotional story (Grusha's) to a political problem (that
of the kolkhozes): "their [Grusha and Azdak's] success can then be transferred *a fortiori* to the more rational kolkhoz situation," he writes (169). Suvin's distinction violates Brecht's careful union of the two. It is more
productive to understand both Grusha's relationship to the fruit-growing
kolkhoz and her relationship to Azdak as dialectical: negotiating these dialectics, the spectator may derive emotional (i.e., rational) insight. The
play's offer of wisdom is thus complex, as Brecht himself had warned,

> *dann ist das Vorspiel als ein Hintergrund erkennbar, der der Praktikabilität dieser*
> *Weisheit sowie auch ihrer Entstehung einen historischen Platz anweist. Das Theater*
> *darf also nicht die Technik benutzen, die es für die Stücke vom Parabeltypus ausge-*
> *bildet hat.* ("Zu 'Der kaukasische' " 342)

> [the prologue is recognizable as a background, which situates the practicability of
> this wisdom as well as its evolution in a historical context. The theatre must not
> use the technique that is developed for parable plays.]

Not a parable, the play presents an "attitude [*eine Haltung*]" toward the disagreement between the kolkhozes and for the spectator's own development.
And, significantly, this development requires a *recognition* of the practicabil-
ity (in our own lives) of the "attitude" that Grusha's story upholds; that is,
Brecht relies on an updated notion of anagnorisis, as Walter Benjamin ele-
gantly concedes: "All the recognitions achieved by epic theatre have a directly educative effect; at the same time, the educative effect of epic theatre
is immediately translated into recognitions – though the specific recognitions of actors and audience may well be different from one another" (25).
The audience's recognitions do not require *identification* with Grusha (a

"*tragische Figur*," Brecht called her in his journal [*Journale* 2: 192]) but rather the cognitive negotiation of various dialectics – a negotiation facilitated by means of a refraction, through the onstage audience and the choric Singer, of their impulse to identification.

The Caucasian Chalk Circle is thus paradigmatic of the epic theatrical mode, which is principally concerned with the "attitudes [*Verhalten*] which people adopt towards one another" (Brecht, "On the Use" 86; "Über die Verwendung" 157). As the story of the dueling kolkhozes makes clear, society's "laws of motion" ideally lead to better communal living among individuals. Brecht had written in 1939 that the theatre should provide "models of men's life together such as could help the spectator to understand his social environment and both rationally and emotionally to master it" ("On Experimental Theatre" 133) – but, by the late 1940s, the once-antonymical categories of "reason" and "emotion" would be fully integrated. Indeed, the play's transformation of its spectators' behaviors – a transformation by which the success of the modern theatre must be judged, according to Brecht ("Kleines Privatissimum" 39) – begins by offering them experiential evidence of this integration in the fable of Grusha and Azdak: as Brecht put it in a posthumously published note, "If a feeling [i.e., attitude (*Gesinnung*)] is to be an effective one, it must be acquired not merely impulsively but through the understanding" ("Notes" 247; "*Katzgraben*" 456).[29] That is, this transformation is effected not through emotional coercion but rather through a clarification that helps spectators refine the beliefs that inform their emotions and, in turn, the ethical "attitudes" that Brecht seeks to transform.

Such a clarification of emotional judgment, then, resembles Aristotelian katharsis, if we follow Golden's interpretation, in which spectators derive experiential pleasure and inductive wisdom from their emotional experience. Brecht's surprising fit with an Aristotelian model is only improved by the cognitivist interpretations put forth by Halliwell and Nussbaum, each of whom views emotions as cognitive and each of whom foregrounds the desire for ethical actions engendered by emotional experiences. If we accept these models, *The Caucasian Chalk Circle* comes close to replicating the form that *The Measures Taken* had parodied. But Brecht's greatest value to Aristotelian commentary inheres precisely in his continued rejection – after he had made concessions to emotion and even recognition – of the formal unity that Aristotle's prescriptions claim to produce. While *The Measures Taken* had put its juridical mock-catharsis onstage ("Demonstrate how it happened and why, and you will hear our verdict," the Control Chorus declares [*Measures* 77]), *The Caucasian Chalk Circle*'s open analogical structure frustrates the closure that should result from katharsis. The space for error that Brecht leaves open at the ending of the play enables but does not guarantee (let alone provide) an emotionally clarifying catharsis. Just as in *Sophocles' Antigone*, we never return to the setting of the prologue; the structure achieves unity only "by its effect on the spectators' reality," as Suvin notes – not only their interpretive negotiation of the play's complexities but also the ethical decisions they make after their emotional experience of it (Suvin 174). As Althusser astutely remarks in *For Marx*, "[Brecht] wanted to make the spectator into an actor who would complete the unfinished play, but in real life" (146). Therefore, Brecht severs katharsis from mimesis and attaches it to praxis, the realm in which he believes that theatre's emotional effects ought to be registered and felt. He thus rescues the spectator from an emotional passivity before the spectacle, facilitating the "attitude" for ethical action – an attitude that, as he had diagnosed in 1935, is no basis for katharsis as formulated by Aristotle.[30]

In this revision, Brecht exposes, *avant la lettre*, the principal drawback of the model of kathartic clarification. Golden and Nussbaum each declare that their model's principal strength is its explicit location of katharsis within mimesis; indeed, Nussbaum claims that this fact recommends "clarification," prima facie, above other translations of the word "*katharsis*" (*Fragility* 388; italics in original). But accounts such as hers necessarily elide the feature of Aristotelian emotion that Brecht most strongly derides: the potential intransitivity or passive function of emotions, whose capacity to incite bodily pleasure is an end in itself, an end guaranteed by the identification that pity facilitates. This capacity is foregrounded in Aristotle's remarks on katharsis in the *Politics*, in which he defines the term in opposition to "mathesis" [instruction or enlightenment], explicitly describing "cathartic" as antithetical to "ethical": the pipes, Aristotle states, "are not an instrument of *ethical* but rather of *orgiastic* effect, so their use should be confined to those occasions on which the effect produced by the show is not so much *instruction* [i.e., *mathesis*] as a way of working off the emotions [i.e., *katharsis*]" (*Politics* 1341a 17; emphasis added).[31] Proponents of "clarification" emphasize the spectator's emotional cognition and, especially in Nussbaum's case, consequent ethical behavior. In so doing, they perform unwittingly the same displacement that Brecht performs intentionally: dramatic closure is made to occur in the spectator's "real life" instead of within the plot, upsetting Aristotle's formalism and ignoring the gap, well theorized by Paul Ricoeur, between Aristotelian poetics and rhetoric.[32] As Martha Husain summarizes, Nussbaum "sees the definitory *telos* of a tragedy as 'the generation of tragic responses' in an audience" that is comprised of agents capable of ethical action (115). However, as Aristotle stresses in *Poetics* 8, the mimetic plot finds its unity within itself. To this plot, characters are subordinated; they are objects and not agents.

Brecht helps us to understand the clarification model's considerable exegetical appeal in spite of its limitations. "Clarification" provides a way of negotiating the *Poetics*' problematic tension between individual and collective spectatorship by highlighting spectacle's capacity for engendering collective harmony among individual agents. Brecht helpfully illuminates the negotiation between the individual and the social in *The Caucasian Chalk Circle* in several ways: by paralleling the claims of individuals (in the fable) to those of collectives (in the prologue) and by demonstrating – in the intersecting emotional and geographical trajectories of Grusha and Azdak – how individual emotional journeys facilitate the harmonious union of individual interests. The cognitivists thus help to defend Aristotle against Platonic charges by describing how emotions can provide illumination and shape the beliefs that ensure better communal living.

Readings such as Nussbaum's also help us to clarify the challenges and concessions that Brecht offers to the *Poetics*. First, they explain Brecht's apparently paradoxical position that theatre should de-emphasize "common humanity" and "divide its audience" in order to facilitate better social living ("Indirect Impact" 60). Thus, their individualist paradigm of spectatorship allows us to reconcile Brecht's anti-Aristotelian desire to refract the audience's identification (by means of *Verfremdung*) with his Aristotelian goal of greater understanding through aesthetic pleasure. Second, they validate Brecht's claim that theatrical experience can transform emotions from "outworn, decrepit, [and] subjective" to "new, manifold, [and] socially productive" ("Little Private" 161) – illuminating his obscure pledge, in a poem from "Der Messingkauf," to transform "*Gerechtigkeit zur Leidenschaft* [justice into passion]" ("Gedichte" 327). Third, and most importantly, their limitations vindicate Brecht's decision to effect this transformation by sustaining his challenge to Aristotelian mimesis. An emotional ethos should be developed, Brecht tells us, from a position of agency – a position of skepticism, even resistance.

At one point in *The Caucasian Chalk Circle*, Michael is permitted by Grusha to play with some other children. The Tallest Boy, whose authority over the others Brecht slyly roots in his physical size, declares: "Today we're going to play Heads-off. *To a fat boy:* You're the Prince and you must laugh. *To Michael:* You're the Governor. *To a girl:* You're the Governor's wife and you cry when his head's chopped off. And I do the chopping . . . *They form a procession. The fat boy goes ahead, and laughs. Then comes Michael, and the tallest boy, and then the girl, who weeps*" (*Caucasian* 56–57). The Tallest Boy intends that his pageant go unchallenged by the other children; he hopes to direct their emotional responses while preserving the only action for himself. In the children's abnegation of their own agency – an abnegation that passive theatrical experience may incite, Brecht warns – The Tallest Boy's script can recapitulate emotional clichés: the Fat Prince laughs because that is what fat princes do, the Wife cries because that is what wives do, and neither gains knowledge of the evaluative beliefs that

ought to inform emotional responses. In this way, they are like the spectators whom Brecht saw in the bourgeois theatre, "somewhat motionless
figures in a peculiar condition . . . True, their eyes are open, but they stare
rather than see, just as they listen rather than hear" ("Short Organum"
187).

In Brecht's theatre, agency was not to be thus inhibited. While the rest
of the children play their parts, the young Michael Abashvili rejects his passive role, and this rejection disrupts the Tallest Boy's grim beheading plot,
steering the script away from tragedy: Michael demands a sword of his
own and then reframes the pageant by comically toppling over (*Caucasian*
57). Brecht too sought to disrupt the old scripts with the unexpected, challenging the doctrine of realism, which he had earlier blamed on Aristotle.
Brecht would rewrite Aristotle in the "Short Organum" (its title ironically
recalling Aristotle's *Organum*): "And we must always remember that the
pleasure given by representations of such different sorts hardly ever de-
pended on the representation's likeness to the thing portrayed" (182). Having thus challenged mimesis, Brecht could end his treatise with a sly wink
at – and an important correction to – the theorist he had dialectically opposed with such vigor:

> [O]ur representations must take second place to what is represented, men's life
> together in society; and the pleasure felt in their perfection must be converted
> into the higher pleasure felt when the rules emerging from this life in society are
> treated as imperfect and provisional. In this way the theatre leaves its spectators
> productively disposed even after the spectacle is over. Let us hope that their thea-
> tre may allow them to enjoy as entertainment that terrible and never-ending
> labour which should ensure their maintenance, together with the terror of their
> unceasing transformation. Let them here produce their own lives in the simplest
> way; for the simplest way of living is in art. (205)

In constructing political representations for the stage, Brecht forces the
audience into engagement by leaving the dramaturgy open: he resists Aristotle's structural prescriptions in the *Poetics*, which emphasize the plot's
completeness. This resistance to closure is meant to be not only aesthetically but also argumentatively productive. While Aristotle had noted in the
Metaphysics that at the end of an argument "[w]e must . . . draw our conclusions from what has been said, and after summing up the result, bring
our inquiry to a close," Brecht preferred also to leave his arguments open –
to force his auditors to connect the final dots by, and for, themselves (Aristotle, *Metaphysics* 1: 401). As he stresses in both *Sophocles' Antigone* and
The Caucasian Chalk Circle, such a state of residual agitation in the audience is not only productive but crucial when the question at hand is open
and its satisfactory answers necessarily time-bound.

NOTES

1 I am grateful to Martin Meisel for his helpful comments on an earlier version of this chapter.

2 Throughout this chapter, I have cited Brecht in English translation for ease of reading; the original German is included where germane or where no published translation exists. Uncredited translations are my own. Citations to *The Measures Taken* refer to Brecht's 1930 version. For variations among Brecht's multiple versions – including variations in this passage specifically – see *Die Maßnahme* (7–209).

3 The reading of Brecht's play as a "tragedy" is common: in addition to Sokel (135– 36), see Orr (53) and Nelson, who explains that "[t]he play's tragic effect is documented by the reaction of audience and critics to the premiere in 1930, by the changes Brecht made in the play, by his later attitude to it, and finally by later scholarly discussion" (570). On the play's 1930 reception, see Steinweg (319–46, 398–99).

4 The comments appeared in *Die literarische Welt*; as Willett notes, the interviewer had paraphrased Brecht (qtd. in Brecht "Conversation" 16). The German text therefore does not appear in Suhrkamp's thirty-volume edition of Brecht's *Werke*.

5 A good consideration of the new view of emotion that has emerged by the "Short Organum" is provided by White's recent *Bertolt Brecht's Dramatic Theory* (231– 37) (reviewed in this volume).

6 That early Soviet theatre theory was strongly marked by the influence of behaviorism and reflexology is widely acknowledged: see, for example, Law and Gordon (36–37, 40–41, 126, 263) and Eaton (40–41, 64). Eisenstein's debt to behaviorism is both more easily discernible and less well documented in English-language scholarship. He explicitly grounded his early theory of montage – which, of course, he formulated in and for the theatre alongside Meyerhold, before he turned to filmmaking – in his understanding of Pavlov and especially Vladimir Bekhterev. See, for example, this assertion from "The Montage of Film Attractions": "[t]he method of agitation through spectacle consists in the creation of a new chain of conditioned reflexes by associating selected phenomena with the unconditioned reflexes they produce" (45). In early writings such as this one, Eisenstein repeatedly cites Bekhterev (e.g., "Montage" 49; "Constantja" 68; "Perspectives" 155), whose works Richard Taylor notes that the director had studied (Eisenstein, Notes, "Constantja " 308 n6). Even in 1936, by which time Eisenstein's views on psychology had become colored by his interests in psychoanalysis and "Oriental" thought, his teaching program for film directors included readings by both Bekhterev and Pavlov ("Teaching Programme" 86).

7 A note about usage: I use "katharsis" in its strictly Aristotelian sense, to denote an apparatus theorized in the *Poetics* as central to the definition of tragedy. I use "catharsis" in its more general senses – that is, as it has been used in post-Aristotelian dramatic theory and everyday parlance.

8 Willett's technically inaccurate translation of "Reflexologen" as "Pavlovians" conveys Brecht's sense well; reflexology like that of Bekhterev evolves out of Pavlovian behaviorism.

9 This text was published only in English, in a translation prepared by Brecht and Eva Goldbeck; his original German typescript is incomplete (Brecht, "German Drama" 81; *Werke* 22: 939).

10 Eisenstein himself seems to have understood this insight as Aristotelian: in a clear reference to *Poetics*, he noted that his 1925 montage film *Strike* should "stir the spectator to a state of pity and terror" (qtd. in Bordwell 61). And, more generally, his prescriptions for aesthetically successful representations – with aesthetic success measured in terms of the spectacle's effect on the spectator – share key features with Aristotelian dramatic theory.

11 Brecht's connection with, and debt to, Soviet artists such as Sergei Tretjakov and Meyerhold (especially at the time of Brecht's work with Piscator) is well documented: see, for example, Arvon (69–73), Eaton (9–37), Lunn (53–55, 101–02, 123–24), and Willett (*Theatre* 109–10). Brecht himself noted the "tremendous impact [*ungeheuere Wirkung*]" on his work of the films of Eisenstein ("Entwurf" 138).

12 This passage is published exclusively in English; see note 9 above.

13 Eisenstein extended Meyerhold's biomechanical method, calling for mechanical duplication of emotional states rather than the naturalistic emotional representations favored by Stanislavsky and his adherents: Eisenstein's notion that an actor could duplicate an emotion by expertly embodying its physical effects persuasively suggests the extent to which behaviorist ideas had penetrated Soviet cultural discourse of the 1920s and 1930s. As Taylor notes, Eisenstein sought to "subjugate the actor's mind and body to the discipline of gymnastic control and the actor himself more completely to the dictates of the director" (Eisenstein, Notes, "Teaching Programme" 366 n10). Eisenstein had even coined a word for such an actor: "*naturshchik* [mannequin]."

14 This comment from 1936 represents Brecht's evolution from his early faith in behaviorist acting precepts like those of Eisenstein: just six years earlier, Brecht had noted that "[j]ust as moods and thoughts lead to attitudes and gestures, so do attitudes and gestures lead to moods and thoughts" [*So wie Stimmungen und Gedankenreihen zu Haltungen und Gesten führen, führen auch Haltungen und Gesten zu Stimmungen und Gedankreihen*]" ("Zur Theorie" 397).

15 As Golden has pointed out, an earlier interpretation of katharsis as clarification [*Aufklärung*] "had no effect on the mainstream of criticism of the *Poetics*" ("Mimesis and Katharsis" 145). Stephan Odon Haupt had proposed in 1915 that "*katharsis* in Aristotle's sense is neither moral nor 'hedonic' nor therapeutic but rather intellectual [*die Katharsis in Aristoteles' Sinn weder ethisch noch, 'hedonisch' noch therapeutisch ist, sondern intellektualistich*]" (18); he quotes a letter he received from Otto Immisch in 1907 as the origin of the idea. But the "clarification" theory of katharsis would have to wait until its cultural moment.

16 "If catharsis is understood as 'clarification' in the intellectual sense of the word, then the final clause of the definition of tragedy in chapter 6 may be translated as, 'achieving, through the representation of pitiful and fearful situations, the clarification of such incidents' " (Golden, "Catharsis" 58). Halliwell writes, "I have therefore concluded . . . that tragic *katharsis* in some way conduces to an ethical alignment between the emotions and reason: because tragedy arouses

pity and fear by appropriate means, it does not, as Plato alleged, 'water' or feed the emotions, but tends to harmonise them with our perceptions and judgements of the world" (200–01). Similarly, see also Nussbaum, *Fragility* (391) and "Tragedy" (282–83).

17   The goal of tragedy, these accounts remind us, is the attainment of pleasure-giving knowledge. Golden writes, "Since tragedy as a species of poetry must involve learning and since, according to Aristotle, it is specifically concerned with pitiful and fearful situations, we must assume that tragedy in some way involves learning about pity and fear" ("Catharsis" 55). Compare Nussbaum and Halliwell:

> For Aristotle, pity and fear will be sources of illumination or clarification, as the agent, responding and attending to his or her responses, develops a richer self-understanding concerning the attachments and values that support the responses. (Nussbaum, *Fragility* 388)

> And because of this integration [of emotion] into the total experience of tragedy, *katharsis* must also be intimately associated with the pleasure derivable from the genre, for this pleasure . . . arises from the comprehension of the same action which is the focus of the emotions. (Halliwell 201)

Nussbaum and Halliwell's shared avoidance of the term "learning" – she opts for "understanding"; he, for "comprehension" – relates to their more fully articulated view of emotions as cognitive. Because of behaviorism, "learning" can still carry the connotation of a nonintellectual process.

18   "Since learning for Aristotle means proceeding from the particular to the universal, we must also assume that tragedy consists of the artistic representation of particular pitiful and fearful events in such a way that we are led to see the universal laws that make these particular events meaningful" (Golden, "Catharsis" 55). Nussbaum gives an example: "The sight of Philoctetes' pain [in Sophocles' *Philoctetes*] removes an impediment (ignorance in this case, rather than forgetfulness or denial), making him [i.e., Neoptolemus] clearer about what another's suffering means, about what his good character requires in this situation, about his own possibilities as a human being. The audience, in the midst of wartime, is recalled to awareness of the meaning of bodily pain for another, for themselves" ("Tragedy" 282). Similarly, see also Halliwell (77–80).

19   Nussbaum's book offers a cogent summary and distillation of several decades of philosophical and psychological writing about the emotions; as she acknowledges, she relies on (among others) William Lyons's 1980 *Emotion*, Ronald de Sousa's 1987 *The Rationality of Emotion*, and Robert Gordon's 1990 *The Structure of Emotions: Investigations in Cognitive Philosophy* (see *Upheavals* 22). For good, if incomplete, surveys of cognitivist emotion theory see Deigh (focusing on the discourse of philosophy) and chapter six of Strongman (focusing on the discourse of psychology).

20   Most post-Cartesian views of emotion presuppose that physiological change in the emotional subject precedes his or her awareness of that physiological change. The reversal of cause and effect (a judgment, then a physiological

change) was initiated by Maranon's adrenaline studies in the 1920s (see Strongman 62) but was principally associated with Schachter and Singer, who established that subjects injected with adrenaline did not consider themselves to be
in an "emotional state" until they were put in an emotion-appropriate context.
Thus, they proposed that "cognitive factors are potent determiners of emotional states" (Schachter and Singer 398).

21   Throughout the 1940s and 1950s, behaviorist psychologists complicated their
     models to fit the complexities of human behavior successfully enough that, as
     late as 1968, Fodor could write, "surely . . . one or another form of behaviorism
     is true" (49). Its dominance would soon slip: see, for example, Gardner (109–11)
     or Lazarus (8–15).

22   Brecht had expressed the same point succinctly in an untranslated essay from
     1935: "[i]nsofar as Aristotle (in the fourth book of the *Poetics*) speaks generally
     about the pleasure of imitative representation and calls it the basis of learning,
     we go along with him [*Solange der Aristoteles (im vierten Kapitel der, 'Poetik')*
     ganz allgemein über die Freude an der nachahmenden Darstellung spricht und
     als Grund dafür das Lernen nennt, gehen wir mit ihm]" ("Kritik" 171).

23   The poem is not included in the play in the Suhrkamp *Werke* (see instead,
     Brecht, *Brechts Antigone* 167). Antigone's words in the original are particularly
     pointed: "*Halt für ein Beispiel.*"

24   "It also follows from what has been said that it is not the poet's business to re-
     late actual events, but such things as might or could happen in accordance
     with probability or necessity" (Aristotle, *Poetics* 1451a).

25   Citations are to Brecht's 1954 version of the play; variant scenes are gathered in
     Hecht (36–54).

26   The story of Solomon is structurally parallel (and its verdict identical) to that
     told in a thirteenth-century play by Li Hsing Dao. Brecht probably did not use
     the Chinese source directly; rather, he cribbed from the popular 1924 adap-
     tation of Kla-bund (Alfred Henschke), itself only one of several Western adap-
     tations (Ritchie 7– 11).

27   Brecht had addressed the issue in his untranslated 1955 dialogue "Ein Umweg":

>   P   Man hat in X vor, den „Weg in die nördlichen Gebirge" zu streichen. Das
>   Stück ist lang, und der ganze Akt, macht man geltend, ist schließlich nur ein
>   Umweg . . .
>   B   Die Umwege in den neuen Stücken sollte man genau studieren, bevor man
>   einen abgekürzten Weg geht. Er mag länger wirken . . . Erstens kommt es im
>   Prozeß nicht auf den Anspruch der Magd auf das Kind, sondern auf den Anspruch
>   des Kindes auf die bessere Mutter an, und die Eignung der Magd zur Mutter. Ihre
>   Zuverlässigkeit und Brauchbarkeit werden gerade durch ihr vernünftiges Zögern
>   beim Übernehmen des Kindes erwiesen . . . In der Magd Grusche gibt es das Inter-
>   esse für das Kind und ihr eigenes Interesse im Widerstreit miteinander. Sie muß
>   beide Interessen erkennen und beiden zu folgen versuchen. (403–04)

>   [P   The people at X want to cut "In the Northern Mountains." The play is
>   long, and they assert that the whole act is really no more than a detour . . .

B   Detours in modern plays ought to be studied meticulously before one takes a short cut. It might seem longer . . . To start with, the trial isn't about the maid's claim to the child but rather about the child's claim to the better mother and the maid's suitability as a mother. Her reliability and usefulness are proven by her reasonable hesitations about taking on the child . . . Within the maid Grusha, the child's interests and her own are in opposition. She must recognize and try to follow both interests.]

28   In 1926, Brecht was said to comment that characters "are not matter for empathy; they are there to be understood" ("Conversation" 15). Brecht did not greatly attenuate this early conviction as he began to rethink the role of emotion in the "non-Aristotelian" theatre. In 1944, for example, Brecht maintained that "[i]t is only opponents of the new drama, the champions of the 'eternal laws of the theatre,' who suppose that in renouncing the empathy process the modern theatre is renouncing the emotions" ("Little Private" 161). Or, as Brecht put it in his unfinished "Der Messingkauf": "Only one out of many possible sources of emotion needs to be left unused, or at least treated as a subsidiary source – empathy" (173).

29   "*Damit Verlaß ist auf die Gesinnung, muß sie nicht nur impulsiv, sondern auch verstandesmäßig übernommen werden*" (Brecht, "*Katzgraben*" 456). Willett's translation of this passage – "If a feeling is to be an effective one, it must be acquired not merely impulsively but through the understanding" (Brecht, "Notes" 247) – is uncharacteristically unsatisfactory. Brecht stresses the reliability of a spectator's attitude (*Gesinnung*) that is to be engendered through emotion – that is, through impulses but also understanding.

30   Brecht had written in his "Kritik der 'Poetik' des Aristoteles" that "*[e]ine völlig freie, kritische, auf rein irdische Lösungen von Schwierigkeiten bedachte Haltung des Zuschauers ist keine Basis für eine Katharsis*" (172).

31   The haste with which Nussbaum dismisses (in a footnote!) these remarks in the *Politics* may betray their problematizing impact on her argument: "The brief remarks are indeed unclear. *Katharsis* is linked in some way with medical treatment; but it is also linked to education . . . There is no obstacle to the translation 'clarification,' and no reason to suppose that at this time Aristotle had any very precise view of what clarification, in this case, was" (*Fragility* 503 n18). Golden has also dismissed the *Politics* passage ("Purgation Theory" 474–77), as Halliwell himself has pointed out (355).

32   Ricoeur writes,

Aristotle defines it [rhetoric] as the art of inventing or finding proofs. Now poetry does not seek to prove anything at all: its project is mimetic; its aim . . . is to compose an essential representation of human actions; its appropriate method is to speak the truth by means of fiction, fable, and tragic *muthos*. The triad of *poiesis–mimesis–catharsis*, which cannot possibly be confused with the triad *rhetoric–proof–persuasion*, characterizes the world of poetry in an exclusive manner. (Ricoeur 13)

Belfiore makes a similar point, contrasting the emotions that are elicited by a rhetorician (as prescribed, for example, in the *Rhetoric*) with those elicited by the tragic poet (as prescribed in the *Poetics*). Belfiore acknowledges the cognitive aspect of the tragic emotions, but she is careful to note that "tragedy, unlike rhetoric, does not have an immediate, practical goal, but leads us to contemplate imitations for their own sake" (253).

WORKS CITED

Althusser, Louis. *For Marx*. Trans. Ben Brewster. London: Allen Lane, 1969.
Aristotle. *Metaphysics*. Trans. Hugh Tredennick. Loeb Classical Library. Vols. 17–18. Cambridge:Harvard UP, 1953.
———. *Poetics. On Poetry and Style*. Trans. G.M.A. Grube. Indianapolis: Hackett, 1989.
———. *Politics*. Trans. T.A. Sinclair. Rev. ed. New York: Penguin, 1981.
Arvon, Henri. *L'esthétique marxiste*. Paris: Presses Universitaires de France, 1970.
Belfiore, Elizabeth S. *Tragic Pleasures: Aristotle on Plot and Emotion*. Princeton: Princeton UP, 1992.
Benjamin, Walter. *Understanding Brecht*. Trans. Anna Bostock. London: NLB, 1973.
Bordwell, David. *The Cinema of Eisenstein*. Cambridge: Harvard UP, 1993.
Brecht, Bertolt. "Alienation Effects in Chinese Acting." *Brecht on Theatre* 91–99.
———. "Anmerkungen zur Oper 'Aufstieg und Fall der Stadt Mahagonny.' " Brecht, *Werke* 24: 74–84.
———. "Amerkungen zur ‚Mutter'." Brecht, *Werke* 24: 150–90.
———. *Antigonemodell*. Brecht, *Werke* 25: 73–168.
———. "Appendices to the Short Organum." Brecht, *Brecht on Theatre* 276–81.
———. *Brecht on Theatre: The Development of an Aesthetic*. Ed., trans., intro., and notes John Willett. London: Methuen, 1990.
———. *Brechts Antigone des Sophokles*. Ed. Werner Hecht. Frankfurt am Main: Suhrkamp, 1988.
———. *Briefe*. 3 vols. Brecht, *Werke*. Vols. 28–30.
———. *The Caucasian Chalk Circle*. Trans. James and Tania Stern, with W.H. Auden. London: Methuen, 1996.
———. "Conversation with Bert Brecht." Brecht, *Brecht on Theatre* 14–17.
———. *Der Dreigroschenprozeß: Ein soziologisches Experiment*. Brecht, *Werke* 21: 448–514.
———. *Der kaukasische Kreidekreis*. Brecht, *Werke* 8: 93–191.
———. " 'Der Messingkauf': An Editorial Note." Brecht, *Brecht on Theatre* 169–75.
———. *Die Maßnahme: Kritische Ausgabe mit einer Spielanleitung von Reiner Steinweg*. Frankfurt am Main: Suhrkamp, 1972.
———. "Ein Umweg." Brecht, *Werke* 23: 403–04.
———. "Entwurf einer Vorrede für eine Lesung." Brecht, *Werke* 22: 138–40.
———. "The Film, the Novel, and Epic Theatre." Brecht, *Brecht on Theatre* 47–51.
———. "Formal Problems Arising from the Theatre's New Content." Brecht, *Brecht on Theatre* 226–30.

————. "Formprobleme des Theaters aus neuem Inhalt." Brecht, *Werke* 23: 109–13.

————. "Gedichte aus dem Messingkauf." Brecht, *Werke* 12: 319–31.

————. "The German Drama: Pre-Hitler." Brecht, *Brecht on Theatre* 77–81.

————. *In the Jungle of the Cities.* Trans. Gerhard Nellhaus. *Collected Plays.* Vol. 1. Ed. John Willett and Ralph Manheim. London: Methuen, 1970. 117–78.

————. "Indirect Impact of the Epic Theatre." Brecht, *Brecht on Theatre* 57–62.

————. *Journale.* 2 vols. *Werke.* Vols. 26–27.

————. "*Katzgraben*-Notate." *Werke* 25: 401–90.

————. "Kleine Liste der beliebtesten, landläufigsten und banalsten Irrtümer über das epische Theater." Brecht, *Werke* 22: 315–16.

————. "Kleines Organon für das Theater." Brecht, *Werke* 23: 65–97.

————. "Kleines Privatissimum für meinen Freund Max Gorelik." Brecht, *Werke* 23: 37–39.

————. "Kritik der ‚Poetik' des Aristoteles." Brecht, *Werke* 22: 171–72.

————. "A Little Private Tuition for my Friend Max Gorelik." Brecht, *Brecht on Theatre* 159–63.

————. "Masterful Treatment of a Model." Brecht, *Brecht on Theatre* 209–15.

————. *The Measures Taken. The Jewish Wife and Other Short Plays.* Trans. Eric Bentley. New York: Grove, 1965. 75–108.

————. "The Modern Theatre is the Epic Theatre." Brecht, *Brecht on Theatre* 33–42.

————. "Notes on Erwin Strittmatter's Play '*Katzgraben.*' " Brecht, *Brecht on Theatre* 247–51.

————. "On Experimental Theatre." Brecht, *Brecht on Theatre* 130–35.

————. "On the Use of Music in an Epic Theatre." Brecht, *Brecht on Theatre* 84–90.

————. "Short Description of a New Technique of Acting which Produces an Alienation Effect." Brecht, *Brecht on Theatre* 136–47.

————. "A Short Organum for the Theatre." Brecht, *Brecht on Theatre* 179–205.

————. *Sophocles' Antigone.* Trans. Judith Malina. New York: Applause, 1990.

————. "Theatre for Pleasure or Theatre for Instruction." Brecht, *Brecht on Theatre* 69–77.

————. "Über die Verwendung von Musik für ein episches Theater." Brecht, *Werke* 22: 155–64.

————. "Über rationellen und emotionellen Standpunkt." Brecht, *Werke* 22: 500–02.

————. *Werke: Große kommentierte Berliner und Frankfurter Ausgabe.* Ed. Werner Hecht et al. 30 vols. Frankfurt am Main: Suhrkamp, 1988–2000.

————. "Zu ‚Der kaukasische Kreidekreis.' " Brecht, *Werke* 24: 341–48.

————. "Zur Theorie des Lehrstücks." Brecht, *Werke* 21: 397.

Deigh, John. "Cognitivism in the Theory of Emotions." *Ethics* 104.4 (1994): 824–54.

Dickson, Keith A. *Towards Utopia: A Study of Brecht.* Oxford: Clarendon, 1978.

Eaton, Katherine Bliss. *The Theater of Meyerhold and Brecht.* Westport, CT: Greenwood, 1985.

Eisenstein, Sergei. "Constanta (Whither 'The Battleship Potemkin')." *Selected Works 1:* 67–70.

————. "The Montage of Film Attractions." Eisenstein, *Selected Works 1* 39–58.

————. Notes. Eisenstein, "Teaching Programme" 366–69.

————. Notes. Eisenstein, "Constanta" 308.

————. "Perspectives." Eisenstein, *Selected Works 1* 151–60.

————. *Selected Works 1: Writings, 1922–34.* Ed. and trans. Richard Taylor. Bloomington: Indiana UP, 1988.

————. *Selected Works 3: Writings, 1934–47.* Ed. Richard Taylor. Trans. William Powell. London: BFI, 1996.

————. "Teaching Programme for the Theory and Practice of Direction: How to Teach Direction." Eisenstein, *Selected Works 3.* 74–97.

Fodor, Jerry A. *Psychological Explanation: An Introduction to the Philosophy of Psychology.* New York: Random House, 1968.

Gardner, Howard. *The Mind's New Science: A History of the Cognitive Revolution.* New York: Basic, 1985.

Golden, Leon. "Catharsis." *Transactions and Proceedings of the American Philological Association (TAPA)* 93 (1962): 51–60.

————. "The Clarification Theory of Catharsis." *Hermes* 104 (1976): 437–50.

————. "Mimesis and *Katharsis.*" *Classical Philology* 64.3 (1969): 145–53.

————. "The Purgation Theory of Catharsis." *Journal of Aesthetics and Art Criticism* 31.4 (1973): 473–79.

Halliwell, Stephen. *Aristotle's Poetics.* Chapel Hill: U of North Carolina P, 1986.

Haupt, Stephan Odon. *Wirkt die Tragödie auf das Gemüt oder den Verstand oder die Moralität der Zuschauer? [Does Tragedy Affect the Mind, the Understanding, or the Morality of the Spectators?].* Berlin: Leonard Simion, 1915.

Hecht, Werner, ed. *Materielen zu Brechts "Der kaukasische Kreidekreis."* Frankfurt am Main: Suhrkamp, 1966.

Husain, Martha. *Ontology and the Art of Tragedy.* Albany: SUNY P, 2002.

"Katharsis [καθαρσιος]." *Greek-English Lexicon.* 9th ed. 1940.

James, William. *The Principles of Psychology.* Vol. 2. Cambridge: Harvard UP, 1981.

Law, Alma, and Mel Gordon. *Meyerhold, Eisenstein and Biomechanics: Actor Training in Revolutionary Russia.* London: McFarland, 1996.

Lazarus, Richard S. *Emotion and Adaptation.* New York: Oxford UP, 1991.

Lunn, Eugene. *Marxism and Modernism: An Historical Study of Lukács, Brecht, Benjamin, and Adorno.* Berkeley: U of California P, 1982.

Nelson, G.E. "The Birth of Tragedy Out of Pedagogy: Brecht's 'Learning Play' *Die Massnahme.*" *German Quarterly* 46.4 (1973): 566–80.

Nussbaum, Martha C. *The Fragility of Goodness: Luck and Ethics in Greek Tragedy and Philosophy.* Cambridge: Cambridge UP, 1986.

————. "Tragedy and Self-sufficiency: Plato and Aristotle on Fear and Pity." *Essays on Aristotle's Poetics.* Ed. Amélie Oksenberg Rorty. Princeton: Princeton UP, 1992. 261–90.

————. *Upheavals of Thought: The Intelligence of Emotions.* Cambridge: Cambridge UP, 2001.

Orr, John. "Terrorism as Social Drama and Dramatic Form." *Terrorism and Modern Drama.* Ed. John Orr and Dragan Klaicð. Edinburgh: Edinburgh UP, 1980. 48–63.

Ricoeur, Paul. *The Rule of Metaphor: Multi-disciplinary Studies of the Creation of Meaning in Language.* Trans. Robert Czerny, with Kathleen McLaughlin and John Costello. Toronto: U of Toronto P, 1977.

Ritchie, James MacPherson. *Brecht: Der Kaukasische Kreidekreis*. London: Edward Arnold, 1976.

Schachter, Stanley, and Jerome E. Singer. "Cognitive, Social, and Physiological Determinants of Emotional State." *Psychological Review* 69.5 (1962): 379–99.

Silk, M.S. "Aristotle, Rapin, Brecht." *Making Sense of Aristotle: Essays in Poetics*. Ed. Øivind Andersen and Jon Haarberg. London: Duckworth, 2001. 173–95.

Sokel, Walter. "Brecht's Split Characters and His Sense of the Tragic." *Brecht: Critical Essays*. Ed. Peter Demetz. Englewood Cliffs, NJ: Prentice-Hall, 1962. 127–39.

Steinweg, Reiner. "Zeugnisse der Rezeption." Brecht, *Die Maßnahme* 319–469.

Strongman, K.T. *The Psychology of Emotion: Theories of Emotion in Perspective*. New York: John Wiley, 1996.

Suvin, Darko. "Brecht's *Caucasian Chalk Circle* and Marxist Figuralism: Open Dramaturgy as Open History." *Critical Essays on Bertolt Brecht*. Ed. Siegfried Mews. Boston: G.K. Hall, 1989. 162–75.

White, John J. *Bertolt Brecht's Dramatic Theory*. Rochester, NY: Camden House, 2004.

Willett, John. *The Theatre of Bertolt Brecht: A Study from Eight Aspects*. London: Methuen, 1959.

12

Jane Harrison and the Savage Dionysus: Archaeological Voyages, Ritual Origins, Anthropology, and the Modern Theatre[1]

JULIE STONE PETERS

In March of 1888, Jane Ellen Harrison and a large party headed toward the Greek islands and the coast of Turkey, chartering a black ship to "see all the places Pausanias pretended he had visited" (qtd. in Stewart 11). The trip's official purpose was research for *Mythology and Monuments of Ancient Athens*, the edition of Pausanias-turned-travel-guide that (dubbed the "Blue Jane") was to become the intelligentsia's *Blue Guide* to Athens.[2] But Harrison was also drawn by what she later described as "the irresistible tide of adventure" (*Reminiscences* 83), which began to bring her regularly to Italy, Greece, and Turkey in the last decades of the nineteenth century, partly as a scholar-adventuress, partly as a seeker of lost relics, partly in search of the occult origins of theatre. Wandering about the site of the old Theatre of Dionysus, Harrison suddenly understood a Greek vase she had seen in Naples (Figure 1) (*Mythology* 288, fig. 29(a), fig. 29(b)).[3] One side of the vase showed "all the ordered splendour and luxury of a regular dramatic representation – masks, tripods, costly raiment; while Bacchus and Ariadne watch the preparation of the chorus from their sumptuous couch." The other side showed "the wild dance of Maenads and Satyrs" around a sacrificial goat, "such a dance as went on by many a rustic altar." What suddenly became clear was that the dancing Maenads and Satyrs, the sacrificial goat, and the primitive god were the key to the "ordered splendour and luxury of [the] regular dramatic representation" (288). The Maenads and Satyrs were transformed, as one turned the vase, into the chorus. The goat (*tragos*), with his dying song, was abstracted into the tragedy itself, to which he "gave his name" (*tragoedia*) (Harrison, *Mythology* 288).[4] And the primitive god worshipped at the "rustic altar" metamorphized, on the other side of the vase, into none other than Dionysus–Bacchus, presiding god of the drama. The figures of the ritual

Figure 1: "[A]ll the ordered splendour and luxury of a regular dramatic representation" with "the wild dance of Maenads and Satyrs"; *Mythology and Monuments* 288.

dance were theatre's pre-history (the vase was telling her), its origins and *raison d'être*.

In the ruins of the old Theatre of Dionysus, looking past "the rough-looking wall [that] looks like some rubbish heap," the seats, and even the stage itself, she found a faint trace of what must have once been there: a simple circular orchestra with a stone boundary line like those she had seen at Epidaurus and Oropus (*Mythology* 285–86, 290). And she could suddenly see before her not only "*the old original orchestra on which the plays of Aeschylus were performed*" but, still further back in historical memory, "the early Dionysiac dance." The "theatre of the Greeks," she realized, "was originally an orchestra, or dancing-place," an "altar and a level place about it, circular because the worshippers danced round in a ring," "*that and nothing more*, yet enough for Dionysos the Dance-lover" (285–86; emphasis in original). Here, "ritual was perfectly simple," and "all were worshippers ... none were actors, none spectators." It was only in the drama's "days of decadence" that the stage had begun to "encroach on the orchestra." As long as the Greek drama was "worth anything at all, it was an act of worship" (290). Standing in that one-time place of worship, she could imagine she saw before her a scene she had seen on a cylix by Hieron in the Berlin Museum: "the ancient upright image, half a post, half a man," a totemic pillar-god with "ivy boughs and fruits" spilling over his shoulders, "about his neck ... a garland of dried figs," the "simple god of the vine and the fruits of the earth." Around "an altar ... flecked with the blood of the slain goat" circled "the ring of Maenads ... dancing their simple *contre-danse*, with lively gestures of hands uplifted to salute the god, and bodies bent to invoke the mother earth" (286–87).

***

Harrison is primarily known as a classicist, centre of the group of scholars later to be known as the "Cambridge Ritualists."[5] An academic star at Newnham College in Cambridge (where she was among the first women students in the 1870s), she nonetheless took a disappointing second in the Classical Tripos. Denied a lectureship, she moved to London in 1880 to study archaeology at the British Museum and there began the life of the newly independent metropolitan woman, living in women's residences, supporting herself through public lectures on Greek art and culture (her income supplemented by a small inheritance), travelling to the Continent whenever possible, acting in amateur Greek theatricals, falling in and out of love (with men and women), and taking tea and theatre with London's bohemian intelligentsia. At last granted a position in Cambridge in 1898, she spent the next two-and-a-half decades there, producing scholarship that was a hybrid of classics, art history, archaeology, anthropology, folk-lore, religion, literature, aesthetics, and theatre history, in a self-conscious anti-disciplinarity that acutely irritated her fusty classicist colleagues and helped make her one of the most widely read British academics of the first decades of the century.[6]

All of Harrison's books ostensibly focus on Greek art and religion. But, as she explained in her *Reminiscences*, ritual came to be her "real subject" (84), and most of her work was shaped by her preoccupation with the relationship between ritual and theatre. From her archaeological journeys and her encounter with late nineteenth-century anthropology emerged her vision of theatre's origins in archaic ritual, which became an essential source for the primitivist rhetoric of modern theatre. Treating teaching as a performance practice and an opportunity for multimedia spectacle, she did lecture-hall re-enactments of archaic rituals that were themselves proto-types for modernist dramaturgy. As a crucial contributor to the intellectual foundations of theatrical modernism in England, Harrison was pivotal in the transformation of theatre from the narrative and socially mimetic insti-tution that it had been since the Renaissance into the anti-mimetic organ it became for the twentieth-century avant-garde. As important, her work offered a model for modern theatre historiography: challenging the written text as privileged vehicle for performance knowledge and docu-mentation, positioning the artefact as the central actor in the symbolic drama of theatre history, and showing theatre history to be intimately linked to the broader history of human performance. She was thus instrumental in formulating the twentieth-century conception of theatre as part of a broader continuum of performance practices, to be studied in relation to one another. And so one might see, in theatre history's marriage with the larger study of cultural performance, the belated emergence of what she helped to make possible.

In the period after her death in 1928, Harrison tended to be smirkingly dismissed for what amounted to scholarly hysteria, while her work was silently assimilated by scholars who had supposedly superseded her.[7] Later, she was often cast as merely one of the Cambridge ritualists, themselves followers of J.G. Frazer (see, e.g., Smith 43). But her first major book on myth and ritual – *Mythology and Monuments of Ancient Athens* – was published in 1890 a month or so before *The Golden Bough*.[8] It (along with her popular lectures) helped give currency to ritualist ideas a decade or two before Gilbert Murray or Francis Cornford (who were as much her disciples as her colleagues) started writing about ritual.[9] While her work was very much a product of the primitivist longings and projections of the era, and while she acknowledged her debt to Nietzsche, Freud, Durkheim, Bergson, and Frazer himself,[10] she may be seen as having produced one of the most influential early formulations of the ritualist idea.

Harrison's importance for modernism has been sporadically recognized, and classicists have recently begun to look at her importance for the history of their discipline.[11] But her vital place in the disciplinary history of theatre and avant-garde performance has gone unrecognized.[12] On the one hand, my goal here is to recover her for theatre history, elevating her status from that of footnote to that of central figure in the creation of theatrical modernism (at once influential and emblematic) and identifying the consequences and meaning of her work not only for twentieth-century theatre but also for the development of theatre history and (eventually) performance studies as academic disciplines. At the same time, Harrison was doing theatre anthropology *avant la lettre*, and, in this sense, I view this essay as a contribution to a broader history of the anthropology of performance (still to be written), as well as to the study of the multiple trajectories of ethnographic modernism more generally.

AESTHETIC HELLENISM AND THE GREEK THEATRICAL

Studying Classics at Newnham in the 1870s, Harrison had already become something of a celebrity. Looking back, friends described the dramatic impression she made – her "willowy figure" arrayed "in 'bluery-greenery' Burne-Jones draperies," a Pre-Raphaelite vision, "exceedingly striking to look at in those days – tall, a little swaying, graceful," with a "splendid head of hair & bright eyes."[13] She herself proudly recalled being visited by George Eliot in her Cambridge rooms, which she had just repapered "with the newest thing in dolorous Morris papers," and Eliot's comment: "Your paper makes a beautiful background for your face" (*Reminiscences* 45–46). The kind of dramatic self-presentation that helped make Harrison such a personage at Newnham – dressing in pre-Raphaelite gowns, posing against her Morris wallpaper – also helped make her something of a star in the recondite world of the late Victorian amateur Greek theatrical, that nexus of tweedy academia, naughty bohemia, and high society.[14] Harrison had been at the vanguard of what became a tradition of college Greek performances when, in 1877 at Cambridge, she tried to mount a production of Euripides' *Electra*.[15] As one of the originators of the scheme, she taught the choruses their dances, designed the costumes, and played both the messenger and *paidagogos*. Unfortunately, the production was called off because the principal of the college was appalled by the idea of women acting as men and performing with bare arms and legs.[16] In 1883, however, three years after she had established herself in London, she had her chance again when George Warr, professor of classical literature at King's College, asked her to play Penelope in a theatrical concoction entitled *Tale of Troy*, a compilation of key moments from the *Iliad* and the *Odyssey*, linked by a series of tableaux, to be performed both in Greek and English (on alternating nights).

The production – four performances in May of 1883, in the private Greek theatre that had been specially built in Cromwell House, the London home of Sir Charles and Lady Freake – was a spectacular affair.[17] Frederic Leighton had created the overall design, specially commissioning such artists as Edward Burne-Jones, John Everett Millais, Edward Poynter, G.F. Watts, and Lawrence Alma-Tadema to design the tableaux that linked the scenes. There was "The Pledge of Aphrodite" (arranged "after an ancient bas-relief"), a "view of the Trojan plain, the sea, Imbros, and the sacred height of Ida as beheld from Hissarlik" (adopted in deference to the archaeologist Heinrich Schliemann), "the Ilian plain by moonlight," and the "beautiful archaic palace of Alcinous" where "[t]he maidens of Nausicaa" tossed a ball from hand to hand (*"Tale," Saturday Review*). Along with Harrison as Penelope, the cast of nearly eighty actors included J.K. Stephen, Florence Stoker (Bram Stoker's wife), Lionel Tennyson (Alfred Lord Tennyson's son), Leonora Blanche Lang (Andrew Lang's wife), and that great theatrical couple Herbert Beerbohm Tree and his wife Maud. In the audience were such celebrities as Leighton, Prime Minister Gladstone, and Tennyson (the poet himself).

In the *Tale of Troy*, the architecture of the sets, the objects used onstage, the folds of the costumes, the choreography, the very postures of the performers aimed at capturing the ideal beauty that was the particular province of Greek culture. This fashionably aesthetic Hellenism (the production's "sympathetic [and] refined appreciation of the beauty of Greek art," in the words of the reviewer from the *Times* ["*Tale*," *Times*]) was fused with an antiquarianism that was its scholarly counterpart: "each scene was in itself a work of art," wrote the *Athenaeum* reviewer, "and the accessories were not only ... archaeologically accurate, but beautiful" ("*Tale*," *Athenaeum*). This was due, in part, to the various classical archaeologists on board, who fussed over the historical details of costuming, hair-styles, and pediments, eager to represent the latest archaeological findings correctly to the audience of leisured intelligentsia. Charles Newton, keeper of Greek and Roman antiquities at the British Museum and Yates Professor of classical archaeology at University College, London, was a consultant. Charles Waldstein, reader in Greek art and classical archaeology at Cambridge, who had been involved with Sophocles's *Ajax* there in 1882 (the first Cambridge Greek play), coached the actors.[18] As the *Saturday Review* pointed out, "The attire of the heroines, nymphs, and goddesses was reproduced from ancient vases and gems," modelled on "relics of Phoenician and Assyrian art." In preparation for the performance, Harrison and her friend Elinor Ritchie spent hours at the British Museum looking at vases to find inspiration for costumes and poses.[19] While it was "impossible to obtain the actual Pelian spear" wielded by Achilles (as the *Saturday Review* commented dryly ["*Tale*," *Saturday Review*]), Charles Newton lent precious gold jewellery (borrowed from the museum?) to Eugénie Sellers, who was playing Helen in English and Cassandra in Greek.[20] Maud Tree recalled the erudite primping backstage: "What about my [*chiton*]?"; "Please drape the folds of my [*himation*]" (18–19).

This sort of "five o'clock antiquity" (as it was called in the 1880s) (see Mirrlees, Draft) was not a lone experiment. Soon after the *Tale of Troy*, Charles Newton wrote to Eugénie Sellers of "our idea of bringing out the scenes of the Shield of Achilles in a series of tableaux."[21] Warr presented scenes from the *Oresteia* in Princess's Hall in 1886 and, during the same week, the Irish scholar and poet John Todhunter and the architect–designer E.W. Godwin (Ellen Terry's lover) put on *Helena in Troas* at Hengler's Circus in London, recreating an Attic theatre with a Trojan *mise en scène* based on Schliemann's archaeological discoveries.[22] And there were the college Greek plays, among them the Oxford University Dramatic Society's production of Euripides's *Alcestis* in 1887, with Harrison (opportunely lecturing on Greek sculpture there at the time) in the title role. This production had similar archaeological aspirations (along with some lavish special effects: Apollo came in on flying wires and was accidentally nearly strangled by them; "burst[s] of steam," unfortunately reminiscent of "the occasional volumes of smoke which r[o]se into London streets through the gratings of the Underground Railway," produced an ominous mist around Thanatos; Alcestis was carried offstage on a bier). According to the *Times* review, the society reproduced the "Greek arrangement" for choreographic "evolutions ... with antiquarian precision," following Albert Müller's recently published tome on the Greek stage. The set had marble stairs leading to the stage; "[t]he thymele," or central altar, stood "upon a tessellated pavement; and copies of bas-reliefs from Phigaleia form[ed] the background" (*"Alcestis," Times*). In the eyes of the reviewer for the *Athenaeum*, "[e]very step in the direction of accuracy" produced a "manifest gain in beauty and harmony of effect" (*"Alcestis," Athenaeum*).

For some, Harrison's acting in these productions was insufferably theatrical. In *Alcestis* (according to one of the reviewers), she was "by turns hysterical and stony" (qtd. in Carpenter 45). She kept her voice at "an artificially high pitch" (*"Alcestis," Cambridge*), and (as the *Athenaeum* wrote of her performance in *Tale of Troy*), her "excessive declamation and too great emphasis on unimportant words tend[ed] rather to destroy than create natural effect." But for most, Harrison was a genius at evoking the fusion of scholarly antiquarianism and aesthetic Hellenism for which the Greek theatricals seemed to call. Hope Mirrlees (Harrison's companion in later life) wrote that everything about her performance in *Tale of Troy* – "her classic grace & her incomparably beautiful voice" – was "EXQUISITE" (Draft). If the *Tale of Troy* as a whole showed a "sympathetic [and] refined appreciation of the beauty of Greek art," Harrison herself personified that perfectly Hellenic beauty, as a languid photograph of her in the role of Alcestis was meant to suggest (Figure 2). She was "a truly picturesque Alcestis," according to Charlotte Sidgwick, wife of the classicist Arthur Sidgwick and Harrison's Oxford host during the *Alcestis* production. The Sidgwicks' children recalled her as a "figure of beauty ... a fairy princess," who "came up to our nursery in her Greek dress, all white, with arms bare to the shoulder, and bracelets on her *upper* arms."[23] "Greek things [were] the fashion," wrote Mirrlees, and "she herself was [the ultimate] 'Greek thing'" (Draft).

Harrison revelled in the posing, the publicity, the beginnings of fame.[24] Later, writing of the psychology of ritual, she described the "thrill of speaking to or acting with a great multitude" (*Themis* 43), borne away by the emotions of the crowd. When she began giving lectures in 1882, first at the British Museum, then at the South Kensington Museum, the London Archaeological Museum, the London Society for the Extension of University Teaching, and eventually on tour throughout the British Isles, she discovered the same thrill she had found onstage. All that she learned from the early theatricals she transferred into the sphere of the learned lecture. In the 1880s and 1890s, before the advent of cinema, public lectures were not simply academic exercises but part of the entertainment industry, and Harrison was a consummate entertainer, attracting

Figure 2: Harrison as Alcestis (1887); Newnham College Archives; courtesy of the Principal and Fellows, Newnham College, Cambridge.

huge crowds for lectures on such erudite topics as Attic grave reliefs.[25] When Harrison came to lecture at Winchester, a prefect there described her as "a splendid creature in Cardinal brocade with a Medici collar with her fine head of hair and bright eyes sweeping on to the platform." Mid-lecture, she suddenly "thr[ew] back her head" and "broke into a chorus from Euripides in Greek," at which the spectators "jumped onto their chairs & ... raised the roof with their cheers & for at least a week they talked of nothing else" (Mirrlees, Draft). "I was," she wrote later, "fatally fluent" (*Reminiscences* 63).

Greek theatricals (along with avid theatre-going) had given her a sense of how to use costuming, the grand gesture, the striking tableau. If, at

Cambridge in the 1870s, she had draped herself in pre-Raphaelite gowns, now she dressed in dark drapery or brilliant spangles. At one lecture, she had feathers in her hair and a train (de Buxton 66). Sometimes (as one student recalled) she would wear "a glittering shawl," which she would shrug off "at an exciting moment of recital" and let "fall in shimmering folds about her feet" (Holland 86). Lecturing at Winchester, dressed in blue-green spangles, she struck one young man as very like "a beautiful green beetle" (Harrison, *Reminiscences* 54). "I have a vision of her figure on the darkened stage of the lecture room at the Archaeological Museum," wrote her close friend Francis Cornford, "which she made deserve to the full its name of theatre – a tall figure in black drapery, with touches of her favourite green and a string of blue Egyptian beads, like a priestess' rosary" (Cornford 74).[26]

Dressed in robes, with the lights dimmed in the great lecture hall, Harrison would chant fragments of Greek tragedy to her rapt audiences. Sometimes she arranged that from the back of the hall would emerge an "unearthly noise," an "awe-inspiring and truly religious sound": the sound of primitive bull-roarers, "the magic *whirlers* of the tundun," so that the audience could learn what Aeschylus meant in the *Edonians*. And then she would intone the lines from the Greek: "Bull voices roar thereto from somewhere out of the unseen, fearful semblances, and from a drum, an image as it were of thunder underground is borne on the air, heavy with dread."[27] On other occasions, there were veiled objects on side-tables, which she would suddenly unveil: a *liknon*, or winnowing fan, for instance, "identical in shape and use with the *mystica vannus* she had illustrated from reliefs thrown upon the screen" (Cornford 74). As in the Greek theatricals, she used "a high strained voice," as her friend Alice Dew-Smith described it, "quite different to the voice her friends were accustomed to in her less formal moments" (64): a voice intended to intensify the sublimity of the experience and to capture the eerie magic of the past. "Every lecture," wrote Cornford, "was a drama in which the spectators were to share the emotions of 'Recognition'" (74).

At the centre of Harrison's lectures were her magic-lantern slides: in the pre-cinematic era, the closest thing to a light and sound show that one could get (outside of the theatre).[28] Harrison's artefacts – found in museum collections around the continent, photographed or drawn in stylized form, enlarged, lit from behind, and projected through her lantern – became dramatic visions of shadow and brilliant limelight. As a slide would loom up on her screen, she would narrate in the present tense: "It is Athene [in the Gigantomachia] who with her shield on her arm, her aegis on her breast, is grasping the strong-winged giant by the hair, and she is the victress now as before, for near her floats Nike, the victory-bringer, and conquest is assured" (*Introductory* 283). Teaching her spectators to "nurture their souls on the fair sights and pure visions of Ideal art" (Preface, *Introductory* vii), Harrison used her magic lantern not as a passive technology of representation but as an active player in her pedagogic scenography, crucial to the staging of her objects. As Cornford remarked, her "lectures were designed so that each new light" (intellectual and sensory) "should break upon the scene just when she would have it" (74). Projected by her magic lantern, her artefacts became actors in the drama of ancient history. The relic dug up from the earth – properly staged, transformed into light emerging out of the darkness – could speak the secret messages sent from the world of the past.

THE ANTI-AESTHETIC: VOYAGES INTO THE ARCHAIC PRESENT

Not everyone appreciated Harrison's pedagogic theatricality, the preciosity of her aestheticism, her treatment of classics as connoisseurship, or her performing artefacts. D.S. MacColl, the friend and sometime romantic partner with whom she travelled and collaborated in the late 1880s and 1890s, famously wrote her in early 1887, attacking the combination of aestheticism and sensationalism in her lectures, what Harrison came to refer to (contritely) as her *"Epideiktikos Logos,"* or "display oratory" (Harrison, Letter to D.S. MacColl, "Saturday" 1887; qtd. in Beard, *Invention* 58). Harrison responded (with typical drama) that MacColl's letter had provoked a conversion experience for her:

> I tore it up in the fury of first reading but unfortunately that only made me remember every word of it. I knew from the first that my rage against you was caused by the simple fact that you were right & I was wrong – but it was not till I began my work again that it was borne in upon me *how* wrong – how much more wrong than you could possibly divine – The worst is that all the success I have had has been based on wrongness, I could always hold an audience – any fanatic can – not by the proper & legitimate virtue of my subject or its treatment but by the harmful force of an intense personal conviction – I had grown into a sort of Salvationist for Greek art ... [A]rt has to me taken & more than taken the place of religion & my work for it was I see only another form of an old & I thought long dead personal fanaticism.[29]

Her belief in the redemptive power of Greek art crushed, Harrison claimed that she was unable to continue to produce the spectacular lectures for which she had become famous. She knew (she wrote MacColl) that she ought to follow his advice, "trust the subject to its own value & rid myself of my hateful habit of trying to force upon it meretricious effects." She admired the fact that he had "found for lecturing the 'more excellent way' as remote from dulness [*sic*] on the one side as from sensationalism on the other" and wrote that she envied him "without the smallest hope of emulation." But, without what she called the "sensational element," she felt lost. "[A]ll virtue is gone out of me; lecturing this term has been nothing but a dreary mechanical struggle & if my hearers have not found it out as they soon will it is only that something of the manner of conviction clings."[30]

Harrison was hardly crushed, as is clear from the mix of repentant and playfully unrepentant letters to MacColl in the months that followed: at one point she writes him that, on receiving some photographs from Siena, "[r]eleased from your stern censorship I broke loose into a 'wanton' profusion ... – come and sneer at them when next you have time."[31] Despite her supposed crisis, Harrison continued, throughout her life, to don flowing robes and green glass beads and dazzle her audiences with exquisite objects projected in dazzling light show. And one can find a residual strain of self-dramatizing aestheticism in much of her later work. But, without losing its dramatic flair, her work began to take on an anti-aestheticist cast.[32] Arguably, she gradually began to replace the make-believe of Greek theatricals and the "meretricious" "sensational[ism]" of her equally theatrical lectures with a search for the real thing, to be found in the remains of the ancient world in Southern Europe and at the exotic edges of the Asiatic world. She began to replace the decorative evocation of antiquity with the real excavation of whatever might be left of it, the making of stage sets with the unearthing of ruins, archaeology as purveyor of fine artefacts with archaeology as key to primal truths, the appetite for effects with the search for origins, aestheticism with primitivism, theatre with ritual.

In an 1886 letter to John Todhunter's wife Dora, Harrison had referred to her "long and somewhat bitter experience of amateur performances." She had, she wrote, "come to what was almost a conviction that a Greek play in modern times could never be anything but painful."[33] As she was to explain a few years later,

> Any one who has watched the modern restoration of a Greek play has, if he is honest, been conscious of a sense of extreme discomfort ... The whole is artificial, conventionalised, utterly unlike the simple, large, straightforward freedom that would naturally be expected of a Greek representation ... How absurd Agamemnon and his chariot look, shot half through a side door on a modern Greek stage ... It is only the humble and touching conviction that the effect is "Greek" that enables a modern audience to support the sight without laughter. (*Mythology* 291–92)

One might take Harrison's offhand remark (in early 1888) that she would go to the Haymarket "and chance disgust," for it was "the last theatre I shall enter till I sit with Dionysos himself beneath the 'hill-top,'"[34] as a symbolic leave-taking: a renunciation of the modern theatre for the theatre of the primitive gods. If she could still admire the pantomime art of a Madame Chaumont (a regular performer on the London popular stage), she was now in pursuit of a more primal pantomime, the kind whose memory was preserved only on vases or in Xenophon's "pantomimic myth," which she had just discovered.[35]

A few months later, Harrison was on her way to Greece and Turkey.[36] Touring the excavations and archaeological museums that had been multiplying over the past decades, Harrison and her friends spent long hours on the Acropolis, listening to the lectures of the German archaeologist Wilhelm Dörpfeld ("He would hold us spellbound for a six hours' peripatetic lecture," Harrison recalled [*Reminiscences* 65]). In Thebes, they visited the excavations of a mystery cult, a temple dedicated to the worship of a group of fertility gods (the Kabeiroi), where they found votive offerings, pottery fragments, animal bones, and the remains of an earlier Macedonian temple showing "sacrifices [made] on an open-air altar" (Harrison, "Archaeology" 128–29; see Robinson 95). They visited Prime Minister Charilaos Trikoupis's private collection of antiquities, where, as Harrison was carrying a vase showing the exploits of Theseus back to its place, light falling from a passage window revealed in its interior an inscription – Athenodotos, a "familiar *love-name*" – that had never before been seen (Harrison, "Two Cylices" 232).

After visiting excavations in Eleusis, Delphi, Thebes, and Olympia, Harrison and MacColl ("scandalously") broke away from the rest of the party, travelling *à deux* to Turkey and Sparta and then on a several-day journey by mule to the monastery of Voulcano. (Harrison had a flirtatious interlude with one of the monks there, giving him a "languishing" photo of herself in a ball gown, which he pinned up next to his icon of the virgin, and MacColl almost got them expelled for bathing naked in the courtyard.) Later, they ventured through ravine-filled mountains to Bassae to visit the Temple of Apollo, where, pursued by demons (or so the guide said), they slept in the rain, covered only by Macintoshes, beneath the "[w]ildish night" sky with the sound of "wolf-like dogs" howling in the background.[37] On the way home from Constantinople, Harrison found that she had lost her passport and had to pass herself off as MacColl's wife (with all the risqué implications of the deception). "[W]ho do you think protected me thro' those wilds?" she wrote Elizabeth Malleson soon after the trip. "I know I may venture to tell *you* what I do not disclose to every British matron that Mr. MacColl and I ventured on that pilgrimage alone … Arcadia was just one's dream come to life." In Arcadia, they had "slept in monasteries and strange khans where half the village comes to drink with one and camp round all night – it was a never to be forgotten experience but inconceivably primitive and savage."[38]

In 1888, and repeatedly over the next decades, while seeking out wet nights under the Arcadian sky, "monasteries and strange khans," and all

that was most "inconceivably primitive and savage," Harrison was also
involved in a broader search for traces of the ancient theatre to be found
on journeys through the ruins of the Hellenic world. At Eleusis, she and
her fellow travellers explored the "rock cut theatre in which the spectators
saw the mysteries."[39] In Epidauros, they saw the fourth-century theatre,
with its "circular orchestra with stone boundary line" showing the outlines
of what had once been a dancing place, altar, and site of ritual sacrifice
(Harrison, *Mythology* 293). At the American excavations in Dionyso, she
visited the "centre of worship of the ancient deme of Ikaria," traditionally
identified with the beginnings of Attic comedy and tragedy: "To this
place first in Attica the god Dionysos came, and he certainly could have
chosen no fairer spot; fine woods and tangled ivy are still ready for his
service" (Harrison, "Archaeology" 130). Most important, Dörpfeld showed
her around the remains of the Theatre of Dionysus, where she could at
last "sit with Dionysos himself beneath the 'hill-top'" and imagine she
was watching the birth of Greek tragedy. There, he led her imaginatively
through a production of the *Agamemnon*, "free from the sorry trammels
of a high and narrow Roman stage":

> Enter the watchman on the top of the temporary palace of Agamemnon; ... he
> sees the beacon fire and cries aloud, and forthwith in stream the chorus by the two
> broad paradoi, singing the fate of Troy; and when the long tremendous chant is
> ceasing, they catch sight of Clytemnestra ... and they bid her hail ... [S]ee
> [Agamemnon] come with his train sweeping up the parodos, thronging the
> orchestra, the chorus chanting its anapaests, swaying to either side to make room
> for the great procession.[40]

At the Theatre of Dionysus, she saw not only the remains of the circular
orchestra (once perhaps surrounded by stones like that at Epidauros and
Oropus) but also a large stone altar decorated with masks (now abandoned
behind the stage but perhaps once at the centre of the orchestra). The trip
(she had written to MacColl a few months earlier) would be an expression
of their "conjoint worship of Dionysos" ("one of my 19th century disrepu-
table, heathen ways").[41] Now, transposing the "ring of Maenads" and the
"blood of the slain goat" and the totemic pillar-god covered in "ivy
boughs and fruits" into the ruins, she could imagine herself in the midst
of the "Dionysiac dance," with "folk danc[ing] about the altar, [all] worshippers, [none] actors, none spectators." In Greece and Turkey, everywhere she looked – theatres, excavations, "rubbish heap[s]" – Harrison
began to see evidence of the ritual practices that the Theatre of Dionysus
illustrated and that lay at its origins (*Mythology* 285–86, 290).

Mythology and Monuments, with Harrison's 156-page introductory essay
and 607-page commentary, was completed not long after her return from

Greece and Turkey and published in 1890.[42] It brought her instant international recognition, generating invitations to join the Berlin Archaeological Society and honorary doctorates from Aberdeen and Durham universities (Stewart 12). Here, one can find sketchily outlined what were to develop into more fully elaborated arguments about the origins of myth, religion, art, and theatre in ritual. "I have tried everywhere to get at ... the cult as the explanation of the legend," she writes in the preface:

> My belief is that ... in the large majority of cases *ritual practice misunderstood* explains the elaboration of myth ... Some of the loveliest stories the Greeks have left us will be seen to have taken their rise, not in poetic imagination, but in primitive, often savage, and, I think, always *practical* ritual. (*Mythology* iii; emphasis in original)

Harrison had begun her career bitingly dismissive of budding connections between classics and anthropology. When a new Cambridge collection of plaster casts of ancient sculpture was, by an "accident of space," forced to share a gallery with some of the Cambridge ethnographic collections in 1884, Harrison commented acidly on "the 'squalid savage' with whom Hellas is thus perforce unmetely mated," expressing the hope "that no unfortunate undergraduate will think himself bound to begin his studies in Greek art with a course of Fiji islanders" ("Hellas" 511; qtd. in Beard, *Invention* 121, 206n40). But, travelling in "inconceivably primitive and savage" Arcadia, reading the work of folklorists and historians of religion such as Wilhelm Mannhardt, Andrew Lang, and W. Robertson Smith, listening to MacColl's lectures on "Songs and Ballads,"[43] breathing the air of a changing zeitgeist, she too began to change. In *Introductory Studies in Greek Art* (1885), she had sneered at the overly "ritual[ist]" Assyrians, with their addiction "to obscure rites of divination and incantation, to elaborate and significant gesture and posture, to the letter with little of the life, to mechanical formularies rather than vital expression" (63–64). By 1887, on the brink of her trip to Greece, she had begun to show a tentative interest in ritual, sending MacColl images of the Hieron vase "with dance in honour of Dionysos Dendrites" and the Gallipoli relief, "with dance of Hermes and Charites in a cave to Pan," writing dryly: "I have lots of these sort of *ritual* dances on pots, but I do not know if they are quite in your line."[44] A few years later, in *Mythology and Monuments*, she could claim, with full appreciation, that "[t]he myth-making Greek [w]as a practical savage rather than a poet or philosopher." She began writing the pioneering Cambridge anthropologist Alfred Cort Haddon for tips on primitive worship, taboo, and sacrifice, acknowledging that, while she knew she ought to stick to "Greek facts," "occasionally I succumb to temptation."[45] "[P]rimitive, often savage ... ritual[s]" began to take a place in the centre of her historical vision (Preface, *Mythology* iii).

Looking back, Harrison cast this period as one of revolutionary enlightenment: in her own thinking and in the nature of classics as an enterprise. "We Hellenists were, in truth, at that time a 'people who sat in darkness,'" she wrote (quoting scripture with a touch of irony), "but we were soon to see a great light, two great lights – archaeology, anthropology. Classics were turning in their long sleep. Old men began to see visions, young men to dream dreams" (*Reminiscences* 82–83). There are grounds for some scepticism about this retrospectively triumphalist account of intellectual awakening.[46] But there was unquestionably a change in her thinking, a change reflected in critical appraisals of her work. As one (prototypically racist) review of *Mythology and Monuments* put it,

> The school which holds that a study of the mental condition of savages is the best foundation of a scientific mythology, and that the legends of the Greeks resolve ultimately into traditions from ancestors on a level with Eskimo and Bushmen, can boast of an accomplished adherent in Miss Harrison. (Review 167; qtd. in Robinson 143)

"In matters of ritual," Harrison later wrote, caricaturing her critics' attacks, "I prefer savage disorders, Dionysiac orgies, the tearing of wild bulls, to the ordered and stately ceremonial of Panathenaic processions" ("Pillar" 65; qtd. in Robinson 196). In short, as the *Mythology and Monuments* reviewer put it, she had given up "the spirit of Hellenism" for "the vile conceptions that habitually circle round a wigwam" (Review 167; qtd. in Robinson 143).

Harrison could, throughout her career, flippantly dissociate herself from her own armchair romance with anthropology, mocking fashionable primitivism in a self-parody of European provincialism. "[S]ave for their reverent, totemistic attitude towards animals," she wrote in the introduction to *Themis*, "savages ... weary and disgust me, though perforce I spend long hours in reading of their tedious doings" (xxv).[47] Longing for the "inconceivably primitive and savage" in her travels, she frankly preferred her savages from a distance. When several Buganda chiefs ("enormous, very black men, in flowing white garments") were invited to dine with Harrison and her friends in 1902, precisely in order that they might "expatiate on their one-time heathenish practices, human sacrifice included," Harrison was (reported her host's daughter) "instinctively repelled," while at the same time disappointed that they preferred to discuss the Church Missionary Society.[48] But when she situated her savages in relation to the archaic, pre-Hellenic past, this particular combination of sentimentality and revulsion was lifted, and she could see "savage peoples" – their art, their culture, those "tedious doings" – as, in the end, key to "track[ing] the secret motive springs" of human life (*Ancient* 23–24).

As her thought developed (in the books that followed *Mythology and Monuments*), Harrison came to feel that in just such "doings," formalized as ritual, lay the origins of art and, indeed, of human culture. This view had important consequences for her historiographic methodology, already inflected by the archaeological preference for the artefact over the text. "The habit of viewing Greek religion exclusively through the medium of Greek literature has brought with it an initial and fundamental error in method," she explained in the *Prolegomena to the Study of Greek Religion* (1903). "For literature Homer is the beginning, though every scholar is aware that he is nowise primitive." But "Homer presents ... an almost mechanical accomplishment, with scarcely a hint of *origines* ... sceptical and moribund already in its very perfection." What she sought, instead, was the "substratum of religious conceptions, at once more primitive and more permanent." Archaeology was historiographically necessary but not sufficient to this task. For the primitive substratum was not to be found in literary remains and was not merely to be found in archaeological remains. It was also to be found in ritual. "What a people *does* ... must always be one clue, and perhaps the safest, to what it *thinks*." Ritual could, in fact, be treated as a kind of text, for the "facts of ritual" were "more easy definitely to ascertain, more permanent, and at least [as] significant" as the facts of mythology (Introduction, *Prolegomena* vii; emphasis in original). Archaeological evidence was one means of ascertaining the facts of ritual. The other was close observation of the rituals of contemporary primitive peoples.

RITUAL AND THE ORIGINS OF THEATRE

Giving ritual its "due share of attention" became one of Harrison's central tasks in the *Prolegomena* and the books that followed, in which she came to offer both an analysis of the specific rituals out of which Greek religion, art, and drama had emerged and a theory of the origins of ritual itself. "When a tribe comes back from war or from hunting, or even from a journey," she explained in *Themis* (1912), "the men will, if successful, recount and dance their experiences" (43). But "the action tends to cut itself loose from the particular in which it arose and become generalized, abstracted as it were ... Such a dance generalized, universalized, is material for the next stage, the dance *pre*-done," in which the tribe begins to pre-enact the desired events (44). "A tribe about to go to war will dance a war dance, men about to start out hunting will catch their game in pantomime" (44–45). "Primitive man ... does in pantomime what he wishes done. He wants to multiply his totem, so he imitates the actions of this totem – he jumps like a kangaroo, he screeches like a bat, he croaks like a frog, he imitates the birth of a Witchetty grub" (*Epilegomena* 12). The human-emu "dresses and dances as an emu, that he may increase and invigorate the supply of bird-emus," magically "secur[ing] the multiplication of the totem" (*Themis* 273).

Springing thus from "unsatisfied desire," these dances are (like dreams for Freud) forms of wish fulfilment, "[m]imetic, not of what you see done by another, but of what you desire to do yourself" (*Themis* 45). They are precipitated by pent-up emotion: "The thought of the hunt, the desire to catch the game or kill the enemy cannot find expression yet in the actual act; it grows and accumulates by inhibition till at last the exasperated nerves and muscles can bear it no longer and it breaks out into mimetic, anticipatory action" (45). And they serve as emotional purgatives: ways of dealing with "the thunderstorm and the monsoon," "things of tension and terror": "Tension finds relief in excited movement; you dance and leap for fear, for joy, for sheer psychological relief" (42). Dancing together in a collectivity that allows emotion to "mount to passion, to ecstasy" (43), the individual dancers begin to "sink their own personalit[ies] and by the wearing of masks and disguises, by dancing to a common rhythm, above all by the common excitement, they become emotionally one, a true congregation, not a collection of individuals" (45–46).

Ritual was, then, in its origin, a kind of proto-drama, taking the form of mimetic dances and containing an "element of make-believe." This element did not, however, involve an "attempt to deceive, but a desire to *re*-live, to *re*-present" (*Themis* 43). Rather than being a mere imitative copying of life, it was a conjunction of acting, making, and doing that was essentially performative: a magic invocation of the object of desire, a creation of the event through its pre-enactment, and a collective discharge of pent-up emotion. It was *metheksis* more than *mimesis*, participation or *doing* more than imitation (126). Nonetheless, Harrison writes, "It is a fact of cardinal importance" that the Greeks' word for theatrical representation, *drama*, "is own cousin to their word for rite, *dromenon*; *drama* also means 'thing done' ... [I]n these two Greek words, *dromenon* and *drama*, [in] their relation and their distinction," she explains, "we have the keynote and clue to our whole discussion" (*Ancient* 35–36). "The beginnings of drama and of primitive magical rites are ... intertwined at the very roots" (*Themis* 31).

It was important (she had written in *Prolegomena*) "to understand primitive rites," not merely "from love of their archaism," but because from "[a] knowledge of ... the *milieu* of this primitive material [it] is one step" to the understanding of "its final form in tragedy" (Introduction viii). Ritual was a kind of proto-drama, but, as importantly, the Greek drama proper arose from specific rituals and bore their imprint. As she explained in *Ancient Art and Ritual*, even Aristotle (who "was not specially interested in primitive ritual" and to whom "beast dances and spring mummeries" must have seemed "mere savagery") acknowledged that Greek drama "had in some way risen out of ritual" (75): comedy from Dionysian vegetation rituals and tragedy from the improvisations of the leaders of the Dithyramb, the spring bull-driving ritual celebrating the birth of Dionysus. Traces of the spring ritual remaining in the formal structures of the Greek drama, linking "the Spring and the Bull and the Birth Rite" to "the stately tragedies we know" (118), prove the ritual origins that Aristotle merely suspected. For instance, the "Bull-driving Dithyrambs" sung at the great festival where tragedies were performed were clearly a survival of the bull-driving ritual from which tragedy sprung (100–101). The dramatic chorus was, in fact, a group of men and boys, originally "tillers of the earth, who danced when they rested from sowing and ploughing" (124). And the dance that turned into the Dithyramb and eventually drama was "circular because it is round some sacred thing, at first a maypole, or the reaped corn, later the figure of a god or his altar" (126). That the Greek theatre began with "no permanent stage in our sense, shows very clearly how little it was regarded as a spectacle," how much it was "a *dromenon*, a thing to be done, not a thing to be looked at" (142).

The specific myths enacted in the festival of the Dithyramb – the ritual that had eventually been transformed into tragedy – could offer a key to the ritual significance of the Greek drama (and perhaps of drama more generally). Like the Dionysian mysteries, the festival of the Dithyramb was originally about the birth (or, rather, rebirth) of Dionysus: "Dithyrambos" became a nickname for the twice-born baby Dionysus, and "the Dithyramb was originally the *Song of the Birth*" (Harrison, *Themis* 32). In this version of the myth, Zeus called on the Kouretes – a group of youths – to guard his son, the baby Dionysus from the Titans, instigated to infanticide by jealous Hera. (In another incarnation, Dionysus was called Zagreus, and sometimes referred to as the *kouros*, or babe). The Kouretes (whose name derived either from their own youth or from their task as guardian of the *kouros*) danced and sang wildly, beating with their swords on their shields, to prevent the baby from being discovered and stolen. Nonetheless, the Titans lured the baby Dionysus away with toys and then tore him to pieces (or, in another version, Kronos swallowed him). However, he was resurrected, in some versions because his mother saved his heart and gave it to Zeus, who implanted the heart in his own thigh (or groin), from which Dionysus was reborn (*Themis* 14–15).

This story is closely associated with the myth of the birth of Zeus himself. Indeed, the baby is (interchangeably) "the infant Zeus, Dionysos, Zagreus or the Kouros" (as in the "Hymn of the Kouretes," which had recently been discovered on the eastern coast of Crete [*Themis* 15]), associating the story of the birth of Zeus, through that of Dionysus, with tragedy and the drama more generally. To prevent Kronos from eating his newborn son Zeus, Zeus's mother Rhea enlisted the help of the Kouretes. Harrison quotes Strabo's version:

> They surround the goddess and with drums and with the din of other instruments try to strike terror into Kronos and to escape notice whilst trying to filch away the child. The child is then given over to them to be reared with the same care by which it was rescued. (*Themis* 13–14)

This narrative is enacted in the mysteries of Demeter and Dionysus, which were performed "with orgiastic rites" and with attendants called "Kouretes" (youths who "perform armed movements accompanied by dancing" and are "similar to the Satyrs that attend Dionysos") (*Themis* 13).

Other scholars had seen in seasonal renewal, linked to the food supply, the key to understanding ancient myths and rituals of death and resurrection (the Christian not least). For Harrison, these were personified in a figure, the *Eniautos-daimon* [year daimon], often a baby or young man (the vegetation spirit or corn baby), who was torn apart in winter and returned in spring. However, the real key to understanding the myriad peculiar details of death and resurrection myths and their attendant rituals lay in "the analogy of *primitive rites of tribal initiation*" (*Themis* 16; emphasis in original). To understand the savage Dionysus–Zagreus or Zeus, one needed to look not primarily to Greek harvest cycles but to contemporary initiation rites or *Rites de Passage* (in Arnold Van Gennep's influential formulation) that accompanied successive stages of life: those of the Wiradthuri tribe of New South Wales (*Themis* 18), or the "Narrinyeri" (36), or the "Binbinga of North Australia" (*Ancient* 110), or the East African "Akikuyu," whose photograph is reproduced in *Themis* as evidence of "what a Koures in ancient days must have looked like" (Figure 3) (24–25).

The purpose of the initiation ritual was to transfer the male child from the female world of the mother to the male world of the father. In *Bora* initiation rituals in New Zealand, for instance, "the surrender of the boys by their mother is dramatically represented. A circle is marked out, the mothers of those to be initiated stand just outside it, the boys are bidden to enter the circle, and thus magically pass from the women to the men of the tribe" (*Themis* 38). The child is, in this sense, "re-born" from the male as a means of ridding him of the "infection" of the mother, turning him from a "woman-thing" into a "man-thing":

> Woman to primitive man is a thing at once weak and magical, to be oppressed, yet feared. She is charged with powers of child-bearing denied to man, powers only

Figure 3: East African "Akikuyu" initiation: "what a Koures in ancient days must have looked like" (*Themis* 25, fig. 4; reproduced from Routledge and Routledge 156g [Plate 108])

half understood, forces of attraction, but also of danger and repulsion, forces that all over the world seem to fill him with dim terror. (36)

The central trope of this transfer is the death of the male child and his rebirth as a man, dramatized in a ritual "pantomime" whose particularities may vary but whose basic structure is universal. "[I]n Africa, in America, in Australia, in the South Pacific Islands," writes Harrison,

we come upon what is practically the same sequence of ceremonies. When a boy is initiated, that is when he passes from childhood to adolescence, this panto-mime, this terrifying [*ekplêxis*], this pretended killing of the child, this painting him with clay and bringing him back to life again as a young man, is everywhere enacted. (18–19)

Both the Zeus and Dionysus narratives enact this passage: "In the case of the Kouros the child is taken from its mother, in the case of the Dithyramb it is actually re-born from the thigh of its father" (36).

If the initiation ritual explains the myths that founded the drama, at the same time (in a dizzying *mise-en-abîme*), it figures, in its central narrative event, the transformation of this primal drama into the make-believe that is art. For the second birth from the father in the Dionysus story – and in initiation rituals generally – is, importantly, not real, but a "sham" or "mimetic" birth: "all rites *quâ* rites are mimetic, but the rite of the New Birth is in its essence *the* mimetic rite *par excellence*" (*Themis* 35; emphasis in original). In this sense, Dionysus's first birth figures the birth of ritual in the *dromenon*, and his second birth figures ritual's transformation into dramatic mimesis. If initiation (figured in Dionysus's second birth) involves the imitation of female reproductive power (through the production of the sham birth), it also involves (implicitly) imitation of the male world to which the young male initiate must pretend he belongs (the production of the social self in the world of men). In this sense, in figuring the birth of mimesis, the sham birth at the same time figures departure from the pre-mimetic female world and the entry into the post-mimetic male world, the already fallen social world of representation, the world of secondariness.

Insofar as initiation rites (and the myths and second-order rituals that reference them) enact the passing of the young man from the mother to the father and from the pre-mimetic female world to the post-mimetic male world, they also re-enact metonymically the traumatic pre-historic transition from matriarchy to patriarchy (from "mother-rites" to "father-rites"). For Harrison (writing in the last years of the century under the influence of Johann Jakob Bachofen's *Mutterrecht*), "the earth-goddess, call her Gaia or Demeter or Kore or Pandora as you will," had, in "matriarchal days," been the governing deity. "With the first dawn of anthropomorphism appears the notion that the earth is the mother, and the earth genii tend to be conceived of as her daughters" ("Delphika" 232–33, 205; see, also, Harrison, "Notes"). Goddess worship was essentially a fertility cult in which ecstatic ritual practices – "mother rites" – helped to preserve the collectivity against the threat of individualism. "[W]hen, chiefly through the accumulation of property, matriarchy passes and patriarchy takes its place ... the child is viewed as part of the property of the father ... [and] initiation ceremonies lose their pristine significance." However, "the memory of primitive matriarchal conditions often survive[d] ... in mythology," for instance in "the divine figures of Mother and Babe or Kouros, rather than in that of Father and Son" (*Themis* 41–42). The traumatic transition from matriarchy to patriarchy was memorialized in the "many stories of mothers who hide their child directly after birth" so that the child, "concealed or acknowledged, might remain with its mother for a time" and she might "practise on it her mother-rites" (37): perhaps real stories of resistance to the infanticide regularly practised in ancient times, but also tropes for women's resistance to the transfer of the male child.

Like the myths that underlay it, Greek drama continued to memorialize the overthrow of the matriarchy, hazily recalling its own half-forgotten past. Euripides' Bacchae, for instance (argues Harrison) are residual figures of goddess and fertility worship: "The Bacchants are the Mothers; that is why at their coming they have magical power to make the whole earth blossom ... At the touch of their wands, from the rocks break out streams of wine and water, and milk and honey" (*Themis* 40). Aeschylus's *Eumenides* acts out the death of matriarchy, she argues (following Bachofen): in Athena's tie-breaking vote against the Furies and in favour of Orestes (on the outrageous grounds that "no mother b[o]re" Athena and therefore she "approve[s] / In all ... [t]he man's way"); in the resulting normalization of Orestes' matricide; and in the domestication of the Furies, transformed by Athena into gentle Eumenides with dominion restricted to home and hearth.[49] "Matriarchy died out; Athena was 'all for the father'; hence the scandal caused by the Bacchants" (*Themis* 208). But the drama reminds us of the secret survival of matriarchal practice, for instance in the mysteries represented in the *Bacchae*: "Half mad with excitement [the Bacchants] shout aloud the dogmas of their most holy religion – the religion of the Mother and the Child" (39).

Indeed, the drama itself represented a survival of matriarchal religion, however attenuated. For the festival of the Dithyramb was not merely a generic spring festival but was, at its origins, an annual initiation ritual: "behind the Dithyramb lay a rite, a [*dromenon*], and that rite was one of group initiation," and the group "belonged to the social structure known as matriarchal" (*Themis* 41–42). This ritual was at the centre of a living religion:

> [T]he religion of the Kouros and the Kouretes, and of Dionysos and his *thiasos* [worshippers] are substantially the same. Both are the reflection of a group religion and of social conditions which are matriarchal and emphasize the figures of Mother and Child. The cardinal doctrine of both religions is the doctrine of the New Birth, and this doctrine is the reflection of the rite of social initiation. (*Themis* 49)

The wild dances and songs of the Kouretes in the public festival of the Dithyramb were extensions of the ecstatic religions, public versions of the Dionysian and Orphic mysteries, which themselves were residual forms of earlier ecstatic goddess cults.

Thus, we have in Harrison a set of layered accounts of the origins of drama. Functionally, the origins of a kind of primal drama (drama inseparable from the ritual performative: the *dromenon* [rite], or doing, or *metheksis* [participation]) lay in ritual re-enactment and pre-enactment generally. Structurally, one can find the origins of the drama proper in the initiation ritual – with its traumatic repetition of the crushing of the matriarchy (narrated in the dithyramb, replayed in the spring festival) – and from the ecstatic religions that nonetheless residually preserved the "mother-rites." We also, however, have a more evolutionary account of the process of individuation that transforms the ritual *dromenon*, via religion, into the drama. At some point in the evolution of a culture, "[t]he whole group ceases to carry on the magical rite, which becomes the province of a class of medicine-men." In Greece, "the specialized Kouretes ... supplant[ed] the whole body of Kouroi" until "[f]inally the power [was] lodged in an individual, a head medicine-man, a king whose functions [were] at first rather magical than political" (*Themis* 127). The "leader of the band of *kouroi*, of young men, the real actual leader," eventually became "by remembrance and abstraction ... a daimon, or spirit, at the head of a band of spirits" (*Ancient* 115). On the one hand, the leader became a god. On the other, he became the choral leader who would evolve into the dramatic hero.

In Greece, this evolution was the result of specific socio-historical transformations: the "migrations [and] the shifting of populations," travel, and the new cosmopolitanism that grew from these, which began to destroy local cultures.

> Local ties that bind to particular spots of earth are cut, local differences fall into abeyance, a sort of cosmopolitanism, a forecast of pan-Hellenism, begins to arise. [Now] [w]e hear scarcely anything of local cults, nothing at all of local magical maypoles and Carryings-out of Winter and Bringings-in of Summer. (*Ancient* 161, 160)

Perhaps it was no accident that Dionysus (in his late civilized guise) was a cosmopolitan traveller, coming from the east, "[w]inding, winding to the west," accompanied by "a train of barbarian women [who] chant their oriental origin," bringing with him the drama (*Prolegomena* 372).[50] As the old tribal group began to disaggregate, "the mass of the people, the tribe, or the group [became] but a shadowy background" (*Ancient* 159). Society was "cut loose from its roots" (161), and what arose in its place was a cult of heroic individualism more hospitable to the Homeric stories than to local myths and the collective ritual practices associated with them. The "ancient Spring *dromenon* [had become] perhaps well-nigh effete" when, in the middle of the sixth century, "the life-stories of heroes" were added to "the old plot of Summer and Winter." (146). As the heroic, god-like individual became the focus of contemplation (rather than the leader of collective action), he started to be separated from the chorus and transformed into a dramatic hero. Little by little,

> out of the chorus of dancers some dancers withdrew and became spectators sitting apart, and on the other hand others of the dancers drew apart on to the stage and presented to the spectators a spectacle, a thing to be looked *at*, not joined *in*. (193; emphasis in original)

"[A]nd thereby arose the drama" (146).

In her explicit account of the disappearance of ritual into theatre proper, Harrison pays lip service to the "amazing development of the fifth-century drama" (*Ancient* 164). But, at the same time, the birth of drama (and of art more generally) represents a tragic falling off from the intensity, the desire, the power, the engagement, the collectivity, the magic of ritual enactment. In a sense, when ritual drama becomes drama proper, it begins to lose its essential identity. In the separation of spectator from object, a "community of emotion ceases," the spectator is "cut loose from immediate action," and an "attitude ... of contemplation" takes over (*Themis* 46; *Ancient* 193; *Themis* 46). With detached contemplation (inherent in the nature of art) comes a loss of the sacredness of the ritual *dromenon*:[51]

> If drama be at the outset divine, with its roots in ritual, why does it issue in an art ... purely human? The actors wear ritual vestments like those of the celebrants at the Eleusinian mysteries. Why, then, do we find them, not executing a religious service or even a drama of gods and goddesses, but rather impersonating mere Homeric heroes and heroines? (*Ancient* 13–14)

This secularizing tendency transforms embodiment into mere impersonation, creation into "mere copying":

> It is easy to see that as the belief in magic declines, what was once intense desire, issuing in the making of or the being of a thing, becomes mere copying of it; the mime, the maker, sinks to be in our modern sense the mimic; as faith declines, folly and futility set in; the earnest, zealous *act* sinks into a frivolous mimicry, a sort of child's-play. (48; emphasis in original)

Ultimately, writes Harrison, "Greek drama ... betrays us" (14).

In a wistful essay entitled "Crabbed Age and Youth," written (she explains) in the wake of work on "[s]avage initiation ceremonies" and "the rise of Greek drama" ("Crabbed" 4), Harrison draws a distinction between "acting" and "masquerading":

> Acting is sinking your own personality in order that you may mimic another's. Masquerading is borrowing another's personality, putting on the mask of another's features, dress, experiences, emotions, and thereby enhancing your own. (9)

Harrison's ambivalences in this essay complicate a straightforward reading, but her language here tracks her description in *Themis* of the primitive dancers who "sink their own personalit[ies]" in order to become "emotionally one, a true congregation" (44) and suggests a parallel: acting (doing) decays into masquerading, just as ritual decays into drama.

In a telling passage, she draws an analogy between the marginalization one experiences in old age and the transition from ritual into Greek drama. Greek drama "arose out of the chorus, which then differentiated into chorus and spectators, and ultimately into actors and spectators. This is what happens ... in life" ("Crabbed" 12–13):

> [The] chorus of ... Youth differentiates into actors, each specialized, in all humility, to a part. But last there is a third stage. Some withdraw from the stage into the *theatre-place* and become spectators ... [D]ischarged from life, they behold it. It is the time of the great Apocalypse. ("Crabbed" 13–16; emphasis in original)

Harrison may describe ritual's pre-mimetic *dromenon* as a kind of proto-drama. But she nonetheless casts drama as the enemy of ritual, standing in opposition to it both ontologically and historically. Ritual – archaic, collective, anti-aesthetic, tending to the ecstatic, identified with matriarchy and thus in some sense prior to the shamming of patriarchy – is ultimately killed off by the drama. It is instructive, here, to look at the layered tropes of death and birth in Harrison's discussion of the origins of drama, for they reverberate in her discussion of the death of ritual and its rebirth as institutional drama. The death and dismemberment of the baby Dithyrambos, leading to his rebirth as Dionysus, is explicitly a figure for the "death" of the boy and his "rebirth" as a man in the initiation ceremony. And the initiation ceremony is a figure for the broader historical death of matriarchy and the birth of patriarchy. As we have seen, both of these instances of death and rebirth (or, rather, sham birth) figure the birth of mimesis generally, and thus we can see them as also figuring, for Harrison, the death of the ritual *dromenon* and the birth of the institutional drama. Just as the initiation ritual re-enacts, over and over, the central trauma of human history – the suppression of matriarchy and the rise of patriarchy – so we re-enact, over and over, the sad substitution of "mere copying," "folly and futility," "frivolous mimicry," "a sort of child's-play" – that is, theatre – for the primal *dromenon* that was ritual and remains the true essence of the drama.

RITUALISM, MODERNISM, AND THE THEATRE ANTI-THEATRICAL

Harrison's turn, in the late 1880s, from the "make-believe" of Greek theatricals and the aesthetic ideas that were their counterpart had become, two decades later, a full-blown distaste for the theatre, at once theoretical and deeply personal: "I am always aware that there is a passion in you quite left out in me – that dramatic one," she wrote to Gilbert Murray while he was working on a production of the *Medea* in London in 1907:

& it is very strong in you for it makes you bear so much incidental squalor. I also
believe that one reason why you can bear it is that you either are or have trained
yrself to be less easily irritated & upset by merely sensuous tawdriness – both in
sights & sounds – you live so much by the inward eye ... I know what I feel is –
here are these lovely words, altogether lovely which I read by myself in great &
pure joy & they are going to be presented in a medium both muddy & violent.
(Harrison, Letter to Gilbert Murray, n.d.; qtd. in Robinson 202)

The theatre, "both muddy & violent," with its "sensuous tawdriness" and its
"incidental squalor," could cause Harrison intense revulsion: she reportedly once became violently ill on seeing a torture scene and had to be
taken from the theatre (Mirrlees, Notebook). But it also seemed in sad contrast to the Dionysian glory from which it had arisen. During preparations
for a Cambridge production of Comus for the Milton Tercentenary in 1908,
she wrote Murray again: "I am weighted down by Comus ... I wrestle with
my loathing of things theatrical & I see the Beast-Rout in a vision which will
never be accomplished – what beautiful preposterous stuff it is" (Harrison,
Letter to Gilbert Murray, n.d.; qtd. in Robinson 202).[52] The "vision" Milton
offers of the "Beast-Rout" – the "rout of Monsters, headed like sundry sorts
of wild Beasts" attendant on Comus (son of Bacchus-Dionysus and Circe)[53] –
seems to evoke, for Harrison, the ecstatic Dionysian rituals of the past. But
this vision "will never be accomplished," for it has been overtaken by the
theatrical – by Cambridge undergraduates, preposterously performing
Dionysian mysteries in fancy dress – that is, by a theatricality that filled
her by turns with mirth, by turns with loathing. As she acknowledged wist-
fully in another letter to Murray, "my savage heart is more at home in ritual,
that is the real difference between us (inter alia!) – that you have pushed
right thro into art. I am still in the ritual stage" (Harrison, Letter to
Gilbert Murray, n.d.; qtd. in Robinson 257).

As it turned out, however, Harrison was not alone in "the ritual stage."
For, like the secret practices of the undying matriarchy, ritual (the essential
drama) lived on in the interstices of culture, to be found still by the cosmopolitan traveller in search of its remains. Others' eye-witness accounts of
still-surviving ritual had long served Harrison as crucial evidence of the
ritual underpinnings of Greek mythology and art.[54] But she began,
herself, in her later years, to find ritual practices everywhere she travelled,
claiming (with a certain degree of melodramatic revisionism) that it was
"ritual dances ... ritual drama" that "I was all my life blindly seeking"
(Reminiscences 86). A "ritual dance, a ritual procession with vestments
and lights and banners," she wrote, "move me as no sermon, no hymn,
no picture, no poem has ever moved me" (84). At the cathedral in
Chartres, she participated in the festival of Notre Dame du Pilier [Our
Lady of the Pillar], a survival of Cretan or Olympian pillar (or tree) cults:

a matriarchal festival during which a throng of young girls dressed in blue, with long white veils and carrying lit tapers, went in procession to worship the "Vierge du Pilier," the Maiden of the Pillar ("It was the old pagan thing back again, the maidens worshipping the Maid – *their* Maid. My matriarchal soul was glad in me," she commented) (Harrison, "Pillar" 68; see, also, Robinson 196–97; emphasis in original). When she travelled to Seville during Carnival, she saw the dance of the Seises before the cathedral's high altar, accompanied by a prayer to the setting sun for light and healing. Its origin was (as the Catholic Church admitted) *"perdue dans la nuit des temps* [lost in the darkness of time]", but Harrison saw in it the remains of "the dances of the Kouretes of Crete to Mother and Son":

> I felt instantly that it was frankly Pagan ... It is decorous, even prim, like some stiff stylised shadow. But it is strangely moving in the fading light with the wondrous setting of the high altar and the golden grille, and above all the sound of the harsh, plangent Spanish voices. Great Pan, indeed, is dead – his ghost still dances. (*Reminiscences* 84–85)

In the celebration of the Orthodox Mass, she found traces of the pre-history of theatre: the "real enacting of a mystery – the mystery of the death and resurrection of the Year-Spirit which preceded drama" (86). In the still surviving mummers and sword-dancers one could find traces of the Kouretes (*Epilegomena* 17). The folk-play or fertility drama lived on in children's games and peasant festivals (24). The cult of Dionysus survived in the modern carnival in Thrace (22). "The ritual dance is all but dead, but the ritual drama, the death and the resurrection of the Year-Spirit, still goes on" (*Reminiscences* 86).

If migration and cosmopolitan travel (figured in Dionysus's journey from east to west) were responsible for the transformation of ritual into drama, migration and cosmopolitan travel could, in a sense, reverse that transformation by bringing still-surviving primitive ritual (studied by anthropologists and travellers to the colonial hinterlands) back to modern art, thereby returning it to its origins and, indeed, its true self. In the theatre, this could, for instance, be seen in what Harrison (with comic glibness) lists as "Reinhardt productions, Gordon Craig scenery, Russian ballets ... Impressionists, Post-Impressionists, Futurists" (*Ancient* 208), "'Miracles,' and Russian Ballets, and 'Oedipus Rexes'" ("Crabbed" 10). It could be seen in the kind of "ritual play" that MacColl composed and sent to Harrison soon after she'd published the *Epilegomena*.[55] Above all, it could be seen in the "revival of the ritual dance" (*Ancient* 207). Harrison had made her own small contribution to this revival by reciting the Greek at Isadora Duncan's performances of the "Hymn to Demeter" and the *Idylls of Theocritus* at the turn of the century (see "Miss Duncan's").[56] A decade or so later, such work had blossomed into the "strenuous, exciting, self-expressive dances of to-day," some "of the soil and some exotic," dances based on and constituting a true resurrection of "very primitive ritual." With this resurrection, possible because "[t]o-day ... life grows daily fuller and freer, and every manifestation of life is regarded with a new reverence" (*Ancient* 206–07), one could renounce the passive spectatorship that was art and return to emotion lived with a primitive immediacy:

> [T]he life of the imagination, and even of the emotions, has been perhaps too long lived at second hand, received from the artist ready made and felt ... With this fresh outpouring of the spirit, this fuller consciousness of life, there comes a need for *first-hand* emotion and expression, and that expression is found for all classes in a revival of the ritual dance. (*Ancient* 206–07; emphasis in original)

"Art in these latter days," she writes, "goes back as it were on her own steps, recrossing the ritual bridge back to life" (*Ancient* 207).

In this passage, one can find the romantic ideology of "spirit," immediacy, freedom, and expressive emotion transformed into a compendium of modernist performance aesthetics, or, rather, anti-aesthetics (that peculiar grafting of romanticism onto an avant-garde suspicion of "art" to be found in so much of modernism). Art (theatre) was a mistake, Harrison implies, producing a life of second-hand imagination and second-hand emotion. But, through a return to its exotic origins in the soil and in primitive ritual – a return made possible by rupturing the civilized boundaries of Europe (geographical and historical) – art could turn itself back into the kind of ritual performance that it was always meant to be.

As important, one can find at work in this passage a dynamic that turned out to be crucial to modernist performance: the dynamic between anti-theatricality and ritual. Here, "loathing of things theatrical" becomes a foundation for theatre's wished-for antithesis: the kind of performance that reaches back to theatre's origins, captures its essence, but somehow emerges free of theatre's theatricality.[57] The *raison d'être* of ritual performance, from this point of view, is to undo theatre in an attempt both to return to a time before theatre and to move beyond theatre to the artwork of the future. Here, ritual performance becomes an antidote to or cure for theatre. But, at the same time, theatre is the essential vehicle for the return to primal performance. In this sense, ritual theatre works something like the *pharmakon*: in Harrison's rendering (in the *Prolegomena*) a "healing drug, poison, and dye," a form of "savage 'medicine'" (108), in which theatre becomes a necessary means of expelling or purging theatre from ritual. That is, theatre becomes necessary to its self-catharsis.[58]

Despite her "loathing of things theatrical," Harrison continued on occasion to dabble in theatre, notably in 1904, in what one might think of as a quasi-ritualist production (somewhere between the Victorian theatrical and the more radical experiments of theatrical modernism): Harley Granville Barker and Gilbert Murray's *Hippolytus*. Harrison's *Prolegomena* had just been published, with a powerful passage quoting Euripides in conjunction with an Attic relief, ostensibly representing Aphrodite and Hippolytus, but actually illustrating "a superposition of cults," a much more primitive "contest ... between a local hero and Aphrodite" (354). There is no specific evidence that Granville Barker read the *Prolegomena* (though Murray read and commented on the proofs). But Harrison helped with preparations for the production, and Murray was in constant correspondence with both Granville Barker and Harrison, passing her ideas on to the production team.[59] As an expert on Euripides and on primitive goddesses, Harrison was commissioned to design the statues of Aphrodite and Artemis, which flanked the stage and were intended to offer a symbolic frame for the play.

In keeping with her vision of the production, Harrison insisted that the goddesses be archaic rather than classical and that their faces be made of masks based on the Athenian *korai* (female versions of the *kouros*): "Artemis shall have a bow & Aphrodite shall be divinely stiff with a dove & a flower & a smile. Oh such a smile!" (Figure 4) (Harrison, Letter to Gilbert Murray, n.d.; qtd. in Robinson 173).[60]

Mischievously, Harrison wrote an unsigned review for the *Cambridge Review*, echoing her *Prolegomena* and praising the goddesses, with their "strange archaic smile[s]":

> The play is the conflict of two passions – two goddesses ... – and these two passions, these goddesses stood incarnate, two lovely graven images on the stage. That is a thing not easily realised in the reading; they are there, they who tangled the whole human coil; they stand immutable, implacable.[61]

If the production was archaic (at least in part, thanks to Harrison's goddesses), it was, at the same time, "indisputably modern," as the *Times* reviewer reported ("New Century Theatre" 4): in its Ibsenism, in what Desmond MacCarthy referred to as its avoidance of the "archaeologically sentimental" (12; see, also, Kennedy 42–43), in its rejection of realism, and in a certain anti-aestheticism. "It would have been better for the pictorial effect," wrote one reviewer, "if the dresses could have been draped a little more artistically, and, perhaps, included a few brighter hues," and if the odes had not been recited in a "monotone, as though they were a series of Gregorian chants" ("Euripides' *Hippolytus*" 7). Better for the pictorial effect, perhaps. But worse for the production's underlying ritualism.

If Harrison was directly involved in Granville Barker and Murray's archaic–modernist *Hippolytus*, one might equally (if somewhat more

Figure 4: Drawings for the Aphrodite and Artemis statues for Harley Granville
Barker's and Gilbert Murray's *Hippolytus* (1904); reproduced from Robinson 174

tenuously) trace her presence in modern drama, theatre, and dance more
generally. Shaw's *Getting Married* and *Major Barbara* were deeply influenced by Murray's turn-of-the-century translations of the Greek plays,
which drew heavily on Harrison's *Prolegomena*.[62] Yeats certainly knew
her work when he was engaged in his own ritualist theatrical experiments.
(He may have lectured at her house in Cambridge in 1905, and they shared
a close connection to Florence Farr.)[63] Eliot read *Themis* as an undergraduate (along with the work of Murray and Cornford) and cited Harrison
repeatedly in his dramatic criticism, and her influence can be found
throughout *Sweeney Agonistes*, *The Family Reunion*, and *Murder in the
Cathedral*.[64] In constant correspondence with Murray, Harrison was (arguably) in the background of all of Granville Barker and Murray's numerous
collaborations, from the *Hippolytus* to the highly ceremonial productions
of *Iphigenia in Taurus* and *The Trojan Women* in the Yale Bowl and
Harvard Stadium in 1915. One can hear her behind Murray's comment

on Max Reinhardt's *Oedipus* at Covent Garden in 1912 (in a letter to the
Times, a few months before *Themis* was to appear): the Oedipus story, he
wrote,

> belongs to the dark regions of pre-Hellenic barbarism [. . . and] Professor
> Reinhardt was frankly pre-Hellenic, partly Cretan and Mycenaean, partly Oriental,
> partly – to my great admiration – merely savage. The half-naked torch-bearers
> with loin-cloths and long black hair made my heart leap with joy. ("Oedipus")[65]

And one can hear her meditations on the initiation rite as the origin of
the drama in what Granville Barker was to write years after his Greek
productions: "All arts are mysteries, the way into their services is by
initiation . . . and the adept hugs his secret" (17).

But I am less interested in Harrison as a specific influence or a site of
specific origin (ever-receding as origins always are) than as a template for
reading the nexus of preoccupations, desires, projections, and loathings
that gave rise to some of the central strains of theatrical modernism and
its off-shoots. Through the lens of her work, one can see with particular
clarity how the fundamental aesthetics of theatrical modernism were
articulated through the transformation of the Greek play from the perfected
world of ideal beauty, staged by the amateur Greek theatricals of the last
decades of the nineteenth century, to the archaic world of primitive mysteries, staged by avant-garde directors in the first decades of the new
century. If Harrison's work gives us a deepened understanding of the emergence of the conceptual and visual rhetoric of theatrical modernism
(infused with the broader primitivist zeitgeist) and of the trajectories of
turn-of-the-century archaeology and anthropology, it also captures two historical changes crucial to our own disciplinary objects and methodology:
the twentieth-century creation of an artefact- and performance-based historiography, which came to define theatre history in its life as a formal discipline in the twentieth century and continues to dominate it as a practice;
and the move from the transhistorical study of theatre to the cross-cultural
study of performance, which was crucial in the creation of performance
studies in the last decades of the twentieth century and continues to play
an important role in its ongoing emergence as a discipline. One might
trace the first through the beginnings of the formal institutionalization of
theatre in the university: in the work of such scholars as Brander
Matthews (named the first professor of dramatic literature in the United
States in 1900), whose "Dramatic Museum" – the collection of artefacts
and theatre models he housed at Columbia – was crucial to his teaching
of theatre history; or in the work of A.M. Nagler, whose collection of documents and images, *A Source Book in Theatrical History* (1959), is still used
in many theatre history classes. One might trace the second more broadly

through the joint work of anthropology and theatre history in the first decades of the century; the naturalization of ritualist ideas in theatre studies in the work of such critics as Francis Fergusson; the simultaneous rejection of origins theory and embrace of the cross-cultural study of performance in the work of Richard Schechner, Victor Turner, Erving Goffman, and others; and the formal institutionalization of "theatre anthropology," identified most notably with the work of Eugenio Barba.[66] Thus, in their shared origins, one might see theatre history and performance studies not as antithetical enterprises (as they are often seen today) but as enterprises with deeply linked conceptual roots.

Equally important, Harrison's work offers an exemplary case of the ritualist anti-theatricality that continues to shape avant-garde performance, even long past the explicitly ritualist productions of the middle decades of the twentieth century: the sense (imbibed, consciously or not, from an earlier avant garde) that, while institutional theatre may have emerged from ritual, it is deeply spiritually antithetical to it; the sense that ritual somehow transcends the frivolously ornamental make-believe of theatre but that, by recapturing the history of ritual at its heart, theatre can finally transcend itself. Looking, that is, at Harrison's rendering of the historical transformation of ritual into theatre and theatre back into ritual, traced through with her passions and loathings, we can better understand the relation of insistent antithesis and inexorable bondage between theatre and its ritual and performative others that continues to haunt us.

NOTES

1   I would like to give my grateful thanks to my indefatigable research assistant Michelle Knoetgen, to Annabel Robinson, who generously sent me not only her photocopies but her personal transcriptions of Harrison manuscript materials, and to Anne Thomson, whose assistance in the Newnham College Archives was invaluable. All letters cited can be found in the Jane Harrison Collection, Newnham College Archives, Cambridge, UK, unless otherwise noted. Letters are also cited to published sources where available.
2   For an extensive discussion, see Beard, "'Pausanias'"; for the title "Blue Jane," see Stewart 12.
3   For her 1881 trip to Naples, see Harrison, Letter to Elizabeth Malleson from the Hotel Britannique in Naples, 17 Dec. 1881. I am grateful to Clemente Marconi for supplying me with a wealth of information on the history of this vase (later referred to as the Pronomos vase, and still in the Naples Archaeological Museum).
4   It is worth noting that Harrison later rejected the view that the etymology of tragedy was *tragos*; see, e.g., Harrison, "Is Tragedy?"
5   The phrase comes from Robert Ackerman, who discusses the close collaboration and shared ideas of the "group": Harrison (at the centre), Francis Cornford,

Gilbert Murray, and Arthur Bernard Cook (with James G. Frazer at the margins); see also Calder. For a dissenting view, see Beard, *Invention* 109–14 (there was no formal "group" and ritualist ideas were already part of the classical curriculum); and see my discussion in note 28 below.

6 For further biographical details, see Robinson; Beard, *Invention*; Peacock. The evidence about Harrison's sexuality is hard to disentangle. She fell unambiguously in love with men (some of them decades younger) throughout most of her life. She also seems to have had (at least) crushes on a series of women, and there are hints of potentially scandalous, unidentified romances in the 1870s and 1880s. From about age 60 to the end of her life, she became the companion of Hope Mirrlees, 37 years her junior, with whom she lived and shared pet names. She referred publicly to Mirrlees as her "ghostly daughter, dearer than any child after the flesh" (*Reminiscences* 90). But in letters, Mirrlees was the "younger wife" and she the "older wife" of their stuffed bear (Harrison, Letters to Mirrlees undated; 2 Apr. 1912; 4 Aug. 1914; 25 Dec. 1914; 26 Mar. 1918; see Peacock 111– 15). According to Virginia Woolf, they had a "Sapphic flat somewhere" and could be seen "billing and cooing together" when she visited them in Paris; see Letter to Molly MacCarthy 22 Apr. 1923 (the phrase "Sapphic flat" is omitted from Woolf's published letters, but see Beard, *Invention* 154); Letter to Jacques Raverat 5 Feb. 1925, Woolf 3: 164; also qtd. in Beard, *Invention* 154; and see Beard's discussion of Harrison's "sexuality" (*Invention* 152–57). Tellingly, Harrison burned most of her correspondence when she left Cambridge in 1922. It might be tempting to make a case for Harrison as a first-wave feminist, but, although she would speak out occasionally about women's issues (particularly women's unequal treatment in the university), she was not a suffragette and resisted efforts to bring her into the movement. Harrison's work – her championing of the matriarchy and the power of the goddess – might be thought of as an early version of cultural feminism and has been unconsciously absorbed into the cultural feminist consciousness (mainstreamed as New Age feminism). But she was always uncomfortable around anything she considered anti-male or too political.

7 Arthur Pickard-Cambridge's *Dithyramb, Tragedy, and Comedy* (published the year before Harrison died) was thought to have demolished many of Harrison's arguments about the birth of tragedy in the Dithyramb, although subsequent archaeological evidence suggested that a modified version of her thesis was correct. For an assessment, see T.B.L. Webster's preface and notes to the second edition of Pickard-Cambridge; on her continuing influence, see Calder, Preface v.

8 Frazer can arguably be seen as one of the first to place ritual at the centre of investigations of the history of religion, and he was unquestionably the most influential. But Harrison's earliest discussions of ritual precede the publication of *The Golden Bough*, and she and Frazer were developing their ideas about the role of drama more or less simultaneously. In the 1890 edition of *The Golden Bough*, Frazer does include extensive discussion of European folk festivals as survivals of primitive rituals, and he looks at "magical" or "sacred" drama at various points in the twelve-volume 3rd edition (published 1911–15). But the explicit discussion that one editor has seen as "the fountainhead of the ritualistic view of drama"

appears only in Frazer's 1922 abridgement of *The Golden Bough*, published nearly a decade after Harrison's popular formulation of her dramatic theories in *Ancient Art and Ritual* (1913); see *Golden Bough* (1998) 651 and Robert Fraser's note, 835n. Frazer insultingly omits *Themis* and *Ancient Art and Ritual* from the extensive bibliography in the third edition of *The Golden Bough*, though he was clearly influenced by them.

9　Murray was sixteen years younger than Harrison, and Cornford twenty-four years younger. Their contributions to *Themis* in 1912 might be considered their first true "ritualist" works, with Cornford's only book on Greek drama published two years later. Harrison's first ritualist thinking is contemporary with Andrew Lang's *Myth, Ritual, and Religion* (1887), which was certainly an influence.

10　Harrison cites the *Birth of Tragedy* once in her *Prolegomena* (1903) 445n4, and in the 1927 edition of *Themis*, she proclaims herself a Nietzsche "[d]isciple" (viii). For her acknowledgment of Bergson and Durkheim, see *Themis* xii–xiii. For her acknowledgment of Freud, see *Themis* viii; *Reminiscences* 80–82.

11　There have been three relatively recent biographies (Peacock; Robinson; and Beard's critical anti-biography, *Invention*); one book on Harrison's influence on Eliot, Woolf, and Joyce (Carpentier); and a number of further essays on her contribution to classics (Beard, "'Pausanias'"; Fiske), her place among the Cambridge ritualists (Robert Ackerman), her influence on modernism (K.J. Phillips; Cramer; Radford), and her gender and sexuality at the borderland between the Victorian and the modern (Prins; Arlen; Torgovnick).

12　Harrison herself is mentioned, if at all, only in passing in most theatre histories, but one can trace the persistent (if sometimes veiled) influence of her work on such theorists as Francis Fergusson, Northrop Frye, Kenneth Burke, Richard Schechner, and Victor Turner (this influence unsurprisingly intensified with the rise of structuralism and waning under the influence of post-structuralism). The most explicit acknowledgment is that of Fergusson (26–27); see also the discussion below and in note 66.

13　Mirrlees, Draft; quoting, in part, Dew-Smith 63; de Buxton 66.

14　"Bohemia was still an exciting & romantic world," wrote Mirrlees, "from which occasionally (tho' the Dowagers preferred it not to be on Sunday – 'what would the servants think?') fascinating creatures, like Ellen Terry, would emerge for a luncheon-party. But the way to make the most, so to speak, of both worlds, was amateur theatricals, & amateur theatricals were the most exciting of all fashionable amusements, still preserving, one fancies, a slight tinge of daringness" (Draft).

15　Regular Greek productions were launched in Oxford in 1880 with the *Agamemnon* and in Cambridge in 1882 with the *Ajax*; see Easterling, "Early."

16　On the cancellation of the production, see Mirrlees, Draft, citing Harrison's friend Margaret Merrifield; see, also, Robinson 46.

17　For my account of the *Tale of Troy* and Harrison's other theatricals, I am indebted to Beard, *Invention*, 37–53, which offers a detailed discussion; Robinson 81–84; letters in the Harrison papers; and contemporary reviews.

18　Mirrlees, Draft; and see Elinor Ritchie Paul, Letter to Mirrlees, 13 June 1934.

19   Elinor Ritchie Paul, Letter to Mirrlees, 13 June 1934; also cited in Peacock 63, 259n16.
20   See Newton, Letter to Eugénie Sellers, 12 June 1883; cited in Beard, *Invention* 52. Newton was anxious to retrieve the gold jewellery lent to Sellers.
21   Newton, Letter to Eugénie Sellers, 22 Aug. 1883; qtd. in Beard, *Invention* 52.
22   See Stokes 52–55; "*Helena in Troas.*" For an overall discussion of the Greek plays of the 1880s, see Hall and Macintosh 462–87.
23   Charlotte Sidgwick, Letter to Ethel Wilson, 18 May 1887; qtd. in Beard, *Invention* 49.
24   See Mirrlees, Draft, on the "'publicity'" (Mirrlees's scare quotes) the theatricals gave Harrison.
25   Harrison claimed to have gotten an audience of 1600 people for one such address in Dundee; see "Woman's View" 2; also mentioned in Robinson 80–81; Beard, *Invention* 56.
26   To refer to Cornford as her "close friend" is something of an understatement. They spend much of the first decade of the century travelling and working together, in an erotic friendship that appears not to have been overtly sexual. She claimed to have realized that she was in love with him only when he became engaged to her former student, Frances Darwin, an engagement that threw her into a deep depression; see Robinson 200–06.
27   Cornford 74; see, also, M.E. Holland's similar recollections (87) (and for "unearthly noise"); and Harrison's discussions of this passage in *Themis* 61; *Ancient* 47–48.
28   See the discussion in Robinson (79) of Harrison's use of lantern photos, shown by means of oxy-hydrogen light, and of the difficulty of preparing them. On the history of the magic lantern, see Terpak; on the hugely popular magic-lantern shows of the nineteenth century (the large-screen narrative photographic entertainments capable of such special visual effects as dissolves, superimpositions, or the simulation of motion), see Barber.
29   Harrison, Letter to D.S. MacColl, 6 Feb. 1887; qtd. in Peacock 70–71. This letter has become a touchstone in the critical literature on Harrison, seen as initiating a crisis and conversion to ritualism for Harrison; see, e.g., Stewart 115; Robert Ackerman, 223–24; Peacock 70–75; Mirrlees, Notebook. Challenging this view, Beard argues that Harrison must have been accustomed to such critiques, citing an earlier letter from Vernon Lee to Charles Newton in 1886 in which Lee apparently attacked Harrison for excessive idealism ("Ideality" in Harrison's habitual nomenclature). Beard also notes that Harrison continued, on occasion, to invoke the language of aestheticism (in the book on Greek vase paintings she wrote with MacColl, for instance). It would be hard to disagree with Beard that "[t]his was no 'watershed' after which 'everything was new.'" We need not put too much weight on Harrison's flirtatious response to MacColl. And it seems correct that ritualism was in the air in the 1880s. Beard notes that the Cambridge Classical Tripos of the 1880s included not only a new archaeology section but questions about rites and ceremonies well before Harrison published *Mythology and Monuments*. (In 1888, "Paper 2" was given the title "Mythology and Ritual," changed in 1890 to "Myth, Ritual and Religion"; see

Invention 57–58, 90–94, 119–20, 125–27). But it is also impossible not to see a significant change in Harrison's work in the year or so that followed.

30   Harrison, Letter to D.S. MacColl, 13 Nov., 1887; qtd. in Peacock 74; undated; 6 Feb. 1887; qtd. in Peacock 71.

31   Harrison, Letter to MacColl, 30 Sept. 1887.

32   The reverse-aestheticism of what became one of her favourite lecturing devices encapsulates this anti-aestheticism. As Gilbert Murray described it, "We were gradually led to expect a revelation, and then with a slightly hushed voice Jane heralded as 'an exquisitely lovely creature' the appearance on the screen of a peculiarly hideous Gorgon, grinning from ear to ear" (*Jane* 565); see, also, Alice Dew-Smith's recollection of Harrison announcing "[t]his beautiful figure which I will now place before you," after which "would appear some very archaic figure with arms pinned to its sides" (qtd. in Mirrlees, Notebook). Years later, Harrison offered a brutal portrait of the "aesthete" that surely refers back to this period and has some element of autobiographical self-flagellation in it: The aesthete does not produce, or, if he produces, his work is thin and scanty ... He has no joy, only pleasure. He cannot even feel the reflection of this creative joy. In fact, he does not so much feel as want to feel. He seeks for pleasure, for sensual pleasure as his name says, not for the grosser kinds, but for pleasure of that rarefied kind that we call a sense of beauty. The aesthete, like the flirt, is cold. It is not even that his senses are easily stirred, but he seeks the sensation of stirring, and most often feigns it, not finds it. The aesthete is no more released from his own desires than the practical man, and he is without the practical man's healthy outlet in action. He sees life, not indeed in relation to action, but to his own personal sensation. By this alone he is debarred for ever from being an artist ... The aesthete leads at best a parasite, artistic life, dogged always by death and corruption. (*Ancient* 214–16) See, also, Harrison's description of *Ancient Art and Ritual* as "all a tilt against art for art's sake"; Letter to Gilbert Murray, April 1913; qtd. in Payne 190.

33   23 May 1886 (Todhunter papers); qtd. in Beard, *Invention* 48. This comment is actually in a fawning letter to Dora Todhunter, commending her husband's production of *Helena in Troas*.

34   Harrison, Letter to D.S. MacColl, undated; qtd. in Peacock 70. Harrison is referring to *Partners*, starring Herbert Beerbohm Tree, which opened at the Haymarket on 5 January 1888.

35   See Harrison's undated letter to MacColl, recommending that he go see Madame Chaumont and saying that she has "found an account of a pantomimic myth – just the thing wanted – re pots and dances" (presumably for their joint work on Greek vase paintings). She is probably referring to Celine Chaumont, an actress in light French comedies (thanks to Richard Schoch for helping me to identify Madame Chaumont).

36   For discussions of this trip, see Beard, *Invention* 70–74; Robinson 92–100; Peacock 83–86; D.S. MacColl, Letters to Lizzie MacColl (copies in the Harrison archive, titled "Diary of a Greek Journey"); Harrison, "Archaeology."

37   D.S. MacColl, Letters to Lizzy McColl, Mar.–May 1888; see, also, Robinson 96, 99, 100.

38   Harrison, Letter to Elizabeth Malleson, 6 June 1888; qtd. in Peacock 86; Beard,
     Invention 73. See the rather more sceptical account of this trip in Beard,
     Invention 70–71. (The guide probably did not relish the thought of a night in the
     rain; the "inconceivably primitive and savage" path was well trod by English
     scholars.)
39   D.S. MacColl, Letter to Lizzie MacColl, 5 April 1888; qtd. in Robinson 94.
40   *Mythology* 292; see, also, Harrison's note, attributing this reconstruction "to a
     lecture given by Dr. Dörpfeld in the Athenian theatre." In *Mythology and
     Monuments* (and elsewhere), she championed Dörpfeld's "revolutionary" views
     that the Theatre of Dionysus dated not from the fifth century but from the
     fourth; that therefore its raised stage represented a late development; and that,
     during the great period of Greek tragedy, the actors and chorus had performed
     on the same level; see *Mythology* 271–95; Harrison, "Dr. Dörpfeld"; Beard,
     Invention 66–68; Robinson 250.
41   Harrison, Letter to D.S. MacColl, 30 Sept. 1887.
42   Harrison had already sent a complete list of illustrations to Macmillan by August
     1888; see Harrison, Letter to F.(?) Macmillan, 28 Aug. 1888; cited in Beard,
     "'Pausanias'" 315 n68.
43   There is a typescript "syllabus" (summary) of these lectures (provenance
     uncertain) in Letters to D.S. MacColl, Harrison Papers, 1/5/2, Newnham College
     Archives. Borland (60) identifies them as part of an Oxford University Extension
     course given in the summer of 1889, though she also mentions Oxford
     Extension lectures (perhaps the same) in the winter of 1887–88 (51); see
     Harrison, Letter to D.S. MacColl, "Septuagesima Sunday" (29 Jan) 1888 referring
     to these. MacColl's emphasis is more folkloristic and more interested in song
     than in ritual per se, but there is some similarity between these lectures and the
     ideas that Harrison was developing in *Mythology and Monuments*. In the
     description of lecture 2, for instance, on "Ceremonial or Ritual Songs," MacColl
     writes, "Behind the Dance gone through as play we must look for Dances gone
     through with a religious object; and for the origin of the movements in the
     religious or ritual dance, we must go back to the various occupations they
     symbolised by imitative gesture."
44   Harrison, Letter to D.S. MacColl, 31 Oct. 1887. On the Gallipoli relief, see
     Prolegomena 291.
45   Harrison, Letter to Alfred Cort Haddon, Haddon papers, Haddon Box 3,
     Cambridge University Library (two letters, undated but apparently written while
     preparing the *Prolegomena* manuscript). These letters have not, I believe, been
     previously uncovered by Harrison or Haddon scholars.
46   See Beard, "Invention"; *Invention* 125–27. And see note 29 (above).
47   See, similarly, Harrison's *Reminiscences*: "By nature, I am sure, I am not an ...
     anthropologist – the 'beastly devices of the heathen' weary and disgust me"
     (83). And see Harrison's biting remarks in *Ancient Art and Ritual* on "the cult of
     savagery," which "simply spells complex civilization and diminished physical
     vitality" (236).
48   See Stewart 43 (Stewart's father was the host); see, also, Harrison's comment to
     Gilbert Murray: "I have read somewhere that you do not allow any crude

statements about colour, but they really are blacker than any hat, and I simply adore them" (Harrison, Letter to Gilbert Murray, June 1902; reproduced in Stewart 43).

49 Aeschylus 239 (*Eumenides* 5.731–47). Harrison credits two other scholars with the identification of the Erinyes with goddess-worship: C.O. Müller and Erwin Rohde; see "Delphika" 206–07.

50 This is, in part, a quote from Murray's translation of the *Bacchae.*

51 On detached contemplation, see, e.g., *Ancient Art and Ritual*: "that peculiar contemplation of ... life which we call art" requires "remoteness from immediate action" and transforms the work of art into "a 'possession for ever'" (205, 165, 167).

52 The fact that Cornford, who played Comus, was becoming romantically entangled with Frances Darwin at this stage may have played some part in Harrison's "loathing" here.

53 Milton 92, stage direction following line 92. Harrison's comment is perhaps somewhat more ambiguous and ambivalent than this reading would suggest. Her reference to the "Beast-Rout" evokes the double meaning of "rout" (the crowd of beasts and their flight upon defeat). Do Comus and his rout represent theatre? or do they represent its ritual antithesis? Is the vision nirvana? or is it nightmare?

54 See, for instance, her discussion of James Theodore Bent's *Cyclades, or Life among the Insular Greeks*, an ethnological account of Bent's travels in the Cyclades in the 1880s (*Mythology* xxxvii, xliii).

55 Harrison, Letter to MacColl, 1 Jan 1922 ("It was nice of you to send me your ritual play").

56 In the 1890s, she was already thinking about dance as a "lost art" (in a column she wrote for a hotel newspaper), mourning "this great and goodly gift the gods have given us," which we have "misused," "curtailed," losing "all its delicate gradations, its subtleties, its instinct life and manifold variety"; see "On Dancing as a Lost Art," clipping in the Harrison papers 1/5/2 (letters to D.S. MacColl), Newnham College Archives (for its dating and provenance I rely on a ms. note on the clipping).

57 On various permutations of this dynamic, see the essays in Ackerman and Puchner; see, similarly, Eleanora Duse's comment (as remembered by Arthur Symons): "To save the theatre, the theatre must be destroyed, the actors and actresses must all die of the plague ... It is not drama that they play but pieces for the theatre. We should return to the Greeks, play in the open air" (Symons 336).

58 See Harrison's more extended discussion of the Pharmakos (the sacrificed or expelled scapegoat) in *Prolegomena* 95–114; "Pharmakos."

59 At one point, Harrison offered to meet with Granville Barker to discuss the production in Murray's stead, which suggests that she had, perhaps, been part of other production meetings; see Harrison, Letter to Murray, 25 Mar. 1904; qtd. in Robinson 175.

60 Harrison's student Jessie Crum (Stewart) made the masks and statues, and Harrison must have been responsible for transporting them, for one Newnham

student recalled seeing her wheeling an old-fashioned pram through the streets of Cambridge "in which was a Greek statue of a female figure, I suppose of a goddess, [with] an outstretched left arm ... held up to high heaven"; see Brown 50; Robinson 173; see, also, the letter from Harrison to Murray, insisting that "Mr Barker *must* look at the Goddesses to see if they are right from the stage point of view. If you are very tired I will take him alone" (Harrison, Letter to Gilbert Murray, 25 Mar. 1904; qtd. in Robinson 174–75; emphasis in original).

61   Harrison continues playfully, explaining that the goddesses were made in Cambridge and that "[i]t was no stage carpenter who modelled those austere faces, and froze the strange archaic smile on those deathless lips"; "Hippolytus" 372. The review is attributed to Harrison in Farr 14.

62   See Hall and Macintosh 490–508; Easterling, "Gilbert Murray's" 123–25. Shaw is, of course, explicit about his debt to Murray's *Bacchae* in *Major Barbara*, famously representing Murray as Adolphus Cusins.

63   W.B. Yeats, Letter to Lady Gregory, 10 Nov. 1905, Yeats, *Collected* 4: 218–19, 219n4; and Florence Farr, Letter to William Butler Yeats, June or July 1913, Yeats, *Yeats* 300–01, wishing he could send "a good Pagan like Jane Harrison" to help Farr in her teaching in Ceylon.

64   Eliot advised Hallie Flanagan that it was important to read Cornford's *The Origin of Attic Comedy* before she produced *Sweeney Agonistes* (Flanagan, *Dynamo* 83; see, also, Smith 62–63n40). On Eliot's undergraduate paper, in which he cites *Themis*, see Gray 141n128; see, also, his laudatory references to Harrison and the other Cambridge ritualists in "A Dialogue on Dramatic Poetry" (32); "Euripides and Professor Murray" (75–76). See also the discussion in Carpentier (106–14), drawing links between Eliot's claims about ritual and ideas that (she argues, perhaps somewhat dubiously) are exclusive to Harrison, and the more general discussion of Harrison's influence on *Sweeney* (101–32) and *The Family Reunion* (133–70).

65   On the anthropological elements in Murray's translation (used for this production), see Easterling, "Gilbert Murray's" 121. While she presumably liked the primitivism here, Harrison reacted badly to this production's portrayal of Jocasta, who was "noisome to me all thro & most in the 'great tableau' of the dominant mother, overhanging him, I nearly fled – its womanliness made me sick" (Harrison, Letter to Gilbert Murray, Jan. 1912; qtd. in Peacock 178).

66   Turner and Goffman were not formally part of the formation of performance studies, as Schechner, Brooks McNamara, Michael Kirby, and Barbara Kirschenblatt-Gimblett were, but their work was conceptually important to the array of academic endeavours that we might associate with it from the 1970s on. It would take another essay to trace Harrison's influence on performance studies, but Schechner's extended (hostile) evaluation in his seminal "Approaches to Theory/Criticism" (20–28) suggests how important it was for early performance studies theorists to situate themselves in relation to the Cambridge ritualists. (See also Rozik's belated attack on largely logical grounds [25–68]). In a revision of "Approaches to Theory / Criticism," Schechner himself acknowledged: "whatever my quarrels are with the Cambridge thesis, a number

of productions of Greek tragedies have exploited it, including my own *Dionysus in 69*" (*Performance* 28n1); see also note 12.

WORKS CITED

Ackerman, Alan, and Martin Puchner, eds. *Against Theatre: Creative Destructions on the Modernist Stage.* Basingstoke, UK: Palgrave, 2006

Ackerman, Robert. "Jane Ellen Harrison: The Early Work." *Greek Roman and Byzantine Studies* 13 (1972): 209–30.

"The *Alcestis* at Oxford." *Athenaeum* 28 May 1887: 712–13.

"*Alcestis* at Oxford." *Cambridge Review* 25 May 1887: 345–46.

"The *Alcestis* at Oxford." *Times* [London] 19 May 1887: 7 Col. F.

Arlen, Shelley. "'For Love of an Idea': Jane Ellen Harrison, Heretic and Humanist." *Women's History Review* 5:2 / (1996): 165–90.

Barber, Theodore X. "Evening of Wonders: A History of the Magic Lantern Show in America." Diss. New York U, 1993.

Beard, Mary. "The Invention (and Re-invention) of 'Group D': An Archaeology of the Classical Tripos 1879–1984." Stray 95–134.

———. *The Invention (and Re-invention) of Jane Harrison.* Cambridge, MA: Harvard UP, 2000.

———. "Pausanias in Petticoats, or the Blue Jane." *Pausanias: Travel and Memory in Roman Greece.* Ed. Susan E. Alcock, John F. Cherry, and Jas Elsner. Oxford: Oxford UP, 2001. 224–39.

Borland, Maureen. *D.S. MacColl, Painter, Poet, Art Critic.* Harpenden, UK: Lennard, 1995.

Brown, E.G. "In Newnham Walk." Ann Phillips 50.

Calder, William M., III, ed. *The Cambridge Ritualists Reconsidered: Proceedings of the First Oldfather Conference.* Atlanta: Scholars Press, 1991.

———. Preface. Calder v–vii.

Carpenter, Humphrey. *OUDS: A Centenary History of the Oxford University Dramatic Society 1885–1985.* Oxford: Oxford UP, 1985.

Carpentier, Martha C. *Ritual, Myth, and the Modernist Text: The Influence of Jane Ellen Harrison on Joyce, Eliot, and Woolf.* Amsterdam: Gordon and Breach, 1998.

Cornford, Francis. Untitled obituary. *Newnham College Letter* (Jan. 1929): 72–78.

Cramer, Patricia. "Jane Harrison and Lesbian Plots: The Absent Lover in Virginia Woolf's *The Waves.*" *Studies in the Novel* 37.4 (winter 2005): 443–63.

de Buxton, Victoria. Untitled obituary. *Newnham College Letter* (Jan. 1929): 66–70.

Dew-Smith, Alice. Untitled obituary. *Newnham College Letter* (Jan 1929): 62–65.

Easterling, Patricia E. "The Early Years of the Cambridge Greek Play: 1882–1912." Stray 27–47.

———. "Gilbert Murray's Reading of Euripides" *Colby Quarterly* 33.2 (1997): 113–27.

Eliot, T.S. "A Dialogue on Dramatic Poetry." *Selected Essays 1917–1932.* New York: Harcourt, 1932. 31–45.

———. "Euripides and Professor Murray." *The Sacred Wood: Essays on Poetry and Criticism.* London: Methuen, 1960, 71–77.

"Euripides' *Hippolytus.*" *Daily Telegraph* 27 May 1904: 7.

Farr, Florence. *The Music of Speech, Containing the Words of Some Poets, Thinkers, and Music-Makers Regarding the Practice of the Bardic Art.* London: Elkin Mathews, 1909.

Fergusson, Francis. *The Idea of a Theater: A Study of Ten Plays – The Art of Drama in Changing Perspective.* 1949. Garden City, NY: Doubleday, 1953.

Fiske, Shanyn. "The Daimon Archives: Jane Harrison and the Afterlife of Dead Languages." *Journal of Modern Literature* 28.2 (2005 Winter): 130–64.

Flanagan, Hallie. *Dynamo.* New York: Duell: Sloan and Pearce, 1943.

Frazer, Sir James George. *The Golden Bough: A Study in Comparative Religion.* 2 vols. London, 1890.

——. *The Golden Bough: A Study in Magic and Religion.* 3rd ed. London: Macmillan, 1911–15.

——. *The Golden Bough: A Study in Magic and Religion.* 1922. Ed. Robert Fraser. Oxford: Oxford UP, 1998.

Granville Barker, Harley. *On Dramatic Method.* New York: Hill, 1956.

Gray, Piers. *T.S Eliot's Intellectual and Poetic Development 1909–1922.* Atlantic Highlands, NJ: Humanities Press, 1982.

Hall, Edith, and Fiona Macintosh. *Greek Tragedy and the British Theatre 1660–1914.* Oxford: Oxford UP, 2005.

Harrison, Jane Ellen. *Ancient Art and Ritual.* New York: Henry Holt and Co., 1913.

——. "Archaeology in Greece, 1887–1888." *Journal of Hellenic Studies* 9 (1888): 118–33.

——. "Crabbed Age and Youth." *Alpha and Omega.* London: Sidgwick and Jackson, 1915. 1–26.

——. "Delphika. (A) The Erinyes. (B) The Omphalos." *Journal of Hellenic Studies* 19 (1899): 205:51.

——. "Dr. Dörpfeld on the Greek Theatre." *Classical Review* 4.6 (June 1890): 274–77.

——. *Epilegomena to the Study of Greek Religion.* Cambridge: Cambridge UP, 1921.

——. "Hellas at Cambridge." *Magazine of Art* 7 (1884): 510–15.

——. "Hippolytus Crowned in London." *Cambridge Review* 15 (June 1904): 372.

——. Introduction. Harrison, *Themis* xi–xxv.

——. Introduction. Harrison, *Prolegomena* vii–xv.

——. *Introductory Studies in Greek Art.* London, 1885.

——. "Is Tragedy the Goat-Song?" *Classical Review* 16.6 (July 1902): 331–32.

——. *Mythology and Monuments of Ancient Athens.* London, 1890.

Rev. of *Mythology and Monuments of Ancient Athens,* by Jane Harrison. Athenaeum 2 Aug. 1980: 166–67.

Harrison, Jane Ellen, "Notes Archaeological and Mythological on Bacchylides." *Classical Review* 12.1 (Feb. 1898): 85–86.

——. Preface. Harrison, *Introductory* v–viii.

——. Preface. Harrison, *Mythology* i–clvi.

——. "The Pillar and the Maiden." *Proceedings of the Classical Association* 5 (1907): 1–13.

——. "The Pharmakos." *Folklore* (30 Sept. 1916): 298–99.

——. *Prolegomena to the Study of Greek Religion.* Cambridge: Cambridge UP, 1903.

——. *Reminiscences of a Student Life.* London: Hogarth Press, 1925.

———. *Themis: A Study of the Social Origins of Greek Religion*. Cambridge: Cambridge UP, 1927.

———. "Two Cylices Relating the Exploits of Theseus." *Journal of Hellenic Studies* 10 (1889): 231–42.

"Helena in Troas" Advertisement. *Times* [London] 14 May 1886: 12, col. B.

Holland, M.E. "The Suffrage March." Ann Phillips 86–87.

Kennedy, Dennis. *Granville Barker and the Dream of Theatre*. Cambridge: Cambridge UP, 1985.

MacCarthy, Desmond. *The Court Theatre 1904–1907*. London: Bullen, 1907.

Milton, John. *Comus. Complete Poems and Major Prose*. Ed. Merritt Y. Hughes. Indianapolis: Odyssey Press, 1957. 86–113.

Mirrlees, Hope. Draft biography. Jane Harrison Collection, Newnham College Archives, Cambridge, UK.

———. Notebook. Jane Harrison Collection, Newnham College Archives, Cambridge, UK.

"Miss Duncan's 'Dance Idylls.'" *Times* [London] 17 Mar. 1900: 11, col. F.

Murray, Gilbert. *Jane Ellen Harrison: An Address*. Cambridge, UK: Hetter, 1928.

———. "*Oedipus* at Covent Garden." *Times* [London] 23 Jan. 1912: 8, col. C.

Nagler, A.M. *A Source Book in Theatrical History*. New York: Dover, 1959.

"New Century Theatre." *Times* [London] 27 May 1904: 4, col. F.

Payne, Harry C. "Modernizing the Ancients: The Reconstruction of Ritual Drama 1870–1920." *Proceedings of the American Philosophical Society* 122.3 (June 1978): 182–92.

Peacock, Sandra. *Jane Ellen Harrison: The Mask and the Self*. New Haven: Yale UP, 1988.

Phillips, Ann, ed. *A Newnham Anthology*. Cambridge: Cambridge UP, 1979.

Phillips, K.J. "Jane Harrison and Modernism." *Journal of Modern Literature*. 17.4 (spring 1991): 465–76.

Pickard-Cambridge, Arthur. *Dithyramb, Tragedy, and Comedy*. Ed. T.B.L. Webster. 2nd ed. Oxford: Clarendon Press, 1962.

Prins, Yopie. "Greek Maenads, Victorian Spinsters." *Victorian Sexual Dissidence*. Ed. Richard Dellamora. Chicago: U of Chicago P, 1999. 43–81.

Radford, Andrew. "Hardy's *Tess*, Jane Harrison and the Twilight of a Goddess." *Thomas Hardy Journal* 21 (2005 Autumn): 27–57.

Robinson, Annabel. *The Life and Work of Jane Ellen Harrison*. Oxford: Oxford UP, 2002.

Routledge, W. Scoresby, and Katherine Routledge. *With a Prehistoric People, the Akikuyu of British East Africa*. London: Arnold, 1910.

Rozik, Eli*The Roots of Theatre: Rethinking Ritual and Other Theories of Origin*. Iowa City: U of Iowa P, 2002.

Schechner, Richard. "Approaches to Theory/Criticism." *Tulane Drama Review* 10.4 (1966): 20–53.

———. *Performance Theory*. New York: Routledge, 1988.

Smith, Carol H. *T.S. Eliot's Dramatic Theory and Practice, from* Sweeney Agonistes *to* The Elder Statesman. Princeton: Princeton UP, 1963.

Stewart, Jessie. *Jane Ellen Harrison: A Portrait from Letters*. London: Merlin Press, 1959.

Stokes, John. *Resistible Theatres: Enterprise and Experiment in the Late Nineteenth Century*. London: Elek, 1972.

Stray, Christopher, ed. *Classics in 19th and 20th Century Cambridge: Curriculum, Culture, and Community*. Cambridge: Cambridge Philological Society, 1999.

Symons, Arthur. *Studies in the Seven Arts*. London: Constable, 1906.

Terpak, Frances. "Magic Lantern." *Devices of Wonder: From the World in a Box to Images on a Screen*. Ed. Barbara Stafford and Frances Terpak. Los Angeles: Getty Research Institute, 2001. 297–306.

"*The Tale of Troy*." *Athenaeum* 2 June 1883: 710.

"*The Tale of Troy*." *Saturday Review* 9 June 1883: 723–74.

"*The Tale of Troy*." *Times* [London] 31 May 1883: 5.

Torgovnick, Marianna. "Discovering Jane Harrison." *Seeing Double: Revisioning Edwardian and Modernist Literature*. Ed Carola M. Kaplan and Anne B. Simpson. New York: St. Martin's Press, 1996. 131–48.

Tree, Maud. "Herbert and I." *Herbert Beerbohm Tree*. Ed. Max Beerbohm. London: Hutchinson, 1920. 1–170.

Webster, T.B.L. Preface. Pickard-Cambridge vi–viii.

"A Woman's View of the Greek Question: An Interview with Miss Jane Harrison." *Pall Mall Gazette* (4 Nov. 1891): 1–2.

Woolf, Virginia. *The Letters of Virginia Woolf*. Ed. Nigel Nicholson and Joanne Trautmann. 6 vols. New York: Harcourt, 1975–80.

Yeats, William Butler. *The Collected Letters of W.B. Yeats*. 4 vols. Ed. John Kelly and Eric Domville. Oxford: Clarendon Press, 1986–97.

———. *Yeats and Women*. Ed. Deirdre Toomey. 2nd ed. New York: St. Martin's Press, 1997.

Contributors

Alan Ackerman is associate professor of English, University of Toronto. His recent books include *Just Words: Lillian Hellman, Mary McCarthy, and the Failure of Public Conversation in America* (Yale UP, 2011) and *Seeing Things, from Shakespeare to Pixar* (U of Toronto P, 2011), and he is editor of the journal *Modern Drama*.

Richard Begam, Professor of English at the University of Wisconsin-Madison, has published articles on modern and postcolonial literature, Irish literature and literary theory. He is the author of *Samuel Beckett and the End of Modernity* (Stanford UP, 1996), co-editor of *Modernism and Colonialism: British and Irish Literature, 1899–1939* (Duke UP, 2007), editor of *Modernism and Opera*, a special issue of *Modernist Cultures* (2007), and co-editor of *Text and Meaning: Literary Discourse and Beyond* (Düsseldorf UP, 2010). He is completing a book entitled *Beckett's Philosophical Levity*.

Bilha Blum teaches in the Department of Theatre Studies at Tel-Aviv University. She has published extensively on theoretical issues concerning play and performance analysis, modern drama, theatre and media, poetic drama, and specifically, the drama of Federico García Lorca. Her book, entitled *Between Playwright and Director: A Dialogue* (2005), discusses aspects of cultural transference, canonization processes, and audience reception of canonical plays. She is also the author of *The Quest for Self-Realization: Modern Drama Re-considered* (due summer 2011), which places the analysis of modern drama upon the background of modern philosophy. Since 2004 she has served as co-convener of the Performance Analysis Working Group at the International Federation of Theatre Research.

Allison Carruth is the Associate Director of the STS program at Stanford University, where she teaches and conducts research in the areas of science and technology studies, twentieth and twenty-first-century literature, and the environmental humanities. Her completed book manuscript is entitled *Global Appetites: American Power and the Imagination of Food.* She is currently working on two book projects: "Bio-Art: Environmental Ethics, Life Science and the New Avant Garde" and "Alimentos: Food Routes through Literature and Culture" (co-authored with Amy Tigner). Recent publications include essays in *Modern Drama, Modern Fiction Studies* and *Modernism/Modernity* as well as collections from Oxford UP and Routledge.

Nicholas Crawford is Associate Professor of English at the University of Montevallo, where he teaches courses on Shakespeare, Renaissance literature, and playwriting. He also maintains broad interests in modern literature and has published on such figures as Virginia Woolf, Harold Pinter, and Sam Shepard. His essays appear in *English Literary Renaissance, South Atlantic Review, Cahiers Charles V,* and other scholarly journals and collections. His current book project studies metaphor and subjectivity in early modern drama.

R. Darren Gobert is Associate Professor of English and Theatre Studies at York University. He has published articles on writers such as Michel Marc Bouchard, Molière, and Tom Stoppard, as well as on dramatic and performance theory, in venues including *Journal of Dramatic Theory and Criticism, Modern Drama,* and *Theatre Survey.* He has two books in progress: *The Mind/Body Stage,* about Cartesianism and theatre history, and *The Theatre of Caryl Churchill.* He won the John Charles Polanyi Prize for Literature in 2007.

S.E. Gontarski is Robert O. Lawton Distinguished Professor of English at Florida State University His most recent books are: (with C. J. Ackerley) *The Faber Companion to Samuel Beckett: A Reader's Guide to His Works, Life, and Thought* (London: Faber and Faber, 2006), *Krapp's Last Tape and other Short Plays,* ed. and with a "Preface" and notes on the texts by S.E. Gontarski (London: Faber and Faber, 2009), and *A Companion to Samuel Beckett,* ed. and with an Introduction by S.E. Gontarski (Oxford: Wiley-Blackwell, 2010).

Julie Stone Peters is Professor of English and Comparative Literature at Columbia University. Her publications include *Theatre of the Book: Print, Text, and Performance in Europe 1480–1880* (Oxford UP, 2000) (winner of the ACLA's Harry Levin Prize, English Association's Beatrice White Award, and honorable mention from ASTR for the best book in theatre history), *Women's Rights, Human Rights: International Feminist Perspectives* (co-edited, Routledge, 1995), *Congreve, the Drama, and the Printed Word* (Stanford UP, 1990), and numerous articles on the history of drama and performance and the cultural history of the law. She is currently working on three book projects: a study of turn-of-the-century "obscenity" and theatrical modernism; a study of theatre and anthropology between the eighteenth and twentieth centuries; and a historical study of legal performance and the law's fraught relationship to its own theatricality.

Joseph Roach, Sterling Professor of Theater and English at Yale University, is the author, most recently, of *It* (2007), a study of charismatic celebrity and ageless glamour, and the editor of *Changing the Subject: Marvin Carlson and Theatre Studies, 1959–2009* (2009), both from the University of Michigan Press.

Nick Salvato is Assistant Professor of Theatre and a member of the graduate faculty of English at Cornell University. His first book, *Uncloseting Drama: American Modernism and Queer Performance* (Yale University Press, 2010), is part of the series Yale Studies in English. His articles have appeared in such journals as *Camera Obscura*, *Journal of Dramatic Theory and Criticism*, *TDR: The Drama Review*, *Theatre Journal*, *Theatre Survey*, and *Modern Drama*, where he guest-edited a special issue on "Gossip" and where he is the book review editor.

Tanya Thresher is an Associate Professor in Scandinavian Studies at the University of Wisconsin, Madison. Professor Thresher has her PhD in Scandinavian Studies from the University of Washington (1998), an MA and BA from the University of East Anglia, Norwich, United Kingdom. In addition to articles on Ibsen and contemporary Norwegian dramatists, she has published *Cecilie Løveid: Engendering a Dramatic Tradition* (2005) and was the editor for *A Dictionary of Literary Biography: Twentieth Century Norwegian Writers* (2004). Her research and teaching interests include modern Scandinavian drama and film, women's writing, and Scandinavian postmodernity. Currently Professor Thresher is working on a book about the relationship between Henrik Ibsen and melodrama along with an introduction to Henrik Ibsen for Cambridge University Press.

Myka Tucker-Abramson is a PhD candidate at Simon Fraser University. Her PhD dissertation is on the American novel and the rise of neoliberalism.

Hana Worthen, Assistant Professor of Theatre and European Studies at Barnard College, Columbia University, is the author of *Playing "Nordic": The Women of Niskavuori, Agri/Culture, and Imagining Finland on the Third Reich Stage* (Univ. of Helsinki, 2007). Her articles on modern dance and the Third Reich, on the use of political allegory as a strategy of theatrical resistance during the German occupation of Czech lands, on Czech dissident theatre in the 1970s, and on the ethics of allegory in contemporary theatre have appeared in *Theatre Journal, Modern Drama,* and *GRAMMA: Journal of Theory and Criticism*. Worthen's review articles on the denial of Finland's contribution to the transnational Holocaust appeared in *East European Jewish Affairs.*

W.B. Worthen, Alice Brady Pels Professor in the Arts, is Chair of the Department of Theatre at Barnard College, Columbia University, and Co-Chair of the Ph.D. in Theatre at Columbia, where he is also Professor of English. He is the author of several books, most recently *Drama: Between Poetry and Performance* (Wiley-Blackwell, 2010) and *Print and the Poetics of Modern Drama* (Cambridge, paperback 2009); recent work on Shakespeare, contemporary performance, and performance studies appears in *Shakespearean International Yearbook, Postmedieval,* and *Shakespeare Quarterly.*

Index